More Than Bollywood

MORE THAN BOLLYWOOD

Studies in Indian Popular Music

Edited by Gregory D. Booth

and

Bradley Shope

OXFORD
UNIVERSITY PRESS

OXFORD
UNIVERSITY PRESS

Oxford University Press is a department of the University of Oxford.
It furthers the University's objective of excellence in research, scholarship,
and education by publishing worldwide.

Oxford   New York
Auckland   Cape Town   Dar es Salaam   Hong Kong   Karachi
Kuala Lumpur   Madrid   Melbourne   Mexico City   Nairobi
New Delhi   Shanghai   Taipei   Toronto

With offices in
Argentina   Austria   Brazil   Chile   Czech Republic   France   Greece
Guatemala   Hungary   Italy   Japan   Poland   Portugal   Singapore
South Korea   Switzerland   Thailand   Turkey   Ukraine   Vietnam

Published in the United States of America by
Oxford University Press
198 Madison Avenue, New York, NY 10016

Library of Congress Cataloging-in-Publication Data
More than Bollywood : studies in Indian popular music / edited by Gregory D. Booth and Bradley
Shope.
    pages cm
Includes bibliographical references and index.
ISBN 978–0–19–992883–5 (hardcover : alk. paper) — ISBN 978–0–19–992885–9
(pbk. : alk. paper)   1. Popular music—India—History and criticism.   2. Motion
picture music—India—Mumbai—History and criticism.   I. Booth, Gregory D., editor of
compilation.   II. Shope, Bradley, editor of compilation.
ML3502.I4M47 2014
781.630954—dc23
    2013009314

CONTENTS

LIST OF FIGURES

LIST OF COMPANION MEDIA

In this book, the symbol ⊙ indicates a video accessible on the companion website (see p. xvii for details). The video numbers given in the text correspond to items on the website, listed below.

LIST OF CONTRIBUTORS

Shalini Ayyagari completed a Ph.D. at University of California, Berkeley in ethnomusicology and a Mellon Postdoctoral Fellowship in the Humanities at Dartmouth College. She has conducted extensive field research on regional music in North India.

Jayson Beaster-Jones has published research on Indian cultural and media histories in *Ethnomusicology, Popular Music,* and *South Asian Popular Culture.*

Gregory D. Booth is the author of *Behind the Curtain: Making Music in Mumbai's Film Studios* (OUP 2008) and *Brass Baja: Stories from the World of Indian Wedding Bands* (OUP 2005), and numerous articles on music, film, industry and culture in South Asia.

Stefan Fiol received his Ph.D. in Ethnomusicology from the University of Illinois at Urbana-Champaign. His research on the commercialization of folk culture and music in the Uttarakhand Himalayas has been widely published.

Joseph Getter's research on South Indian music culture has been published by Wesleyan University Press and elsewhere. He is an active performer of the South Indian classical flute, and a disciple of the late Sangeeta Kalanidhi Dr. T. Viswanathan.

Paul Greene is co-editor, with Jeremy Wallach and Harris M. Berger, of *Metal Rules the Globe: Heavy Metal and Globalization* (Duke, 2011) and with Thomas Porcello, *Wired for Sound: Engineering and Technologies in Sonic Cultures* (Wesleyan, 2004).

Niko Higgins completed his PhD at Columbia University on contemporary practice of Carnatic fusion in Chennai, India, with support from the Fulbright Hays Program. He studied Carnatic vocal music with T. Viswanathan at Wesleyan University and with Smt. Rama Ravi in Chennai.

Stephen Putnam Hughes earned his PhD in Social and Cultural Anthropology at The University of Chicago. His research and publications revolve around a various topics of media history including film, sound media, religion and politics.

Peter Kvetko has a Ph.D. in ethnomusicology from the University of Texas-Austin. His primary research concerns the relationship between popular music and globalization in urban North India.

Kaley Mason is finishing a book that examines how a subaltern performer caste merged feudal traditions of ritual servitude with modern practices of musical work and mobility in Kerala. His current research traces the intersection of radical socialism and song in Malayalam popular music scenes since Indian Independence.

Anjali Gera Roy has published several essays in literary, film and cultural studies, including a monograph *Bhangra Moves: From Ludhiana to London and Beyond* (Aldersgate: Ashgate 2010).

Natalie Sarrazin holds a Ph.D. in Ethnomusicology from the University of Maryland and is the author of numerous works on the music of the Hindi cinema and on children's musical worlds.

Anna Schultz earned her Ph.D. in Ethnomusicology from the University of Illinois in 2004. Her book, *Singing a Hindu Nation: Marathi Devotional Performance and Nationalism*, was published by Oxford University Press in 2012.

Bradley Shope received his degree in Ethnomusicology from Indiana University. His most recent publications are found in *South Asia: Journal of South Asian Studies*, *South Asian Popular Culture*, and the *Journal of Imperial and Commonwealth History*.

Timothy D. Taylor is the author of *Strange Sounds: Music, Technology and Culture* (Routledge, 2001), *Beyond Exoticism: Western Music and the* World (Duke University Press, 2007), and *The Sounds of Capitalism: Advertising, Music, and the Conquest of Culture* (University of Chicago Press, 2012).

ABOUT THE WEBSITE

www.oup.com/us/morethanbollywood

This is the companion website for *More Than Bollywood: Studies in Indian Popular Music*. This title provides essays on the scope and depth of popular music in India, and includes many of the leading scholars currently working on Indian popular music and culture. The volume offers a wide perspective on contemporary and historical popular music in India. Oxford University Press publishes this website to accompany the book. It offers additional information, downloads, and supplemental materials to augment the printed publication.

More Than Bollywood

Introduction

Popular Music in India

GREGORY D. BOOTH AND BRADLEY SHOPE

In March of 2011, Asha Bhosle, the legendary Indian vocalist, finished a short Asia-Pacific tour with a concert in Auckland, New Zealand. At 78, Bhosle had retired from her career as a playback singer recording songs for films, primarily in Hindi, that had begun in 1948. Nevertheless, this was her first appearance in Auckland, and the event attracted roughly four thousand members of the local Indian community. Some had spent their college years listening to Bhosle's hits; others were small children during the height of her career but had experienced her songs as their parents' favorites; others, still younger, were familiar with remix versions of her hits.

Bhosle's tour was titled "Rahul and I," a reference to film song composer Rahul Dev Burman (1939–1994) with whom she was closely associated, both personally and professionally. Consequently, all the film songs she performed that night were composed by Burman and recorded by Bhosle under his supervision in Mumbai's film studios. The 11-piece band that accompanied her was directed by percussionist Nitin Shankar and featured veterans of Mumbai's film studios (especially in the horn section), as well as some younger guitar-playing rockers.

The latter's influence was quite perceptible in some of the arrangements that combined Bhosle's featured songs with famous hits from the American rock repertoire. A performance that began with the Eagles' "Hotel California," for example, segued quite neatly—if unexpectedly—into

Burman's early "Chura Liya Hai Tumne Jo Dil Ko" ["You've Stolen My Heart"].

In addition to film songs, Bhosle sang four items from a broad category of songs historically referred to as "non-film." The significance of such a label is highly instructive and is discussed below. In this case, Bhosle selected four songs from popular repertoires that are associated—by language and regional style—with four of India's major northern cultural communities (Panjabi, Bengali, Gujarati, and Marathi), each of which was well represented in the audience that night. Early in the performance, a *bhangra* song inspired a number of Panjabi audience members to dance their way to the front of the hall.

Toward the end of the program, Bhosle acknowledged her own Maharashtrian heritage by singing a pair of *lavanis*, the often risqué Marathi-language songs associated with the more vaudevillian musical theatre traditions of western India. This provoked an even larger rush to the stage by the Marathis who were present. The crowd grew larger again when Bhosle moved on to one of her most famous film recordings, Burman's nod to psychedelic rock, "Dum Maro Dum" ["Take Another Hit"]. After her final number, Burman's masterful and complex "Piya Tu, Ab To Aaja" ["Lover, Come Soon"] Bhosle left the stage. At that point, her band segued smoothly and loudly into an arrangement of "Soul Sacrifice," an instrumental number from the 1969 debut LP of the Latin-rock band Santana.

This concert in Auckland (though it could have been almost anywhere in the Anglophone world) embodied many issues and complexities. Three of these issues stand out: first, the inescapable importance of the songs produced by Mumbai's commercial film industry (now commonly referred to as "Bollywood") in Indian popular culture; second, the regional and linguistic diversity of India that has played such a role in the shaping of the popular music market; and third, the longstanding interactive relationship—across colonial, postcolonial, and global periods of Indian history—between Indian popular music and the songs of the globally powerful Western music industries. We consider each of these issues in turn here.

FILM SONG (AND ONLY FILM SONG)

The basis of Asha Bhosle's success was her career as a playback singer for the Hindi cinema. She provided the musical voice of more than 20 important film actresses who emoted, mimed, and danced their way across Indian screens. Despite the fact that she was heard much more than she was seen for most of her career, and despite the increasingly nostalgic quality of her songs and image, Bhosle remains one of India's most important popular singing stars; the appeal of her film songs remains both pan-generational and global.

India's popular music and its popular culture history were conditioned by the subcontinent's historical relationships with colonialism, imperialism, slavery, the transnational market economy, local governmental factors, international conventions, and a host of other circumstances. At the heart of India's popular music culture, however, is the fact that India's commercial filmmakers often wielded the most direct financial interest in and control of Indian popular song. Across India's print, cinematic, and broadcast media, those songs were imbued with powerful and complex semiotic, cultural, and industrial connections to the images, emotions, and ideologies of the films of which they were a part. Because India's popular music culture has been so enmeshed in the needs and symbol systems of a commercial cinema, it is impossible to approach Indian popular music simply as if it were an Indian version of the culture, industries, and processes that produce Western popular music.

Scholars have gradually come to accept the logic of the seemingly self-evident argument that "film songs are not a tradition of music independent from the cinema" (Morcom 2007, 13). Yet, as Asha Bhosle's concert demonstrated, "independence" (or the lack thereof) is a slippery concept in this (or almost any) cultural context. Film songs in India *did* function very much in the manner of popular songs elsewhere: They were mediated expressions of romantic love to which young (and not-so-young) Indians responded emotionally; they were the materials of popular slang and shorthand social communication; they were the songs people sang or listened to at parties and social gatherings; and at times they were (and are still) the songs to which people danced, both socially and on stages.

MANY LANGUAGES, MANY INDUSTRIES

Bhosle's Auckland concert also demonstrated the ongoing reality of India's cultural diversity and the ways that diversity has affected its popular music culture. After her opening number, Bhosle asked the audience a question that might be translated into English as "Who all is here?" She meant, of course, which of India's many specific linguistic/cultural groups were represented in this particular Indian audience. She then singled out four groups: Gujaratis, Panjabis, Marathis, and Bengalis. These communities would have been well represented in almost any audience that she confronted. Bhosle's explicit acknowledgment of the audience's diversity, however, both reified and essentialized that diversity while simultaneously constructing a unified whole. (Indeed, some members of the audience responded by shouting "Indian" in response to her question, intentionally rejecting Bhosle's division of the audience into regional/linguistic components.)

The divisive potential of the "Indian" audience has long been a matter of much debate, and one that has required quite careful handling in all mass-media forms. By confronting community identities in this way, Bhosle expressed direct recognition of each group, facilitating the accessibility of her linguistically specific songs for the audience as a whole. More than the simple fact of her performance of songs representing specific regional and linguistic identities, however, our awareness of Bhosle's management of the cultural diversity within this (or almost any) Indian audience helps refine our understandings of the relationship between India's popular music culture and industry and the subcontinent's diversity.

India's music, theatre, and film industries, from their inception in the live stage-theatre traditions of the latter 19th century, have had to survive in a culture with linguistic, religious, and regional distinctions that sometimes seem to be endless. As Bhosle's *lavani* performance demonstrated, regional styles in regional languages have the power to call attention, usually in a very positive way, to individuals who are simultaneously Indian and also Tamil, Bengali, Konkani, and so forth. Multilingual vocalists such as Bhosle, as well as an often-fragmented music industry, have embraced this impossible diversity. An enormous range of potentially genre-defining factors, most clearly language and regional style, but also devotional content, relationships to "traditional" or to "Western" models, or relationships to visual images and narrative have made for an extremely diverse popular music culture. This diversity of music has influenced individuals involved in music creation, composition, performance, production, and distribution. Multiple industries have catered to India's diversity and incorporated diversity in performances, mediated content, and industrial structures and practices.

Despite the subcontinent's linguistic and cultural diversity, and despite political protests in the 20th century, Hindi is today India's national language. In consequence, the Hindi-language cinema has often been seen as acting in support of a pan-regional Indian nationalism (Chakravarty 1993; Vasudevan 2000; and Rajadhyaksha 2009). Furthermore, the Hindi film and music industry was initially the largest of all the linguistic industries and has been the most consistently influential nationally. In what remains a fragmented market, regional film industries have often followed the stylistic, technological, and commercial practices of Mumbai's composers and film producers. Bhosle's performance in New Zealand demonstrated both the Hindi dominance and the regional diversity that have been replicated across a transnational Indian culture.

"EAST" AND "WEST"

Finally, the performance in Auckland demonstrated that "East is East and West is West" has never been the rule in Indian popular culture. From the later 19th century at least, and often in direct response to the pressures and opportunities of British (and Portuguese and French) colonialism, Indian artists have been part of a globalizing popular music culture. With the establishment of film song's hegemony in the mid-20th century, globalizing forces converged in the cinema industry and exposed masses of Indians to a synthesis of what were once distinctly Indian and non-Indian styles.

The complexity of India's cultural referents is clear from the very cover of this volume. The original version of the image on the cover was created by a young Indian named Darryl Kirby in 1965 as the program cover for a dance (the Thunder Ball) that was being put on by two young men from Mumbai at the prestigious Crystal Room located in Mumbai's landmark Taj Mahal Palace Hotel (see Chapter 10). One of bands featured at the Thunder Ball was the Jets, whose lead guitarist was Kirby's younger brother Mike (see Chapter 11). The cover was one of many that Kirby, then an art student at South Mumbai's Campion High School, produced for local rock and other events in the first half of the 1960s.

It is indicative of the closeness of the South Mumbai "western" music scene that Darryl Kirby's art teacher was Alex Correa. When he was not teaching art, Correa was also playing drums in the city's leading jazz band, led by his brother Mickey. The Correas were also regular performers at the Taj. It is a further indication of the interconnected-ness of South Mumbai's popular music world that Correa's daughter, Fran, was a member of Mumbai's only "girl group", the Pop-Pets.

In addition to the Jets, the Thunder Ball line-up featured included other early Indian rock or pop acts such as the Beatroutes, the Satellites, Unit 4+1 and Lone Trojan. Biddu Apaiah was the last survivor of the Trojans, another very early Indian rock band. When the Trojans broke up in 1964, Apaiah spent a year or so in Mumbai performing as the Lone Trojan before moving to the U.K. and subsequent fame as a pop song writer and producer. Thunder Ball itself was an early example of a growing trend in India's popular music culture, in which young people (almost always young men) from the city's elite schools and colleges acted as part-time entrepreneurs to produce events at which they could share their enjoyment of the new popular music with their friends and (hopefully) make some money as well.

The event that resulted in the design on this volume's cover, however, leads us back to Asha Bholse's Auckland concert. The connections are certainly tenuous, but nevertheless instructive; they demonstrate clearly India's role in the multi-lateral cultural interactions that we now call globalization. It was the younger fans of bands like the Jets and the Trojans who responded so positively to the Indian release—by Polydor Records in 1970—of the three LP-set that chronicled the 1969 Woodstock Music and Art Fair (Woodstock) and to the subsequent release of the film in 1971. Given the relative scarcity of western recordings in India during the 1960s and 1970s, the songs and artists featured on the Woodstock recordings became disproportionately important for Indian rock fans. Accounts of local rock performances during the early 1970s, which built on the success of 1965's Thunder Ball, are laden with reports of Indian bands playing the songs performed in up-state New York in 1969. When Asha Bhosle's Auckland musicians closed their concert with Santana's "Soul Sacrifice"—a band and a song that featured prominently in the Woodstock recordings— the Indian audience in Auckland was hearing distant echoes of the impact of an American event on an earlier generation of Indians.

Many of the musicians onstage in Auckland in 2011 that night had personal (if still professional) connections—as Indians—with jazz, rumba, rock, hip-hop, and other musical styles. At the same time, they had all recorded film music at least occasionally during their professional careers. Because of these longstanding interactions, it is frequently difficult (and often pointless) to try to assert the specifically "Indian" or "Western" meanings of songs, instruments, or even genres. In the first decades of the 21st century, we are confronted with a cultural context in which songs by the Eagles or by Santana may contribute successfully and almost unremarkably to a quintessentially Indian performance.

As is already apparent from this brief discussion, the three issues highlighted by this concert interact in endless ways in Indian popular music and culture. This volume argues that these three issues are fundamental. We explore a broad range of styles and meanings in India's popular music from the 1930s and '40s to the first decades of the 21st century; but, like Asha Bhosle's career and her Auckland performance, our research is based on the premise that to perform—or to think, speak, or write about—popular music in South Asia is to confront, in one way or another, the unique and overwhelming importance of the songs of India's commercial cinemas. Similarly, our various chapters (each contributed by a different author) acknowledge India's linguistic and cultural diversity. We examine film songs and non-film songs sung in Hindi but also consider songs sung in Panjabi, Tamil, Malayali, and Marathi, which are only a small proportion of India's linguistic diversity. Finally, most of our chapters confront, in some fashion or other, aspects of the very real mixtures and the sometimes artificial distinctions that maintain the "East and West" paradigm in various syncretic popular music repertoires.

Despite this linguistic, historical, and stylistic range, however, we (like Asha Bhosle) are never too far from the dominant film song repertoire. Using the English-language metaphor, film song is the elephant in the room at a party. In the Hindi version of that metaphor, film song is the *safed hathi*, the white elephant. In either language, this elephant stands out in the crowd (in Hindi, he even stands out in a crowd of elephants). We may choose to admire or to ridicule his impressive girth and unusual color; we may complain about the amount of room he demands or even try (however futilely) to pretend that he simply does not exist. No matter what form our response takes, however, we must somehow acknowledge and account for the elephant's presence: We know he is there and even if the object of our research is quite distinct (as it is in some of these chapters), we cannot help glancing over our shoulders at the behemoth.

Despite our acknowledgment of the elephantine reality, it is one our goals to underscore the fact that music and commerce in India have never been entirely subsumed within the domain of film songs and the film industry. Popular music outside the film industry existed in India before, during, and especially after the years of film song's more complete dominance, in more diverse and vital forms than the undifferentiating (and rather dismissive) qualifier "non-film" would suggest, even though this label has been routinely used by those in the music and film industries. Some chapters in this volume directly address musics that have achieved some popularity among heterogeneous audiences outside of the cinema. We address the integrity and sustainability of music at the margins of the film industry, and reiterate the suggestion that even the representation of music in films solely as "film music" is problematic. From the consumption of jazz during the colonial period, to an emerging rock scene in the 1960s, to more contemporary "Indipop" or fusion hip-hop styles, we claim that meaning in India's popular music has been closely linked to historical patterns of the various forms of capitalism and semi-capitalism in Indian music production and to industrial frameworks that often—but not always—shadow the dynamic growth of the cinema.

To extend our pachydermal metaphor to cover all of India's popular music, the authors and editors of this volume are rather like the blind men and women who, when confronted with an elephant, each reported an animal of different shape and size, based on their quite different anatomical experiences with the tail, trunk, legs, and so on. Given the breadth and diversity of popular music as a phenomenon in India, it is not realistic to expect unanimity of perception or interpretation. Nevertheless, our individual accounts are not as disparate as they may appear. As the metaphor implies, the specific and even localized studies in this volume collectively offer a view of popular music on the subcontinent that is both more comprehensive and more detailed than has heretofore been available.

DANCING (AND NOT) WITH THE ELEPHANT

India's popular music, as a whole, remains understudied. In the first couple of decades after independence, film song was India's only locally produced, mass-mediated popular music, but it was firmly embedded in India's commercial and chaotic film-production system. The composers who produced film songs, their music production workshops, and the recording studios where those songs were recorded—indeed, the film industry as a whole—operated at a frenetic pace in a relatively closed world. Yet only after the musical and industrial changes and growing diversity that occurred either immediately before or (more commonly) after the beginnings of economic liberalization in the late 1980s (cf. Guha 2007) did ethnomusicologists begin to gradually engage with popular music on the subcontinent, producing research that, by and large, addressed new developments rather than the past. Although a number of chapters in this volume are historical, the book as a whole does not (and cannot) fill the historical gap in scholarly studies addressing the popular music of the pre-liberalization era. The years of late colonialism through the 1970s still require extensive primary research by ethnomusicologists. At best, we strive here to create a coherent link between the pre- and post-liberalization periods.

Popular music is directly connected to processes of commodification, reproducibility, mass production, and mass consumption of live performances, sound recordings, and broadcasts. Radios, gramophones, cassettes, CDs, MP3s, sheet music, films, and other entertainment commodities produced capital that enabled the growth of a wide variety of entertainment. In India, these processes and media sometimes took place within, and often connected to, the historical context of British colonialism from the 19th century onward. Especially after the appearance of recorded sound, local popular music production was sometimes dependent on technologies and media that were initially under the control of the entertainment industries of the British and Europeans, discussed by Booth, Hughes, and Shope in this volume. Wallis and Malm (1984) and Manuel (1993) have examined these issues at global and local levels.

Beginning in the mid-19th century, the global products of the transnational music industry in India were produced by companies located primarily in Britain and the United States, whose influence arose from their embedded positions within the structures of European colonialism and American hegemony. Performers and recordings associated with that industry flowed through India as through the world, carried by the power of colonialism and industrialization, and consumed largely by those following the paths of colonial control. These processes resulted in two streams of music: one transnational and the other local, one catering largely to Europeans or local elites and the other almost exclusively to local mass audiences, one often sung in colonial languages and the other almost always in vernacular languages. Each musical stream flowed alongside the other, and both were constrained by borders that were cultural rather than national. By the mid-20th century, the scope of global music in India was no longer defined by European or colonial culture.

In many ways, India's economic and regulatory environment has been a key factor in the postcolonial history of its popular music. In 1950, India was a newly nonaligned and socialist nation that sought to manage industry and development centrally through carefully prepared economic plans. The Indian Planning Commission's second five-year plan in 1956 sought to encourage indigenous industrialization through government control (Guha 2007). It banned or severely restricted the importation of almost all consumer goods and much technology, imposed high tariffs on all imports, required the licensing of all new private companies, and, most significantly, required almost all Indian-registered companies to have at least 60 percent Indian ownership. This body of legislation, known as the "License Raj," had an enormous effect on Indian business and culture. As Stephen McDowell has argued, "[I]n the first 35 years of its independence from Britain, India pursued national and international economic and political policies that left it truly situated at the margins of the world economy" (1997, 59). There is no evidence that the Indian government thought seriously about its culture industry in terms of development, but the legislation did "indigenize" the music industry by forcing foreign-owned music companies out of India. From 1956 or so onward, India was not part of the world music (or film) economy; this economic isolation had the concomitant effect of severely limiting the impact of external media culture on the Indian audience. Despite the difficulties and limitations imposed by the License Raj, India's isolation created an environment in which its indigenous popular music and culture (both generated by the film industry) could flourish without significant competition. When Prime Minister Rajiv Gandhi initiated the process of economic liberalization in the late 1980s, India's culture industries (along with the rest of the country) embarked on the road toward globalization. Most of the chapters in this volume detail specific outcomes of that journey.

Readers will note that we focus primarily on musical, cultural, and technological innovation in Indian popular music from the 1980s onward, when India's popular culture was characterized by rapidly expanding diversity in such matters as musical style, industrial logic, and technologies of sound and film recording, with India's increasing economic liberalization centered firmly in the background. The popular music of India's colonial era and first few years of independence has received relatively little scholarly attention generally, as we have noted, with the exception of work by Shope (2007, 2008), Hughes (2002, 2007), and Fernandes (2012). Hughes and Shope both provide chapters in this volume (chapters 5 and 10); Booth's study of the key figures contributing to the formation (and formalization) of the Hindi film song style between 1948 and 1952 also examines this era. Otherwise, and with the partial exception of Booth's examination of Indian rock bands (chapter 11), the research in this volume focuses on developments that began with liberalization. The limited historical scope of this volume highlights both the need for more research and the difficulties in conducting historical explorations into the early years of India's popular culture. Our post-liberalization focus also explains this volume's ahistorical organization.

FILM MUSIC BEFORE AND AFTER (LIBERALIZATION/GLOBALIZATION)

As Gregory Booth outlines in chapter 1, the specific (and syncretic) nature of film song during the first two decades after independence (or longer) was formalized and reinforced by a group of music directors (composers), singers, and arrangers who came to prominence in the later 1940s. This group established film song as a genre that was independent from the songs of India's musical stage and integrated into the technological process of producing a musical film. Music directors like Naushad Ali, the duo

Shankar-Jaikishan, C. Ramchandra, and many others often used traditional and classical melodic materials in their compositions, but they also pioneered the use of global popular musics.

The beginnings of liberalization at the end of the 1980s witnessed the first appearances of a major technological shift in Indian film and sound production. By the late 1990s, even newer sound and film production technologies significantly impacted Indian films and film songs. Musical instrument digital interface (MIDI) systems and other computer-based technologies increased filmmakers' use of background music and encouraged a new generation of recording studios, resulting in higher production values across the film- and music-production process. Digital technology also created new opportunities for illegal retailers who began producing cheap audio discs using MP3 formatting.

Natalie Sarrazin continues Booth's focus on the Hindi cinema in chapter 2. She examines the relationship between digital technologies and the expanded scope of film music production and consumption in the post-liberalization cinema. More specifically, she proposes that new digital technologies have significantly broadened access to music from around the world for Indian composers and producers, creating a newly global "digital aesthetic" that has reconfigured patterns of film score composition. She also suggests that the increasingly global quality of the Hindi film song aesthetic is not necessarily a process of "Westernization," but represents yet another development in India's ongoing production of an independent popular culture.

Although Indian music culture has long been affected by global flows of entertainment commodities, the increased level of interaction between Indian popular music and global culture, brought about in part by digital technology, has become increasingly multifaceted. Processes of film song composition have extended well beyond the influence of the "West" on Indian popular music, perhaps best illustrated in the recent work of film composer A. R. Rahman, an international figure who represents India's important function in the global flow of popular music. Sarrazin considers some of Rahman's work for the Hindi cinema. Her chapter is complemented by Joseph Getter's consideration of "Kollywood" in chapter 3, the Tamil-language film industry located in the Kodambakkam area of Chennai, where Rahman began his film-music career.

In chapter 3, Getter offers a study of regional film music. The linguistic diversity of India that we previously discussed produced a quasi-national popular cinema in the Hindi language production center of Mumbai, but it also produced regional centers dedicated to the production of Tamil-language films in Chennai, Telugu-language films in Chennai and

Hyderabad, and Malayali-language films in the south, in addition to films produced in Bengali, Gujarati, Bhojpuri, and other northern languages. Getter examines recent developments in Tamil film song and investigates the impact of online communities in connecting Tamil film music fans globally. He suggests that new patterns of digital circulation reconstitute Tamil film music as a global sound and force us to question our capacity to solely attribute film music to the Indian domestic geographic space.

In chapter 4, Kaley Mason moves beyond the industrial processes in song development, commoditization, and dissemination that Booth, Sarrazin, and Getter develop. Mason addresses a relationship between film songs (and song scenes) and local understandings of gender. As he sorts through newly crafted images of gender in the musical sensibilities of the Malayalam film industry located in Kerala in Southwestern India, he suggests that music and on-screen visual images reflect subjects that reach well beyond the purely musical, or even the purely expressive. His exploration of gender details a thoughtful example of a social matter that informs audience understanding of music, narrative, and images.

AUDIO CULTURES, MUSIC VIDEOS, AND FILM MUSIC

Before the 1980s, Indian audio culture was largely limited to the cinema and the radio. For primarily economic but also infrastructural reasons, recorded sound discs and records played very little part in most people's lives. Popular music might be fancifully said to have a natural relationship with mediated modes of production, dissemination, and reception; but in truth, those modes were limited to broadcast and public display formats. The individual ability to own the means of music playback as well as individually chosen music commodities only came within the reach of most Indians beginning in the late 1970s during what Manuel has called the cassette revolution (1993).

Audiocassette technology first reached India in the mid-1970s, initially in the form of portable "two-in-one" cassette player-recorders, but professional recording and duplicating technology was in place by the end of the decade. Audiocassettes were robust and easy to mass-produce and could be played on portable battery-powered players. Cassette technology significantly increased the number of consumers who could afford to buy and listen to recorded music and was indeed a "revolution, which fundamentally restructured the commercial-music industry and the nature of Indian popular music in general" (Manuel 1993, 37). The relative low cost and ease of cassette production created an industrial and cultural space for new music companies and new patterns of consumption outside the context of the cinema hall or the radio.

Because of cassette technology, popular non-film musical genres increased exponentially in the 1980s. Despite the sudden diversity and choice available to consumers, however, film songs did not disappear from the market. Old and new record companies began to produce compilations of older popular songs that had not been easily available or accessible. "Version songs," re-recordings or reproductions of old melodies, also made an impact in the 1980s. This new genre used film song melodies as the basis for new arrangements that added contemporary rhythms to familiar songs.

As technologies changed, television gradually became a significant force in India's mediascape. By 1984, the government-owned Doordarshan (literally, tele-vision) was available to 70 percent of the population; in 1991, the privately owned Star Asia satellite network first offered consumers direct, privately controlled access to global television content. MTV and other music channels took advantage of these developments and exposed audiences to the music and media of the world economy. Part two considers some of the developments during this period of increasingly rapid change. We examine audio and video phenomena and the ways mediated cultures have developed around popular practices, genres, artists, and marketing practices.

In his consideration of genre in Indian popular music in chapter 5, Jayson Beaster-Jones connects the range of film song traditions discussed in part one to a variety of non-film popular musics. Cassettes made possible an economically viable mass market that allowed Indian popular music producers to begin a process of genre differentiation that had long characterized the world music economy (Walser 1993). Beaster-Jones takes a broad perspective on the fundamental changes that began in the 1980s, examining global flows of technology as a primer to understanding the development of a *filmi* aesthetic in North India. He assesses the extent to which genre categories in the Indian popular music industry have become even more nebulous in the face of new patterns of composition and production.

In chapter 6, Stephen Putnam Hughes suggests that early Indian entrepreneurs embraced foreign gramophone technology to construct an Indian, and explicitly Hindu, popular music in the late 1920s and early 1930s. Hughes suggests that the complex role played by iconography in Hinduism helped locally owned and managed subsidiaries of the major global recording companies (primarily Columbia and the Gramophone Company of India) construct an ideology in which the image of the gramophone itself and the technological innovations it embodied were incorporated into a modernist Hindu outlook. He argues that commoditizing a conspicuously

Hindu manner of conceptualizing religious music corresponds to the moment that South Indians were for the first time becoming involved in the music recording business. A new business model involved a kind of Hindu makeover for a gramophone industry that lasted for almost a decade until the advent of film music. In these years before the dominance of film song, Hughes teaches us that popular music became a modern reorientation of traditional devotional practice.

Like Beaster-Jones, Anjali Gera Roy traces a connection between film song and non-film popular song. In chapter 7, she addresses the famous, if contested, popular song and dance genre called *bhangra*. Widely known as a "traditional" form of Panjabi performance culture from Northwestern India, Roy examines the early incorporation of *bhangra* as a symbol of Indian identity in the Hindi cinema during the mid-1950s. She then considers how Panjabi migrants living in Britain developed *bhangra* into a pop style eventually repatriated to India, and examines *bhangra* as it has been shaped and transformed through continuous negotiations between the aesthetic and stylistic norms of MTV and Hindi film song scenes.

In the 1990s, with no local examples or models to follow (other than film song), many pop artists such as Alisha Chinai, Remo Fernandes, and others turned to Western pop music and artists for inspiration. Peter Kvetko's (2005) research on this topic offers the first comprehensive study of popular music in India from the 1980s onward. In chapter 8, Kvetko continues his work and examines the career and recordings of one of the most important stars in the first wave of Hindi pop (sometimes called Indipop), rapper Baba Sehgal. Kvetko asserts that Sehgal reconfigured the music of globally familiar rap stars (as hip-hop was then known) to produce Indipop songs that successfully appealed to a new youth identity.

The continuing development of a non-film popular music market that began in the 1980s and '90s included new markets for popular devotional genres, regional musics, stylized folk and folk narratives, as well as romantic songs based on light-classical models (after the turn of the millennium). Stefan Fiol offers a detailed example of regional popular music development in chapter 9. He provides a close-up look at non-film folk song production in the context of the dramatic growth of Garhwali *geet*, from the hill region (Garhwal) of the northern state of Uttarakhand. Following these developments into the 21st century, Fiol details the ways that new technologies, requiring much smaller investments in production infrastructure, have increased the viability and popularity of regional styles. This story has been replicated in many regions of India, as India's mono-genre popular music culture has exploded and diversified in all directions.

LIVE MUSIC, PERFORMANCE CULTURES, AND REMEDIATION

With the important exception of musical theater, venues for the live, commercial consumption of popular music—such as concert halls, nightclubs, or dancehalls—were not "traditional" components of Indian culture. As much as the music itself, the development of a popular music culture in India involved the development of new, live forms of popular music production and consumption beginning in the early 21st century. Part three examines live music and performance cultures of popular music in India. This section also considers the interaction of pre-mediated live performance traditions with the world of recorded popular music.

In chapter 10, Shope unpicks the multi-textured entertainment networks that dominated European social life in colonial India. He shows that as early as 1865, these flows washed the songs and performance culture of American black minstrelsy onto Indian shores, but he focuses on the global flow of popular culture in the early and middle 20th century. Those flows brought the popular music and musical cultures of Europe and America, vaudeville, jazz, and their related forms to British India; but, as he shows, those flows spilled over into the film song stream. In particular, he traces the presence of Latin American music in Mumbai from the 1930s to the 1950s.

In the first decades of the 20th century, the local colonial population supported theaters and ballroom venues that booked touring minstrels, burlesques, vaudeville acts, masquerade dances, "follies," and cabaret routines. Shope suggests that by the end of World War I, a global jazz craze appeared in India, as almost everywhere else. Listeners enjoyed jazz on imported gramophone discs and witnessed live jazz performances by local orchestras and foreign touring groups. He focuses on live cabaret performances, which increased exponentially between the 1930s and 1940s, and argues that they were heavily influenced by Hollywood representations of Latin American music and dance, including the work of Carmen Miranda.

Colonial India thus became an import market for an increasingly global music (and film) industry. When sound recording technology (and industry) appeared in India, it did so in a context that was inherently transnational. European audiences enjoyed exposure to global patterns of music movement, including imported recordings of "opera, comic songs, military band music, marches, waltzes, classical and church music catered primarily to European tastes" (Hughes 2002, 446). These early industries were designed to cater to European and elite Indian populations, and often reinforced social status.

By mid-century, a number of developments radically altered the cultural, political, economic, and regulatory contexts for popular music in India. Indian independence led to the departure of most of the British (and other Europeans) residents who had been the primary audience for the global stream of India's popular music culture. Outside of Mumbai and Kolkata and a few other urban locations, the social behaviors and entertainment economies that provided the basis for the live performance of Western-style popular music ended. The new government of Prime Minister Jawaharlal Nehru sought to move the new, economically destitute country toward a more egalitarian, socialist model of society. Among other consequences of this shift was a decline in Western-style cabaret nightlife and the consumption of alcohol, both of which were officially frowned upon. Meanwhile, the Indian government began to regulate the import of foreign culture and technology, limiting Indians' access to global trends. These developments led to a decline in (although by no means the complete obliteration of) the market for, and availability of, "English" popular music, especially outside India's large urban centers.

Despite these daunting conditions, some young Indians—mostly urban and enrolled in English middle schools—became fascinated by British and American rock music in the early 1960s. Those for whom it was especially attractive found no alternative but to make the music (and sometimes their instruments) themselves. Following global developments in youth culture in the later 1960s and early 1970s, these young enthusiasts sought to develop a viable rock music culture, usually in explicit opposition to the sounds and ideologies of film song. In chapter 11, Booth offers three case studies of rock bands from Mumbai, in the context of changing media and access to foreign musical content. Although rock music's distinctly oppositional ideology was attractive to some young Indians, it was not embraced by the country as a whole or by the Indian music industry. As they had in the 1950s, English-language lyrics limited the appeal of rock. Struggling to overcome the challenges of locating instruments and equipment and finding venues that would support them, Booth suggests that most bands found the struggle to survive overwhelming.

Niko Higgins, in chapter 12, examines the history and contemporary outcomes of another development in popular music that began in the 1970s, when Indian classical and folk musicians, seeking to expand their musical and/or financial horizons, began collaborating with Western musicians (from similarly diverse backgrounds and with similar goals) to produce a genre that the Indian industry labeled "fusion." The group Shakti combined the talents of three young Indian musicians with those of a jazz/rock/blues guitarist and recorded some of the most influential discs of this new style. In his examination of fusion as popular music, Higgins suggests that genre boundaries in contemporary fusion music in Chennai are created through politically charged, irresolute strategies of classification. In this instance, conflicts between broad "Indian" and "Western" categories are apparent, as are "modern" or "traditional" designations and their associated links to the Indian/West binary.

A number of regional styles of popular music came about from interactions between traditional Indian music forms and the recording studio. In chapter 13, Shalini Ayyagari explores the work of Manganiyar folk musicians and emphasizes the role of industry in regional music development. Her study of these hereditary musicians in Western Rajasthan focuses on two recording studios that engaged in divergent approaches to infusing world music into local song traditions. She explores changing ideas about creativity and innovation among Manganiyar musician communities, and traces a shift from diverse traditional song practices to more expansive markets beyond local patronage and tourism markets.

In yet another chapter addressing a regional style of music, Anna Schultz examines popular manifestations of regional devotional songs in chapter 14. Schultz explains that a diversity of live performers, including classical performers, embraced devotional song styles and used their classical reputations to record popular and devotional songs for record companies. Schultz traces the ongoing shifts in identity and ideology in the Marathi- and Kannada-language devotional song recordings of Pandit Bhimsen Joshi. In doing so, she helps us follow the historical flow of devotional songs, sometimes highly visible and sometimes almost totally submerged by the overwhelming presence of film song.

Finally, in chapter 15, Paul Greene addresses a new style of music production called "remixing" in which club DJs layer vocal lines from Bollywood film songs and remix them over dance beats. Remixing has engendered a reorientation of the politics of music production in the Bollywood industry and expanded the film song market to youths in dance clubs who otherwise might not usually listen to original Bollywood versions. DJs sell these remixes and take advantage of the widespread popularity of older film songs, while still appealing to young audiences who, increasingly, want to dance to contemporary rhythms. This process expands the reach of film songs into a larger demographic market while crossing over into a new style of film music.

CONCLUSION

Throughout the studies of Indian popular music offered here, the presence and importance of film music (and more broadly, music in dramatic narrative) has wandered very much like the elephant of our metaphor: His big feet have sometimes badly muddied (and perhaps even diverted) the stream of India's popular music culture. Film song (and theatre song before it) often dominated the locally produced popular music, sometimes to the exclusion of everything else. As we have made clear, during the nearly three decades of the License Raj, it had relatively little outside competition.

Despite film song's locally produced identity, its instrumental and musical and stylistic content have long been the grounds on which Indian music producers have engaged with the sounds and trends of the globally dominant music industries of Britain and the United States. Historically, film song itself has been the music of (almost) all Indians; but the music of those foreign industries has often been the elite alternative, either in the context of colonialism and its "locally foreign" audience or in the context of globalization and the increasingly transnational "ears" of the elite domestic audience.

Popular music in India has long existed between and been shaped by local and global trends. The pull of those poles has sometimes affected the degree of dominance enjoyed by our *filmi* elephant and has routinely colored the musical specifics of sound and style. Today, the power of globalizing forces is clear for all to hear and see in Indian popular music of all genres and in the videos that often accompany them. That power is also perceptible in the survival strategies of most Indian musicians. Nevertheless, in the first decade of the 21st century, the legal consumption of "international" music, which is to say international popular music, was still well under 10 percent of all Indian music revenues according to the figures of the Indian Music Industry (2005). A listen to India's growing FM radio soundscape suggests that the elephant is in no danger of imminent demise. The studies in this book present a range of detailed perspectives on multiple aspects of a complex phenomenon, one that is uniquely reflective of the cultural, political, and economic interactions of the global world of the 20th and 21st centuries.

PART ONE

Perspectives on Film Song

CHAPTER 1

A Moment of Historical Conjuncture in Mumbai

Playback Singers, Music Directors, and Arrangers and the Creation of Hindi Song (1948–1952)

GREGORY D. BOOTH

The first 15 years of Indian film song (1931–1946) witnessed a number of significant aesthetic and professional transitions. Composers, singers, actors, directors, and technicians of all sorts confronted the relocation of music dramas from the live stage to the screen; the technological innovation that allowed filmmakers to record sound and image separately and later synchronize to make a film product; the separation of acting and singing in both the places and times of recording and the professional roles that defined these components of the filmmaking process; and the growth of film orchestras and the need for arrangers who notated compositions, orchestrated and harmonized melodies, and often composed some of the instrumental music. Other changes appeared on the horizon at the end of this period, including the decline of the studio production system, a growing sophistication in the cinematography of song scenes and in the use of music in narrative, and a change in the sound of the male voice in film songs (Arnold 1991, Booth 2008a, Ranade 2006). During this period, film song also gradually took on a role as India's most important popular song form. (Note: Throughout this chapter and book, all Indian language film titles are translated except for those consisting solely of proper nouns or proper nouns joined by a conjunction.)

In the five years following Indian independence, from roughly 1948 through 1952, many of these incremental changes and other, still more recent developments coalesced into a set of sonic, stylistic, industrial, and cinematic norms that came to define the music of the Hindi cinema over the subsequent 20 or more years. This chapter focuses on these five years in which the fundamental musical, aesthetic, and cinematographic nature of Hindi film song was established, and on a small group of musicians—composers, singers, and arrangers—who undertook two complementary roles during this period. The individuals who are the focus of this study—Naushad Ali, Shankar-Jaikishan, C. Ramchandra, Lata Mangeshkar, Antonio Vaz, and Sebastian D'Souza—are listed in figure 1.1. These musicians led the consolidation of the developments outlined above that had been taking shape during the preceding ten years. They were also innovators, however, playing active roles in establishing new aspects of film song style, including the consolidation of the film song form, the explicit engagement with both classical Indian and foreign popular styles, the increasing sophistication of film song orchestration, and the redefinition of the sound of female playback singing, among others. I suggest that these five years were a moment of historical conjuncture that brought together these seven key musicians in such a way that their individual efforts and their collaborations with each other and with other film production figures empowered them to effect this degree of change.

Having said this, I must acknowledge that historical circumstances and systemic developments within the Indian culture industry certainly helped these individuals to achieve their positions of historical power. The concept of the historical conjuncture, as Sahlins (2004) defines it, has an element of the "right person in the right place at the right time." My concern here is with how this notion of "right" person, place, and time can be defined in musical and music/film industry contexts and how individual strengths, inclinations, and skills acted to shape the fundamental musical, aesthetic, industrial, and social patterns of Hindi film production.

Naushad Ali, Shankar-Jaikishan, C. Ramchandra, Lata Mangeshkar, Antonio Vaz, and Sebastian D'Souza collaborated among themselves, creatively and professionally, in various combinations, from time to time. They were never (and never expected to be) a single professional unit, but they were members of a slightly larger oligarchic group who, despite often competing among themselves, effectively controlled the production of Hindi film song. It should be noted at this point that although composers

Figure 1.1. MUSICIANS RESPONSIBLE FOR THE FORMALIZATION OF
HINDI FILM SONG, 1948–1952

Musician	Date of Birth	Professional Role*	Film of First Impact	Active
Antonio Vaz	1906–67	Arranger	*Shehnai* (1947)	ca. 1947–1960
Sebastian D'Souza	1916–96	Arranger	*Awaara* (1951)	1948–1986
Chitalkar Ramchandra	1918–82	Music Director	*Sukhi Jeevan* (1942)	1942–1978
Naushad Ali	1919–2006	Music Director	*Rattan* (1944)	1940–1993
Shankar Raghuvanshi Jaikishan Panchal	??–1987 1929–71	Music Director	*Barsaat* (1949)	1949–1986
Lata Mangeshkar	*b.* 1929	Singer	*Majboor* (1948)	1947–2004

*The dates shown in these columns define careers in terms of the role specified and in terms of the Hindi cinema only.

Shankar and Jaikishan were indeed two people, they worked as a team throughout their career and are here treated as a single entity.

The key figures in figure 1.1 came to the world of film song from a variety of cultural/linguistic backgrounds: Eastern Hindustani/Urdu, Marathi, and Goan (Portuguese/English and Konkani). Many had at least some training in Indian classical music. Lata Mangeshkar and Shankar-Jaikishan had strong connections to the worlds of Indian musical theatre (albeit with different theatrical genres) that involved a range of traditional music styles. Mangeshkar and C. Ramchandra both began their film careers as actors, rather than musicians; for much of his career, Ramchandra not only composed songs for films but sang many of them in the recording sessions as well. Vaz and D'Souza came from Goan and Christian backgrounds. As such, they had received early training in Western classical music and theory from the church-based education system in place in Portuguese Goa. Their subsequent careers (and public demand) involved them in the world of American jazz and dance bands. Collectively, then, this group embodied three of the most central contributing traditions that helped create the syncretic aesthetic of the Hindi cinema in the 1950s—Indian classical music, theatre music, and Western dance band music. For most of them, the period of 1948–1852 marked what are widely understood to have been "turning points" in their individual careers (e.g., Ali 2004b, Kabir 2009, Majumdar 2001); but these events also demarcated turning points in the music of the Hindi cinema. From these individuals' musical sounds and professional practices were constituted the sounds and practices of Hindi film song over the next 30 or more years.

Popular discourse (and even some scholarly discourse, such as Rajadhyaksha and Willemen 1995) in the Hindi cinema tends to define career turning points by the film in which musicians are understood to have made their first major impact. As figure 1.1 shows, most of these musicians made their first impact on the world of Indian film music in the late 1940s. Unique personal circumstances and economic need were naturally factors in each of their career choices; for some at least, film music was neither their preferred life choice nor their preferred musical choice. Each came with different forms of previous training and experience and with specific cultural and personal identities. Each established a distinctive set of professional and personal relationships with the other musicians listed in figure 1.1, as well as with others working in film song production. What they shared, other than the simple fact of being engaged in the same business, was their achievement of significant industry status during the period specified.

As shown, these seven individuals embodied three specific professional and musical roles: music directors (as composers were called), playback singers, and musical arrangers (sometimes referred to as assistants). These seven were by no means the only musicians who occupied such roles, but from the 1950s forward, their work defined and consolidated the professional practices associated with these roles. As I have described elsewhere (Booth 2008a), these roles described informal professional relationships that could extend for years (as they did in some cases here) or remain limited to the recording of a specific song for a specific film. Although there was an implied theoretical hierarchy in which music directors had the most importance, other factors such as age, popularity, and gender could alter the relative status of individuals in these roles.

The musical and professional patterns that were established between 1948 and 1952 remained almost completely unchanged and entirely dominant at least until 1970. Although changes are clearly perceptible after 1970, those changes were relatively superficial. For a further 20 years, until roughly 1990—despite some challenges from non-film popular music genres and the rise of a new generation of musicians playing a significant role, largely replacing the figures I discuss here—Hindi film song maintained a remarkable continuity of sound, style, and genre that must certainly be one of the longest periods of relative continuity in the history of popular music.

"Historical storytelling is the retelling from the beginning of an outcome already known" (Sahlins 2004, 131). Broader questions regarding the nature of "outcomes" in musical or cultural history and regarding the role of individual rather than systemic agency are beyond the scope of this chapter, as are the beginnings of film song in India in 1931, the year of the first Indian sound films. The changes on which I focus were at the heart of an industrial structure that was also changing. They were of such magnitude as to represent a "new beginning" in Hindi film song and were in large part responsible for the long period of relative continuity in the musical styles and practices and the industrial structures of Hindi film song beginning around 1950.

THE "OUTCOME ALREADY KNOWN"

Individual musicians, who formed an oligarchy of music directors, singers, and arrangers, were at the heart of this continuity, although it was also encouraged by the film producers who were their employers and who were overwhelmingly concerned with commercial success. The number of composers who dominated Hindi film song production was quite small relative to the number of films released and began to decline around the time of Indian independence (1947). That decline can be demonstrated, to some extent, by examining the ratios of composers whose soundtracks were heard in more than one film released in any given year. In 1947, the composition of the songs for the 177 films released that year was distributed among 108 music directors; 36 percent of these music directors had more than one soundtrack released that year. Although two or three soundtracks were the most common output that year for these busy composers, Khemchand Prakash, A. R. Qureshi, and C. Ramchandra were especially productive, with five, six, and eight soundtracks respectively. By 1952, however, the percentage of music directors with multiple releases in a year had risen to 62 percent. This figure hovered around 50 percent for the following ten years before dropping back to 30 percent in 1967. Between 1952 and 1992, the number of music directors with releases in any given year averaged less than half of the number of films released in that year. Over the 15 preceding years (1932–1947), that same proportion had been 62 percent (Booth 2008a, 98). Collectively, these figures give some sense of the musical oligarchy in place in Mumbai's film music production world in these years.

The place of the three music directors on whom I focus—C. Ramchandra, Naushad Ali, and Shankar-Jaikishan—is equally clear. Of the 60 highest net grossing films from 1947 to 1957, 19 (32 percent) were released in the middle five years (1948–1952); the scores for 13 of these 19 films were the work of these three music directors.

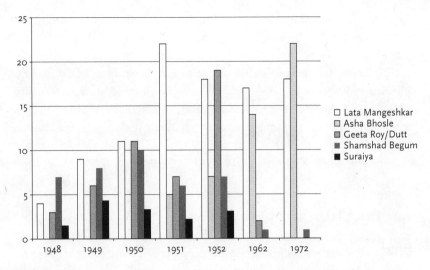

Figure 1.2
Songs recorded by leading female playback singers shown as a percentage of total film songs recorded per year (including male-voiced songs and male-female duets).

The shrinking size of the oligarchy in the world of playback singers is equally pronounced. Among male singers, Mohammed Rafi and Kishore Kumar became increasingly dominant (although Kumar's years of peak importance are after the period of my immediate concern). Nevertheless, there was a greater number of important male singers during and after this period than female singers, where the shift was both more dramatic and more extreme. Mishra notes that "1952 could be seen as the year that brought to an end the richly textured and individually timbered voices of an earlier tradition of film music that included... [singers such as] Amir Bai, Noor Jehan, Suraiya and Shamshad Begum" (2002, 166). Figure 1.2 provides a degree of quantitative definition to Mishra's assertion.

The chart shows the percentage of total film songs per year (including male-voiced songs and male-female duets) recorded by Lata Mangeshkar, Asha Bhosle (b. 1933), Shamshad Begum (b. 1919), Geeta Roy/Dutt (1930–1972), and Suraiya (Suraiya Jamal Sheikh, 1929–2004), the five numerically dominant female vocalists of the Hindi cinema in these years. The data on which this chart is based were drawn from the *Hindi Film Geet Kosh* [Hindi Film Song Dictionary] of Harmandir Singh (1980, 1984, 1986, 1991). Other female singers were responsible for between 1 and 2.5 percent of the songs recorded in these years. The chart shows the same information for ten and 20 years beyond this period. No new female singers have been added; this is because no new female playback singers appeared as numerically significant voices in Hindi playback singing until after this period.

As Mishra suggests, the wide range of distinctive female vocal timbres heard in the voices of singers such as Amir Bai Karnataki, Khurshid, Uma Devi, Rajkumari, and other popular singers (and singing actresses) of the 1930s and 1940s began to shrink in 1950 and was obliterated by the 1960s (cf. Majumdar 2001). The two numerically significant representatives of older vocal styles, Shamshad Begum and the singing actress Suraiya, predominate in 1948 and hold their own in 1949. The rise of the new vocal style is clear by 1950, however, in the prominence of Lata Mangeshkar, with her high, pure soprano voice, and Geeta Dutt, whose voice, although certainly quite distinct from Mangeshkar's, was nevertheless representative of the new vocal trend. The following year shows the strength of the new vocal sound and the beginning of the personal domination of female film singing by the women of the Mangeshkar family, primarily Lata Mangeshkar and her younger sister, Asha Bhosle. The two women, together with Geeta Dutt, recorded slightly over a third of all the songs recorded in 1951. The physical and personal collapse of Geeta Dutt in the late 1950s left the field almost completely in the hands of Mangeshkar and Bhosle, who recorded 31 percent of all Hindi film songs in 1962 and 40 percent in 1972, undeterred by the long-lived persistence of Shamshad Begum who, although ten years older than Mangeshkar, continued to record a small proportion of film songs into the 1970s.

In addition to these quantitative indications of a shrinking oligarchy and stylistic stability, I examine other, more interactive musical, aesthetic, and industrial practices below. I have considered elsewhere many of the specifically instrumental and orchestral aspects of this stability (2008b); in this study, I include the vocal consistencies mentioned above, the increasingly sophisticated integration of song scenes into plot elements, and the adaptation of song scene cinematography and musical structure to the technology of the cinema. Collectively, these factors constitute the musical foundation of the outcome that I seek to explain in this chapter.

HISTORICAL CONJUNCTURES IN POST-INDEPENDENCE HINDI FILM SONG

In his consideration of historical change and the power to effect change, Marshall Sahlins seeks to balance systemic or general trends with individual motivations and abilities. He argues that for individuals to have historical effect, "they have to be in a position to do so" (2004, 155). He continues by arguing that "'position' means a place in a set of relationships," and that it is these positions that empower individuals so that their actions and goals do have historical effect. In this chapter, I try to outline how, during the period I have identified, many specific and often quite personalized conjunctures developed in the system that produced Hindi films and film songs and how the resulting careers influenced film song production. For this influence to have been achieved, the individual skills (specific vocal timbres, musical training and skills, social and personal relationships, and so on) that each musician possessed had to become part of a broader cultural and industrial system of film song production.

In gauging the importance of individual careers, we are immediately confronted by the extra-musical factors that are rampant in a consideration of popular responses to film song. Naushad Ali (hereafter Naushad, as he is most commonly identified) is understood to have established his position in film music through the extremely successful score for the film *Rattan* (1944) (Ranade 2006). This film is also understood to have established the career of its director, M. Sadiq (Rajadhyaksha and Willemen 1995). *Rattan* was the second most commercially successful film of the 1940s[1]; but this two-sided dynamic (a hit for/of the composer, a hit for/of the director) illustrates the impossibility of completely disentangling the interactions that lead to a positive popular response. There is no question, however, that the mutual successes of the film and the score began to position Naushad as an important innovator in Hindi film song.

"Naushad...succeeded in meaningfully tightening the musical concept of a 'film song' as distinct from 'singing in a film'" (Ranade 2006, 195). Ranade identifies Naushad's treatment (and standardization) of instrumental interludes, tempo, orchestral size ("about 100 musicians became an established feature"), recording techniques, and the professionalization of film singers as the basis of "a kind of Naushad-led standardization" and also proposes that in this process, Naushad increased the level of musical repetition (ibid., 195–196).

Naushad's song "Dhar Na Mohabbat Kar Le" ["Don't Be Afraid, Fall in Love"] (video 1.3) appears early in *Andaz* (1949), a film that generated the sixth highest adjusted net gross of the 1940s. The film featured major stars of the period and focused on a romantic triangle involving the two heroes, played by Dilip Kumar and Raj Kapoor, and the film's central female character, played by Nargis, who is simultaneously part of a second romantic triangle (hinted at in this scene) in which she and Cuckoo compete for Kumar's attentions. "Dhar Na Mohabbat" is a female duet, sung by that year's two leading female vocalists, Shamshad Begum and Lata Mangeshkar. Mangeshkar's voice comes first, while Nargis mimes; Shamshad Begum's voice is used for the second heroine, Cuckoo, constructing clear timbral contrast between what was about to become the "old" (and narratively unsuccessful) voice of Shamshad Begum and the "new" and (at this point in the narrative) victorious voice of Lata Mangeshkar.

The song is typical of Naushad's work as described by Ranade, but also illustrates the incremental nature of the transition from earlier musical styles. Rhythmically and melodically, the opening phrase ("*Dhar na mohabbat kar le*") is clearly defined and almost entirely syllabic. After a single complete repetition, Mangeshkar moves on to a contrasting phrase that is distinctly melismatic and more rhythmically ambiguous. Following Ranade's argument, this consequent phrase is more "old-fashioned" than its predecessor. It nevertheless manages to wander its way back to the "*Dhar na mohabbat kar le*" melody, which serves as a refrain throughout the song, this time sung by both women. The musical distinctions between these melodic phrases are minor, but they nevertheless are part of the changes that Naushad and some of his colleagues initiated between 1948 and 1952.

Naushad's position was powerful enough by 1946 that he could contribute to the success of other musical careers, including that of Mohammed Rafi, who would become one of the Hindi cinema's most popular male playback singers. His enormous popularity notwithstanding, Rafi was not a vocal innovator in the same way that Lata Mangeshkar would be (see below); he was following in the smoother, softer, almost crooning vocal style, as Ranade (2006) calls it, introduced by K. L Saigal in the early 1940s. Nevertheless, as a consequence of his classical music training (which Saigal did not have), Rafi became an important symbol of the "professionalization" of Hindi film song that Ranade attributes to Naushad. Further, Rafi's classical orientation aligned with Naushad's own classical training and musical inclinations, so that when Naushad began to advocate the importance of Indian classical music in film scores (a position he developed from roughly 1950 onward), Rafi became the male voice of that position (Naushad Ali, pers. comm. 2004).

Naushad used Rafi as a vocalist in his songs for the 1952 film *Baiju Bawra*, which Naushad subsequently argued was an intentional defense of Indian classical music (Ali 2004a). *Baiju Bawra* was among the top ten commercially successful films of the 1950s, but is today "remembered mostly for its music" (Rajadhyaksha and Willemen 1995, 304). Using Rafi's voice as a primary instrument, Naushad formalized a popularized "*filmi* classical" music that became a standard component in Hindi film vocabulary and operated as something like a musical genre at least in Naushad's films, if not others. Naushad sought to construct a distinct ideological position for the identity of Hindi film song based on these classically flavored popular songs. He continued to produce classical film scores for films such as *Shabaab* (1954) and, most famously, *Mughal-e-Azam* (1960), the highest adjusted net grossing film of the 1960s. In his advocacy of Indian classical music, Naushad was positioning himself in opposition to another music director who, in hindsight, may have been on the "winning side" in the debate so clearly articulated by Naushad. Music director Chitalkar Ramchandra (most commonly known as C. Ramchandra) was, from his very first film scores, an enthusiastic fan of foreign popular styles.

There had been some form of interaction between Hindi film song and foreign (primarily American and British) musical influences almost from the inception of Indian sound film. Naushad himself was an important innovator in his use of orchestral instruments, but Ramchandra's score for *Shehnai* (1947) appears to be the earliest Hindi film score to explicitly use melodic materials from foreign popular song. That film's comic song scene "Aana Meri Jaan, Sunday Ke Sunday" ["Please Come to Me, My Dear, Every Sunday"] was based on melodic fragments taken from older, popular Anglo-American songs; it established Ramchandra's reputation as a composer with a "penchant for American pop" (Ranade 2006, 127). Ramchandra's enthusiasm for what Bose (2008) has called the "Indianisation" of Western popular music was solidified in subsequent films, especially the enormously successful *Albela* (1951).

Like Naushad, Ramchandra found a suitable collaborator for his musical goals, although in Ramchandra's case, that collaborator was not a singer but an arranger. Jazz musician and dance band leader Antonio Vaz had a successful career outside the film world (as Shope explores in chapter 10). Ramchandra's fascination with Vaz's band and their music led him to recruit these musicians for his film scores. Vaz worked as an arranger or assistant (in fact a collaborator) on many of Ramchandra's film scores, providing stylistic expertise (at least) in composing and recording. Ramchandra's scores introduced Latin-styled jazz melodies and dance band arrangements to film music production. Unusually, Vaz and some of his band appear in the *Albela* song scene "Deewana Yeh Parwana" ["An Intoxicated Moth to the Flame"], miming to their own recording (an excerpt from this song scene is included in chapter 10).

Unlike Naushad's single-handed development of the "classical" style of film song, the changes that are represented by the C. Ramchandra scores of this period would not have been possible without Antonio Vaz, who brought to the undertaking musical skills and preferences that were, at that time, unique for the film industry. Ramchandra and Vaz, in other words, were both innovators; both had historical effect. If Ramchandra's power was the result of his position as a famous music director, which gave him the ability to employ Vaz, Vaz's power to change film song existed in potential only, until Ramchandra's personal enthusiasms for foreign popular styles and professional interests in his own career put Vaz in a specific "place in a set of relationships" (as per Sahlins 2004) from which he also could effect musical change. Like Naushad's use of Indian classical materials, Ramchandra (in collaboration with Vaz) set a pattern for the distinctly Indian and distinctly *filmi* use of global popular song materials. However popular the music style was, such formalization needed more than simply musical, stylistic change. Film music production was a large, complex industrial system involving many musicians and other figures and a wide range of physical infrastructural resources; for musical change to succeed, industrial and technological change—which were the outcomes of other moments of conjuncture—was also required.

Both classical and foreign pop-style film songs were popular in post-independence India (the latter perhaps more than the former). Success led the commercially minded film/music industry to pursue the formalization of an increasingly syncretic musical style, in which specific content from, and markers of, other musical styles (such as Indian folk and regional styles) were applied to a generic musical core. Music directors Shankar-Jaikishan are the final composers in this chapter. More prolific over a longer period of time than either Naushad or Ramchandra, their career was tied to that of an iconic figure of India's postcolonial cinema: actor/director/producer Raj Kapoor.

Shankar Raghuvanshi and Jaikishan Panchal began their professional careers as theater musicians, working at the central Mumbai playhouse Prithvi Theatre; it was there that they apparently first met Kapoor, the son of the theater's owner. After working as assistants on Kapoor's first film, Shankar-Jaikishan were chosen as music directors in late 1948 for his second film, *Barsaat* (1949), one of the top five commercial successes of the 1940s. The success of *Barsaat* and the subsequent ongoing success of the "Kapoor brand" as both actor and producer/director positioned Shankar-Jaikishan to effect historical change because it encouraged other film producers to hire them as well; the pair was among the most prolific composers of the 1950s and early 1960s.

Unlike the other two music directors studied here, Shankar-Jaikishan did not introduce new styles directly. For example, the pair took up Naushad's classically flavored style in their score for the 1956 release *Basant Bahar* and Ramchandra's Western rhythms and stylings in "Sunte The Naam Hum" ["I Heard His Name"] in *Aah* (1953). Although it is certainly true that not all their films were major successes, the simple fact of the high annual demand for their work over a long period of time allowed them to establish the industrial practices I have described elsewhere (Booth 2008a). An initial historical conjuncture positioned Shankar-Jaikishan to effect historical change through (and later because of) their successful work with Raj Kapoor. But having achieved this position of musical power, they (like the other music directors above) also effected musical change by "sharing" their power.

In 1947, the same year that the score for *Shehnai* introduced the Indian audience to the beginnings of a foreign popular music element in film song, another Goan dance band musician (like Antonio Vaz) appeared in Mumbai. Sebastian D'Souza had been working in Lahore, the Panjabi capital, playing in nightclubs and doing some work for music directors in that city; but in 1947, when Lahore became part of the new nation of Pakistan, many musicians, D'Souza among them, returned to India (Victor D'Souza, pers. comm. 2004). Like Vaz, D'Souza secured work as an arranger for music directors in Mumbai's film music industry. His son attributes fundamental changes in the sound of the Hindi film song to his father's work: "Before him there was not arrangement. Only they played the melody. So he changed everything" (ibid.).

D'Souza worked with a wide range of film composers through the 1970s; but because arrangers and assistants have been inconsistently listed in film credits, there is no way to know with certainty the actual number of film scores with which he was involved. D'Souza's longest and most consistent professional relationship was with Shankar-Jaikishan, who provided the turning point in his career when they hired him for the (uncredited) arrangements for their second film, *Awara* (1951). D'Souza's skills and impact were broader than those of his colleague Antonio Vaz; whether he in fact changed "everything" or not, he set in motion the integration of Western chordal harmony with explicitly Indian melodic content, and he standardized the film studio orchestra in a range of ways. I have considered D'Souza's work in the context of *Awara* and the musical impact of the Shankar-Jaikishan-D'Souza conjuncture elsewhere (Booth 2008b).

All three of the music directors I have discussed here feature in another important historical conjuncture that resulted in musical change in Hindi film song—the career of playback singer Lata Mangeshkar. The impact of Mangeshkar's voice on the Hindi cinema is something that many scholars have addressed (e.g., Majumdar 2001, Srivastava 2004). Although her first hit song was released only in 1948, the meteoric nature of her rise justifies Ranade's assessment that "by 1950 Lata was a legend" (2006, 403).

As figure 1.2 shows, Mangeshkar's output more than doubled in the 12 months after her debut, recording 122 songs for 1949 releases (9 percent of all film songs—male and female—recorded for that year). Her training as a vocalist, her personal connections with music drama (Kabir 2009), and the sheer appeal that her voice projected were major factors in that success. At the same time, however, over 10 percent of the 122 songs she recorded for 1949 were from two of the most successful films of the 1940s, scored by Shankar-Jaikishan and Naushad; in addition to *Barsaat*, which reported the fourth highest adjusted net gross of that decade, Mangeshkar sang for Naushad in *Andaz* (sixth highest). She recorded 72 songs in the 30 highest performing films in the 1948–1952 period, 11 of which were scored by the three music directors under consideration. Mangeshkar's impact on the history of Hindi film song was unique. That impact, however, was magnified by the strong personal and professional connections she maintained with the three music directors discussed here.

In this admittedly selective account of human agency in Hindi film song production, I have argued that the potential to effect historical change in Hindi film song—latent in individual combinations of human talent, training, and vision—was empowered by the conjunctures I have described. Certainly, the individuals studied here did effect cultural/musical change. Ashok Ranade (2006) and others such as Biswarup Sen (2008) have generally described the history of Hindi film song in precisely these kinds of "evenemential" terms. Sahlins appears to have developed this term to identify the "radical humanist" approach to historical change (2004, 128–143), which focuses on issues of human talent and creativity. But Ranade could not fully avoid acknowledgment of "developmental" change, the deterministic power of economics, technology, and cultural systems that Sahlins fancifully calls the "leviathan" (ibid.). Ranade acknowledges that the changes he (and I) describe—the decline of the "old-fashioned" female voice, the formalization of film song form, and the growing syncretic blend of music styles—may have been "inevitable" (Ranade 2006, 196) regardless of who had participated in the process, which is to say, determined by the impersonal factors of the collective system. The "leviathanology" of India's culture industry is of sufficient size and complexity as to place it beyond the scope of this chapter. In the conclusion of this chapter, however, I offer a systemic, determinist view of cultural change in the period and the context of the personal histories set out above and in the context of a single technological development and its impact.

THE "LEVIATHANOLOGY" OF CHANGE IN CULTURE INDUSTRIES

Systemic change is inevitably more gradual and more incremental than change driven by the sudden conjuncture, for instance, of a jazz band leader and a popular music director. My final argument, therefore, examines the longer sequence of historical changes resulting from the introduction of a new technological process in film production: the appearance of dual-strip film dubbers in India in 1934/35. These relatively simple mechanisms enabled the separate but synchronizable recording of sound (especially music) and image, described in Booth (2008a). Kolkata's New Theatres studio was probably the first to use the new technology, but it is hard to argue that they were empowered to effect historical change. The immediate implications of this technology for the film production process, which had already been in operation in Britain and America for several years, were widely and immediately understood; it was only a matter of time (and timing) before the new technology was taken up by the entire Indian industry. There was a "first" film made using these separate recording processes (probably *Dhoop Chhaon*, 1935), but the change had, so to speak, already taken place in the minds of India's more globally aware technicians and filmmakers who implemented the technology as soon as they were able to acquire it.

One direct outcome of this change was the development of "playback singers" as a professional role separate from that of "actor." The separation of the recording processes initially allowed the actors themselves to sing their songs in recording sessions, then mime them in front of the cameras; this transitioned, over a period of roughly ten years, to a splitting of acting and singing—both in terms of personnel and temporally—into two distinct professional roles. Almost as an aside, and in the context of this systemic history of technological change, Lata Mangeshkar's emergence onto the playback scene in 1948 appears perfectly, if conjuncturally, timed. Just as she sought to abandon her role as a child actor and assume a new professional career as an adult more in line with her skills, training, and personal inclinations, the leviathan obligingly provided one.

There were other outcomes arising from this technological change that had to do with the nature and expressive potential of the song scene as a cinematic component, manifesting as changes in ways that song scenes were positioned within films and utilized within the narrative structure. These were not as easy to perceive as the growth of playback singing or the "meteoric" rise to fame of Lata Mangeshkar; furthermore, they were complexly conjunctural, requiring both music directors and film directors to have both the creative vision and historical effect. Beginning in 1935 (when the technology became available), makers of film and film music began to reconsider the realist principles and aesthetics that they had inherited from various forms of staged music drama that played so important a role in the development of the Hindi cinema as a music-drama form. Early Hindi song scenes had been filmed as complete performances with characters that both acted and sang simultaneously, rather like the performances that had, still earlier, been taking place on the musical stage. The technological ability to record sound and image separately gave film-makers the power to construct a coherent whole from disparate and asynchronous visual and audio elements.

Mishra argues that the new ability of the song scene to serve as "a unifier of otherwise (quasi) disparate shots" was an "event," first evident in the song scenes of Naushad's 1952 release *Baiju Bawra*, and that in these song scenes, "the song may be what holds different narrative events and elements together" (2002, 164). Nevertheless, the systemic, technology-driven process of change was more incremental, more gradual than this "evenemential" understanding suggests. The transformation of the Hindi song scene from a relatively static emotional soliloquy or staged performance to a component with the potential to serve as a unifier of both cinematic and narrative content was implemented during the 1948–1952 period and became an essential convention of the Hindi cinema that continued to develop. By way of conclusion, therefore, I offer an example from the body of films, directors, and composers already discussed, specifically the 1949 film *Barsaat*.

By all accounts, director Raj Kapoor was fascinated by music's emotional power (Chatterjee 1992) and narrative potential. The musical and cinematic results of his collaborations with Shankar-Jaikishan demonstrate the ongoing development of a narrative/musical aesthetic based on the "productive nature of space occupied by the song syntagms in the text" (Mishra 2002, 161). The first three song scenes of *Barsaat* illustrate this approach.

Barsaat is a story of two romantic relationships—one ultimately successful, the other ultimately tragic—involving "modern" urban male characters and unsophisticated women from hill villages. During the film's first 30 minutes, three song scenes (all sung by Lata Mangeshkar) take place that establish the weak nature of Gopal, the secondary protagonist (played by Premnath), and the more idealist nature of the film's hero Pran (played by Raj Kapoor). This introductory portion of the story also makes clear the inherently doomed quality of Gopal's ultimately tragic relationship with his stationary, isolated (and therefore helpless) paramour Neelam (played by Nimmi). Each of the three songs is "sung," which is to say mimed, by a female character, whose beauty is reinforced by the charms of the forests and mountains of her environment. Each scene is bounded to some extent by the movement of Gopal's impressively large car, which is clearly represented as his means of consummating his mountain affairs and escaping their consequences.

As the heroes drive along the mountain road, the narrative's first song, "Hawa Mein Udtha Jaye Mere Lal Dupatta" ["My Scarf Has Blown Away on the Breeze"] (video 1.4), begins. After Gopal's attempted seduction of the unnamed woman whose scarf has indeed blown away, the car starts up again and the two heroes flee the situation. "Jiya Beqarar Hai" ["Life Is Restless/Uncertain without You"] (video 1.5) introduces the narrative's tragic heroine Neelam as she waits for Gopal to return. The song, which speaks of love and Neelam's longing ("please come quickly, beloved, I am waiting for you"), begins as Pran and Gopal drive toward Neelam's village and Gopal boasts that he has someone waiting for him. The scene shifts directly to Neelam, herding her goats, who "sings" the song. When the melody ends three minutes later, the accompanying music continues, as the joyful Neelam sees Gopal's car coming up the mountain road. The scene cuts back to the car.

The final song of this initial musical trio, "Barsaat Mein Humse Mile Tum" ["You Met Me in the Rains"], is staged as an ersatz mountain folk dance. It again features Neelam, this time with a cohort of male drummers and female dancers. It begins as a song of love and celebration in which Neelam reflects on her first meetings with Gopal and her expectations of marriage, but then degenerates into sadness as she realizes Gopal is leaving. In a reverse of "Jiya Beqarar Hai," this song ends with the car once again on the road, this time moving away from the stranded heroine, who chases after it for some distance. The film's first 30 minutes are not only densely musical; they also make use of what Mishra (2002) calls the "productive space" constructed by the songs to define Gopal's untrustworthy and tragic romance. What is more, the three songs construct an emotionally and narratively distinct space that isolates the relationship between Gopal and Neelam from the more innocent romance of the central characters Pran (Raj Kapoor) and Reshma (Nargis). In order to make clear this separation, a full 15 minutes of narrative unfold before the first romantic song featuring these characters.

These three songs illustrate a fundamental change in the nature and role of the Hindi film song scene when compared to the song scenes of the 1930s and 1940s. In this particular instance, the scenes were the result of the combined creative efforts (and visions) of director Raj Kapoor and composers Shankar-Jaikishan, as expressed by Lata Mangeshkar and a whole troupe of actors. As I have argued throughout this chapter, a series of historical conjunctures positioned these individuals to effect such change. However, in this conclusion, I have also suggested that these songs scenes are simply a few examples of the outcome of a leviathan-like change that was potentially possible any time after 1935 and that developed gradually and systemically over a period of ten years in multiple, barely perceptible increments. In this view, Shankar-Jaikishan, Kapoor, and others were simply fulfilling the potential of the technology. Despite the popularity and cultural importance of these songs, singers, composers, and so on, these scenes illustrate "how history makes the history-makers," even in the culture industries (Sahlins 2004, 155).

NOTES

1. All the financial performance statistics reported in this chapter are based on the figures reported by Box Office India (http://www.boxofficeindia.com/), which offers two assessments of film performance: "Net Gross," defined as the gross minus the various entertainment taxes on box-office receipts, and "Adjusted Net Gross," defined as "theatrical business judged against the release size which we believe is the best way to judge a success of a film." For more on what constitutes a cinematic hit in India, see http://www.boxofficeindia.com/showProd.php?item Cat=321&catName=V2hhdCBJcyBBIEhpdA.

CHAPTER 2

Global *Masala*

Digital Identities and Aesthetic Trajectories in
Post-Liberalization Indian Film Music

NATALIE SARRAZIN

INTRODUCTION

Hindi film music has, in a sense, always been inquisitive in nature, with eclectic forays in instrumentation, style, and borrowed idioms from a wide range of cultural sources. In *Behind the Curtain* (2008), for example, Booth recounts how music directors viewed Hollywood films and listened to Western popular music in order to absorb new styles and find compositional inspiration. Over the decades, Indian audiences, both domestic and abroad, demonstrated an appreciation for film music's multiplicity of instruments and styles.

After economic liberalization, Indian pop music underwent unprecedented cultural, technological, and artistic change. Hindi film music in particular entered a rapid and intense era of increased visibility and globalization, fueled by aggressive international marketing and a rise in world consumption of Hindi films and film songs. The change in Hindi film music during this time was nothing short of revolutionary. Songs exhibited an increasingly globalized and cosmopolitan musical sensibility informed by a myriad of styles and approaches to popular music. At the most fundamental level of vocal timbre, for example, the extensive vocal reverb that was routinely added to the high soprano of playback singer Lata Mangeshkar and others in film songs through the 1980s waned in favor of a cleaner, more intimate, and more global pop sound, even as Mangeshkar's voice ceased to dominate the female playback scene. Overall, vocal styles took on a distinctly Western pop affectation while waves of world music genres influenced instrumentation and composition.

In this chapter, I discuss some of the changes in Hindi film music's aesthetics, along with the global, technological, and postmodern forces that drove them in a post-liberalization India. What impact did technological developments have on musical creativity? How have genre construction and stylistic identity been affected? I examine how these factors influenced the propagation of sound itself as a primary marker of Indian global identity in service of both resident and non-resident Indians (hereafter RIs and NRIs respectively). Additionally, I consider some of the consequences of globalization and ways in which cosmopolitan sensibilities found in film sound negotiated space for contested identities, futuristic visions, and nostalgic revivals for the middle-class and diasporic Indian audiences.

POST-LIBERALIZATION AND THE CREATIVE DIGITAL CONVERSION

By the early 1990s, a series of significant political and economic events coalesced, ushering in unprecedented transformation within the Indian nation-state. Primary among these was India's 1990–1991 financial crisis, which forced the government to undertake increased economic liberalization. Led by Prime Minister P. V. Narasimha Rao and his Finance Minister Manmohan Singh between 1991 and 1996, the Indian government initiated reforms of the financial system, expanding Indian import/export markets, freeing international trade, and accelerating the process of economic (and consequently cultural) globalization across the subcontinent. Foreign goods became increasingly available and normalized in Indian culture, and gradually, the last vestiges of a nationalist negativity that had been directed at Western objects, goods, and particularly sounds disappeared.

Strong privatization efforts encouraged private production in television and cinema, increased use of consumer goods such as the VCR, and technological innovations such as satellite and cable—all products that were eagerly consumed by a growing domestic Indian population. Hindi film music was both transformed by these changes and able to capitalize on them—greatly expanding film's national presence and influence. As one of the primary standard bearers of mass-mediated Indian cultural identity, Hindi film benefited from the technological innovations resulting from economic liberalization and played a significant role in cementing and promoting the zeitgeist of the new era (M. Sen 2011).

Through its unique semiotic qualities, sound is amorphous and flexible enough to encompass multi-vocality, meaning, and identity, playing a critical role in capturing complex expressions necessary for each generation. Biswarup Sen has observed that of the three major genres of Indian music, Bollywood, classical, and folk, only Bollywood was able to win the hearts of the masses through its capability of "play with otherness and difference so crucial to modernity and its expressions" (89, 2008).

The technological revolution of the latter 1990s shifted the music scene of the Indian cinema from a focus on film and recording studio production aesthetics toward audience values and tastes. Furthermore, it transformed the creative production process itself. The digital conversion in Indian recording studios, however, occurred rather slowly. Initially, only a handful of technologically savvy music directors owned or had access to the equipment or were knowledgeable enough to take advantage of it.

In a 2006 interview, music director A. R. Rahman, the composer par excellence of post-liberalized India, recalled a decisive moment early on in his career as he began work on what would become the soundtrack for Mani Ratnam's *Roja* (1992), a film of groundbreaking importance, simultaneously launching Rahman into music stardom and ushering in a new era of Hindi film song from which the new global eclecticism and aesthetic emerged. Rahman now sees *Roja* as a landmark soundtrack because of the *way* in which it was recorded. He told me, "At the time, there were these huge recording halls, with 50 violins. But I was doing commercials in my own studio. When Mani (Ratnam) wanted me to do the music, I said, 'Let's do it at my place.'" Rahman considers the small studio to be essential to his somewhat bricolaged compositional style; he states that his "limitations accidentally helped in the way that I approached composition in the early days. If I had the luxury of a full orchestra, I might have gone about composing in a traditional way...but I was producing in my studio at home and needed to use whatever was available to me and make it work" (Kabir 2011, 83).

In addition to reducing the studio space required to record, digital recording technology offered techniques to manipulate and control sound that were complete, extensive, and unparalleled, allowing composers, sound engineers, and musicians license to negotiate musical nuance and detail and integrate individual creativity in a way never before possible. Music directors like Rahman, who were able to master digital technology and synthesizers early on, revolutionized Hindi film sound by innovating their way out of previously entrenched musical soundtrack conventions. Rahman recognized his own early compositional complicity in what he refers to as working in the "heart of the cliché" (pers. comm. 2006), and went on to consciously compose background and song music in keeping with a more contemporary global aesthetic based on technical innovation and his own personal experiences playing in a rock band.

Digitalization not only allowed sound to be manipulated one instrument at a time, but also one note at a time—a piecemeal approach to recording that increased musical precision, intimacy, and nuance. Rahman was able to record each musician and vocalist separately, completing one small section to perfection and later synching together limited sections or fragments to create his aural vision and optimal sonic outcome (Mathai 2009, 201–202).

The idea that an entire soundtrack could be produced in a small studio using only digital equipment and a handful of musicians was anathema to Indian film studio music recording practice at the time. The new approach to production became more "individual-centered" and gradually reduced input from a larger music community. By essentially dispensing with the studio orchestra through sampling and synthesizers, music directors were able to consolidate control while more extensively exploiting the talent and creativity of individual artists or small groups of musicians. The ability to record in short bursts, to quickly and easily re-record over errors, and add synthesized sounds, additional countermelodies, counterpoint, layers of sampled rhythm tracks, as well as sampled sounds of all kinds at will with the help of specialized equipment and editing software, allowed composers freedom to experiment with sound at their convenience and go to comparatively innovative lengths.

SONIC VISUALIZATION: COMMERCIAL COMPOSITION TECHNIQUES

As film audiences grew accustomed to the use of synthesized and other digital enhancements that dramatically improved recording quality and noise reduction, they also came to expect yet another contemporaneous aesthetic—the pithy, intense, and hard-hitting music propagated by advertising and marketing campaigns. Rahman, and others, whose compositional roots began in the ad world composing jingles, introduced song-styling techniques befitting a 30-second commercial: condensed, inventive, and instantly captivating.

Commercial ad or jingle writer-composers apply a myriad of techniques to elicit immediate emotional responses. Given the extremely short duration of ads and limited production time, writers must compose concisely, using short hooks and remarkable and memorable musical material. Their music must connect instantly with the audience, hence the predilection for contemporary music; it must also convey the proper mood of the song, as well as the narrative in general. To accomplish this, composers employ highly persuasive devices known as "hits" (i.e., musical accentuation used to enhance a specific visual event such as the appearance of the product being advertised), as well as new thematic material, a high level of variety, tempo or modal changes, ostinati and drone to create tension, and even short musical themes for character identity (Zager 2003, 62). An immediately accessible sound, of course, requires the immediacy of a visual impact. Film picturizations were always about the visuals and music, but now composers, with the help of computer software, were able to focus extraordinary attention on the integration of music with visual imagery backed by the digital technology that allowed the two elements to be fused.

In 1992, Rahman applied these synergistic techniques to Ratnam's *Roja*; these are described in detail in the following analysis. In "Roja Jaaneman" ["Roja, My Love"], the introduction alone provides a glimpse into the possibilities of precision that resulted from the new technologies (figure 2.1). The two main scenes in this introduction depict the narrative's hero looking out of a window and a forest scene in which the heroine will eventually enter. Musically, the opening seconds (0:00–0:05) immediately grab the audience's attention in an unmetered intro with only two sounds—a raw, high-pitched yet androgynous and linguistically indeterminate synthesized human voice and a hauntingly airy flute. The sounds are digitally processed to the point where the voice is almost unidentifiable as human, leaving the listener with an uneasy feeling.

Nonetheless, the vocals and flute combine to produce a highly memorable melodic hook of four short phrases. In the first two phrases, the melody ascends in major and descends in minor, contributing to the disquieting mood. Phrase one of the melody corresponds with a camera framing and slowly zooming in on the hero's anxious gaze out of a window. By 0:05 seconds, however, the already unsettling melodic phrase is interrupted by a threatening electric bass drone, the use of which highlights mounting tension. The bass's entrance immediately coincides with a dramatic change in cinematography as the camera, placed at a low angle, erratically slinks through the tall forest grass as though looking through the eyes of a wild animal pursuing its yet-unidentified prey. The visual pace increases as the camera alternates shots between the frantic pursuit through the woods and the hero's gaze as he stands motionless, searching the horizon; this segment is accompanied by a melodic line continually and subtly shifting in and out of major and minor modalities. As audience members, we are not yet sure how to connect the melody to the visual, and we are kept guessing as to its identity.

In the climax of the introduction (0:18), the camera returns to the forest, and for the first time, we catch a glimpse of the heroine. Melodic phrase three accompanies her run through the forest as the voice softens, descends, and becomes more obviously identifiable as female. We now realize that the melodic hook identifies and embodies the heroine's character. Still unmetered, however, at 0:18, the electric bass drone changes to a rather menacing pulse, suggesting a threatening uncertainty for the heroine. The camera further heightens this tension through the use of a lowered angle, which frantically pursues her through grass and trees as she runs.

The electric bass pulse continues until 0:26 when not one but two rhythms appear—a slow rock beat played on a drum set and more ornamental, improvisational-sounding rhythms on the *tabla*. Above these, a somewhat foreboding synthesizer plays minor tremolo chords. Visually, the threatening mood is dispelled at this point, as the camera's close-up shots reveal a sweet, coy heroine as she playfully covers and then shows her face. Interestingly, the "hit effects," or emphases, coordinate the sustained synthesizer chords with the heroine's slow, gentle, and playful movements instead of tying them to the rock beat. After a series of close-ups focused on both hero and heroine, the hero's emotional longing is finally revealed as the song begins at 0:36. Delicate, organ-like synthesized chords change with two-beat regularity supporting the melody and lyrics.

Rahman and Ratnam applied this almost unprecedented precision of editing, in which musical change aligns tightly with each visual change in emotional content throughout the *Roja* soundtrack. They also attended quite closely (and innovatively) to the film's sonic design, in which music itself creates not only a mood but a visual image. For example, in "Yeh Haseen Waadiyan" ["These Beautiful Valleys"], also from *Roja*, the close synergy between sonic and visual enters a new realm as Rahman sonically emulates the vastness of a snowy mountain range flagged by jagged cliffs and bare trees and shrouded in a rolling mist. Rahman paints the scene with a fast-pulsed, deep, drone-like electric bass and two lines of delicate, minimalist, polyphonic melodic fragments (melody and countermelody) rendered in a *santoor*-like timbre. As the couple takes in the stunning view, the background melodies are cleverly reminiscent of a *pahari dhun* or hill folk melody. At 0:12, the *santoor*-drone backdrop is suddenly eclipsed by wind chimes, a full, sweeping synthesized string sound, and a high-pitched drone followed by an ethereal choir at 0:21. At 0:40, just as the voice enters, all but the electric bass drone electronically dissolves and dissipates into nothingness.

Figure 2.1. INTRODUCTION TO RAHMAN'S ROJA'S "ROJA JAANEMAN"

Time	0:00-0:05	0:06-0:09	:10-12	:13-15	:16-17	0:18-0:27	0:28-0:38	:38—
Storyboard	Window: Male lead downward gaze	Forest: tall grass, trees, etc.	Window: downward gaze	Forest: tall grass, trees, etc.	Window: male upward gaze	Forest: Female lead in white dress—runs from camera	Forest/Window alternating shots; Female faces camera, acts playfully	Interior Room: Male in silhouette against window
Cinematography	Low angle; slow zoom; medium close-up	Low angle; handheld; through grass	Slow zoom in; close-up	Eye-level angle; downward gaze; handheld	Slow zoom cont'd	Eye-level angle; first glimpse of heroine; camera pursues heroine	Extreme female close-up; male close-up	Wide shot
Music Melody	:01-:07 Phrase 1 Vocals w/ flute		:10-:15 Phrase 1 rep. Vocals, flute cont'd			:18-22 Phrase 2 Vocal timbre "female" :23-:27 Phrase 2 repeats	Male vocal solo w/ lyrics begin	
Bass, Synthesizer	〈〈〈〈〈〈	〈〈 (:06) Drone begins	〈〈〈〈〈〈〈〈 〈〈〈〈〈〈〈	〈〈〈〈〈〈	〈〈〈〈〈	〈〈〈〈〈〈〈〈〈 (:18) Drone pulsates	Synthesizer sustained minor chords	Synthesizer chords
	〈〈〈〈〈	〈〈〈〈〈		〈〈〈〈〈	〈〈〈〈〈	〈〈〈〈〈〈〈〈〈〈	〈〈〈〈〈〈〈	〈〈〈〈〈〈〈

Rhythm	Unmetered			(:28) Rock beat begins <<<<<<< Tabla begins <<<<<<<	Rock, cont'd <<<<<<< Tabla, cont'd <<<<<<<
Jingle/ Editing Devices	Concise, memorable melodic hook; vocal, instrumental ambiguity is digitally created	Drone interrupts melody creating tension	Phrase 1 repeat coordinated with window shot	Pulsation technique accelerates tension; second phrase of melody repeated	Use of contemp. rock rhythm track; "hits" coordinate synthesizer with heroine's movements (:28-30), (:33-:35)	Alternating major/minor synth chords create musical "bed" for lyrics
Mood-Emotive Elements	Unmetered; vocally, ambiguity signifies vagueness	Drone interrupts melody creating tension		Emotional high point of intro: uncertainty elevated by "chase," pulsation coordinated with female	Tension released w/ rock beat and playful heroine	Both major and minor modes express anxious romantic intent

Other songs in the soundtrack use varieties of world music genres to illustrate the mood of a scene. Rhythmic playfulness is encapsulated in a reggae beat in "Chinna chinna asai" ["Little, Little Desires"], reinforcing the lighthearted nature of the heroine's character and the narrative moment (see also Getter's comments on this song in chapter 3).

The editing techniques introduced in *Roja*—including the use of intense hooks, tension-building devices, and intimate, quick shifts in visuals, mood, and instrumentation—are evident throughout these songs, demonstrating a musical recording precision available via computer technology, synthesizers, and a background in commercial ad music composition. Of particular note is the prioritizing of the visual over the aural in "Roja Jaaneman" as the playful movements of the heroine belie and dispel the tense, anxious mood created by the music. Typically, film audiences have been trained to believe the music over the visual. Such careful attention to each vocal and instrumental timbre, pitch, and rhythm, and its relationship to the visual and narrative became an integral part of the audiovisual aesthetic—an aesthetic only made possible through digital recording technology and an increased synchronicity in modes of perception.

AESTHETIC DECISIONS

The institutionalization of this level of aesthetic and technological sophistication in the recording studio was not without consequence, however. As digital recording became more commonplace in the 1990s, standard roles and relationships between producers, engineers, and musicians began to change. With sound engineers and others having extensive music editing software and digital audio workstations (DAWs), "the distinctions among composing, arranging, and recording blurred significantly" (Booth 2008, 84). Satish Gupta, a veteran sound engineer and eight-time International Indian Film Academy recipient, told me in 2009 that he feels that technology has made artists dispensable—a sentiment borne out in theory by Andrew Leyshon, who confirms a radical transformation in the recording industry as technology and software vertically disintegrate production in the recording process (2009), and in practice by music directors such as A. R. Rahman, who have significantly altered the requirements for creating a professional soundtrack.

Consider the following scenario that I observed at Mumbai's Premier Digital Mastering studio that demonstrated to me the changing aesthetics and positions of power in the recording process. Sound engineer Alok Punjani was seated at the keyboard of a DAW in a soundproofed control room, surrounded by floor-to-ceiling monitor speakers, a mixing console, and a musical instrument digital interface (MIDI) system. Alok concentrated intently on the bank of monitors as he recorded an "up-and-coming" pop and playback singer who was located in the isolation booth in front of him. The 22-year-old singer, from a wealthy family, had traveled from Delhi with hopes of breaking into the pop music scene. His father bankrolled both the trip and the recording session. As the young man sang his own compositions, Alok not only recorded, but also scrutinized every sonic facet through his headphones. Acting, in essence, as the producer as well, the engineer made all of the decisions in the session, from details of vocal delivery—dictating pronunciation, range, dynamics, pitch changes—to the song's arrangement in which he digitally manipulated instrumentation, reverb, depth, and special effects. Alok even offered suggestions to change the form of the song.

Perhaps oblivious or indifferent to the power he was relinquishing, the young singer was thrilled at the opportunity to be able to record. Having been turned down by almost all of the major recording companies in Mumbai, the singer finally had access—at least for a price—not only to a high-tech recording studio, but also to the level of aesthetic decision-making and technology used in big-budget Hindi films. He came away from the session with a completely professional accompaniment and recording quality without having to hire or rehearse a group of musicians.

Additional "democratizing" effects of digital technology where the aesthetic decision-making power is redistributed continued after this recording session as Alok returned to work on a new film soundtrack by Himesh Reshemmiya, a popular and well-known film composer whom he had recorded earlier in the week. As he fiddled with the accompaniment for one of the tracks, he discussed ways in which he would like to make the supporting orchestration seem fuller, and experimented not only with audio sweetening or enhancement techniques, but with the instrumentation itself to essentially fill in a gap he perceived in the song's arrangement.

Also in the studio was Satish Gupta, who worked with Alok on a re-edit of the background score for a massive stage production at one of India's top tourist destinations. Satish felt empowered yet underappreciated by the new recording process—empowered, as studios began to rely on fewer and fewer musicians, with more control in the hands of music directors and sound engineers, and underappreciated in the lack of credit given to his work (pers. comm. 2009). Satish remarked that "the real work is done in the studios by sound engineers who edit and add a lot of color, effect, pause and oomph that add to the moods and build the required ambience and feel for a song" (IT Acumens Discussion Board, Sept. 9, 2009).

Technology in the form of digitalization (synthesizers, software, and sampling), combined with pithy and concise ad-driven sonic urgency and an awareness of the slick, synergistic requirements of a globally mediated picturization, created unprecedented space for musical creativity. Possibilities opened up for more complex arrangements, more significant genre borrowing, increased musical layering, and dramatic and precise alterations in orchestration and accompaniments. The sonic flexibility and small-group, personalized vibe that emerged easily captured the expressive and globally curious spirit of India's burgeoning youth population.[1]

The result was an aesthetic that features technologically intricate song arrangements and melodies privileging the overall effect of the song. Pastiches of color, sound, and embedded moods took precedence over any one musical element (e.g., a dominant vocal line; see Zuberi 2002). Furthering the notion of the increasing importance of sonic color over any single musical component, directors began using playback singers based on their vocal timbre rather than their sonic believability in relation to the protagonists. The well-established playback singer-actor vocal association (e.g., Mukesh singing for Raj Kapoor) that had helped paper over the discontinuity between on-screen visual and off-screen voice in older Hindi films became secondary to the full and proper recognition of the sonic properties in toto along with their required emotion. It is this more nuanced and sophisticated treatment of the song as an independently crafted and polished jewel that most dramatically altered film song aesthetics and listener expectations—a shift that privileged the "sound" and "mood" of the song over the sum of its constituent structural elements. Any notion that a film song merely supported or propped up lyrical sentiment was put to rest by the autonomous "packaging" of music as a substantial force in creating the picturization's overall synergy.

THE GLOBAL IMPACT: CREATIVITY, SENSITIVITY, AND AUTHENTICITY

By the late 1990s, world interest in Hindi film increased dramatically due in part to vast improvements in audio sound quality, an enhanced global distribution system for video discs, an increasingly sophisticated Indian middle class, and an increasingly nostalgic Indian diaspora. Hindi films faced the daunting task of satisfying the viewing pleasure of these extended audiences as they demanded sound re-imagined for their postmodern, media-savvy sensibilities. Manuel's assertions regarding pre-liberalization film music continued to be salient in that the music retained "the impression of novelty to the urban Indian who no longer fully identifies with traditional India," while using traditional elements to "satisfy a sense of cultural nationalism and lend familiarity to new songs" (1988, 168). For many, nostalgia and emotion were expressed and satisfied through fantasy escapism and musical eclecticism as Hindi films provided a "cherished link to the lost motherland" while simultaneously including scores that "freely plagiarize sounds from the global style pool" (Manuel 1997, 24). As Hindi films found audiences all over the globe, however, they underwent significant paradigm shifts that reflected the aesthetics of global sensitivity in terms of musical creativity, eclecticism, authenticity, and their approach to physical and psychological character construction, particularly that of the hero.

Heroes began to display a dramatic departure from traditional Indian masculinity, both in physical appearance and personal characteristics. In Derné's in-depth look at masculinity and modernity in movies, one of the responses of male hero construction was to appease and accommodate Indian males' concerns about the "uncertainties of modernity" including the "effete abandonment of masculine power...placing women on an equal footing with men" (2000, 3). Exploration of personal independence and creativity on-screen became of interest to the postmodern Indian film industry as one way to mitigate these concerns. A significant change in masculinity had already become solidified in Western films of the early 1990s, in a shift from "violent to vulnerable" and emphasizing intelligence, vulnerability, and sensitivity (Kimmel and Aronson 2003, 185). These images retained enough masculinity for the Indian male viewer for this new construction to begin to find its niche alongside more traditional depictions, particularly regarding family and financial situations.[2]

Heroic characters also exhibited self-awareness and sensitivity as creative and artistic agents capable of functioning in a postmodern world. In discussing the role of creativity in constructing the character Nikhil, the hero in *Salaam Namaste*, for example, Deckha writes, "Nick's affirmation of creativity is part of a self-stylized and self-realized identity that is severed from the family...and is emblematic of the imagined optimism and opportunity encountered by the younger generations of post-liberalized, globalized India...whose imagined selves extend globally" (2007, 66).

Beginning in the early 2000s, films such as *Dil Chahta Hai* (2001) became narratively and musically emblematic of a globally extended creativity. One of the film's heroes is portrayed as a sensitive artist, whereas another radically transforms his cynical and self-absorbed character to be more self-actualized, cosmopolitan, mature, and emotionally in touch with himself. His pivotal transformation in the film occurs while he is listening to an opera. The soundtrack revels in a postmodern pastiche of world music sounds, timbres, and instruments. Celtic and bluegrass timbres and melodic content inflect the song "Woh Ladki Hai Kahan?" ["Where's That Girl?"], while a choir and an Australian Aboriginal didgeridoo are featured in "Jane Kyon" ["Wonder Why"]. The subtlety with which the soundtrack integrates styles was groundbreaking at the time. Consider "Tanhayee" ["Loneliness"], which begins with an electronically manipulated dance beat supported by a traditional *dhol* rhythm, with a melancholy flute counter-melody, seamlessly intertwining the production of emotional representation through explicitly Indian musical sounds with equally unmistakable global sounds and content.

CREATIVE ECLECTICISM: FUSION AND FOLK

Hindi film music's well-established eclecticism continued to develop as on-screen creativity was matched with off-screen imagination when increased technological capabilities provided new opportunities for expression. Music directors composed syncretic combinations based on world music sound samples. Fusion, which had long been problematic outside the film music scene, became increasingly popular from the 2000s onward, blending cool or hot jazz, pop, rock, gospel, hip-hop, reggae, disco, dancehall, and particularly electronic dance and trance music. Fusion easily extended to indigenous Indian and world musics, mimicking what was occurring in global pop music. For example, regional folk or *qawwali* songs might be intermingled with heavy metal, techno, or a wide range of other world pop or world folk musics and sounds. Instead of maintaining the kinds of stylistic uniformity of sound that characterized many tracks of the pre-liberalization cinema (in which, for example, a Latin rhythm track would remain throughout the song), music directors composed in more of a creatively eclectic manner, experimenting with digital and sampled sounds and genres from a variety of sources, weaving them together or sometimes placing disjunctive sounds as striking sonic curiosities in a song or background score. World styles, instruments, and timbres from South African *isicathamiya*, Japanese *Noh* theatre, Algerian *rai*, gospel, blues, opera, and Panjabi, Bengali, Bhojpuri, and Malayalam Indian folk, as well as digital processes such as distortion, vocoding, Auto-Tuning, voice-boxing, sampling, and endless varieties of world percussion were inlaid into the accompaniment or graced the vocal line. Such poly-stylistic and eclectic pastiches might encapsulate the core identity of the song or an aspect of its picturization (e.g., South African vocal harmonies in Rahman's "Mastam Mastam" ["Unrestrained Joy"] from *Yuvvraaj*, 2008) or might be utilized as an exotic ornament (e.g., Japanese *Noh* vocalizations in Rahman's "Shakalaka Baby" from *Nayak: The Real Hero*, 2001).

A more active inclusion of world folk music resulted in increasing awareness of musical issues regarding performance practice and authenticity. Hindi film music found itself amid a world music scene that had long grappled with such issues concerning its use of synthesized sound and borrowed styles. Film composers demonstrated increasingly sophisticated ideas regarding the use of sonic authenticity and sound (styles, instruments, and timbres) with an eye toward faithful reconstruction in keeping with the notion of cinematic realism. This idea primarily concerned depictions of folk music performance practice, and vocal and instrumental timbres, using indigenous instruments and rhythms.

Such attention to authenticity was simultaneously supported by India's middle-class and nostalgic diaspora, which demanded and helped usher in a revival of regional folk genres, instruments, rhythms, and timbres to accompany its newly inspired neo-traditional visuals (see Livingston 1999). Folk song styles, a staple in the *filmi* soundtrack, reemerged as an essential element, capable of satisfying identity and longing. Malayalam vocals in Rahman's "Jiya Jale" ["My Heart Burns Up"] from *Dil Se* (1998), and Rajasthan's Langa-Manganiyar inspired "Nimbura" ["Little Lemon"] in music director Ismail Darbar's score for the groundbreaking 1999 production *Hum Dil De Chuke Sanam*, among others, provided audiences with re-envisioned folk timbres, styles, and instruments to fulfill nationalist desires through a celebration of the motherland's folk music offerings.

Films such as *Paheli* (2005), based in Rajasthani folklore, and *Lagaan* (2001), a period film located in Gujarat, seem to be obvious choices to include folk-inspired songs; the use of folk was widespread and used in romantic comedies such as *Bunty aur Babli* (2005), the soundtrack of which relied heavily on regional folk roots. Reviewers described the score by Shankar-Ehsaan-Loy as an over-the-top, uninhibited, rustic-with-teasing-spices musical *masala*, thoroughly infused with the flavor of Indian folk (Verma 2005). The soundtrack for *Bunty aur Babli* is a loosely coherent pastiche of "folk item numbers," with the "folk feel" accomplished with a nod to authentic folk *tala* and *raga* references, but primarily concerned with instrumentation and playback singing timbre. During the first song "Dhadak, Dhadak" ["The Train Clatters"], the film's hero and heroine escape from their small villages in Bihar. The song exhibits a vague, general folk-song feel on top of an onomatopoeic train-track rhythm. The scene's visuals and the song's lyrics make explicit the small town/village character implied by the music. The folk style of the song, loosely representing Bhojpuri folk music, is expanded to imply a folk mood writ large—creating a character of rustic, rural, and "pure" India as it introduces a particular small-town feel of the hero and heroine to the audience.

These re-imagined folk numbers reflected new dimensions of authenticity as standardized arrangements and timbres of folk songs or *filmi* folk were replaced by more authentic renditions. The songs "Genda Phool" [Marigold Flower"] from *Delhi-6* (2009), a popular Chhattisgarh wedding folk song, and "Madhorama Pencha" ["Which Girl Should We Pick"], a Punjabi wedding song from Mira Nair's *Monsoon Wedding* (2001), depict more traditional vocal style and performance practice. The latter of these songs is sung without melodic accompaniment, with appropriate Punjabi dialect, inflection, and seemingly untrained rustic voices emulating proper pitch placement and vocal timbre. The song is accompanied by a simple *dhol tala* and handclapping. Rahman's "Genda Phool," however, places Rekha Bharadwaj's highly authentic folk vocal performance practice and timbre against a female solo/group response over a highly contemporary funk bass and distorted wah-wah synth sound representing the American origins of the hero Abhishek Bachchan. In both cases, folk wedding songs—and their vocal timbre in particular—were used to bring an authenticity to the picturization, replete with emotional and sub-cultural associations of marriage that could not be garnered from anywhere else.[3]

TRADITIONAL FANTASY MEETS POSTMODERN NOSTALGIA

Now in their second, third, and even fourth generations, globally sophisticated RI and NRI audiences steeped in global cultures and aesthetics began to seek out alternative narratives and sonic ties to the homeland. Legions of young RIs weaned on Hindi cinema and global connectivity were now in a position to create, produce, direct, and effect film production. Some films, such as *I Hate Luv Storys* (2010) and *Mujhse Fraaandship Karoge* (2011), downplay the use of songs and song scenes as distinct narrative components. Songs are increasingly separated from their cinematic contexts and are more consistently used as part of the background, abandoning the mimed singing of previous decades. For 20-something Delhi-ites, Mumbai-ites, etc., the emphasis on marketing and the increased non-diegetic role for songs are in keeping with contemporary urban and highly cosmopolitan lifestyles, postmodern nonchalance, and world-weary cynicism. Other films, however, took a different path, and celebrated picturizations. For them, film music needed to negotiate a musical space that spoke to a globally mediated, postmodern music scene sensitive to their unique desires, identity, and position.

The film *Bbuddah Hoga Terra Baap* (2011), for example, provides ample space in which to combine nostalgia, globalization, and technology. Directed by Puri Jagannath with music by Vishal-Shekhar, the film was a vehicle for superstar and veteran actor Amitabh Bachchan. In an attempt to extract as much off-screen and on-screen essence as possible, Bachchan not only starred as the film's lead, but also sang four out of the five songs from the soundtrack himself. In the song "Bbuddah Hoga Terra Baap" ["Your Dad Might Be Old"], the actor performed, along with son Abhishek, both the a cappella and dubstep versions. The sound of Bachchan's voice is one of the most renowned vocal cinematic timbres in Indian film; its gruff, gravelly, and austere tones remind many listeners of his earlier famous cinematic soliloquies and his forays into playback singing (covering 29 films in all). Here, his voice is anachronistically surrounded by a blend of London-European dubstep, techno, funk, and even hardcore dance sub-genres, accentuated with DJ scratches. Interestingly, in terms of timbre, Amitabh's voice does simulate an industrial music edge implicit in the music, albeit perhaps unintentionally. The film's soundtrack also provides the large Panjabi NRI and Indian community with their fix of folk with a *bhangra*-inspired track, "Main Chandigarh di star" ["I'm Chandigarh's Star"].

The trajectories insinuated by this soundtrack are revealing. The film, which directly states in a written message on the final screen shot that it misses the "angry young" Amitabh, evidenced a breach in the diachronic cultural narrative of India's film history. Resuscitating a past hero (and his voice) from the 1970s and 1980s and recasting him as a current hero for a new generation suggests a jarring combination of painful longing for an imagined cinematic past with a desire for hope in an uncertain future. It is as much part historical re-signification and part collective eulogy as it is wishful thinking that Amitabh, as a weighty cultural and iconic entity, can assuage India's futuristic and global anxieties in celluloid perpetuity.

In keeping with the general zeitgeist of postmodernism—the "combination and juxtaposition of elements from disparate discourses and subjectivities" (Manuel 1995, 229)—music directors such as A. R. Rahman intentionally recoded Hindi film soundtracks through nuanced positioning of disparate musical elements. Film music's eclecticism (seemingly random inclusion of voices, sounds, riffs, instruments, and timbres) is intentionally re-signified, through authenticity and creativity, to embody intimacy and meaning in sounds that are unfamiliar and exotic. The success of A. R. Rahman, Shankar-Ehsaan-Loy in the 1990s, and others like Saleem-Sulaiman and Himesh Reshammiya can be attributed to their agility in combining musical familiarity and novelty cloaked in a postmodern sensibility firmly grounded in transnational and ambient sounds from an eclectic sonic palette.

SCI-FI: INDIA'S EMERGENT SONIC FUTURE

One could argue that versions of utopia have always existed in India (e.g., Hinduism's golden age of Rama during which Lord Rama ruled peacefully for 11,000 years after defeating Ravana; Gandhi's utopian vision for a newly minted post-independent nation) and in the Indian cinema; but while many Indian films offered utopian visions of various kinds (e.g., the typical, peaceful Indian village, the elite mansion, the happy Muslim *muhalla*), for the most part, they concentrated on developing and reliving "emotions in the moment," rather than offering overtly whimsical or deterministic visions of India's future. Younger RIs and increasingly influential NRIs, however, continued to vie for their own unique cinematic expressions and imagined communities. In some recent films, however, instead of manifesting as "traditional," these imagined utopias took shape through a relatively new or rather newly rediscovered genre in the Hindi film world—science fiction. The fact that sci-fi emerged as a viable entity long believed to be outside the cultural reference of the Indian audience (Thomas 1995, 26) speaks to greater access to and acceptance of technology rooted in the success of India's computer software industry and in cultural aspirations for a brighter Indian future.

Similar to its foray into technology, Hindi film's excursion into sci-fi has also been relatively slow, with only a few scattered films along the way. *Mr. India* (1987), for example, offered audiences a hero with powers of invisibility and an outrageous Indian take on the Bond villain Dr. No. More recently, *Koi...Mil Gaya* (2003) featured an animatronic head on the robotic alien Jadoo, based on a combination of *Close Encounters of the Third Kind* (1977) and *E.T.* (1982). In 2008, Harry Baweja's *Love Story 2050* displayed a stunning, technologically sophisticated version of a futuristic Mumbai utopia. With sci-fi still relatively new in its conception, its heroes and villains remain relatively conservative in their construction and often resemble Hindu deities and/or other characters from the great epics. One 2006 release, *Krrish*, featured a hero whose name (also the name of the film) resembled that of India's great romantic hero and deity Krishna. More recently, the archetypal Indian villain (or in some interpretations, anti-hero) Ravana was reconfigured in *Ra.One* (2011).

A futuristic-sounding soundtrack, however, does not seem to automatically accompany a sci-fi film narrative. For Anubhav Sinha's *Ra.One*, the most expensive and technologically advanced Hindi film to date according to BBC News South Asia (2011), music directors Vishal and Shekhar do not mirror the on-screen digital pyrotechnics with an overly indulgent futuristic, electronically generated score as one might expect. Although there is some vocal audio processing (i.e., Auto-Tuning or vocoding, techniques wildly popular in folk music found in Rajasthan) and electronically generated material in the soundtrack (i.e., computer/video game, sci-fi, laser, and vehicle sound effects), the score, for the most part, heads in a completely different and rather "retro" direction instead, challenging the boundaries of eclectically sourced music assimilation in significant and surprising ways.

The soundtrack includes 15 songs, of which seven are originals, four are remixes, and three are instrumentals. The song "Dildaara" ["O Beloved"] is based on Ben E. King's 1961 R&B hit "Stand By Me," itself inspired by an African American spiritual. At the same time, the musical lynchpin song of *Ra.One*'s marketing campaign, "Chammak challo" ["Flashy Girl"] has three versions: as a Panjabi mix, a club mix, and an "international" mix.

The range of genres that provided inspiration for the soundtrack is based on an increasingly expanded world dance and pop music base, including electronic dance music (reminiscent of the music of Swedish-born Liquid Stranger), techno, hardcore, trance, and dubstep, as well as hip-hop, ska, big band, swing, R&B, gospel, rock, jazz, and the aforementioned R&B hit, with multiple genres often occurring in the same song. For example, the song "Raaftarein" ["Swiftly"] lays syncopated 1940s big band swing over a techno bass and hardcore vocals. The energetic and rather ominous-sounding bass guitar riff for "Raaftarein," based on a minor third, evokes characteristic images of 1960s British and American spy heroes, while the call and response of the upper brass parts seems to respond and comment on each line of text in unison, bringing to mind the swing era's zoot suit. The subtleties in the background score are surprising as well. In addition to a fair amount of swing, muted trumpets, and big band, there is a jazz feel mixed with unison choruses reminiscent of Orff's *Carmina Burana* as it dissolves into anxious, arpeggiated violins evoking Danny Elfman's *Spider-Man* (2002) score.

The most curious aspect of the *Ra.One* soundtrack, however, is the vocal appearance of Senegalese-American R&B singer Akon, who sings playback for two of the songs, "Chammak challo" and "Criminal." Although the use of non-Indian playback singers is not entirely new, it remains rare given the highly personal nature of the voice. The selection of Akon's voice for actor Shah Rukh Khan is unusual not only in the timbral dissimilarity between Shah Rukh's speaking voice and Akon's singing voice, but also in its cultural significance. The voices are so strikingly different, in fact, that Akon's voice renders the pretense of playback singer-actor relationship almost irrelevant, perhaps foreshadowing a trend yet to come. In addition, Shah Rukh's on-screen persona now embodies the international cachet and Western aesthetic of an American-identified R&B/pop singer with a highly distinctive sound and a rather interesting reputation (known for songs such as "Smack That" and "I Just Had Sex"). In the opening seconds of the song "Criminal," the notion of cooptation is visually realized as Shah Rukh aggressively grabs a black male in order to steal and don his slick, tight, black leather "hip-hop-gangsta" outfit, complete with Ray-Ban aviator sunglasses.

Critics of the film cite its derivative nature and mish-mash of references, plot devices, and characters. The soundtrack is no exception. The large orchestra makes a comeback as Vishal and Shekhar employ the Prague Philharmonic Orchestra to perform a score that borrows heavily from Hollywood blockbusters' standard superhero fare, including a riff quite similar to Hans Zimmer's *Dark Knight* theme. Song lyrics, like the dialogue, are linguistically mixed, containing English, Hindi-Urdu, Panjabi, and Tamil ("Criminal," the breakout electronic dance number, contains 35 percent English and 65 percent Hindi, while the lyrics of "Chammak Challo" are 55 percent English, 35 percent Hindi, and 10 percent Tamil).

Other than the occasional use of electronic sounds and vocal processing techniques, the soundtrack to *Ra.One* bears little resemblance to what one might expect for a futuristic sci-fi narrative. Instead, it bridges historically grandiose genres, timbres, and styles, albeit with profound confidence. This compositional confidence does, however, express a new level of comfort and intimacy with world music styles and sounds from multiple global sources, indicating the fruition of a cosmopolitan sensibility begun by music directors such as S. D. Burman decades ago, developed and made globally acceptable by A. R. Rahman in the 1990s, and further developed and realized through technological advancements in the studio and the continuing experimentations of newer composers. Films such as *Love Story 2050, Koi...Mil Gaya, Krrish,* and *Ra.One* speak to a culture coming to grips with and harnessing the power of its own technology and its implications for new utopian visions of society.

Ra.One's impact, however, does not end with the film or its soundtrack, but continues in the boldness and extent of its global distribution. The Hindi film industry is now one of the primary, if not *the* primary, exporters of Indian culture; it is responsible for a massive change in world perceptions of India. In 2008, Shah Rukh Khan, upon visiting Berlin to promote his film *Om Shanti Om,* entered a country that, because of Bollywood and the Indian IT industry, has gradually changed its clichéd images of "bullock cart India," with its limbless beggars, sacred cows, corrupt politicians, and catastrophes (Daily News & Analysis India 2008). Many of the films spearheaded by Shah Rukh Khan, such as *Om Shanti Om* (2007), *My Name is Khan* (2010), *Devdas* (2002), and *Veer-Zaara* (2004), were aggressively promoted on a worldwide scale, as were other films like *Lagaan* (2001) and *Jodhaa Akbar* (2008). These films represent a triumph of global marketing, distribution, and aesthetics, and support the idea that Bollywood is a separate and relatively new culture industry designed to integrate the "packaging of big-budget Hindi films across an array of international promotional sites" (Govil 2008, Rajadhyaksha 2003). In the ultimate coup combining globalization, nostalgia, tradition, and fantasy, Shah Rukh Khan announced plans for an international version of the *Mahabharata* epic, something along the lines of *Avatar*, in conjunction with 20th Century Fox (Sawf News, Jan. 18, 2012).

As increasing numbers of Indians and non-Indians interact daily with an active global music scene based on sonic connectedness, Hindi film music and films link with international expansion and rising worldwide sync opportunities. Film music utilizes distribution channels in multiple formats, while iTunes, CD Baby, Pandora, film licensing opportunities, video games, and apps are all global fair game for imitation and inspiration, as are the artists themselves, eroding the idea that countries or cultures can claim musical genres entirely as their own.[4]

CONCLUSION

India's post-liberal economy, escalating globalization, and increased application of digital technology resulted in a perfect storm, bringing in new aesthetic production techniques and new pathways for using them. Digital equipment and software spurred creative innovations, altering methods of recording and editing, and increasing musical democratization and artistic freedom. Music director-composers mastered technology and replaced entire orchestras, focusing energy on a handful of musicians in small studios, while perfecting the aesthetics of song. Playback singers, once staples of the cinema, are now interchangeable for their timbral qualities, emphasizing the mood of a scene rather than vocal continuity. Composers, inspired by the ability to digitally record, edit, and manipulate sound, now include audio effects, world music style and instrument sampling, and world beat sounds and global rhythms that move Hindi film music beyond the idea of eclecticism. Changes such as increased individual control and creativity were compatible with the sensibilities of musicians (weaned on Western and world music) who often cut their musical teeth in high school or college bands.

For some, the aesthetic changes discussed above reinforce the notion that film song's musical construction is less informed by Indian classical music (as was the case in prior decades) and is now more Western in its musical perspective, aesthetics, and orientation (Ranade 2006). A concern over musical homogeneity is inevitable in Indian film, even more so in the face of the processes of globalization. The fear that an already monocultural (Mumbai-based) Indian film industry would distribute a highly homogenized Western pop sound is easily understandable, particularly as Western musical sensibilities became increasingly acceptable among audiences. And while increased usage of Westernized sound has come close to the cataclysmic perils of a complete "cultural grey-out" (Lomax 1968), eradicating all traces of Indian characteristics in film music, it is really the *processes* of creation, rather than the film songs themselves, that have undergone significant aesthetic changes. Music directors like Vishal-Shekhar, for example, reflect the trend of composing a musically integrated rather than "grafted" soundtrack, with ample space for various world music possibilities and global inspirations. Soundtracks like *Tees Maar Khan* (2010), *Bbuddha Hoga Terra Baap* (2010), *I Hate Luv Storys* (2010), and *Ra.One* (2011) are not imitating or borrowing global genres per se, as much as they are musically assimilating them.

However, technology, coupled with a piqued interest in globalization, not only changed film song aesthetics, but also allowed them to keep pace with higher musical expectations and identities, at home and abroad. Attitudes toward authenticity and creativity changed under consumer scrutiny, as ever more savvy audiences demanded more thought behind production values, as those values became technologically available. The new "sound" of film music (vocoding, Auto-Tuning, etc.) began to signify both NRIs' and RIs' need for entertainment, expression, and self-identity in a consumer-driven culture, alongside a growing diasporic need for deep-seated nostalgia in a postmodern world. Electronic and digital film sound and new film genres, such as sci-fi, successfully captured the attention of both RI and NRI audiences through use of regional and novel idioms, while appealing to their postmodern, global requirements.

India's desire to become a world superpower, combined with enhanced technology and worldwide marketing opportunities, has opened up new possibilities for Hindi film. Hindi film music must project carefully crafted identities and desires onto the world stage, embodying Indian values in musical idioms palatable to an international music market and appealing to interested non-diasporic audiences. India's active embrace of and enactment upon the promise of globalization require new Indian sonic agents, ones that portray India's current energy, as well as its image as a suitable global economic partner. Such music, to be successful, must create space for dreams and desires of Indians and NRIs, while offering up musical fantasy escapism to the rest of the world.

NOTES

1. According to the latest Indian census, 65 percent of Indians are under the age of 35.
2. Physical changes enhanced the global popularization and marketing of films, including an increased sexualization of the *male* body—an increasingly popular phenomenon prominent in modeling and advertising. Film promos, such as those for *Salaam Namaste* (2005), began displaying more images of heroes than heroines. A hairless and muscular physique became the norm, and such men, especially those who came from the modeling world, were given the moniker "chocolate boys," a term used regularly by the likes of *Times of India* beginning in the mid 2000s to describe a male's light skin, attention to appearance, and beautiful, almost effeminate characteristics (similar to the concept of "metrosexuality").
3. Inclusion of actual folk songs in films continues to be a challenge to both the industry and audiences who have come to expect *filmi* folk-composed songs. Song credits still list the film's music director and lyricist rather than employing a label such as "traditional folk."
4. Billboard charts currently list 30 percent of their artists as international.

CHAPTER 3

Kollywood Goes Global

New Sounds and Contexts for Tamil Film Music in the
21st Century

JOSEPH GETTER

Often referred to as Kollywood, the Tamil film and film music industry is centered in the Kodambakkam area of the Chennai metropolis.
Tamil films form the largest of India's regional-language film repertoires;
their songs have developed into a significant linguistic and musical genre
(or sub-genre) of popular film music throughout South Asia and the many
global communities of Tamil speakers. As Sarrazin argues in chapter 2,
India's post-1990 economic liberalization and increasingly globalized
position have unleashed forces that produced many substantial changes
to India's economy, media, and society. Under the impact of those forces,
the sounds and timbre, methods of recording, industry marketing, and
global dispersion of Tamil film song and music have all undergone significant transformations. The growth in numbers and importance of the Tamil
diaspora and the possibilities offered by a range of social/media networking have enabled Tamil song audiences to modify their responses to and
uses of Tamil film songs, song scenes, and videos. In the first decades of the
21st century, the music, stories, and images of Kollywood's Tamil films are
enjoyed widely within and outside of India, and have an impact far beyond
the immediate world of Tamil language speakers. Although this chapter
begins with a brief consideration of Tamil film song as such, I mainly focus
on the newly expansive musical and mediated processes in which film
songs have been manifested and transformed.

Film composer A. R. Rahman has been at the forefront of musical changes in the Tamil cinema, the Hindi cinema, and Indian popular music more broadly. He is widely regarded as a pivotal figure in Indian post-liberalization popular music. In chapter 2, Sarrazin examines Rahman's music for *Roja*, a Tamil film dubbed into Hindi and other Indian languages. Rahman's innovative production and compositional techniques arose from professional experiences as a composer and producer of music for advertising jingles for television, as a keyboard player in film composer Ilayaraja's studio, and as a performer in an Indian rock band. These diverse musical experiences provided him with an expanded technical perspective on music composition that helped him produce music that was broadly accessible at national and global levels, and achieved significant success with worldwide audiences of listeners beyond the Tamil-speaking communities. In a blog post likely written in the mid-1990s, Gopal Srinivasan commented:

> The music of [*Roja*] would be a phenomenal success that would revolutionize modern day Indian film music....Five years ago, what did teenagers dance to at discotheques? What else but...the latest Western dance hits of the day. But one man singlehandedly changed all that. With his universally appealing tunes, A. R. Rahman has demolished all conventional rules in Indian film music (Srinivasan 2002).

Despite Rahman's many contributions to popular Indian film song, the majority of those contributions, especially those specifically directed toward film song as such, took place in the 1990s. In this chapter, I study Rahman's more recent and more global musical activities, as well as other contemporary developments in Tamil film song, to show how separate and distinct linguistic communities make use of songs, fitting them into new contexts. I consider how music circulates by means of borrowing, mimicry, cover song productions, viral marketing, and other means. I am also concerned specifically with how the Internet facilitates these processes, moving music instantly and anonymously across the globe, making Tamil film song a global phenomenon.

TAMIL LANGUAGE AND MEDIA

There are over 66 million people in the world who speak the Tamil language. Most are located in the Southeastern Indian state of Tamil Nadu and in parts of Sri Lanka, with diasporic communities that are spread across much of the world, including large populations in Malaysia, Singapore,

South Africa, Fiji, Europe, the Middle East, North America, and elsewhere. Although many characteristics distinguish these various communities, the Tamil language serves to unite them all. Although this is equally true for other linguistic communities of India, Tamil's political history is distinctive in its relationship to the national dominance of Hindi. During the 20th century, as debates about national languages raged, Tamil attained a status as a strong literary, cultural, and political platform—understood to be numerically significant and largely independent of the Sanskrit etymologies of many other Indian languages—from which to oppose the national dominance of Hindi. The Tamil film industry has occupied a similar position as the leading oppositional force to the dominance of Hindi cinema. Indeed, the output of Tamil films has always rivaled and often exceeded the number of Hindi films produced in a given year. Thus, the Tamil language has an especially prominent unifying and distinguishing quality.

The audience for Tamil films, as in other linguistic film industries, watches movies in cinemas and exhibition spaces; but since the mid-1990s and the explosion of satellite channels, television has become an important avenue for connecting films and film music to a more expansive but still linguistically defined audience. Jayson Beaster-Jones suggests that throughout India, "[t]he sheer number of music-oriented [television] channels that have emerged since the mid-1990s cannot be understated" (2009, 432). This growth in the linguistic diversity of Indian television broadcasts has led to groups of channels offering programming content that includes new and old films, foreign and local music videos, news, television dramas, live arts broadcasts, "reality TV" contests, devotional content, and so on, delivered in an equally diverse array of languages including Hindi, Telugu, Kannada, Malayalam, Tamil, Bengali, Urdu, Gujarati, Marathi, and others. Regional and linguistic variance naturally change the offerings on a market-by-market basis; but if viewers wish to pay for the channel, they can watch Bhojpuri television in Chennai and Tamil television in Kashmir. Viewers may select from music video programming in multiple languages according to the individual's linguistic orientation.

This massive shift in India's mediascape was the result of the same governmental economic and regulatory policies that other authors in this book have described. Changes beginning in the late 1980s included deregulation of the communications and technology sectors and increased foreign investment and economic globalization (Sharma 2011). The growth of India's computer industry and widespread access to the Internet are other outcomes of economic liberalization and the collapse of the "License Raj." Following liberalization, India became a well-known center for the development of computer-based services and software. Web access gradually became available in Indian homes, schools, offices, businesses, institutions, and cyber cafés. On December 31, 2011, India was ranked third in the world in terms of the number of Internet users, with 121 million people having online access, or 10.2 percent of the population (Miniwatts Marketing Group 2012); and earlier that year, in March 2011, it was estimated that there were over 11.89 million Internet connections in India (Telecom Regulatory Authority 2011 2). Though the ability to access the web may not have reached the majority of Indians, many millions of people are going online for work, business, worship, and entertainment; the Internet has thus emerged as an important cultural force and communications tool in India.

CHANGES IN TAMIL FILM MUSIC PRODUCTION

Another change that followed liberalization was the gradual digitalization of production practices and consumption formats across India's culture industries (cf. Manuel 1993, Meintjes 2003). In Chennai, as in other production centers, older large studios continued to exist, but computer-based technologies and procedures had the effect of relocating much creative work to smaller professional and home recording studios, from which files could be transferred digitally to larger production centers. The creation of songs and background scores has been transformed into a nonlinear process in which the use of sound sample libraries and synthesized instrumental sounds began to play a bigger role. In digital studios, the music is routinely stitched together from fragments of recordings originally created at various times and places. As elsewhere in India (and the world) and as Booth (2008) has described for film music recording in Mumbai, the large ensemble "live" recording practices of the past are no longer necessary, although in many cases, Chennai studios continue to record some instrumental configurations—especially string sections—in large groups. "Comp tracks" are composite recordings assembled from small portions of many recording takes. For example, a singer might record lines or phrases one at a time, and then studio engineers select the best to compile together. Track comping is a very common recording procedure used in computer-based studios in Chennai and around the world.

The shift from analog tape to computer-based digital audio workstations (DAWs) has changed and improved the production standards of Indian visual and audio recordings. Compared to older releases before the 1990s, newer sound recordings often exhibit greater frequency range, less distortion, and expanded dynamic range (the contrast between loud and soft audio levels in a recording, though this range may be compressed when played back over loudspeakers, audio systems, and so forth). An important aspect of the sound palette of Tamil film songs and background music is the use of audio effects such as frequency equalization, time-based delays and reverberation, pitch correction, and dynamic compression (as a technique for recording individual voices or instruments, as well as in mastering, the final stage of audio production). Singers' voices may be processed with Auto-Tune technology that subtly adjusts any pitch discrepancies or can be used with extreme settings to create any special effects. Although studio effects have long been used in Tamil film music, with the advent of computer technology, the quality, clarity, and sophistication of effects have risen to international standards. Many studios have been newly built or upgraded with high-quality technology, so when compared to music recordings from the 1930s through the 1980s, Tamil songs produced in the 1990s and 2000s have a noticeably different audio signature and often possess a clear and subtle sonic quality.

The instrumental sounds heard in Kollywood film songs have also changed over time. Composers, called music directors in Chennai as elsewhere in India, are responsible for crafting melodies and overseeing the production of the music, and they manage the work of a team of arrangers, assistants, engineers, vocalists, instrumentalists, and others. The music director and arranger must choose instrumentation that supports the narrative situation of the film (Getter and Balasubrahmaniyan 2008). Tamil songs often feature traditional acoustic sounds, including South Indian classical instruments like the *nagaswaram* (double-reed keyless wind instrument), *vina* (fretted stringed instrument), and *mridangam* (pitched two-headed barrel drum), as well as Tamil folk instruments such as the *urumi* (friction drum) and the generically ambiguous *kural* (bamboo flute). Western and other non-Indian instruments—acoustic and electric guitars, accordion, drum set, trumpet, vibraphone, and bongos—are also commonly used. Electric guitars and other electronic instruments have been widely used in film songs since the 1960s. In an early example, music director M. S. Viswanathan's 1964 hit song "Anubavam Puthumai" (video 3.1), an electric guitar plays the melody in the song's introduction, accompanied by drum set, a string section, accordion, vibraphone, Latin percussion, and other instruments.

Tamil film songs produced in the 1970s and 1980s by music director Ilayaraja reinvigorated an elderly genre, making extensive, innovative, and newly syncretic use of both global popular music styles and a wide range of folk music sounds from Tamil Nadu. Illayaraja's music combined bamboo folk flutes with guitars, keyboards, brass instruments, classical Indian music, and a wide variety of percussion. This composer also extended the application of South India's classical, modal *raga* system. Regarded as a master of *raga*, Illayaraja based his newly popular songs on these classical structures. His 1981 hit song "Andhi Mazhai" (video 3.2) is considered by fans to be a masterpiece in part because of the composer's use of the Karnatic *raga* Vasantha as the basis for the melody. The song's instrumentation includes a string section, flute, vibraphone, guitars, and other instruments, with rhythmic accompaniment by both *mridangam* and *tabla*; the arrangement weaves together Indian classical music styles with a rock music sound. One of the main characters in the film is a blind musician, presenting an opportunity for the picturization of the song to show film musicians at work, including a keyboardist, conductor, string section, studio engineers, and (quite unusually) playback singer S. P. Balasubramaniam. The scene appears to have been filmed at Chennai's Prasad Recording Studio, where Ilayaraja recorded much of his music over the years.

Tamil film music of the 21st century demonstrates both levels of continuity with the past, as well as the affinity for novelty and contemporary fashion that other Indian film song repertoires also demonstrate. The songs produced by contemporary Kollywood music directors feature the latest colorful and striking new sounds of the day and follow the shifting trends of popular music from around the globe by incorporating elements of Latin music, electric guitars, drum machines, synthesizers, Auto-Tune, rap vocals, and hip-hop rhythms. Simultaneously, composers have often quoted, referenced, or borrowed from past hits and trends in film songs, and certainly film musicians are knowledgeable about the work of their predecessors. Since the advent of sound film in the 1930s, many songs have creatively combined Western and Indian musical elements, creating a new hybridized sound based on music genres that originated in local, regional, and international sources.

The overall role of film songs within the film industry has been consistent over the history of Indian cinema, as songs support the film's narrative, provide entertainment for mass audiences, and serve as a marketing tool for upcoming films. Like the exchange and marketing of music recordings in many places around the world today, the business of selling recordings of Tamil film music has also experienced a shift to computer-based networks. However, the old patterns of circulation have not been entirely eclipsed by the new, in that audio CDs and cassettes are still available for purchase, despite revenues having declined due to piracy from unauthorized copying and file-sharing (Indian Music Industry 2005). Although there has been a near-complete displacement of the older analog tape-recording methods by computer-based studios, distribution in India relies on older physical media, as well as the Internet.

GLOBALIZATION AND THE "A. R. RAHMAN STYLE" IN TAMIL FILM SONG

For many listeners (such as Gopal Srinivasan, above), the Grammy- and Academy Award-winning music of A. R. Rahman represents a confluence of the new sounds and studio methods of song production that developed after 1990. Rahman's debut as a film music director was with the Tamil film *Roja* (1992), and even though it was his first film score, it was an immediate success, winning the National Film Award and the *Filmfare* Award for best musical score of the year. He was suddenly popular on a national scale in India, especially when *Roja* was dubbed into Hindi and several other languages. The hit song "Chinna, Chinna Aasai" ["Little, Little Desires"] (video 3.3) from the film exemplifies some of the characteristics of the new sounds that emerged in early 1990s Tamil film music. The sparse texture of the instrumental arrangement combines both acoustic and electric instruments, many of which are modified by reverberation effects that are conventionally used in Indian cinema to give sonic reinforcement to images of large outdoor spaces, but which also convey a somewhat dreamlike soundscape. Some sounds and musical content are clearly Indian in style, such as the melodic ornamentation of string melodies, whereas other sounds, such as guitar, bass guitar, and sustained synth pads, originate in international popular music. Playback singer Minmini made use of the conventionally "sweet" vocal timbres pioneered more than 40 years earlier by Hindi playback singer Lata Mangeshkar. *Roja* was also the first of many soundtracks on which Rahman sang some of his own songs or added vocal overdubs to tracks by other singers. In "Chinna, Chinna Aasai," he added his voice in his own characteristic way, singing short phrases without text, somewhat quieter in the mix, with reverberation added. Here in one of his first hits, Rahman articulates many of the sonic and musical qualities that have continued to comprise his personal style as a music composer and producer.

Rahman's personal studio complex at his home in Kodambakkam, originally named the Panchathan Record Inn, is the primary studio where he developed his sophisticated methods and innovative sounds. The studio is known for its top-quality audio gear and productions, and has been described as "arguably one of Asia's most sophisticated and high-tech studios" (Cellini 2009). The song "Pachchai Nirame" ["The Color Green"] (video 3.4) from the romantic film *Alaipayuthey* (2000) is a song that exemplifies his style in the early 2000s. The soundtrack was very well received by audiences and critics, and received a number of awards. Reverberation again plays a major role in the song's timbral identity, reinforced by the careful balance of instruments in the mix, with a light percussion sound, softly strummed acoustic guitar, and Rahman's signature layering of both acoustic and synthesized versions of the same instrument, such as percussion, flute, and violins. The lead vocal was provided by noted film, *ghazal*, and fusion singer Hariharan, with harmony support vocals by Rahman and Clinton Cerejo. This instrumentation and its delicate timbral components were understood by many viewers and listeners to reinforce the scenic nature of the song's picturization, shot in various village, lake, and forest locations in Kashmir and also at the Taj Mahal.

By and large, fans of Tamil film songs have embraced these new sounds while fondly remembering the older styles. However, some involved in Tamil film music have criticized the sounds of recent music, especially louder songs with raucous rhythms, like the sub-genre known as *gaana* songs, which feature lively percussion with very fast-paced melodies in triple-pulse beats. Vairamuthu, one of the leading lyricists of Tamil film songs who has penned words to several thousand songs, in an interview was asked, "There is a widespread criticism that today's movie songs are very noisy and in that noise the words of the lyric are mutilated. What do you think about that?" Vairamuthu replied, "You need to understand one thing. The world is becoming noisy. The vehicles of today, war cries in the world, the noise of machinery, the noises of life surround the man. So he expresses noise in a noisy way.... For this, the youth seeks music. In such a situation, noise is unavoidable" (Tamizhselvan 1998). Vairamuthu's comment also pointed out a generational divide that exists in Indian music and society. In the rest of this chapter, I consider a number of recent examples of film and film-related songs in the increasingly global, mediated, and interactive environment in which Tamil film song has come to operate.

The Global Travels of "Shakalaka Baby"

By 1999, Indian film songs were demonstrating a new level of engagement with the practices and content of global popular music culture. The Tamil film song "Shakalaka Baby" illustrates this and shows how Tamil film songs circulate among audiences in both audio and visual media. "Shakalaka Baby" is the first song in the hit film *Mudhalvan* (1999), for which

A. R. Rahman won the *Filmfare* magazine award for best music director for a Tamil film. The song's success also helped to launch the career of vocalist Vasundhara Das (Bimbi 2001). The film was produced in Chennai and initially released in Tamil and Telugu in 1999 (the Telugu version was entitled *Oke Okkadu*), so that from its inception, the song was known in versions in two different languages. Later the film was remade in Chennai as a Hindi language film titled *Nayak: The Real Hero* (2001).

Structured diegetically as a music video shoot within the narrative and musical frame of the cinema, the song offers an obvious contrast with the two examples discussed above; despite its diegetic rationale, "Shakalaka Baby" (video 3.5) is an "item number," an upbeat song featuring a dancer who is not otherwise featured in the narrative (and who may never be named in the script). The song "reminds one of an MTV music video," according to one review (Balasubramaniam 1999). It features an upbeat tempo, electric guitars, dense and exciting rhythms, and various electronic and synthesized sounds. Vocalist Vasundhara Das trades phrases with a male chorus. The song lyrics and visuals reference the desires of the younger generation to succeed in the modern, competitive world; the lyrics also combine English language phrases with Tamil in a mixture of the two languages known as Thanglish (also spelled Tanglish).

"Shakalaka Baby" became a part of the Andrew Lloyd Webber musical production *Bombay Dreams* (video 3.6) in 2002, for which the song was rearranged, with new instrumental tracks and new lyrics in English. This show ran for two years in London, and then moved to Broadway in 2004 for a shorter run in New York. The London stage show cast recording, which features vocals by Preeya Kalidas, overall retains a song structure and arrangement similar to that of the original Tamil and Hindi film versions. However, the cast recording differs in that the density of sounds is significantly increased, with distorted guitars and thickly layered percussion and electronic sounds that recall styles of music such as techno and hardcore breakbeats. There is a frenetic energy in this music that distinguishes it from the original.

The musical show's version of "Shakalaka Baby" (video 3.7) soon began to circulate widely in several contexts around the world; it became, among other things, the basis for new dance routines created by professional and amateur dancers, teachers, and choreographers. In the increasingly circular fashion of interactive media culture, some of these individuals have uploaded their home videos to the video-sharing website YouTube, inspiring further new creations. There is a wide geographic spread among these dance performances: A dance school group in Finland performed to Rahman's music at a competition (Milquiiq 2008); a school group in Malaysia danced to the song at their Teacher's Day festival (SMKDU 2008); dance schools and university groups in the United States and Britain have also danced to the song (Hogan 2008; Hsett 2007). On other videos uploaded to YouTube, it is possible to watch an exercise class work out to the song (Fit Haven 2007) or view the cross-dressing "Sweepy Skirt Girl" (Daniels 2008) as she dances to the song. Though the famous dancing prisoners of the Cebu Provincial Detention and Rehabilitation Center in the Philippines have yet to choreograph this song, they have danced to his still more famous song "Jai Ho" (*Slumdog Millionaire*, 2008). Tourists who watched the performances have uploaded their videos of the dance to YouTube (CPDRC 2009).

"Shakalaka Baby" did not achieve this global attention solely on the basis of its inclusion in the Tamil film of 1999. Rather, by shifting from the Indian cinema to the Western musical theatre—in collaboration with a widely known figure in the Broadway musical genre—Rahman's music was exposed to an audience that was both culturally and socio-economically distinct from the Indian film audience (and from the relatively small Western audience of Indian films). This shift moved Rahman into a broader international spotlight, in part due to the musical's massive promotional campaign. The song was seen on morning television shows in the United States, for example—a place where Tamil film songs are not generally heard and discussed. On his fan blog, Srinivasan gushed, "The publicity for *Bombay Dreams* touched a feverish pitch with Webber managing to get nearly every publication of note to do a feature" (Srinivasan 2002).

The transformation of an Indian film song into a global hit in the Western musical theater genre was hardly the end of this song's media-based transformations. In 2007, the Singapore-raised, Taiwan-based pop singer Kelly Poon Kar Lai created a song using parts of Rahman's melody from the *Bombay Dreams* version of "Shakalaka Baby." When Indian fans heard the "new" song, many were outraged that it quoted so much of Rahman's song without appearing to credit the composer. Rahman's name did eventually appear on the music video by Kelly Poon, after her song had been "mired in controversy" (Wong 2007). Thus, in the case of "Shakalaka Baby," the original Kollywood song left its niche in the Tamil-speaking world, first in the usual manner of crossing Indian language divides, then making the leap to English and audiences in Europe and North America, and eventually to a version for Chinese and Southeast Asian audiences. The song is truly a border-crossing global phenomenon.

The 2004 tsunami that struck Indian Ocean coasts in Southeast and South Asia resulted in extensive death and displacement throughout the region. In 2005, the song "Indian Ocean" (video 3.8) was released by Yusuf Islam, the socially conscious British pop star formerly known as Cat Stevens. For this song, Islam solicited musical contributions by A. R. Rahman, who added tracks to the final version of the song. "Indian Ocean" was released on iTunes with proceeds donated to charity and was subsequently released as the only new song on a two-disc CD album of Yusuf Islam's older pop hits. According to the singer-songwriter's official website, "The song he composed for that occasion, Indian Ocean, was the first official song Yusuf wrote and recorded with instruments after a break of [26] years!" At the time, Yusuf Islam had only recently begun to perform again after a hiatus of many years, having previously given up his pop music career after converting to Islam at the height of his popularity.

When "Indian Ocean" was recorded in January 2005, the devastation of the previous month was the biggest news story in India and was very much on the minds of many people. Although the Chennai metropolis had experienced some effects of the tsunami, most of the losses of life in India had occurred farther south. It was in the aftermath of this devastation and with considerable awareness of the situation that Rahman's team recorded the parts that would be added to "Indian Ocean." As they created the keyboard lines and set the equalization on some tracks, the engineers at Chennai's Panchathan Record Inn Studios, S. Sivakumar and H. Sridhar, explained to me how they and Rahman had gone about actually collaborating on the song, because Yusuf Islam was not actually present in the studio in Chennai. The procedure involved the transfer of audio files back and forth from the studio in India to other facilities in Britain via an Internet-based file-sharing service. Rahman had been given some artistic freedom to build the accompaniment tracks, and he added parts that he felt were suitable for the song; Yusuf Islam had not dictated exactly what Rahman should do.

The song responds to the issues and problems that arose in the aftermath of the tsunami, and thus represents a significant departure from most film music, where lyrics support the film's narrative and usually dwell upon romantic love. Despite the fact that the story of "Indian Ocean" clearly lies outside the world of film music, the song clearly illustrates the increasingly global nature of both the creative process and the artists (the composers, studio musicians, and engineers) who also create film song. The song's production relocates Tamil film song in a global context outside the relatively closed world of the pre-liberalization cinema and its music. Their engagement in these kinds of global collaborations inevitably provides them with a more global perspective on musical creation, production, and performance. Furthermore, the song's audience, like the audience for Tamil film song, is a transnational one.

ONLINE MARKETING AND THE "WHY THIS KOLAVERI DI" VIRAL VIDEO PHENOMENON

A number of authors in this volume refer to the impact of television in the 1980s and satellite television in the 1990s. By the beginning of the 21st century, although television continues to be an important social medium, more recent and more interactive online media are capable of reaching a worldwide mass audience with an almost endless variety of content in the forms of blogs, fan-sites, download sites, and other fora. A wide variety of Tamil-language websites now make it possible to view current and past Tamil films, film songs, and programs about films, such as reviews, interviews, contests, and news. Such online visual, audio, and text materials are readily accessible from computers anywhere on the planet and also exist for the other regional cinemas in India. While broadband web access is relatively inexpensive in cyber cafés in India, it is often beyond the reach (or at least the daily access) of people at the bottom of India's socio-economic spectrum. As with all digital media, however, online distribution easily facilitates unauthorized distribution and viewing of content. In contemporary India, some media companies (e.g., Shemaroo, Eros, Rajshri) are learning to work with the Internet, making their content formally available on dedicated YouTube "channels" and other similar formats to encourage legal consumption. The website TamilPeek launched a Facebook fan page, where over 6,000 people clicked the link to demonstrate they are fans of the company, but generally it is difficult to know who is watching Tamil films and songs online. Though the viewers of online Tamil film songs may not necessarily be a group with a shared experience and identity, it is possible for them to communicate with one another by posting comments on videos and through chat and discussion on websites such as Forumhub.com.

In late 2011, the new Tamil film song "Why This Kolaveri Di" ["Why this Rage against Me Girl"] (video 3.9) was uploaded to YouTube by Sony Music India to promote their then-forthcoming film 3 (2012). Composer Anirudh Ravichander's catchy song featured nonsensical lyrics delivered in Thanglish, a linguist mix especially important for younger Tamil speakers. The instrumentation of the song includes acoustic guitar, bass guitar, *urumi* and percussion, synthesized keyboard and sustained pad sounds, *nagaswaram*, and soprano sax. The *nagaswaram* sound is obviously utilized as a loop in some parts of the song, in which short phrases are played back repeatedly, lending an artificial quality to the resulting musical sound. Extreme pitch correction with Auto-Tune is added as an effect on the vocal part in some places, further imparting an intentionally unnatural yet pleasing and modern musical atmosphere. It is a downtempo *gaana* song with a slow triple-pulse rhythm.

The video became a viral sensation and on November 17, 2011, was the most searched-for and played video on YouTube in India, according to a Twitter post by the composer that day (Ravichander 2011). The song and music video were recorded in Chennai at A. R. Rahman's personal studio; the facility underwent a major expansion in 2006 and was renamed as A. M. Studios. The studio logo was clearly visible in the music video (figure 3.10), which showed music director Anirudh Ravichander playing a synthesizer, lyricist and vocalist Dhanush performing with a microphone, and film director Aishwarya Rajnikanth Dhanush and others in the studio. Soon after the release of the video, dozens of other videos were uploaded to YouTube with cover versions, tributes, and parodies of the song. These included cover versions in Panjabi, Hindi, Bengali, and English that usually mimicked the studio location for the song, the apparent drunkenness of the vocalist, and the small group of appreciative listeners in the studio. Other videos featured flash mobs singing and dancing to the song at shopping areas, campuses, and in the street.

Figure 3.10
Audio engineer P. Anbu records music for *Ayya* at AVM Studio, Chennai, India (2005). (Photo by Joseph Getter.)

CONCLUSION

Tamil film songs of the 21st century circulate more widely than ever before possible and have the potential to be heard by diverse audiences around the world. Elements of Kollywood songs have been reconfigured, transformed, and translated, in some cases by people who possess few ties to Tamil culture or India. Although A. R. Rahman has not been directly responsible for all these developments, which are ultimately driven by changing technological circumstances, his popularity and early commitment to innovative sounds, state-of-the-art musical technology, and global artistic relationships have clearly played a role in the acceptability of the process. These examples of Tamil film music as a syncretic expressive form present interesting cases as we try to understand Indian music and culture. Perhaps the foremost problem presented by such material is that there is no satisfactory way to assess the size and identity of the audience for these new interactive forms, or locate them within a physical community. Moreover, the web can be a space for people to act anonymously or with assumed identities, so it may be difficult to put "people back in the picture," as Anthony McCann has recently described the ethnomusicological goal (2002).

The circulation of Kollywood's music is complicated when it moves online. Contemporary exchanges of films, music, and ideas are mediated through computer networks, where flows can take place simultaneously alongside prior forms of (offline) circulation rooted in geographically situated communities and older forms of media. The example of the song "Shakalaka Baby" illustrates how separate and different communities can take an interest in a song and rework it for new purposes, all the while ignoring the context and intent of the original version. Musical borrowings and transformations constitute some of the fundamental methods for the circulation and transmission of music, but in the case of online film song, the sounds can instantly span the globe for anyone else to anonymously reuse as they wish. Aspects of Tamil film song also demonstrate the growing importance in India of the younger generations and the middle classes as significant forces in commerce and culture. The promotional YouTube video for "Why This Kolaveri Di" focused attention on a forthcoming film by displaying youthful musicians boisterously performing in a high-tech recording studio, thus presenting a fashionable and cutting edge image for Tamil cinematic culture. The songs discussed here are particular to Tamil culture, with the sounds of folk instruments like the *urumi* and the poetry of Tamil (and Thanglish) lyrics. But the songs also allowed listeners to experience their own music, all the while setting trends in modern global popular music.[1]

NOTES

1. Many people have contributed to the final form of this chapter. In Chennai, thank you to Premeela Gurumurthy, B. M. Sundaram, Neeraja Chandrasekaran, Srimushnam V. Raja Rao, V. A. K. Ranga Rao, Sandhya Kumar, Charubala Natarajan and Suresh Gopalan, P. Unnikrishnan, Thotta Tharani, Vamanan, Film News Anandan, Arun Kumar Bose, Lakshminarayan, S. Chandra Kumar, Bharathwaj, Dhina, A. R. Rahman, S. Sivakumar, and the late H. Sridhar, Noell James, Rajiv Menon, and M. S. Viswanathan. Thanks are also due to Gregory Booth, Bradley Shope, Stefan Fiol, Karim Gillani, Aaron Paige, Zoe Sherinian, David Nelson, Mark Slobin, Su Zheng, and B. Balasubrahmaniyan for their encouragement. An earlier version was presented as "Share, Steal, Transform and Mistranslate: The Circulation of Tamil Film Music in the New Media Era," at the 54th annual meeting of the Society for Ethnomusicology, Mexico City, November 19, 2009.

CHAPTER 4

On Nightingales and Moonlight

Songcrafting Femininity in Malluwood

KALEY MASON

Beneath the coconut palm canopies of cities, towns, and villages in the southwestern Malayalam-speaking state of Kerala, film songs animate the labor of everyday life. Along with the sounds of wet laundry smacking on washing stones, sizzling onions and spices, and the gruff calls of fishmongers, the voices of playback singers fill the tropical morning air in rural communities like the one where I lived during fieldwork stints that began in 2002. Whether playing on the radio, satellite TV, or mobile phones, film songs provide the soundtrack for daily activities like these, amplifying sentiments of love, devotion, innocence, heroism, and pathos for communities at work in coastal Malabar.

Affectionately known as Malluwood or sometimes Mollywood, the Malayalam-language film industry is the primary producer of popular music in Kerala (Thoraval 2000; Menon 2009). As in other commercial cinemas of South Asia, the prominence given to song-and-dance sequences in film reflects oral storytelling practices that refashion, amplify, synthesize, and complement narrative themes and formulae (Nayar 2004). Whereas some scholars have shown how these sequences enrich and advance film narratives (Dudrah 2006), others have noted how songs provide a space for transgressing normative social roles (Gopinath 2005). Still others have shown how music serves extra-narrative purposes by linking the plot and characters to wider South Asian mythic, religious, and political worldviews (Rajadhyaksha 2009). Away from the melodrama on screen, songs take on social lives of their own: through public radio broadcasts, cassette culture, digital media, festivals, weddings, public concerts, private music-making, and television programs like "Idea Star Singer," a popular reality music contest show sponsored by Idea Cellular Limited and broadcast on the Malayalam-language channel Asianet.

A decade after my first encounters with Malayalam cinema, the film song continues to be among the most popular forms of entertainment, as well as an important medium for telling stories that matter to Kerala's listening publics. The stories and characters amplified through song do more than reflect the way society sees itself, though; they also shape the mutually constitutive processes of individualization and gendering that feminist theorist J. Devika cogently describes as "en-gendering" individuals (2007). Music directors and their creative collaborators mobilize musical strategies to perform a variety of femininities and masculinities. Their stylistic choices inform ways of organizing sound in song forms and non-diegetic incidental music that re-inscribe or challenge aesthetic sensibilities associated with normative gender roles, relations, and behaviors.

Building on social histories and ethnographies of Indian popular music, this chapter examines generational shifts in the embodiment of musical taste through the prism of two Malayalam film songs at the turn of the millennium: "Karmukil Varnnante Chundil" ["On the Lips of the Dark-Clouded One"] and "Karuppinazhaku" ["Black Is Beautiful"]. Rather than analyze these songs as isolated texts, however, I draw on Stokes's recent work on Turkish popular music as a model for thinking about how songs and their significance serve as vehicles for cultural intimacy "in the historical context of versions and interpretations, both prior and subsequent" (2010, 6). By tacking between the collaborative creative work of the professional musicians who produced the original recorded versions and the subsequent social life of their songs, I hope to distill some preliminary thoughts on how stylistic features become associated with new forms of intimacy and feminine personae, and how evolving generational and gendered tensions inform how women experience film songs in Kerala's public cultural sphere. An important theme that cuts across these lines of inquiry is "cosmopolitanism," both in the sense of worldly urban elites, sophisticated consumer lifestyles, and trans-local alliances, as well as discrepant and critical cosmopolitan perspectives from below (Clifford 1997; Mignolo 2000). For our purposes here, I use the term in some instances to characterize a social group or identity, as in a cosmopolitan middle class or subaltern subject position (Turino 2000), and at other times to invoke aesthetic values that inform creative acts of mixing musical materials of different origins (Manuel 1995). Such practices of mixing are in some cases classically cosmopolitan, as in the coalescence of genres that evolved over long periods of time through networks of elite courtly and temple patronage (Pollock 2000; Schofield 2010), or eclectically cosmopolitan, as in the rapid emergence of new styles that juxtapose and layer contrasting sonic elements drawn from both indigenous and global sources (Arnold 1988; Greene 2001b).

With these distinctions in mind, I focus on a key moment in the history of the Malayalam film song when some music directors and playback singers used eclectic musical strategies to expand the range of possibilities for gendering musical expression between 2002 and 2004. Until the late 1990s, the singing voices of female and male characters in Malayalam cinema followed a predictable set of timbral qualities and classical stylistic features. This dominant style was buttressed by the success of classically trained playback singers such as K. J. Yesudas, a Malluwood film music legend who defined the scene for more than three decades. In the mid-1990s, a new generation of music directors, playback singers, and cine-musicians began accessing positions of creative influence in the industry, and suddenly a wider range of feminine and masculine identities entered Kerala's public cultural arena. New musical sensibilities provoked passionate responses from those who lamented the demise of a golden age of feminine and masculine ideals in popular song on one hand, and a younger generation that embraced global cultural hybridity on the other. Characterized by greater emphasis on duple meters and electronic percussion, extensive use of synthesizers and sound cards to widen the palette of instrumental timbres and textures, and shorter declamatory vocal phrasing in lower ranges, the turn away from classically inspired film songs created new possibilities for sounding feminine on the screen and beyond it. At stake were the shifting contours of patriarchy and its musical mediation between the socio-religious conservatism associated with classical music, nation-building, and older cosmopolitan narratives of the "composite culture" that emerged from Kerala's historical Indian Ocean encounters (Menon 1978), and new aspirational tastes for urban consumer lifestyles and globally sourced eclectic cultural forms (Osella and Osella 2000; Lukose 2009). Who were the musical agents and co-agents that challenged musical orthodoxy? How did they handle Kerala's conflicting desire to appear both open and regionally distinctive to the world? If social transformation works "through the constant production, contestation, and transformation of public culture, of media and other representation of all kinds, embodying and seeking to shape old and new thoughts, feelings, and ideologies" (Ortner 2006, 18), how do we account for the creative influence of professional women performers on song craft in South Indian cinema?

Critics have often reverentially compared exceptional female play-back singers (*pinnanigayika*) to songbirds, a metaphor that celebrates their vocal artistry even as it draws attention to the limited scope for women's musical agency in the industry. Any rethinking of the social and aesthetic implications of borrowing and mixing musical ideas from other traditions, therefore, must address how such intercultural discourses are gendered. By examining how women performers shape the creative process of mixing musical practices in unconventional ways in spite of patriarchal constraints, we reveal how disparaging and celebratory narratives of stylistic hybridity reinforce normative gender roles. We also bring into critical relief shifting intergenerational views on the uncertain compatibility of new cosmopolitan lifestyles with respectable ways of sounding feminine.

Leading feminist scholars question why elite and vernacular cosmopolitanisms regularly exclude women (Werbner 2008). They interrogate commonly held assumptions that only men are capable of seeing the world from a different perspective, becoming a global citizen, or transcending the tension between universalism and historical difference (Chakrabarty 2000, 82). Critical feminist perspectives situate women as creative agents who not only draw on universal ideals associated with interculturalism, but more important, engage in "a process of redefining and reimagining" such values as local forms of modernity (Stivens 2008). For example, there are now many ethnographic cases of rooted cosmopolitan women who manage to work within postcolonial patriarchal structures of belonging like the nation-state while also advancing feminist and womanist identity politics (Ram 2008). Women playback singers in South Indian commercial film industries add a specifically music-centered perspective to this discourse, one that highlights how musical performance can serve as a vehicle for mixing sound materials that challenge conservative gender roles, interventions that one might call *cosmofeminist* musical acts (Pollock et al. 2000, 8). Some women playback singers are working together with progressive male music directors to complicate binary oppositions that continue to locate feminine respectability in the domestic private sphere rather than the public mainstream, or "malestream" as some have put it (Stivens 2008). Together, these creative collaborations are expanding the possibilities for sounding feminine and cosmopolitan in Kerala, a region that despite international praise for its human development achievements, nonetheless remains one of India's most conservative societies.

Throughout the history of Malayalam popular film music, playback singing—the art of performing the voice of a character visually embodied by an actor who mimes to prerecorded tracks on-screen—was the only available role for women. Even then, most female playback singers in the Malayalam industry came from other South Indian states until the stigma associated with women who perform music in public began to relax in the 1960s. Although Kerala may have one of the most conservative cinematic traditions, the state must be situated in relation to broader patterns of limiting roles for women in the entertainment fields of postcolonial India (Qureshi 2006). Amanda Weidman reminds us that music "brought women into the public sphere in a particular way, as the voice of tradition. They were not perceived as innovators, much less as performers" (Weidman 2006, 139). Today, women are still widely perceived to contribute little in the way of creativity to the process of performing and recording songs composed by male music directors. Their job, according to conventional belief and some insider accounts, is to follow the composer's instructions with as little personal interpretation as possible. Yet even within these constraints, playback singers exercise creative agency when they employ a range of techniques to embody the appropriate voice for a given character or mood behind the curtain. For example, in a 2011 interview held in Thiruvananthapuram, Rajalakshmy, the 2010 playback singer of the year at the Kerala State Film Awards, described for me how she responded to a director's request to bring innocence to a character's voice while recording her award-winning song "Olichirunne" ["Hiding"] (video 4.1) for the film *Janakan* (2010).

Rajalakshmy's vivid illustration of the skills required to establish a mood or embody a heroine underlines the significant individual artistry women playback singers bring to the project of recording a hit song. She elaborates in the following excerpt from our conversation (video 4.2):

> KM: And so in this case, he [the music director, M. Jayachandran] wanted you to bring innocence to your voice.
>
> RAJALAKSHMY: Yes.
>
> KM: How do you do that...as a singer?
>
> RAJALAKSHMY: I am innocent [we both laugh].
>
> KM: Sure...but even if you weren't innocent, and somebody asked you...how do you respond to that?
>
> RAJALAKSHMY: Professionally...with my experience I know how to bring innocence, or how to bring pathos to the music...how to bring funny elements to music. I know that. And it comes like that. I don't know how to express it.

KM: But you know you could demonstrate. You know you demonstrated husky....

RAJALAKSHMY: Husky. Romantic.

KM: Romantic. But for innocence, you wouldn't sing like that.

RAJALAKSHMY: Innocence means... "Olichirunne" ["Hiding"].... Have you heard that song?

KM: Yes.

RAJALAKSHMY: [She sings] *Olichirunne onnicholichirunne* [Hiding, we were hiding]....*Muttathethum chethi poovil olichirunne* [Hiding in the chethi flowers in the courtyard].... Very innocent words. Then, we laugh while singing... [she demonstrates].... You see the difference?

KM: It changes the sound.

RAJALAKSHMY: These are all techniques.... If I sing... [she demonstrates the effect of laughing while singing the above lines again]. You see the difference.

KM: I see the difference. I hear the difference.

RAJALAKSHMY: Then if we have a pathos song. Just cry. We'll get the emotions.

KM: So you actually try to physically change your facial expressions based on the emotions.

RAJALAKSHMY: We are actors. We are acting in front of the mic.

The above dialogue reveals how a playback singer conceptualizes her creative agency in the process of giving voice to different feminine characters. Still, it is rarely assumed that an actor's craft and bodily presence are vital for becoming a character in a purely audible transformation. Nor is it widely acknowledged that performing the voice of a character picturized miming on-screen necessarily involves using bodily techniques like facial expressions and subtle gestures to bring that character to life. Likewise, in Kerala's celebrated classical dance-drama tradition, Kathakali, all eyes are on the performers who visually embody the characters with stunning costumes and sophisticated vocabularies of facial expressions, hand gestures, and stylized movements. Yet the visual spectacle alone cannot achieve *rasa*—the perceived flavor, sentiment, or mood in Indian aesthetic theory—without the singers who sonically embody the characters' speech and song from their positions in the background. The body-mind theory of how Kathakali actors conceptualize the interrelation of mind, body, and emotion in the process of merging their identity with a character seems equally applicable to artists who render characters audible on-screen (Zarrilli 2000). Following Noland's definition of gesture as "the organized form of kinesis through which subjects navigate and alter their worlds" (2009, 4),

Figure 4.3
Rajalakshmy plucking the strings of a *tambura* at her home in Thiruvananthapuram (2011).
(Photo by Kaley Mason.)

and in light of Rajalakshmy's insider account of the role theatricality and
movement play in her artistry, we can begin to see the potential for playback singers to draw on bodily techniques to intervene aesthetically and
socially in the creative process. Indeed, Rajalakshmy (figure 4.3) credits her
theater training for her success as a playback singer, suggesting that singers without a foundation in the dramatic arts inevitably find it even more
difficult to enter the field.

Having gained a sense of how women playback singers mobilize embodied knowledge to en-gender specific characters and moods, we now return
to Kerala's popular music scene in the early 2000s. How did two Malayalam
film songs from opposite ends of a stylistic continuum ranging from conservative classicism to bold eclecticism gain widespread currency? In the
next section, I consider the range of musical strategies that musical actors
deployed to articulate conservative and liberal gender values in dramatic
situations on-screen at the turn of the millennium.

A TALE OF TWO SONGS

Etched in my memory of daily encounters with commercial cinema in Kerala
are two songs in particular that evoke strikingly different feminine subjectivities: "Karmukil Varnnante Chundil" ["On the Lips of the Dark-Clouded
One"], hereafter "Karmukil," and "Karuppinazhaku" ["Black Is Beautiful"].
Both were released shortly after the millennium (2002 and 2003 respectively); both were picturized in situations featuring young women singing

sentiments of love; and both enjoyed considerable success. The similarities between the songs end there, however, as they diverged aesthetically and generically, evoking different moods, relationships, and feminine roles. Although much of the stylistic contrast can be linked to the artistic practices of the music directors and the specific situational demands of the film director's narrative, the playback singers also played an important role in shaping their distinctive sounds.

The most popular song from the award-winning film *Nandanam* (Ranjith 2002), "Karmukil" was composed by Raveendran and sung by K. S. Chitra, two towering figures in the history of the Malayalam film song with highly refined classical sensibilities. So pervasive and beloved is Chitra's musical presence in popular media today that she is known throughout Kerala and India as the Nightingale (*vanambati*) of South India (Nair 2001). The second song, "Karuppinazhaku," from the film *Swapnakoodu* (2003), was remarkable for the extent to which it rejected classical Indian film music aesthetics in favor of global popular music influences. Unlike "Karmukil," "Karuppinazhaku" was crafted by a younger generation of film music artists, including music director Mohan Sithara and young playback singer Jyotsna, whose voice and charisma some critics have compared to moonlight, following the Sanskrit meaning of her name and the Malayalam word for moonlight (*nilaval*) in the title of her first hit "Sukhamanee Nilaval" ["Moonlight Feels Good"], from the film *Nammal* (2002). Compared to the classical standard set by established artists like Chitra, Jyotsna's lower tessitura, tersely delivered rhythmic phrases, and unconventional timbre were considered bold and experimental at the time. But before we see how some artists' stylistic innovations defied tradition, we need to know something about the musical conventions that were common practice in Malluwood prior to the early 2000s.

CLASSICIZING DOMESTICITY

"Karmukil Varnnante Chundil" is a devotional hymn to Lord Krishna, the Hindu deity at the center of *Nandanam*'s narrative. A familiar tale of impossible heteronormative love between a man and a woman from different social backgrounds, the plot follows Balamani, an orphaned domestic servant girl in an affluent Hindu household and a passionate devotee of Lord Krishna, to whom she turns for guidance in despair when her love for middle-class Manu seems hopeless. Although Manu's feelings for Balamani are mutual, his extended family is determined to arrange a marriage with someone from his own social standing, namely someone of his caste and class. This marriage tension dramatizes the gendered binary tropes of collectivity over individuality, duty (*dharma*) over desire, tradition over modernity, private over public, and local over global affinities (Chatterjee 1993). Educated in the United States, Manu is presented as a well-traveled son with worldly experience who returns home to reconnect with his faith, family, and culture. Balamani, in contrast, plays a local self-sacrificing, virtuous, and spiritual unmarried woman who personifies all that is natural and pure about the nation (Ramaswamy 2010), which in this case implies Kerala rather than India. Another theme the film explores is the ambiguity of romantic and devotional love associated with the *bhakti* tradition and the Puranic stories of Krishna's love for Radha. Balamani's playful, affectionate relationship with Manu parallels her private relationship with Krishna throughout the narrative, leaving the viewer with a contemporary interpretation of the longing for divine love expressed in Jayadeva's 12th-century lyric poem, the *Gita Govinda*. For Malayalee viewers, this devotional tradition is associated with the film's setting in the Kerala temple town of Guruvayoor, one of the most important pilgrimage sites for Krishna devotees and an important center for classical music training. Given the film's setting, characters, and narrative themes, the director and composer understandably envisioned drawing on Karnatik classical conventions in the process of crafting songs for specific situations. One of the most memorable moments in *Nandanam* is the scene in which Balamani is pictured singing "Karmukil" (video 4.4). In this example, we see and hear how devotional-classical stylistic features can be used in a song sequence to amplify conservative gender roles and characters.

The narrative builds to a climax after Manu's arranged marriage appears to be past the point of no return. Leaning on the shoulder of Manu's grandmother in a bedroom, she swells into song, beginning with a short unmetered introduction in the style of the opening section of a classical Karnatik performance when the soloist reveals the framework for the raga (*alapanam*), which in this case resembles Harikambhoji. Wearing a plain blouse and long skirt (*pavada*), the actress playing Balamani, Navya Nair, is pictured singing while moving slowly and gracefully through the wooden teak interior of Manu's aristocratic ancestral home (*taravad*). K. S. Chitra hums a series of smooth melodic phrases in dialogue with a synthesizer imitating bowed strings. She begins the *pallavi* (refrain) section, her voice swaying gently in a triple meter with rhythmic (tabla) and melodic (bamboo flute) accompaniment:

> In the flute at the lips of the one who has the color of the dark cloud
> Oh the gently sleeping Sriragam. The Lord forgot to awaken you.

Raveendran's decision to emphasize the flute complements the lyricist's image of Krishna while drawing on a common "musical cultural code" that associates the popular Hindu deity with the flute for listeners who share an Indian mythical frame of reference (Sarrazin 2008). Light textures give prominence to the voice, text, and melodic instruments, all features that point to conventional songwriting for classical sensibilities. Following the first *pallavi* (literally, "sprouting") section, a musical interlude featuring the flute and the sitar (known as background music or BGM) respectively accompanies a series of flashbacks to moments of intimacy and playful affection between Balamani and Manu. The first BGM also serves as a transition to the *anupallavi* section, which is sung in a higher register before concluding with the *pallavi*. A second BGM section ensues as a dialogue between the flute and the strings ushers in more sentimental flashbacks. A *charanam* section adds another verse in roughly the same tune as the *anupallavi*, before descending back to the *pallavi*. The song then intensifies the pathos of the situation as simulated orchestral strings begin a series of angular, highly ornamented, and pulsed rhythmic phrases that suggest a Western classical dance idiom. The shift in instrumentation and style accompanies five sustained calls for Krishna that rise in pitch through implied major and minor tonal areas before landing on an unusually high stable tone (high A), after which Balamani, kneeling with hands clasped, collapses before a bronze statue of Krishna, utterly surrendering herself to the deity. Meanwhile, the extended family members have gathered around the altar with sympathetic facial expressions as they witness Balamani's passionate plea and *bhakti* (devotion).

Yet despite the dignified and sympathetic portrayal of Balamani's character in this song sequence, the picturization still serves to highlight her status as socially inferior, uneducated, and symbolically confined to the domestic space of the home. By reinforcing the modernist gender binary of men/public versus women/private, the song and its picturization give credence to the Indian feminist argument that women in Kerala have been increasingly marginalized from the public sphere. Many scholars have challenged narratives of women's liberation in Kerala that fail to mention how social reforms replaced traditional family arrangements with new gender roles for men and women in public and domestic life respectively (Devika 2007, 11; Mukhopadhyay 2007). In response to literature on the region's human development achievements (Jeffrey 1992), Devika counters that women only really gained access to a highly gendered and gendering public space as "subjects of a certain Womanliness" (Devika 2007, 11). Instead of eliminating female domesticity, modernity "instituted new forms of family and female domesticity, which did open up agency for women, but were by no means politically neutral" (ibid.). Through education, radio, television, and film, music contributed to instituting a new patriarchy by reconfiguring womanly duty (*streedharmam*) in the modern postcolonial project of nation-building. Training in Indian classical music and dance became an important avenue for improving a daughter's social standing through private and carefully regulated public expressions of respectable womanhood. It follows then that film songs adhering more closely to classical musical aesthetics would be more strongly associated with feminine respectability and clearly defined gender roles and spaces. Indeed, "Karmukil" is an exemplary song that most middle-class parents would be proud to hear their daughters sing.

While living in Kerala, I heard many renditions of "Karmukil" in the domestic spaces of homes I visited. One version, partially reconstructed from my fieldnotes and a video recording, is especially vivid in my recollection. I remember meeting a middle-class family in a village on Kerala's northern coast in the Kannur District in the sweltering heat of late May 2004. That the family valued classical music was immediately evident by the colorful bas-relief of Saraswati, the Hindu goddess of learning and music, playing her veena high above on the side of the chimney. We were invited to sit in comfortable chairs in the hall, a room typically located at the entrance where guests are welcomed. After a few minutes of polite conversation, the topic turned to music and my reasons for traveling to Kerala, which led my friend Suresh to encourage one of the daughters of the family (around ten years of age) to sing a song. Dressed in a simple white frock and wearing a discreet silver chain with matching earrings against her dark shoulder-length hair, she sat on the edge of an elaborately carved chair that was much too deep for her slender form. Eyes closed and hands folded on her lap, she began to sing the opening *pallavi* of "Karmukil" in a low whispering voice without accompaniment. Suresh quickly added rhythmic support, tapping the first and second pulses of the triple meter (*talam*) on the side of his chair. As the song progressed, her confidence increased and she unfolded the remaining verses with a fuller investment in the words, even handling the challenging ascending line and crescendo at the climax with grace. After her quiet concluding statement of the opening line, we clapped and showered her with praise, prompting her to grin bashfully and sink into the back of the chair.

This ethnographic vignette reveals how younger generations embody film songs in the private intimacy of family occasions. Yet the placement of this song through performance in a middle-class home also highlights how popular music serves as a vehicle for en-gendering individuals in families with upwardly mobile aspirations. Although not as esteemed a musical act as performing a *kriti* (classical song form) from the Karnatik repertoire, singing a classically inspired devotional film song for guests is also an embodied presentation of youthful feminine bourgeois respectability.

FEMINIZING MOBILITY

Compared to K. S. Chitra's eloquent musical characterization of Balamani in a classical devotional idiom, Jyotsna's bold performance of "Karuppinazhaku" evokes worldly women who move, work, and play in the public sphere. Unlike Balamani, the heroines in *Swapnakoodu*, Kamala and Padma, are positioned as cosmopolitans from the margins. As the story unfolds, we learn that they help their widowed mother manage a guest-house in the former French territory of Puducherry, a setting that brings them into regular contact with European languages and lifestyles through interactions with tourists. Soon the two young sisters meet three carefree Malayalee men enrolled at a local hotel management college, and romances bloom with all the melodramatic lows, highs, and shenanigans that characterize this youth-centered genre of fun-loving college flicks. Although the narrative eventually reaffirms Kerala's patriarchal values when calamity strikes and the heroines become dependent on the heroes, with Kamala eventually returning to Kerala, the music suggests an alternatively modern femininity, one that values mobility, assertiveness, and a Westernized cosmopolitan sensibility.

The picture begins with "Karuppinazhaku" (video 4.5) introducing the main characters on a holiday dream sequence in an Austrian alpine landscape. With the plot yet to get underway, the mood is pure fun and frivolity with sensual overtones. Beginning with a short accordion riff, the instrumental hook soon interrupts the opening pastoral scene with a regular dance beat and pounding synthesizer bass in a duple meter and upbeat tempo. In contrast with K. S. Chitra's long conjunct melodic phrases in a mid-to-high register, Jyotsna sings short punchy lines in an unusually low register, thereby creating the effect of punctuating the musical texture with her voice:

> The beauty of black, Oh, The beauty of white, Oh,
> The misty shower of dawn, It's beautiful to be seventeen.
> The beauty of eyes Oh, The beauty of speech Oh,
> My passion to touch has a hundred beauties to the mind.

Meanwhile, on the screen, the Malayalee sisters dance on Vienna's streets and Austrian ski slopes in a variety of European attire, from colorful trousers and dresses to winter outerwear. Rhythmically rather than melodically driven, "Karuppinazhaku" expands the usual palette of instrumentation to include an accordion, a distorted electric guitar (power chords and melodic riffs), a European fiddle, and synthesizer string pads and beats. Sithara's decision to privilege low-pitched declamatory singing, a variety of metallic timbres, and unconventional stylistic idioms frames the main characters in a way that departs significantly from typical constructions of femininity. When asked about his creative choices for this particular song in a 2011 interview in Thrissur, Sithara explained that the director wanted to emphasize the Westernized background of the characters with a fresh sound. The decision to represent Westernized characters with European instruments is hardly new in Malluwood, but what is interesting about this case is that these young women are celebrated for their independence, self-reliance, global outlook, and mobility. This runs counter to the practice of using rhythmically driven Western music to amplify one-dimensional hyper-eroticized women with unconventional tastes in fashion and music in the "item numbers" associated with Tamil cinema.

It was thus hardly a coincidence that Sithara asked Jyotsna—one of few playback singers in the industry with exposure to a wider variety of music abroad—to perform this song. By 2003, they had already worked together on other film projects so he knew what her voice was capable of and, more important, he knew that she had the ability to merge South Indian and international musical styles. Like Padma and Kamala's fictional life stories growing up between Kerala and the cosmopolitan Indian milieu of a former French territory, Jyotsna also spent much of her childhood outside Kerala. Born in Kuwait and raised in Abu Dhabi, she encountered expatriate networks of affluent and working-class migrants from around the world, all drawn to the Gulf in pursuit of job opportunities buoyed by oil revenues (Kurien 2002; Osella and Osella 2000). Through these intersections, she gained an appreciation for a wide range of international music, a point that Jyotsna elaborated on in a phone conversation with me in 2011 about the experience of recording "Karuppinazhaku":

> I think one thing that actually helped me was that because I was abroad, because I was in the Gulf...because it was outside India, you get a little bit more exposure to different kinds of music. I used to listen to a lot of Arabic songs and a little bit of English...so we were open to different kinds of music. So that kind of helped me with my rendition.

Although it was not until her late teens that she began to receive formal training in Indian classical music, Jyotsna came from an actively musical family. Her mother sang and taught dance, and she remembers performing regularly for talent contests at school and cultural programs organized by the Kerala diaspora in the Middle East. It is easy to see why Sithara would have considered her an ideal artist to sing the parts of exceptionally mobile, assertive, and Westernized Malayalee feminine characters in the film.

Many music directors go to great lengths to prescribe exactly how their work should be interpreted. According to Jyotsna, though, Sithara takes a different approach: He encourages playback singers to bring their own interpretation to the piece. In the case of "Karuppinazhaku," he lowered the pitch to enable Jyotsna to open up at the highest notes without using her falsetto and invited her to explore "Western modulations," but more generally, he encouraged her to experiment with her voice in the studio, telling her to do whatever feels right and to hold nothing back. The result was a song that gained its popularity as much for the novelty of its hybrid instrumentation as for Jyotsna's unconventional feminine singing style. Instead of serving as a medium for a male composer's work, Jyotsna acted as a creative co-agent, bringing her background and artistry to the recording in the same way that Rajalakshmy described her role in the studio. Listening to Jyotsna and Rajalakshmy's warm recollections of the social life of making music with music directors, lyricists, arrangers, sound recordists, other singers, and studio musicians brings to mind other ethnographic accounts of the highly collaborative workflows that continue to shape the creative process in commercial film industries despite the impact of computers and digital software on the organization of production and musical labor (Grimaud 2003; Booth 2008).

The rapid success of "Karuppinazhaku" in Kerala's post-liberalization youth culture, however, did not easily garner cross-generational praise. Sithara and Jyotsna were criticized for breaking from conventional film song aesthetics and, by extension, gender norms. Charges of Westernization, lack of classical grace and technique, weak melodies, excessive use of rhythm, and hyper-eroticism have all been leveled at the song's creators. In a frequent expression of condescension, Jyotsna is sometimes labeled an *adipoli* singer, an adjective typically invoked to describe all things trendy, here today and gone tomorrow, or the musical equivalent of an artist who produces seasonal hits rather than evergreen classics. Although not pejorative on its own, the label can carry negative connotations when directed at a profession that involves performing on public stages and moving in male-dominated creative workspaces widely rumored to encourage "loose morals." Songs associated with eclectic mixing, it would seem, have the potential to reinforce as well as complicate normative gender roles in the music industry and society at large. Still, the song was also widely praised by listeners who envisioned participating in a burgeoning youth culture of consumer lifestyles centered around fashion, food, travel, and music, a "celebration of hybridization" that some film critics argue is the new Bollywood legacy (Rajadhyaksha 2009, 55–57). New forms of intimacy are part of this legacy, and the college romances depicted in films like *Swapnakoodu* have arguably widened the horizon of possibilities for self-expression while also blurring the line between public and private domains of experience. As research on the effects of liberalization on youth has shown, the rise of fashion shows and dance talent contests are key sites affording new ways for young women to experience expressive movement in public (Lukose 2009). Whether viewed as the objectification of women's bodies by male-dominated global regimes of consumption, or alternatively as a liberating move away from stifling gender values, changes in popular music have led the way with singing voices and increasingly live performances too.

The immense popularity of "Karuppinazhaku" was largely due to the recorded version's aesthetic novelty, but some people attribute at least some of its success to the trend toward enlivening stage shows in Kerala. A common form of public entertainment throughout the state, public orchestral concerts (*ganamela*) featuring live renditions of film song repertoires have become important sources of revenue for professional musicians. These stage shows are often organized in conjunction with temple and church festivals, which, depending on how generous the funding is, often go to great lengths and expense to hire professional orchestras and celebrity playback singers from the cities. Governments also partner with the private sector to sponsor *ganamela* concerts as part of domestic and international tourism development initiatives in the major urban centers. It was at an event like this in February 2004, at the height of "Karuppinazhaku's" popularity, that I first encountered Jyotsna (figure 4.6) in the Northern Kerala city of Kozhikode. She was one of several playback singers who performed at an elaborate *ganamela* stage show at the end of an annual week-long tourism festival called the Malabar Mahotsavam. The evening concert was held in the Municipal Corporation Stadium on the last day of the festival. The stands facing the long rectangular stage in a half-moon formation were nearly full. Rows of chairs were arranged in a VIP section directly in front of the stage where the orchestra, including strings, flute, guitar, bass, tabla, and synthesizers, was warming up. The crowd flooded the ground floor around the cordoned-off areas, but I managed to find a spot close to the stage after chatting with a couple of journalists who were covering the event. After a series of speeches, one of the most popular Malayalam actors of all time, Mohanlal, lit a tall bronze oil lamp, a welcoming gesture that

Figure 4.6
Jyotsna performing at a concert celebrating the career of playback singer M. G. Sreekumar. The event was held at Al-Nasr Leisureland in Dubai, June 2010. (Photo courtesy of Jyotsna Radhakrishnan.)

often marks the beginning of an auspicious occasion in Kerala. The concert began shortly after this ceremony, and the singers each performed one of their songs. When it was Jyotsna's turn, the crowd roared as the accordion riff signaled the beginning of "Karuppinazhaku," and suddenly the atmosphere became electric, like a rock concert in Bengaluru or Delhi. Whereas the standard practice for singers at *ganamela* concerts in the late 1990s was to stand still behind a music stand with a microphone in hand, Jyotsna and others chose to move to the music while they sang. When I asked her about that concert and this development in the *ganamela* scene in 2011, she had this to say:

> JYOTSNA: I think it was the influence of the media . . . and I think it was the introduction of all these new sounds and new trends. People wanted some live action on stage. They didn't want singers to come and sing and go you know. They wanted singers to move . . . have fun. And they also wanted to have fun. That trend kind of set into Malayalam overnight. It just happened overnight! How this trend just changed completely all of a sudden I don't know. You know Malayalees are generally very conservative . . . especially you know, women dancing on stage . . . that was like a taboo until the late '90s. But then, there were people who actually came up to me and they were like, "you're not doing enough, we want to see you move more." I can't choreograph, I'm just moving with the song. [laughs]

KM: But you also had a background in dance?

JYOTSNA: Yeah, actually it was amateur dancing. My mother had a lot of training in classical dance. When we were in the Gulf my mother used to take [teach] dance classes for children...so I used to join her and learn under her. And at school I used to take Bharatanatyam dance competitions. That was just for the fun of it....Nothing serious at all.

Aided by the growing influence of reality television music contests and more frequent appearances of playback singers on television, the trend toward injecting more energy in live shows has broadened the scope of gestural possibilities for female and male performers in Kerala. My account of a *ganamela*-turned-rock concert suggests that there is more at stake in regional dynamics of popular music culture than the embodiment of particular musical sensibilities. The turn toward experiencing film song as expressive movement in public has unsettled boundaries that previously assigned gender-appropriate behavior to public and private domains. If we accept that kinesthetic experience has "the capacity to produce skilled bodies while inspiring audiences to resonate to dance and other movement performances in acts of empathy that may have an ethical, socializing function in human communities" (Noland 2009, 13), then popular music must indeed be an effective vehicle for creating an intimate idea of Kerala, one that has the potential to challenge official ideas (Stokes 2010, 16).

CULTURAL INTIMACY AND POPULAR MUSIC IN KERALA

A ubiquitous cultural form no less in Kerala than in other regions of South India, film songs reverberate across the intimate recesses of social life. As expressive resources for locating selves vis-à-vis others in society, songs influence how people envision themselves being and becoming, and by extension, they inevitably strengthen or contest gender norms. Working with conventional and unconventional musical parameters, artists craft subjectivities by framing dimensions of experience, and this framing "is central to the way in which music comes to serve as a device for the constitution of human agency" (DeNora 2000, 27). Drawing on ethnographic experience, media sources, and song analysis, I have underlined regional dynamics of musical framing that have both enabled and constrained options for en-gendering individuals and song sensibilities in Southwestern India. By bringing specific classical and eclectic creative strategies into relief, and by following their reworking in embodied performance beyond the screen, we can begin to see how songs participate in the everyday experience of cultural intimacy in Kerala.

Although the term "cultural intimacy" is often used to describe a field of tension between lived experience and wider contours of belonging that citizens of modern nation-states navigate (Herzfeld 2005), the concept is also useful for understanding how citizens of regions complicate, resist, or strengthen top-down versions of group belonging. One way Malayalees essentialize themselves to underline what makes them different from other Indians and others in general is to highlight their distinctive cosmopolitan worldview, one that has reconciled the necessity of global aspirations with the intensity of regionalist sentiment. This cosmopolitanism from below unfolds pragmatically as a popular narrative braiding infinite openness to the outside world with a sense of regional insularity and singularity. Though Kerala cosmopolitans have much in common with other liberalizing societies in India, Malayalee sensibilities have also evolved in response to local dynamics of globalization. Among the historical and contemporary experiences that distinguish modern Kerala from other regions of India are mass labor migration to the Arab states of the Persian Gulf, Hindu and Abrahamic religious pluralism, radical socialism and its nostalgia, Indian Ocean mercantile pasts, and unparalleled human development achievements in health and education. Popular music is an evocative means by which Malayalees engage with these shared frames of belonging while locating themselves in the world as both uniquely Indian and reservedly cosmopolitan.

Just as most regions of South Asia have evolved distinctive spice blends, Kerala has cultivated its own *masalas*, a culinary tradition that extends metaphorically to heightened melodrama and intimacy in culture industries like film and music. But Kerala's musical *masalas* also point to struggles over intimacy and love, as younger generations explore new ways of experiencing sentiments of attachment outside traditional familial alliances. Hence two very different visions of love found expression in "Karmukil" and "Karuppinazhaku" with important implications for thinking about how women in Kerala might imagine participating in South Indian public cultural arenas (Appadurai and Breckenridge 1995).

The difference between the singing voices in these two songs—between nightingales and moonlight—highlights the historical significance of stylistic changes that were taking place in millennial Malluwood. For most of the 20th century, music directors crafted songs that would appeal to listeners with classical music sensibilities and conservative gender values, a formula that remained constant for decades despite the increasing musical eclecticism of the much larger Tamil- and Hindi-speaking commercial film industries (Arnold 1988; Morcom 2007; Getter and Balasubrahmaniyan 2008). This old-is-gold model began to wane when composers, producers, singers, and musicians introduced new arrangements, instrumentation, and vocal styles that borrowed heavily from Western and Black Atlantic popular music influences, a shift that resonated well with the new cosmopolitan lifestyles of an emergent youth culture that began to take shape following economic liberalization in the early 1990s (Lukose 2009).

Like the cassette revolution in the 1970s and '80s (Manuel 1993), the democratization of digital playback and recording technologies—combined with economic policy changes, a new middle class (Fernandes 2006), and the discovery of Bollywood "overseas"—made the last decade of the 20th century a pivotal moment in Indian popular music history. In response to pressure from the International Monetary Fund and the World Bank, the Indian National Congress implemented structural reforms in the early 1990s that opened domestic markets to foreign competition for the first time since Indian independence. The turn away from protectionism toward free market competition had a profound effect on public culture in Kerala, clearing the way for local, national, and transnational entertainment corporations like Surya TV, Asianet, Saregama, MTV, Sony, and Time Warner to capitalize on the advent of satellite television, rising consumerism, and the growth of retail and advertising sectors (Booth 2008; Beaster-Jones 2011). But unlike in other regions of India where liberalization encouraged the development of popular music independent of the film industry in the form of Indipop and other genres (Kumar and Curtin 2002), Malayalees remained committed to film songs. So while the convergence of global market forces, media, and mobilities has yet to establish a robust "Mallupop" industry in the 21st century, new musical *masalas* have nonetheless expanded notions of what respectable femininity and cultural intimacy could sound like in Malluwood's post-liberalization moment.

PART TWO

Audio Cultures, Music Videos, and Film Music

CHAPTER 5

Film Song and Its Other

Stylistic Mediation and the Hindi Film Song Genre

JAYSON BEASTER-JONES

The music of Indian films is remarkably heterogeneous. From the first moments of the genre, music directors and the arrangers who work with them have incorporated instruments and stylistic features of manifold sources from inside and outside of India into a distinctly cosmopolitan musical form that has had enduring popularity in India and abroad. Musical ideas from many Indian musical traditions, including classical and semi-classical songs, regional folk songs, and devotional songs, were fused with musical ideas that had origins as diverse as flamenco, Western classical, big-band jazz, samba, bossa nova, and rock. Despite the diversity of source materials, however, many songs are readily identifiable as film songs, even to casual listeners, on the basis of particular sounds and styles that appear with some regularity. Over time, these musical characteristics have become associated with the Indian film song genre. For example, Booth (2008b) has described what one of his interlocutors called "that Bollywood sound." That is, the conventional features of Indian film songs (from the perspective of a Western music producer) that include

> large orchestras, especially with large string sections playing unison melody lines and rapid passagework with impeccable intonation and ensemble, endless eclectic instrumental combinations of Indian and non-Indian instruments, unexpected harmonies, regular and extreme use of electronic reverberation

effects, an idiosyncratic mix of Western and Indian stylistic features, and a facility with electronic instruments and amplification (85).

Beyond the characteristics identified here, one might also add that the Bollywood sound is equally distinguished by the vocal timbres of a small group of professional playback singers, the frequent use of a choir as a component of the orchestration, and studio production practices that emphasize the vocal track above all else in the recording mix. Although these characteristics are especially evocative of mainstream film songs of the late 1960s through the 1990s, Booth notes that many contemporary film songs still retain the traces of "that Bollywood sound" despite the emergence of new technologically enabled production and compositional techniques. The continued reproduction of certain film song conventions points to the ways that music directors continue to mediate (in the Peircean sense) heterogeneous musical styles and practices based on what they think their audiences expect. Accordingly, film songs have achieved a kind of stylistic continuity that audiences, critics, and musicologists frequently refer to as *filmi* (i.e., evocative of film song style).

Despite the widely recognized convergence of musical practices with heterogeneous styles, however, there are certain film songs that do not "sound *filmi*." From an aural perspective, some combination of musical or stylistic characteristics might lead one to question whether a particular song is, in fact, a film song, even when it appears on a film soundtrack. Reframed in different terms, there are times in which particular songs are classified as film songs on the basis of their musical genre, rather than on the basis of their musical style. Although the terms "style" and "genre" are often conflated by musicologists, I suggest here that they can usefully be distinguished from each other: styles classify primarily musical sound and performance practices; genres classify both musical elements and the discourses that accompany them. While some genre associations emerge from the aurality of songs, others do not. For example, even as there are musical features that are attributed to a *filmi* aesthetic, the repetition of songs in a variety of media, picturization of songs on actors (who usually do not sing them), and use of soundtracks in film marketing campaigns reinforce the association of particular songs with particular films regardless of whether or not a song "sounds like" a film song. Moreover, genre categories are more frequently embedded in—and relevant to—commercial discourses than style categories. By suggesting that film songs are a genre, we assume that there are certain stylistic features that are central, yet not defining, that enable an audience to identify the song as belonging to a defined set of musical practices, as well as expected modes of audience reception and use.

While this stylistic/generic ambiguity is especially true of certain film songs that emerged after the early 2000s (as Sarrazin points out in chapter 2), this ambiguity is also apparent in some earlier film songs, especially at historical moments of stylistic transition. Moreover, unlike film music traditions in other parts of the world, this tension between categories of musical style and musical genre is palpable in Hindi film soundtracks, insofar as the music of film songs is seemingly secondary to their presence in a Hindi film as far as genre categories are concerned. Songs that might otherwise be identified as belonging to another genre of music are labeled "film songs," regardless of their musical content. This classificatory issue stems in large part from the trajectory of the popular music industry in India, because only in the 1980s did new, non-film genres like Indipop and the pop *ghazal* provide mass-mediated alternatives to film songs in the marketplace. Consequently, the issues that accompany genre classification are also relatively recent, and like genres in other parts of the world, the boundaries between film songs and other Indian popular genres can be rather porous. Indeed, songs cannot always be classified solely on the basis of musical content; one must also attend to the genre narratives that circulate along with them.

In this chapter, I contextualize the particular history of film song style and genre by discussing the local category of *filmi* as a kind of semiotic mediation of musical style, as well as a mainstream hegemonic musical practice. In order to address how a film song may or may not sound *filmi*, I unpack the manifold meanings that music can bear, particularly in view of India's unique pop cultural milieu and the ways in which new music genres of the 1990s and beyond positioned themselves in opposition to this conception of a *filmi* mainstream. I then analyze three songs that have appeared in Hindi films in the context of stylistic mediation. I suggest that each song signals a stylistic/aesthetic transition in film song sound that intersects with emergent genre meanings, even as each points to the ways in which music directors mediate musical material in their film soundtracks. Moreover, although each of these songs exemplifies a transitional moment in *filmi* sound, the latter two examples complicate the genre definition of film song. I conclude this chapter by pointing to the malleability of style and genre categories in contemporary India and the ways in which artists transform film songs into non-film songs—that is, even as musical material is transformed to fit a *filmi* aesthetic, later incarnations of this material might be used for very different purposes. Accordingly, I suggest that the conventional wisdom that all songs appearing in an Indian film or soundtrack are necessarily "film songs" might need some revision.

FILMI SOUND: STYLISTIC MEDIATION IN INDIAN FILM SONGS

Film songs have been the dominant recorded music in India since the inception of the sound film in the 1930s. Over the intervening decades, Indian music directors (composers) have developed ways of incorporating diverse musical materials into a uniquely Indian musical style that musicians, audiences, and cultural critics have labeled *filmi*. It is important to emphasize at the outset, however, that the sounds and styles of film songs have changed over time as various musical fashions from India and abroad have been incorporated into film songs. Thus, while the musical content and style of film songs have been dramatically transformed a number of times over the last few decades, the compositional practice of music directors—mediating musical content into songs that they believe their audiences will want to hear—has remained more or less consistent.

The label *filmi* has come to index a range of meanings, many of which suggest a nominally inauthentic mode of performance, both in musical and nonmusical contexts. For example, one might call a romantic relationship *filmi* if it tends toward overblown expressions of emotion and melodrama. In musical terms, it can used to describe a genre or style of Indian music that is adapted for use in film song, leading to hybrid categories such as the *filmi qawwali* (Sufi devotional song), *filmi bhajan* (Hindu devotional song), *filmi ghazal* (Urdu-language poetry set to song), and so forth. For example, Morcom (2007) has described how the music of *filmi qawwali* differs from traditional performance contexts, including the use of pre-composed orchestral interludes, minimal improvisation, shortened vocal performances, and fixed length of refrains. Insofar as *qawwalis* written for films are identifiable as *qawwalis* through certain stylistic characteristics, such as alternation between solo voice and chorus, repetition of key portions of the refrain by the chorus, handclapping, and visual representation of instruments like the harmonium and tabla, audiences recognize that these are *filmi* representations of *qawwalis* rather than "authentic" performances. In a similar vein, while the *filmi ghazal* retains the couplet form and rhyme scheme and draws more frequently from the Urdu poetic lexicon of the light classical *ghazal*, music directors use pre-composed musical interludes rather than the improvised vocal and instrumental passages heard in traditional *ghazals*. Song lengths are much more rigid in the film versions as well. In the cases of both *filmi qawwali* and *filmi ghazal*, certain musical elements are mediated to fit the expectations of a film song audience, even as other musical elements remain that are intended by producers to be identifiable representations (i.e., as film versions of non-film genres).

In addition to its use in describing the absorption of a musical style into a film song, the term *filmi* can also describe stylistic approaches of certain genres of music that do not appear in a film. That is, songs that utilize some of the more stereotypical elements of the Bollywood sound might be referred to as *filmi* because of their vocal style, orchestration, or accompaniment. These *filmi* influences on non-film genres at times provoke expressions of derision or anxiety. For example, cultural critics find the incorporation of film song elements into local folk musics a troubling source of commercial influence on folk expression, if not also of inauthentic folk performance. As music directors mediate ideas from Indian folk musicians, folk musicians mediate ideas from film songs; this has led cultural critics to decry this practice as an ostensible feedback loop of inauthenticity (Marcus 1992; Manuel 1993).

One productive way to address this issue of a *filmi* sound and style in Indian film and non-film songs is in terms of a practice I call "stylistic mediation." By stylistic mediation, I mean the production of a musical representation in which musical material from one set of conventions is framed according to the values of a different set of conventions, even as this material retains some aspects of its original content that index its previous usages. In the descriptions of film *qawwali* and *ghazal* above, for example, certain aspects of these musical styles are retained that index (point to) these song genres, even as these audiences recognize that these song genres have been mediated for a filmic context. It is worth noting in passing that there are several theoretical conceptions of mediation (e.g., Adorno 1976; Negus 1992; Auslander 2008) that define mediation as the encounters of cultural practices like music or theatre with systems of mass communication, and the ways in which these cultural practices are shaped by these encounters. The sense of mediation that I am using here, however, is adapted from C. S. Peirce's notion of "semiotic mediation" (see Peirce 1960; Turino 2008). In his theoretical framework, mediation refers to human cognitive encounters with sign systems, in which signs represent objects, even as they are determined by their objects. The consequence of this paradigm is that everything in human experience is necessarily mediated by, among other things, social conventions and practices, as well as individual human experiences. Accordingly, any adaptation of characteristics of one set of styles, genres, or practices into another set of established styles or practices can be described as mediation.

As a kind of widespread musical practice, there are countless examples of musical mediations of one musical style by another in many music genres around the world. In the context of American music, for example, George Gershwin's mediation of 1920s blues incorporates many elements that, to a Western classical audience, allude to "blues," even as it conforms to Western classical conventions of orchestration, harmony, and performance. Despite being in a "blues style" from the perspective of the conventions of Western classical music, few listeners would mistake Gershwin's version of "Summertime" in the opera *Porgy and Bess* (1935) for a blues song. Rather, in adapting the song for an operatic music context, Gershwin mediates an African American blues style to the conventions of Western classical music. Yet songs that mediate one musical context can be mediated yet again to fit the conventions of another genre. Thus, jazz musicians have mediated this Gershwin song into a jazz standard by codifying chord progressions over which they improvise, making several Gershwin compositions central to the jazz canon. In a similar vein, many Indian classical singers have incorporated "evergreen" (classic) film songs into their repertoire to end concerts or provide an encore. Their renditions of these songs conform to the conventions of light classical performance (e.g., instrumentation, timbres, and classical vocal ornamentation) that make them easily recognizable as Indian classical renditions of film songs, even as a particular song might have originated as a regional folk song that was mediated by a music director to fit into a film, and then later mediated by an Indian classical musician to fit a concert context.

This notion of stylistic mediation thus becomes a useful way to describe the complicated peregrinations of musical ideas beyond merely labeling an idea "borrowed" (see also Marshall and Beaster-Jones 2012). Indeed, musical ideas are never merely borrowed; they are transformed to fit new contexts. As a pervasive musical practice, musicians and audiences use a variety of terms to describe mediation of musical material—"version," "rendition," "cover"—in ways that do not always acknowledge the complexity of this mediation. For example, the song "Aate Jaate Hanste Gaate" from the film *Maine Pyar Kiya* (1989) is frequently labeled a Bollywood cover of the Stevie Wonder song "I Just Called to Say I Love You" (1984). But describing the song entirely in terms of melodic borrowing oversimplifies the inherent complexity of musical sound and reuse, even as it trivializes the music director's contribution to the creative reuse of this melody. "Aate Jaate" might better be understood as *filmi* mediation of a Western pop song—that is, it mediates portions of this melody to make it appropriate for (or palatable to) a different audience in a new generic context. As the song analyses later in this chapter illustrate, unwrapping the layers of this mediation can be quite complicated. Indeed, the musical qualities of a song that might lead a listener to say "that does (not) sound *filmi*" can be based upon subtle perceptions in which the evaluator may not have the language to explain how she came to this conclusion.

MUSIC GENRE AND MEANING BEYOND SOUND

Although musical sound itself carries a range of possible meanings, many other meanings emerge in the nexus between musical genre and musical style. Genre categories are of critical importance to the categorization of music, especially in the marketplace. Genre is also an important way for listeners to structure their experience of music and their sets of expectations about musical content (Feld 1984). From music industry perspectives, genre is a fundamental organizing principle even at the earliest stages of production, as producers anticipate potential audiences and markets, and the audiences themselves are constituted through these genres (Frith 1996; Negus 1992). However, there has been a tendency to conflate musical genre and style by listeners and critics. While there are no hard boundaries between these two ways of classifying music, popular music scholars of Western genres have come to describe style as the aural components of music. In contrast, genre has aurally recognizable components, but it is differentiated as much by its extramusical discourses as it is by its musical elements. Although it would be a bit inaccurate to describe style and genre as simply the extremes of musical sound and its social manifestations, one might understand discussions of musical style as emerging primarily from the "music itself" (music as sound), whereas genre is better understood as the confluence of musical sound and the sociability that accompanies it (Toynbee 2000; Holt 2007). Genres are fluid and often emerge in the context of local historical contingencies. That is to say, genres are locally meaningful, not only providing audiences with information about what to expect from music they might encounter, but also information about the kinds of people who might listen to that music.

In an Indian context, there are a number of well-established music genres, some of which are fairly new (e.g., Indipop, Sufipop, remix, etc.). Yet because of the historically hegemonic nature of Indian film songs, the key generic distinction is made between "film" and "non-film" categories in the context of marketing, radio playlists, recording industry catalogs, and retail store categories. As such, radio and newspaper countdowns distinguish between film and non-film genres based on criteria that might not otherwise be present in the music itself. The Radio Mirchi charts that are published in the *Times of India*, for example, have three categories of music: *Mirchi 20* (Hindi film songs), *Indipop* (non-film popular musics), and *Angrezi* (literally "English," a stand-in for "international," because constituents of that chart might also be in Spanish or other languages). Whether a particular song appears in one or another of these categories is determined more by the marketing strategy of the music company than anything present in the musical sound. Indian music television channels often have clear distinctions between genres, especially during countdown shows. However, during regular airplay, generic categories are often conflated, and channels use different semiotic methods to index the source of the recording. For example, for a non-film song on Channel V, the band or artist is highlighted first, followed by the song, album, and record company. In contrast, for a film song, the film is highlighted first, followed by the song, recording company, etc. Finally, this distinction between film and non-film is built into the ways recordings are packaged for sale, namely the cassette or CD jackets that provide the visual clues that enable prospective buyers to determine the contents of the recording.

Further complicating this notion of genre, different media institutions parcel up the musical-social space in ways that reflect marketing needs and anticipate different types of audiences in ways that do not always align with the sound or style of these musics. The genre "Hindi film song," for example, might be definitively understood as any song that appears on the soundtrack of a Hindi film, regardless of the musical style or language of the lyrics. Hindi film songs are also typically sung by a small number of professional playback singers and are produced largely outside the control of a single author, giving the music director the marquee rather than the musicians or arrangers (Prasad 1998; Booth 2008a). In contrast, musicians of the 1990s genre of Indipop define themselves in opposition to Hindi film song production in ways that are a conscious extension of the rock ideology of creative self-expression (Kvetko 2008). In musical-stylistic terms, these artists view Indipop as a vocally-dominated genre in an Indian language (usually Hindi, Punjabi, or English) that utilizes many of the musical and performative conventions of Western pop music, and in which the star power and authorial credit reside with the singer or band rather than the music director. Yet another recent genre, Sufipop, emerged in the early 2000s as an urban middle-class response to the religious intolerance fomented by certain elements of Hindu fundamentalist movements. Ideally, some component of the lyrics emphasizes an antifundamentalist and inclusive religious cosmopolitanism drawn from Sufi mystical texts. Critics have noted that the Sufi ideology is not always present in the music itself, and some songs are Sufi in marketing only. Musically speaking, Sufipop is quite diverse, and it would be impossible to pinpoint a Sufi musical aesthetic beyond the text of the lyrics. Nevertheless, as a popular music fashion of the early 2000s, Sufipop had a certain kind of social (and marketing) resonance (see also Manuel 2008).

The main point here is that the genres of film song, Indipop, and Sufipop are classified on the basis of characteristics that do not necessarily align with each other and enable a certain degree of musical overlap. Moreover, genre categories are always subject to change based upon the vagaries of musical fashion. Thus, artists that might have been labeled Indipop in the 1990s are now labeled "international" by music store chains, in part instigated by music companies that believed that their target audience perceived greater value in the former than the latter. Insofar as genre categories are malleable, Sufipop might also be re-categorized to accommodate future fashions. Finally, in the context of stylistic mediation noted above, there is no reason to assume that a song that begins its life in a film, Indipop, or Sufipop context might not be mediated to fit some other generic context.

FILM SONG AND ITS OTHER: THREE CASE STUDIES

Even as they have fuzzy boundaries in terms of musical genre and style, the songs that I have selected for analysis in this chapter evoke the tensions between *filmi* stylistic mediation and emergent genre categories, albeit in different ways. Each of the songs below has been incorporated into a film at an important narrative moment and is ostensibly a film song. Although each song is a useful illustration of *filmi* stylistic mediation, I suggest that the latter two songs are only nominally film songs on the basis of the all-encompassing nature of the film song genre. In other words, while the first example mediates musical material according to film song conventions, the latter two songs mediate musical material by non-film conventions in ways that seemingly defy *filmi* mediation.

Each of these three examples features a solo male vocalist that was picturized on a lip-synching male actor. In stylistic terms, each utilizes a song form that is fairly typical of Hindi film songs (i.e., the songs are strophic with four stanzas that alternate between verse and refrain). Unlike many film songs, each of the examples here has a well-defined chord progression that is audible in the recording mix. In each case, the chord progression largely follows Western conventions of musical tension and release, rather than *filmi* approaches that utilize different harmonic strategies of tension and release.

There are a number of differences between these songs, however. For example, while the timbre and performative approach of the first playback singer largely conform to *filmi* conventions, the latter two performances are evocative of non-film styles. Similarly, there are differences in song form. The first two songs follow *filmi* conventions in that they begin and end with a *mukhda* (a lyrical and melodic refrain that is the "face" of the song), whereas the third song uses a verse-chorus form that is most common in Western rock songs. In addition, I suggest that the orchestration and studio production of the latter two songs push the genre boundaries of film song, in some ways sounding like representatives of non-film genres (Indipop and Sufipop) that are present on a film soundtrack. Yet even as these are unconventional songs for their era, in other ways, they herald the sonic changes that would take place in later years. The popular success of these songs would encourage later music directors to experiment with sound. Ultimately, I suggest that each of these songs points to the complexity of musical genre as a site both of musical stylistic change and continuity, even as they exemplify why *film producers* are likely to remain the dominant *music producers* in India. Nevertheless, it is noteworthy that the latter two examples also appear on artist compilations along with their non-film work.

Finally, it is important to address one complicating issue of musical meaning and interpretation of Indian film song before moving to the analysis of these songs: the presumed priority of visuality over aurality (Majumdar 2001). Any discussion of the sound of film songs must acknowledge that some, but certainly not all, meanings of a song might emerge from the accompanying visual narrative. Accordingly, I have provided a brief description of the narrative context to situate each song in its respective film. But as far as the stylistic mediation of musical material is concerned, the narrative context of a song matters less than it might seem. Even though songs are promoted in tandem with their films—and some of the potential meanings are derived from the filmic context—one must not assume that listeners know, or even care about, the visual narrative of the song. Most people will listen to these songs far more times than they watch the film. I would argue that the genre category of the song matters the most in the media contexts in which it is broadcast, the very contexts in which listeners will encounter these songs.

"Mere Rang Mein Rangnewali"

The film *Maine Pyar Kiya* (1989) marked a distinct transition from violence-ridden 1980s films to family films of the 1990s and 2000s that featured narratives centered upon the role of the joint family and filial obligation in contemporary India. Film critics have noted that these family films shifted the musical discourse as well, recreating a place for melody-oriented romantic songs that had been displaced by the narrative needs of 1970s and 1980s films, especially action films. The song "Mere Rang Mein Rangnewali" (hereafter "Mere Rang Mein") (video 5.1) is one example of the kind of romantic song that emerged in this period. In the context of the film narrative, the song appears when the hero and heroine have acknowledged that they have feelings for each other, much to the cha- grin of the boy's super-rich father who suspects that a girl of humble ori- gins has ensnared his son. The boy's father makes a pretext to send the boy off to a factory on the girl's birthday, but the boy celebrates her birthday at midnight by singing this song. Featuring the actors Salman Khan and Bhagyashree dancing on a rooftop, the song presents the distinctly filmi vocal timbre of the singer S. P. Balasubramaniam.

"Mere Rang Mein" begins with four four-beat bars (120 bpm) of acoustic piano playing chords in a percussive style that is augmented by sustained notes in the low strings. A rising chromatic piano flourish introduces four bars of a well-known instrumental theme to the 1986 song "The Final Countdown," originally performed by the Swedish rock band Europe. This melody is played by violins and undergirded by a mixed male and female chorus. The theme continues for an additional 12 bars into an introduc- tory section played by brass and synthesizer. When the singer begins the first stanza, another parodied musical theme emerges: the melody to the instrumental theme from the Hollywood film *Love Story* (1970) written by Francis Lai.[1] The stanzas are fairly conventional for Hindi film songs, beginning and ending the song with the *mukhda* that doubles as the title of the song. Balasubramaniam's voice lightly ornaments the melody, adding a light vibrato at the end of held notes. The melody of the first couplet uses a descending diatonic melody line that introduces the first couplet in four bars. This is followed by a four-bar alto saxophone solo, and then returns to the descending melodic line that combines the first and second couplets in eight bars. As the vocal melody approaches the end of the verse, the countermelody in the string section rises in both pitch and volume until the refrain begins.

Musical interludes in many Hindi film songs carry a lot of stylistic infor- mation and are often the most "eclectic" sections of a song (Arnold 1988). Film directors use interludes to underscore much of the on-screen action. Some melodies used in interludes are as distinct as the dominant vocal mel- ody and provide yet another way for audiences to recognize and remem- ber particular songs. In the context of "Mere Rang Mein," the mediated four bars of "The Final Countdown" theme are similarly distinct, and the melody is repeated and developed in each of the interludes in the song.

The music director, however, uses more than these four bars of "The Final Countdown" in the interludes of "Mere Rang Mein." After the first stanza, for example, the song uses another motif from "The Final Countdown," presenting an instrumental version of the verse of "The Final Countdown" on piano in an arpeggiated chord style, accompanied by a choir singing the melody with a "doo" syllable. A violin flourish returns the song to "The Final Countdown" instrumental theme in trumpets and synthesizers that herald the entrance of the third verse.

Despite these musical transformations of international pop songs, "Mere Rang Mein" retains its distinct Bollywood sound, which is especially notable in the strings and chorus textures below the melodies. Indeed, what makes the use of "Love Story" and "The Final Countdown" especially interesting in this song is that they have been mediated by a conventional *filmi* music aesthetic of the late 1980s, and though informed audiences might recognize the earlier peregrinations of these melodies, the music director Raamlaxman nevertheless transforms these melodies beyond simply "borrowing." Indeed, the musical approach of earlier versions of these melodies, which might not have been palatable to many Indian audiences on the basis of their textural and timbral features, were mediated to accommodate conventions and audience expectations of a Hindi film song. Thus, the song illustrates the ways in which musical material might be mediated to represent the consummate "Bollywood sound" of the 1980s. In the local dichotomy between Western and Indian that Booth (2009) discusses, this song provides a good example of the way in which Western material might be mediated by film conventions.

"Ek Pal Ka Jeena"

Set in Mumbai and New Zealand, *Kaho Naa...Pyaar Hai* (2000) was a very popular film that is best known as the debut of the actor Hrithik Roshan, the son of film director Rakesh Roshan and nephew of music director Rajesh Roshan, both of whom also worked on the film. The first half of the film features the classic "poor boy and rich girl falling in love" theme, with the poor boy working as an aspiring singer on a cruise ship. The twist to the story is that the girl's father is a mafia boss who has the hero killed after he witnesses a murder. The song "Ek Pal Ka Jeena" (hereafter "Ek Pal") (video 5.2) appears in the second half of the film and is ostensibly shot in a dance club in New Zealand where a doppelgänger of the hero (also played by Hrithik) appears, confusing the heroine and changing the trajectory of the story.

Lyrically, "Ek Pal" is four stanzas long, beginning and ending with the *mukhda*, which sandwiches two verses with a different melody. The stanzas are separated by long interludes that feature a distinct guitar and ostinato synthesizer (panpipes) riff. Like "Mere Rang Mein," the rhythm track of "Ek Pal" uses a pop-rock beat in bass and drums and a chord progression that utilizes similar styles of tension and release typical of Western pop songs. Yet an important distinction of "Ek Pal" vis-à-vis other Hindi film songs is the performance by the Indipop singer Lucky Ali. Indeed, what is perhaps most striking about the sound of "Ek Pal" is that despite its use in this film and picturization on a lip-synching actor, the song sounds more like an Indipop song than a Hindi film song in this period of Indian film. Even compared to the other seven songs on the soundtrack, the production aesthetics of "Ek Pal" are distinct. Many of the characteristics that might lead one to describe this as an Indipop song that happens to appear in a Hindi film on the basis of the sound are relatively subtle. For example, like other Indipop artists, Lucky Ali's vocal style eschews the *filmi* vocal inflections that fuse Indian classical ornaments with fast vibrato. The few melodic ornaments he uses in "Ek Pal" are slides between notes evocative of international pop vocal styles, very much in line with his approach to his solo Indipop songs. "Ek Pal" is also unusual because the countermelody in the refrain uses solo male voices, rather than a chorus or violins, as well as the guitar/synthesizer riff in the interludes that index this song as much as the sound of Lucky Ali's voice. Similarly, despite the relatively conventional dimension of the song form, "Ek Pal" has a lengthened refrain that sounds more like a chorus of an Indipop song than it does a refrain of a Hindi film song.

The audible studio techniques also subtly point to a non-film aesthetic. The song is well produced, having a studio-augmented aural presence (brightness) in the upper frequencies and a depth of low frequencies that other Hindi film songs (even on the same soundtrack) do not normally have. Moreover, rather than simply using reverb, vocal effects processing creates the impression that Lucky Ali is singing the melody along with himself. The recording mix uses stereo effects throughout—drums, synthesizers, and backup vocals pan between left and right channels in ways that create an illusion of space that is distinct from the heavy reverb on the singer that permeates so many film songs. Peter Kvetko (2008) has noted the various meanings of Indipop as a "private music," including, among other possible meanings, the production of music to be heard through high-quality speakers or headphones. This presentation of the full range of frequencies perceptible to the human ear is also utilized in "Ek Pal," along with studio effects to create an energy in the song that is not present in the other songs of this soundtrack.

This is not to suggest, however, that the production toolset Lucky Ali's producers brought to the studio is necessarily any more sophisticated than that of other music directors or producers. It is most probable that the same studio techniques were available to both. I am suggesting, rather, that "Ek Pal" utilizes a different set of aesthetic conventions in its production than other film songs. That is, with several notable exceptions, many music directors of this period of film song continued to replicate the sound of "old Bollywood" (Booth 2008a), albeit using studio techniques that enabled them to reduce the number of musicians involved. In this track, however, Lucky Ali brings a different set of practices and expectations to the studio production of the song that index the Indipop sound rather than the Bollywood sound.

Although the compositional credit for this song is given to Rajesh Roshan, the kinds of sonic decisions that the production team made led some listeners to question this attribution of authorship. This in turn has led Lucky Ali to note that the production of the song was a collaborative effort (*Rediff India Abroad* 2001), while still acknowledging his unusual role in producing this film song vis-à-vis other playback singers (*Filmfare* 2001). In terms of audience memory and marketing, "Ek Pal" is frequently listed by interviewers and fans as one of Lucky Ali's most recognizable songs, and indeed it has appeared on Lucky Ali's "Best Of" compilation albums with his other Indipop hits. In a music store, one might find this song either in the film song section or in the Indipop section on a Lucky Ali compilation album. Thus, even as the traits of the song lead to some stylistic ambiguity, so too the generic touchstones are ambiguous in this example.

"Allah Ke Bande"

Waisa Bhi Hota Hai, Part II (2003) was a low-budget, violent comedy that fared poorly at the Indian box office. The film would have quickly been forgotten save for several immensely popular songs on the soundtrack, including "Allah Ke Bande," which propelled the extraordinary music career of the Sufipop singer Kailash Kher. The film features Punit (Arshad Warsi), an advertising executive who almost accidentally saves the life of—and befriends—a mafia hit man named Vishnu (Prashant Narayanan). From his new friend, Punit finds himself learning the practices and ideals of the Mumbai mafia. "Allah Ke" (video 5.3) occurs at a critical juncture in the film's narrative as Punit sits in the ruins of a building on Mumbai's seashore listening to Kailash Kher himself singing a song with Sufi-inspired lyrics.[2]

Like the other examples, "Allah Ke" has four stanzas in which the verse of the first and the fourth stanzas are repeated. Rather than having a *mukhda* like the other songs, however, "Allah Ke" follows the rock/pop conventions of verse-chorus form in which the song title is derived from the chorus that separates and comes after the stanzas. Kailash Kher's voice has a raw, throaty quality that is a departure from the usual polished and supple Bollywood playback voices. Like many other Hindi film songs, the melody is simple, diatonic, and singable by non-musicians, yet lightly ornamented with vocal flourishes. Interestingly, Kher's vocal timbre changes once he shifts to the upper end of his vocal range, dramatically transforming it into a powerful voice that evokes great *qawwali* singers. In "Allah Ke," Kher uses this timbral change to emphasize particular lyrics.[3]

In many ways, the production values of "Allah Ke" are similar to "Mere Rang Mein": The bass is relatively soft in the sound mix, the singer has a lot of reverb added, and the song form is similar. However, other characteristics of the interludes and the singer's voice suggest ways in which "Allah Ke" shares even fewer features of film style than "Ek Pal." For instance, the orchestration is very light, consisting only of acoustic guitar (with effects), electric bass, and shaker. In addition, the guitar strumming is in the "Bo Diddley riff" (a modified clave rhythm) that evokes American blues styles. The interludes are very short relative to most film songs (approximately eight four-beat bars each), more like instrumental bridges between stanzas in a rock song than film interludes. The final refrain features a harmonized vocal line along with two male singers singing in the timbres and high tessitura reminiscent of *qawwali* singers. Indeed, the vocal melisma (ornamentation) at the end of "Allah Ke" resembles the Muslim call to prayer (*adhaan*). The sound of clapping becomes apparent at the end and indexes a *qawwali* atmosphere even as it strengthens the pulse. Along with vocal improvisation in *sargam* (solfège), this musical device is similarly used by music director A. R. Rahman in many of his songs to signal a Sufi ethos.[4]

Discussions of Kher frequently mention the quality of his voice and its resemblance to the voice of the late Nusrat Fateh Ali Khan, as well as his relatively humble origins. Although his voice appears on a number of important film soundtracks in the early 2000s, Kher's career, like that of Lucky Ali, has not been dictated by the needs of Bollywood. He frequently tours nationally and internationally with his band Kailasa, finding great success in the moment of India's Sufi music craze that has been an element of both film and non-film recordings of the mid-2000s. Accordingly, Kher has been one of the rare singers to maintain an identity as a solo artist beyond his occasional roles as playback singer, and "Allah Ke" has become one of his best-known songs in live performances with his band. Here too, the generic context of "Allah Ke" has come to be obscured as this film song is transformed to become a representative song for Kailash Kher's solo career.

NON-*FILMI* FILM SONGS?

As these three musical examples illustrate, it is sometimes difficult to make assumptions about music genre on the basis of stylistic characteristics alone. With its established playback singer, violin section, chorus, and production values that foregrounds the voice in the recording mix, "Mere Rang Mein" fits the description of a film song on the basis of its sonic characteristics, even as it uses several layered melodies from distinctly non-Indian sources. There is more ambiguity in the cases of "Ek Pal" and "Allah Ke," however. With the vocal timbres of the singers, the use of solo voices rather than chorus as accompaniment, musical interludes with small ensembles, and production aesthetics that evoke non-film genres, these songs would not be readily identifiable as film songs if they were not generically marked as such by the Bollywood marketing juggernaut. Nevertheless, each of these songs might also be described as three moments that signal musical change in Hindi films: the "return of melody" in *Maine Pyar Kiya*, the incorporation of the "Indipop sound" into film songs (which became relatively common after "Ek Pal"), and the emergence of a non-film "Sufipop sound." Or they might be seen as moments in which possible pop music challengers to *filmi* hegemony are simply absorbed by the film production machine, and each song reflects a transitional moment in the contemporary Bollywood sound.

If Indian film song is broadly analogous to the generic category "pop" in other parts of the world, then like the pop music category, it be might difficult, if not impossible, to pin down what makes a film song a film song simply on stylistic grounds. Insofar as pop music is the "Other" for other genres in the West like rock or rap (Auslander 2008), so too film songs serve as the Other for other genres like Indipop or classical. Yet as the cases of "Ek Pal" and "Mere Rang Mein" suggest, the boundaries between film and non-film genres are porous. It is worth asking, for example, whether a song appearing in a Hindi film, marketed alongside the film, and distributed in a film soundtrack is necessarily a film song. If, for example, a film director should use guest artists like Snoop Dogg or Kylie Minogue singing in English in an international pop style,[5] is the song still best described as a film song? Similarly, the prerecorded song "Garaj Baras" by the Pakistani rock band Junoon appeared on the soundtrack for the film *Paap* (2003), and the song had a significant narrative role, even if the actors did not lip-synch the lyrics. In slightly different terms, what if a music director should record a song for a film that uses the voice of an artist from another musical tradition in such a way that the song is musically indistinguishable from a non-film song?

I would propose that the use of a song in an Indian film does not necessarily make it a film song. This may seem to be an absurd proposition, but based upon the examples of "Ek Pal Ka Jeena" and "Allah Ke Bande," in addition to recent soundtracks by contemporary music directors like Shankar-Ehsaan-Loy, Vishal Bhardwaj, and Amit Trivedi, this is a relevant consideration. As this chapter suggests, the emergence of "non-film songs in films" occurs much earlier than the contemporary moment, and I suggest that it might be fruitful to begin to discuss genre or style within the context of film songs in slightly different terms, based on the notion of "stylistic mediation" detailed above. In order to adapt this notion of the mediations of the social lives of film songs, would there be utility in considering "Ek Pal" as an Indipop song in a film and "Allah Ke" as a Sufi song in a film, rather than simply being undifferentiated as film songs? If this is indeed a useful approach, there might be some value in looking back at older film songs and applying new categories.

NOTES

1. There are several versions of "Love Story"in existence, most famously Andy Williams's rendition of the song with lyrics. It is unclear whether music director Raamlaxman (or his arrangers) was influenced by any particular version of the song, although elements of a couple of versions are present in "Mere Rang Mein"; the accompaniment in the verses is similar to the rhythm section of Williams' version, as well as the piano flourishes of the solo piano in the instrumental version. Finally, beneath the "Love Story" melody, the pianist also seems to be referencing the melody of the 1954 Bart Howard song "Fly Me to the Moon," famously performed by a number of jazz artists (e.g., Nancy Wilson, Nat King Cole, and Frank Sinatra).
2. In this regard, *Waisa Bhi Hota Hai* is also unusual, insofar as several of the songs are picturized on the singers (Kailash Kher, Shibani Kashyap, Rabbi Shergill) and their real names are used in the film diegesis.
3. For example, he performs the melody of the first verse and chorus in the middle of his vocal range (G below middle C to middle D); while the second verse descends stepwise by a fourth (C below middle C), he suddenly jumps an octave to emphasize the final. This has the effect of suggesting a shift to a different narrative voice, possibly voicing Allah himself.
4. For example, "Kehna Hi Kya" from *Bombay* (1995); "Satarangi Re" from *Dil Se* (1998); and "Ishq Bina" from *Taal* (1999).
5. For example, Kylie Minogue's performance of "Chiggy Wiggy" in the film *Blue* (2009); and Snoop Dogg's performance of "Singh is Kinng" in *Singh is Kinng* (2008).

CHAPTER 6

Play It Again, Saraswathi

Gramophone, Religion, and Devotional Music in
Colonial South India

STEPHEN PUTNAM HUGHES

This chapter considers the relationship between Hinduism and the history of music recording in South India.[1] I argue that over the first decades of the 20th century, the introduction and commercial success of the gramophone business was built around a series of constitutive relations with Hinduism. Record companies in South India not only drew upon Hindu musical traditions and performers, but they also used Hindu iconography to market their records and represent their business practices. Moreover, these companies produced records according to the Hindu ritual calendar, turned the studio recording sessions into a place of worship, and sought to locate gramophone technology within a Hindu theology of sound.

In his landmark book on popular music and recording technology in North India, Peter Manuel made the claim that Hindu religious/devotional music had, before the arrival of audiocassettes in the 1970s, played a marginal role in the output of the commercial recording industry (1993, 109). While acknowledging the importance of long-established traditions of devotional music in India, Manuel was primarily concerned with highlighting how, during the 1980s, a new crop of regionally located music recording businesses used the introduction of the then-new media technology of audiocassettes for Hindu devotional music. Manuel argued that this combination of new recording media along with the popularity of religious music contributed significantly to expand the market for audiocassettes. Thus, the emergence of a new mass medium was, he argued, causally linked to an unprecedented commercial popularity of Hindu devotional music that began in the 1980s. Given the dominant position of commercial film songs in the market for popular music and the state-run monopoly of radio broadcasting in India, Manuel was certainly correct in recognizing that the convergence among the introduction of new technology, a new class of entrepreneurs, and a consuming audience for religious music dramatically altered popular music across the Hindi belt of north India in the 1970s. However, in making this argument, Manuel has underestimated the larger significance of Hinduism in a longer 20th-century history of the music recording industry in India.

Going beyond Manuel's focus on devotional music, this chapter focuses on the earlier historical conjunction of recording technology, business interests, and religion in South India to show that there was a more expansive and constitutive relationship between music recording and Hinduism. The argument in this chapter is structured around a comparison between the early years of the gramophone in South India at the beginning of the 20th century and the 1930s when the music recording business was taken over by local entrepreneurs. I track the changes of how the music business in South India forged a series of constitutive relationships with a variety of Hindu religious practices. I am particularly concerned with examining how in the early 1930s the South Indian gramophone industry explicitly drew upon Hindu traditions as a way of defining a distinctively new public address for a rapidly expanding South Indian market for commercial recordings. Far from being marginal in the years before audiocassettes as Manuel has suggested for North India, religious music and references were of central importance to the development of the music recording industry in South India. For at least a decade from the late 1920s into the 1930s, the local gramophone trade enacted a conspicuous articulation of media technology as religious practice through their choice of music recordings, advertising, record catalogues, and business practices. I argue that before the emergence of film songs as the most popular recordings from the late 1930s, the initial success of the South Indian gramophone trade was predicated upon a religious address.

Both Manuel's argument about the newfound importance of religious music for the audiocassette business, as well as my interrogation in this chapter of the relationship between the South Indian gramophone trade and Hindu practice, can usefully be understood in relationship within a wider context of encounters between religion and media in South Asia.

Babb and Wadley (1995) have called our attention to the longstanding, widespread, complex, and transformative relationship between the mass media and the religious traditions of South Asia. Drawing upon a broad range of scholarship covering printed images, audio recordings, and audio-visual media relating to Hindu, Muslim, and Sikh religious practices, they argue that media have dramatically increased the spatial and social mobility of South Asian religious traditions. Media technology have done this by socially "disembedding" religious practice from its contexts within the family, lineage, clan, caste, village, and neighborhood, making it possible for people to share social, national, and spiritual identities in new ways. However, if Babb and Wadley have only focused on one side of the equation where modern media have transformed religion, Manuel's example has emphasized the other side where religious music has transformed the commercial music industry. In what follows, I explore a more complex encounter whereby new media and traditional religious music were reciprocally implicated and co-constitutive.

EARLY RECORDINGS OF SOUTH INDIAN "NATIVE RECORDS"

Commercial music recording companies catering to South Indian markets have always relied heavily upon religious music. Though this chapter is primarily concerned with the 1930s and does not set out to provide a comprehensive treatment of the earliest years of music recording in South India, my argument starts with the recording of religious music at the beginning of the 20th century.[2] There is a strong case for arguing that it was only through the exploitation of religiously oriented music that international music recording companies were able to create a foothold in the emerging market for gramophone recordings in South India during the first decade of the 20th century. Yet these same record companies never fully embraced the religious content of their recordings as part of their public address, in marked contrast to how South Indian companies reshaped the market in the 1930s.

During the formative years of the recording business ranging roughly between 1900 and 1911, Euro-American companies sent "expeditions" around the world (including India) in a competitive effort to capture the emerging markets (Gronow 1981; Parthasarathi 2005, 4). Starting in 1902, the most famous of these early expeditions was led by Fred Gaisberg of Gramophone and Typewriter Limited, which eventually became better known as the Gramophone Company with its "His Master's Voice" (HMV) line of products (Kinnear 1994). But thereafter, a series of other major companies, including Nicole Frères from London, Pathé from France, the American Talking Machine Company, the International Talking Machine Company with its Odeon label, and Beka from Berlin all joined in the bid for taking their share of the Indian market. These companies sent a series of expeditionary tours out to record Indian music (sometimes in collaboration with small Indian firms), which they brought back to their factories in Europe for pressing and then sent back to India as "native records" for sale. In this manner, they materially inscribed music as a commodity like cotton or jute in the triangular trade of empire.

During this early expedition period, the majority of the "native records" that were produced for the South Indian market were drawn from a well-established religious repertoire. It is, perhaps, not surprising that gramophone companies initially found the connection between music and religion to be a commercially promising direction, because most musical traditions in South India had strong religious associations. When the first recording expeditions arrived in South India, they drew upon four distinct but overlapping musical traditions that had emerged out of the 19th century. The first and probably most prominent was the tradition of devotional songs, now known as Karnatik music, which had been adopted as the court music in the 18th and 19th centuries (Subramanian 2006; Weidman 2006). The second was the instrumental accompaniment associated with temple rituals and festivals (Ries 1967; L'Armand and L'Armand 1983). The third was the music that accompanied dance performances (Soneji 2012). The fourth was the songs from popular musical dramas (Baskaran 1981). Although each of these traditions had its own recognized musical forms, community of performers, appropriate settings, and patrons that sustained it, international record companies brought these altogether in the same catalogues and labeled as them "native recordings."

International record companies used this early emphasis on religious music as part of the promotional pitch for advertising their recordings. For example, as seen in figure 6.1, during 1911, the International Talking Machine Company advertised the intended religious appeal of their South Indian records: "Their subjects comprise of religious songs of Sivites [sic], Vishnuvits [sic] and Christians, Thevarams, Keerthanams, Theatrical songs from Harischandra Vilasanam, Ramayanam and other well-known Dramas, etc." (The Hindu, May 5, 1911, p. 11). This advertisement avoided using a unitary category of Hinduism, but instead chose to recognize the main two South Indian variants associated with the worship of Siva and Vishnu. By naming the Thevarams and Keerthanams, the advertisement referred to the respective traditions of devotional poetic hymns initiated by the Saivite Nāyanārs and the Vaisnavite Ālvārs, which as living traditions, date

ODEON
Talking Machine Records!!

Try our new Tamil and Telugu records taken in India recently by our own European Expert. The subjects comprise of religious songs of Sivites, Vishnuvits and Christians, Thevarams, Keerthanams, Theatrical songs from Harichandra Vilasam, Ramayanam and other well-known Dramas, etc.

New lists of Odeon records sent free on application.

Easy payment system can be arranged for on application.

THE TALKING MACHINE CO., OF CEYLON,
(SOLE AGENTS R ODEON GOODS)

Nos. 3 & 4, Mount Road, Madras.

Figure 6.1
Advertisement from *The Hindu*, May 5, 1911, p. 4.

back to the seventh and ninth centuries. Within this advertisement's list of well-known Hindu musical referents, the theatrical songs represented a relatively more recent musical genre that had been popularized by Parsi-style drama companies in South India during the late 19th century (Baskaran 1981; Hansen 1992). And the listing of the Christian songs appears to have been little more than a token inclusion within a record catalogue that was dominated by musical traditions associated with Hinduism.

Nevertheless, international record companies' explicit categorization of music as "religious" in early advertisements was relatively rare. Instead, the market-leading Gramophone Company advertised their South Indian recordings in terms of their star performers and their aesthetic and expressive excellence without categorizing them as religious. Yet we know from their catalogue of recordings in South India between 1908 and 1910 (Kinnear 2000) that their output was overwhelmingly Hindu in orientation. Of the roughly 400 recordings in the South Indian languages of "Tamil, Telugu, Canarese, Malayalam, and Sanskrit" during this two-year period, over 380 titles were drawn from the four main traditions of Hindu music. Given this high degree of prominence, the religious content of their recordings was a conspicuously unmarked category for the Gramophone Company. So even if the earliest international music recording companies were quick to recognize the commercial value of religious records, these companies had something of an ambivalent relationship with the religious implications of their recordings.

Figure 6.2
Front cover, Record Catalogue, Gramophone and Typewriter Ltd., 1906.

While the Gramophone Company happily embraced a broad range of traditional Hindu musical genres with their choice of recordings, it was not marketed as "Hindu" music per se, and the company did not identify their business as a kind of Hindu practice. Perhaps the closest that the Gramophone Company came during the early years to marking their product as Hindu was by using the 1906 painting (figure 6.2) by G. N. Mukherji of Saraswati sitting on her lotus playing a record on a gramophone machine (Farrell 1993, 42–44).

This image originally appeared on the front of their 1906 catalogue, and thereafter the original was said to have hung on the wall of their Calcutta office. It represented a brief but striking departure from what had already become their iconic logo: Nipper the dog listening to "His Master's Voice" through the gramophone; this had at the time only recently taken precedence over the earlier "recording angel" logo. With this image of Saraswati playing her gramophone, the mechanical technology for reproducing music was relocated into "the aural universe of Indian mythology" (Farrell 1993, 44). It is as if the Hindu goddess of the arts and learning was simultaneously acting as the divine creator/patron of this new musical technology, promoting its use among her followers and joining in the pleasurable consumption of its music.

Farrell read this image and a similar example featuring the goddess Durga as a "mixing of ancient and modern," which depicted the new technology in terms of a "bridge between two cultural domains, the West and India" (1993, 42). Farrell was certainly correct in drawing our attention to the way that the introduction of music recording posed new questions about the articulation of modern technology and Indian cultural forms. As such, we should consider the gramophone alongside other contemporary and parallel new media, such as proscenium stagecraft (Hansen 1992), chromolithography (Pinney 2004), photography, and film (Rajadhyaksha 1993; Hughes 2005), in offering a particularly ambiguous enunciation of modernity. At the beginning of the 20th century, the image of Saraswati playing the gramophone brought into play an unstable and unsettling set of cultural and political dichotomies—spiritual and material, indigenous and foreign, past and present, and sacred and profane.

No matter how suggestive this Hindu iconography of the gramophone may have been to the artist or potential Indian customers, the Gramophone Company never developed this into an explicit business strategy for promoting their products. The Saraswati image was not widely featured in advertisements beyond a very limited use in their earliest catalogues. Moreover, it does not seem to have ever been used in relation to any subsequent South Indian recording catalogues or advertisements. Although the Gramophone Company produced large numbers of traditional South Indian Hindu musical recordings over the first three decades of the 20th century, the company showed little interest in using Hinduism either as a generic category or as an iconography to promote their records. Whatever the reason for this may have been, it is clear that there was a large gap between the Gramophone Company's business plan and the traditional modes of performance of religious music and its forms of patronage, institutionalization, and circulation. This gap was readily apparent among many contemporary South Indian musicians and became a prime target for one of the earliest critics of gramophone music in India.

Ananda K. Coomaraswamy (1909), a prominent scholar and art critic (cf. Mohan 1977), comprehensively denounced the use of gramophone technology to record South Indian music, warning that the machine would eventually lead to the destruction of this music. Though gramophone ownership was still relatively new and quite limited in South India at the time Coomaraswamy wrote, he clearly understood its potential to transform music into a new kind of commodity that would reorganize the performance, patronage, appreciation, education, and circulation of Indian music. In publishing one of the first critical responses to the gramophone in South Asia, Coomaraswamy voiced concerns widely shared among many leading musicians during the first decades of the 20th century on the detrimental relationship between gramophone recordings and South Indian classical Karnatik music. For Coomaraswamy, the gramophone was part of a wider vulgarization of culture under British rule in India, which posed new foreign, commercial, and mechanical threats to Indian music. He felt that gramophone recordings of European music were spoiling the refined musical tastes of South Indians and causing them to lose their love for Indian music. Worse still were the recordings of Karnatik music, which he argued ruined the embodied spirituality of South Indian music in favor of commerce and mechanical industry.[3]

Coomaraswamy closely followed the established discourse on South Indian music in that he started with the premise of the human voice as the original, authentic, and most perfect musical instrument.[4] Thus, Indian music was to be learned through oral transmission from guru to *sisyan* (teacher to disciple), from parent to child, and from priest to novice. Indian music traditions did not use any system of written notation, but were taught and learned through the performative and embodied encounter between hearing and singing. Coomaraswamy argued that the excellence of Indian vocal music depended on the peculiar manner and skill with which the singer dwells on certain notes, which are varied or trilled, "vibrating like a bird above the water before it pounces on its prey" (1909, 172). This is known as the *gamakam* and is produced in stringed instruments by varying the tension of the string by deflection. For Coomaraswamy, this meant that Indian music was always a matter of personal interpretation. It depended on the singer's mood, which no record or any other form of material inscription could adequately interpret. Coomaraswamy reasoned that the uniqueness of a performance was just that and could never be repeated. In every performance, a musician adapted to different conditions and found new subjective expressions through the old form. Thus Coomaraswamy maintained that "[t]he intervention of mechanism between the musician and sound is always, per se, disadvantageous" (205). Coomaraswamy equated the mechanical reproduction of music with the destructive intrusion of modernity under colonial rule, which could only destroy the spirituality and authenticity of South Indian music.

With Coomaraswamy's critical response to the introduction of gramophone technology for the recording of South Indian music, we are again faced with a set of cultural and political dichotomies posing the spiritual against the material, the authentic indigenous against the foreign colonial, and the artistic performance against the mechanical industrial. Coomaraswamy's solution was to argue against the intrusion of modern gramophone technology in order to preserve the possibility of a culture of Indian authenticity in the face of British rule, a plea that was to gain so much importance within the discourses of Indian nationalism during the 20thcentury (cf. Chatterjee 1993, 3–13). However, contrary to Coomaraswamy's warnings, the presumed oppositions between music recording technology and South Indian music traditions were not insurmountable, but over time collapsed into a productive encounter of collaboration and dependency. Almost as if in response to Coomaraswamy's concerns, the emergent South Indian gramophone industry struggled over the first decades of the 20th century to suture the gaps between the spiritual and material, between live performance and mechanical reproduction, between art and commerce. In this respect it is useful to return to the Gramophone Company's image of Saraswati playing the gramophone. For the purposes of this chapter, what makes this image particularly important is that it articulated the potential for the gramophone to be rendered in a Hindu vernacular in a manner that went beyond the dichotomous logic of contradiction. This image represented the gramophone as being *continuous* with Hindu religious practice. And even if the Gramophone Company did not pursue this possibility, it may well have set an important precedent that South Indian entrepreneurs were able to develop more fully during the 1930s.

THE RELIGIOUS CONVERSION OF THE GRAMOPHONE

Up to this point, I have argued that prior to 1930, international gramophone companies were heavily reliant upon the South Indian Hindu music traditions, but they did not develop the religious aspects of their product as part of their commercial strategies. Retrospectively, this reluctance stands out all the more when compared to how quickly and comprehensively this situation changed in the 1930s. In what remains of this chapter, I outline how gramophone companies in South India started to rebrand their businesses and musical recordings as part of a Hindu vernacular. In this sense, the mechanical reproduction and commercial exploitation of religious songs were represented as continuous with other forms of popular religion. South Indian record companies rooted the gramophone within both a religious repertoire, as well as a Hindu theology of sound. In this way, these companies sought to embrace, domesticate, and harness recording technology, business practice, and recorded music as a kind of Hinduism. Yet the material inscription and commercial circulation of Hindu devotional records also helped reorganize both public and private access and availability of religious music performance. The gramophone not only built upon and extended the vernacular experience of Hinduism, it also enabled a new set of constraints and possibilities for addressing a new media public. Thus, after setting up this earlier period as a point of comparison, the main questions I pose in this section are: Why and how after 30 years of being in South India did the gramophone suddenly become a vehicle for Hinduism?

The first part of the answer has to do with the reorganization of the gramophone business in South India and what I have written about elsewhere as the "music boom," which took place during the early 1930s(Hughes 2002). The Gramophone Company began to face increasing competition from other international recording companies, after more than 20 years of enjoying a largely uncontested dominance in the Indian market. Columbia Records with their "Magic Notes" trademark and the then-German-owned Odeon Records began to make new moves into the Indian market. The extension of international companies into South India during the early 1930s was achieved through a series of franchise agreements that, for the first time, enabled South Indians to take a leading role in the recording business. Local South Indian companies supplied the capital, management, and music expertise, and the international record companies provided the brand label and pressed the records at their factories. In less than one decade, the gramophone business went from an HMV monopoly to a new proliferation of gramophone labels (nine by 1935) offering a vastly expanded range of South Indian records and transforming the music recording business in South India into an industry of mass proportions (Hughes 2007). This business development is in some ways comparable to Manuel's example of how audiocassettes in the 1980s enabled a new class of "grassroots" entrepreneurs to restructure the market for popular music (1993, 116). The franchise agreements allowed new business interests with a better understanding of their own regional musical traditions to reshape the market for recorded music.

When South Indians first entered into the business of producing records, it was in part based on their dissatisfaction about how the international companies were providing recorded music for the local market. Record dealers throughout South India had been complaining that there were not enough of the most popular titles to meet demand, and far too many of records they could not sell. The South India record distributors felt that foreign companies did not know how to market South Indian music, did not understand the social settings in which their customers would listen to records, and did not know which artists should sing what songs or how many records to produce (Carati 1983).

Within the short span of 1931 to 1932, local music businesses in Madras started to arrange exclusive distribution rights that made them the agents for the retailing of machines and records throughout the South and for the recruitment of regional recording artists. In 1931, Columbia affiliated with

P. Orr & Sons, the luxury goods manufacturer and dealer, to create Orr's Columbia House. During the following year, two other major international gramophone companies entered into new partnerships with South Indian entrepreneurs. In 1932, Odeon went into business with the music dealer Saraswathi Stores (Carati 1983; Meiyappan 1974), and the Gramophone Company collaborated with Hutchins and Company in the production of Hutchins Gramophone Records. Also in 1932, these new gramophone ventures each launched their own local sound recording studios in Madras with great fanfare and publicity. At first these were temporary studios constructed within large bungalows where foreign sound crews and equipment visited Madras for periods of one or two months. Within a few years, however, these companies went further to establish the first permanent sound studios in Madras. This was the moment, coinciding with the creation of a new and more local music industry, when the gramophone trade made conspicuous efforts to embrace Hindu practice as part of its public address.

In order to elaborate on this point, I focus on the case of the highly successful Saraswathi Stores record company.[5] Started during 1932 in partnership with Odeon Records, the management of Saraswathi Stores went to considerable effort to promote their Hindu credentials. The very choice of the name "Saraswathi" worked to merge the technological and commercial aspects of the gramophone with Hindu religious practice. The name itself ritually invoked the presence of the divine patron of music for blessing the new venture and worked as well to dedicate the venture to the goddess. The record company was in effect announcing itself as a permanent habitation for the goddess Saraswati, where she would imbue their music with a true spirit of devotion. Even though their record releases were not entirely religious in orientation and a significant portion of their intended market was not Hindu, the company had no hesitation in identifying so closely with the Hindu goddess and adopting her image as their logo (figure 6.3). This was in itself enough to immediately distinguish Saraswathi Stores from all other previous recording companies operating in South India.

In a gesture that worshipfully acknowledged music as a gift of the gods, the timing of Saraswathi Stores' first record release was appropriately coordinated with the Hindu ritual calendar, falling on the annual day celebrating the goddess known as the Saraswati Puja. In India, the worship of Saraswati is a very important annual event for Hindus. In the South, it is part of the Navaratri (nine nights) festival, which falls according to the Hindu lunar calendar at some point during the autumn. The climax of this event is conventionally marked by the ritual presentation of books and musical instruments at dawn along with special prayers. In return, the goddess then confers her blessings on to the material objects of learning

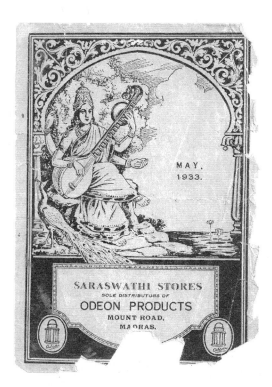

Figure 6.3
Front cover, Saraswathi Stores Record Catalogue, May 1933.

and music. The period of time immediately after this event is considered to be the most auspicious moment possible to begin learning, to start music lessons, or, in this case, to launch a record business.

The timing of their first record launch effectively positioned a business event as part of an important Hindu festival. Moreover, for the occasion, Saraswathi Stores recruited one of the most senior, respected, and orthodox of all contemporary Karnatik musicians, Sangeetha Vidwan Ariyakudi T. Ramanuja Iyengar, for his debut recording (figure 6.4). "Ariyakudi," as he was affectionately known to his fans, had up to this point refused to make any recordings.[6] The framing of the recording event as part of a devotional event worshipping Saraswati was an especially auspicious occasion to finally win the consent of a reluctant artist. Contemporary newspaper reviews of this first release were quick with their praise:

> The first issue of gramophone records at the first session of the Saraswathi Stores forms a welcome addition to the stock of preserved music. Ariyakudi Ramanuja Iyengar and Srimathi Saraswathi Bai are among the very few living

Sangeetha Vidwan Ariyakudi T. RAMANUJA IYENGAR
Makes his debut in the Gramophone World on
SARASWATHI POOJA DAY.

His great Commemoration Song on the
Swadesamitran Golden Jubilee will be released on
SATURDAY NEXT.

Orders registered from To-day.   Price **Rs. 4**

SARASWATHI STORES
Phone: 8206.   ODEON DISTRIBUTORS.   Telegram: ODEOPHONE.
2-159, MOUNT ROAD,   ::   ::   MADRAS.

Figure 6.4
Advertisement from *The Hindu*, October 3, 1932, p. 5.

exponents of Carnatic music of the classic type, who still maintain with distinction the traditions of what might be called the Golden Age of Carnatic Music. The enterprise of the Saraswathi Stores in persuading these front rank artistes (and our South Indian artistes of first class need a lot of persuading in this matter) is commendable (*The Hindu*, December 5, 1932, p. 5).

This was the beginning of a new wave of high-profile Karnatik recordings that continued through the decade.

These new South Indian record companies were much better placed than the earlier European representatives from the international recording companies for understanding how to stage the performative part of the recording session. The new South Indian businesses were able to draw on and build upon the already well-established institutions and forms of patronage for South Indian music. In so doing, they reshaped recording sessions as part of Hindu practice. Though far removed from the royal courts, temples, and salons that had sustained South Indian music throughout the 19th century, the South Indian gramophone companies knew how to serve like traditional patrons of the arts. They would have already had personal links to the leading musicians through their previous involvement with patronage activities and were able to recruit a new class of respected musical figures, who had until then stayed clear of the medium. In general, for Hindu community leaders, the support of musicians was a matter of religious duty and honor within the context of traditional religious practice and obligation (Ries 1967, 18). Moreover, these entrepreneurs understood how to stage a live performance. Each recording session was begun by making a ritual invocation to a presiding deity whose image or statue was installed within the studio. Brahmin ritual specialists were brought into the studio to perform the relevant *puja* ceremonies. The recording sessions themselves would have been performed worshipfully in front of the deity. And after the session was complete, there would be a presentation of gifts and honorary regalia to the performer.[7]

In addition to reorganizing recording sessions on the model of Hindu worship, South Indian recording companies introduced new ways of publicizing their relationships with recording artists. For example, the advertisements printed in the local press in advance of Saraswathi Stores' widely publicized first release included a photograph of Ariyakudi sitting on a platform stage facing into a microphone (figure 6.4 above). These kinds of photographs were for a time during the 1930s a very common feature in South Indian newspapers and gramophone catalogues. They constituted a visual trope for representing the convergence of recording technology and live musical performance. The photographic shot depicting artists in front of the microphone became part of the ritualized practices of the recording sessions and were used to authenticate each recording session as an enactment of the human-machine interface. The photos dramatized the encounter by foregrounding the recording apparatus and freezing the moment of authenticity when the live performance was captured in the very act of its inscription as a mechanical form of reproduction on its way to being transformed into a mass-produced commodity. Thus, Ariyakudi beckons us to take part in his performance through the surrogate of the microphone.

Saraswathi Stores produced a wealth of newspaper advertising and catalogue illustrations, which made use of popular religious iconography of divine figures to represent both gramophone technology and their own commercial activities. In figure 6.5, we see that the company's logo worked into the design of a record dust jacket closely resembled the well-known Ravi Varma painting that had been widely circulated as a chromolithograph for "god posters" and calendar art (cf. Smith 1995). The goddess along with her peacock vehicle and *veena* on her knee routinely adorned the cover of their record catalogues or was decoratively worked into border designs.

For the purposes of my argument, one of the most striking images used for advertising their records depicted the goddess Saraswati giving out the

Figure 6.5
Record dust sleeve, Saraswathi Stores.

Figure 6.6
Advertisement from *The Hindu*, June 8, 1933, p. 9.

gift of music in the form of records (figure 6.6). This image recalls the earlier catalogue image discussed previously in this chapter, but this time the goddess is no longer playing a gramophone. Instead, Saraswati was shown doing the work of the recording company sales agents in handing out records to a representative assortment of readily identifiable South Indian social types, including a Muslim, Brahmin, non-Brahmin, and Christian. The Hindu goddess was represented as ecumenically distributing records to a socially inclusive public of gramophone consumers. The visual link between the goddess and commercial activity was made all the more obvious by the inclusion of the list of approved Odeon dealers throughout Tamil South India that appears at the bottom of the advertisement. There were other South Indian gramophone companies that also made frequent use of similar images depicting Saraswati "giving" (selling?) records to the South Indian public. Figure 6.7 is a particularly good demonstration of how the Hindu goddess was explicitly linked with modern science, electricity, and the business of record distribution to the widest possible demographic of South Indian consumers.

These kinds of images constituted one of the main visual advertising tropes, where both gramophone technology and trade were represented as working in harmony with Hindu deities. In addition to the goddess Saraswati, the South India gramophone companies also used other Hindu

Figure 6.7
Advertisement from *The Hindu*, July 21, 1934, p. 9.

Figure 6.8
Cover *Kiraamapone Kiirttanaamrutham*, P.R.C. Series 22, second edition, Sree Vani Vilas Book Depot, Tirupuliyur, no date.

gods as part of their advertising. For example, in figure 6.8, a private publisher, disregarding copyright, mobilized a musical pantheon as part of a popular series of small booklets of gramophone song lyrics.

This image was from the cover of a Tamil booklet entitled *Kiraamapone Kiirttanaamrutham*, which translates as the "musical ambrosia of the gramophone." The title conveys the common belief that music was both a gift of the gods, as well as a form of communion with them. For my purposes, this image usefully illustrates the range of divine patrons of music, with Krishna and his flute in the center flanked by Saraswati with her *veena* on the right and Naradar with his *tambura* on the left. As the music comes down to earth at the bottom of the page, we see what appear to be two *devadasi* women playing the harmonium and the violin.[8]

Another good example of this trope of gramophone as divine intervention is a series of Saraswathi Stores ads featuring Krishna. In figure 6.9, the young Krishna playing his flute is depicted on top of a gramophone record. Similar to the image of Saraswati handing out records, the material inscription of recorded music was equated with the agency of

छोकानुन्मदयन् श्रुतीमुखरयन् क्षोणीरुहान् हर्षयन्
शैलान्विद्रवयन् मृगान्विवशयन्गोवृन्दमानन्दयन् ।
गोपान् संश्रमयन् मुनीन्मुकुलयन् सप्तस्वरान् ज्म्भयन्
ओष्ठारार्थेमुदीरयन्विजयते वंशीनिनादशिशोः ॥

THE MUSIC OF THE HEAVENS
AVAILABLE AT :
THE SARASWATI STORES, MADRAS

Figure 6.9
Advertisement from *The Hindu*, December 1, 1932, p. 9.

Krishna. But in this instance, the record disc appears as Krishna's vehicle. This emphasis on the divine source of music was further underlined in the English caption at the bottom of the advertisement that portrays Saraswathi Stores as the worldly supplier of "the music of the heavens." With no mention of any vocalist or musician, Saraswathi Stores appears to have claimed Krishna as one of their recording artists and equated their records with the divine power of music. This reference was reinforced in the advertisement through the use of a Sanskrit *śloka* (verse). Even if the vast majority of English daily newspaper readers could not have made sense of the specialist and technical language of this passage, the Sanskrit would have immediately conveyed Brahminical religious authority. The text read:

> Victory to the sound of the child's flute, which delights people, makes musical intervals (*rutis*) resound, makes trees bristle, melts mountains, subdues beasts, gladdens droves of cows, bewilders cowherds, closes the eyes of ascetics, spreads musical notes (*svaras*), and expresses the meaning of the sound Om.[9]

This passage depicts Krishna's flute as both a medium for musical sound and a transcendental subject, while simultaneously elevating the gramophone record to a kind of divine status. In this respect, the gramophone was identified as a central component within a Hindu theology of sound.

There are numerous other examples of this kind, each creatively expressing the divine powers of musical sound, including Krishna at the bathing *ghat* (embankment). In figure 6.10, Krishna in the role of a playful child teases the *gopikas* (cowherds) by stealing their clothes and throwing them in the tree. This image would have been immediately recognizable throughout India as being based on the widely reproduced chromolithograph of a Ravi Varma painting. The text made explicit reference to the power of sound to bring the picture to life through the force of its sonic vibration. The recording not only animated this well-known scene, but offered its audience a firsthand experience of being in the scene. The advertising appeal of this image would have gone something like this: "you all know the story and have seen the pictorial version, now you can live it for yourself for the first time through sound."

SRI KRISHNA AT THE BATHING GHAT.

This scene which Ravi Varma with his painting has immortalised now vibrates with life when you hear record No. C.A. 747 over your machine.

A GREAT RECORD — DO NOT MISS IT.

Figure 6.10
Advertisement from *The Hindu*, July 9, 1934, p. 13.

So far I have given examples about how the new South Indian recording companies reorganized their business, recording, and advertising practices as part of a Hindu vernacular. In addition to this, these companies developed a new range of recorded content that explored ways to represent, reproduce, and extend Hindu religious practice via records. All of the South Indian record companies experimented in the early 1930s with recordings that in various ways sought to recreate the experience of Hindu ritual, worship, festivals, recitations, and pilgrimage through sound enactments. The range of such recordings was comprehensive, almost approximating a full catalogue of Hindu practices appropriate for both festive and everyday situations in both public and domestic settings. These were aural representations of common Hindu devotional practices that offered the chance to re-experience and vicariously participate in these events via sound recordings. These sound representations took on and combined many different representational modes including a kind of realist documentary, humorous parody, nostalgic recollection, and serious devotional styles. These recordings were too numerous and varied to cover in any great detail in this chapter, but in what follows I outline a representative range of examples based on a series of advertisements.

During the first half of the 1930s, South Indian record companies produced a commercial recording for almost every conceivable form of Hindu worship in what was a concerted effort to match their products with the everyday religious lives of their intended audiences. For example, there were numerous recordings of the Vedic chanting associated with the inner sanctum of a Hindu Vaisnavite temple. This chanting would have accompanied the performance of a *puja* in front of the main sculpture of the presiding deity as pictured in the advertisement in figure 6.11. This ritual is a kind of focal point and emotional climax for temple worship that expresses reverence to a god and establishes a spiritual connection with the divine for the worshiper. A particular attraction of such a recording was that it rendered a ritual that would otherwise have been limited to a closed group of Brahmin priests into a public recording that could be played and repeated at will in drastically new settings.

Outside the inner sanctum, other familiar forms of more public worship were recorded. For example, this recording of a Rama *bhajana* (devotional song) party depicted in figure 6.12 would have been a familiar kind of informal group singing of hymns, either as part of pilgrimage or temple processions or in private homes and halls. The image depicted in the advertisement represents what would have been an immediately recognizable everyday street scene around many urban temple precincts (such as Mylapore or Triplicane in Madras), where *bhajana* groups would go on

Figure 6.11
Record Catalogue, Recording Department, Hutchins & Co., August 1934, p. 19.

processions chanting the names of God, singing praises, and offering service and devotion or a form of ballad-like story drawing upon the *puranas* (epic poems), such as the Ramayana with repeated chanting of "Ram-Sita, Sita-Ram" (cf. Cousins 1935, 117; Singer 1972, 199–241). In both of these examples, the record companies were trying to tap into the popular repertoire of everyday Hindu practice of worship with records standing in as both surrogate and vicarious aural experience.

Not all sound representations of worship were strictly oriented toward devotional ends. There were numerous recordings that represented various religious activities in a humorous manner. These lightly poked fun at easily recognizable stereotypical characters. These records were different from the examples discussed above in that they were not so much offering a devotional experience as a kind of observational detachment via a sonic reenactment of familiar religious scenes. These aural representations were composed of a variable mix of social realism, parody, and nostalgic recuperation of public religious events. For example, the record depicted in figure 6.13 on the Vaikunta Ekadesi festival at the famous Sri

Figure 6.12
Record Catalogue, Recording Department, Hutchins & Co., November 1934, p. 18.

Ranganathaswamy Temple promised that "[a] simple, humorous, true-to-life picture of the scene at the temple is portrayed by Record." In this advertisement, which tellingly described the record in visual terms as a picture, also used a visual image of four cartoon-character Brahmins to suggest the humorous quality of the record. This image and the recording it represents asked its viewers/listeners to join along in making fun of these parodied Brahmin characters. We might be tempted to associate this kind of recording with the well-developed tradition of comically insulting Brahmins that was widely shared by non-Brahmins (Pandian 2007). However, the humor here was not entirely derogatory. Rather, this recording seems to have been more aimed at Brahmin Srivaisnavite listeners in inviting them to happily "revive the memory" for those who may previously have attended what was one of the most important annual festivals for the community.

Another example of an explicitly comic representation of another popular form of religious worship, pilgrimage, was performed by the Columbia Comic Party in Tamil. As seen in figure 6.14, the record was described as "a trip to the HOLY TIRUPATHI (from the scene inside the railway carriage to

Figure 6.13
Back cover, Columbia Record Catalogue, Orr's Columbia House, November 1934.

the hills)." Here again, the publicity for this recording stakes a strong claim for its realism in advertising it as a "True to Life Comical Hit." We are told that "the Comic Party have established a reputation for their capacity to depict real life with its comical aspects through Gramophone" (*Columbia Records Catalogue*, 1934, p. 2). Here again, the recording assumes a common and prior firsthand experience of this pilgrimage by its audiences who would be able to recognize and identify the reenacted scenes.

The last example I cite for demonstrating the ways that the South Indian recording industry sought to identify with Hindu practice highlights how the mechanical technology of the gramophone was itself portrayed as a form of Hindu worship. The convergence of the gramophone technology and Hindu worship is particularly well demonstrated by a recording of a Sri Rama Mantram. Figure 6.15 depicts this recording of a song by the eminent artist Chembai Vaidyanatha Bhagavatar about the beneficial power of a well-established South Indian religious practice, referred to as *Nāmasiddhānta*. This doctrine was based upon the belief in the magical power inherent in the recitation of sacred names and in the mantric force

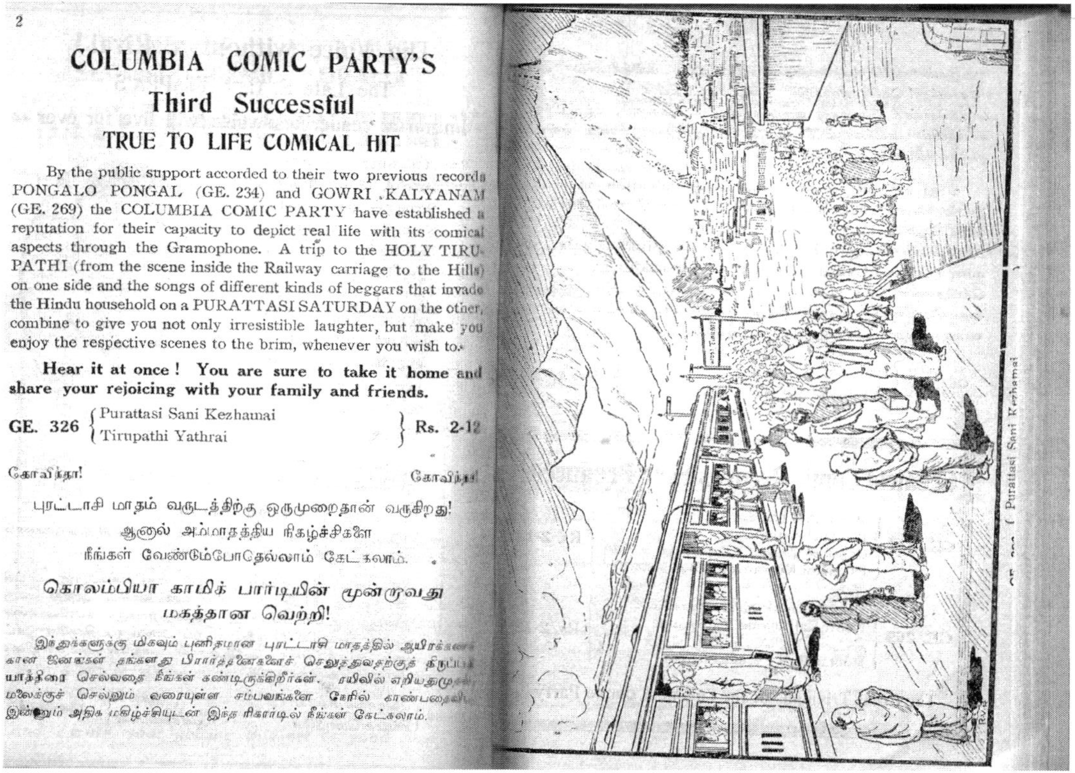

2

COLUMBIA COMIC PARTY'S

Third Successful

TRUE TO LIFE COMICAL HIT

By the public support accorded to their two previous records PONGALO PONGAL (GE. 234) and GOWRI KALYANAM (GE. 269) the COLUMBIA COMIC PARTY have established a reputation for their capacity to depict real life with its comical aspects through the Gramophone. A trip to the HOLY TIRUPATHI (from the scene inside the Railway carriage to the Hills) on one side and the songs of different kinds of beggars that invade the Hindu household on a PURATTASI SATURDAY on the other, combine to give you not only irresistible laughter, but make you enjoy the respective scenes to the brim, whenever you wish to.

Hear it at once! You are sure to take it home and share your rejoicing with your family and friends.

GE. 326 { Purattasi Sani Kezhamai / Tirupathi Yathrai } **Rs. 2-12**

கோவிந்தா! கோவிந்தா!

புரட்டாசி மாதம் வருடத்திற்கு ஒருமுறைதான் வருகிறது!
ஆனால் அம்மாதத்திய நிகழ்ச்சிகளை
நீங்கள் வேண்டும்போதெல்லாம் கேட்கலாம்.

கொலம்பியா காமிக் பார்ட்டியின் மூன்றாவது மகத்தான வெற்றி!

இந்துக்களுக்கு மிகவும் புனிதமான புரட்டாசி மாதத்தில் ஆயிரக்கணக்கான ஜனங்கள் தங்களது பிரார்த்தனைகளைச் செலுத்துவதற்குத் திருப்பதி யாத்திரை செல்வதை நீங்கள் கண்டிருக்கிறீர்கள். ரயிலில் ஏறியதுமுதல் மலைக்குச் செல்லும் வரையுள்ள சம்பவங்களை நேரில் காண்பதைவிட இன்னும் அதிக மகிழ்ச்சியுடன் இந்த ரிகார்டில் நீங்கள் கேட்கலாம்.

Figure 6.14
Columbia Record Catalogue, Orr's Columbia House, September 1934, pp. 3–4.

Figure 6.15
Columbia Record Catalogue, Orr's Columbia House, June 1934, p. 21.

of sound vibration. The mantra sound was supposed to harmonize one with the infinite and eternal hum of the universe (Raghavan 1959). This ritualized repetition of sacred names is one among many other examples of how sound is used as a medium of spiritual realization in Hindu practice. Yet in

Figure 6.16
Cartoon, *Ananda Vikatan*, December 3, 1933, p. 944.

this case, the recording of a song that promotes aural repetition as a form of worship also worked particularly well to co-opt technological reproduction of gramophone playback as a religious practice. The repetitive nature of playing records coincided neatly with the sacred power of repeatedly chanting the name of the deity Rama.

The examples that I have cited above were only a small part of what was a large and varied range of Hindu-themed recordings produced by the new South Indian record companies, all within a few short years at the beginning of the 1930s. These few limited examples help demonstrate how these new companies sought not only to build upon but also extend the vernacular experience of Hinduism. The success of this new alliance between the gramophone and religious practice was such that it became a matter of public comment and even parody. *Ananda Vikatan*, the most popular weekly general-interest Tamil magazine of the day, carried a cartoon (figure 6.16) depicting a poor Brahmin using a gramophone machine and a collection of religious recordings to transform a street water tap into his own temple worship scene. Spread around the machine along the street is a collection of clearly labeled recordings corresponding to major religious events of the Hindu ritual calendar, such as the Saraswati Puja and the Vinayakar (Ganesh) Chaturti. The implication here is that, with the aid of ritual recordings, even the most unlikely of people, the least appropriate of places, and everyday objects can be remade for the purposes of worship. The humor and parody here lie in the recognition that the gramophone machine and recordings have created their own times, places, and occasions for the performance of religious ritual—the technological reproduction has refigured traditional conventions of worship.

I started this chapter by citing Manuel's (1993) example of how new regionally based record companies reshaped the commercial market for popular music with their output of religiously oriented audiocassettes. Using other examples drawn from the history of music recording in South India, I have tried to show that what Manuel has described for North India in the 1980s was not an unprecedented event. At an earlier point in history and at another place in India, South Indian record companies successfully used Hinduism to rebrand their own business practices and record content. In a marked contrast to the globally dominant international record companies that preceded them, the local entrepreneurs used a range of Hindu references, practices, and musical content to reclaim and recast what was once considered to be an imported and foreign gramophone technology. In so doing, the gramophone companies of South India reciprocally implicated the modern and scientific aspects of recording technology with the spiritual devotion of Hindu music traditions.

There was, of course, nothing inherently Hindu about gramophone technology. Instead, I argue that recording businesses articulated the convergence of recording technology and Hinduism as part of a discursive practice that signaled a major transformation in the production of popular music in South India. This transformation may have started as a kind of religious conversion at the beginning of the 1930s. By the end of the decade, however, the public face of the music recording industry in South India had turned to film songs (c.f. Hughes 2007). It was not that these companies stopped recording religiously oriented music, but that they became a much smaller part of a market that was increasingly dominated by film songs.

NOTES

1. I am using the term Hinduism and its cognates to refer to a plurality of distinct religious traditions, rather than a coherent, stable, or unchanging religious system. Though the term is commonly used to refer to one of the major world religions, we must be careful not to essentialize it as a unitary practice. It is a radically decentralized set of changing religious traditions that have coexisted geographically over a long period in South Asia (von Stietencron 2005).
2. Elsewhere I have written about this earlier period in more detail (Hughes 2003). However, Kinnear (1994, 2000) has without a doubt written the most definitive accounts on the early history of music recording in India. I am indebted to his work along with that of several other more recent contributors (Parthasarathi 2005; Das Gupta 2007).

3. Explicitly inspired by the work of John Ruskin and William Morris in England, Coomaraswamy's criticism of the gramophone also shared a similar nostalgia for the lost "aura" of traditional art that Walter Benjamin famously wrote about 20 years later in Weimar Germany. Coomaraswamy's criticism, however, crucially differed in that it was inflected by a struggle for the autonomy and survival of Indian art against its erosion under colonial rule.
4. On this point regarding Coomaraswamy and the primacy of voice, see Weidman 2006, 256–260.
5. When referring to the record company, I use their own transliterated spelling "Saraswathi" that was used on all of their products. In all other instances, I use the now more common spelling "Saraswati."
6. Ariyakudi Ramanuja Iyengar (1890–1967) was a very influential figure who was instrumental in establishing what has become the now standard format for Karnatik music concerts (Subramanian 2008, 47–56).
7. The technical aspects of an early recording session are described in great detail by a newspaper correspondent after having made a visit to an Orr's Columbia House temporary studio (*The Hindu*, Sept. 27, 1932, p. 7).
8. For more discussion of this booklet and the image, see Weidman (2006, 264–266). It is, however, important to note that Weidman has mistakenly identified Naradar as the classical Karnatik composer Tyagaraja and the *devadasis* as housewives.
9. I am indebted to James Benson for his translation from Sanskrit.

CHAPTER 7

Filming the *Bhangra* Music Video

ANJALI GERA ROY

INTRODUCTION

Bhangra is derived from a Panjabi performance tradition of the same name, largely found in western Panjab (Gera Roy 2010), consisting of short couplets that performers insert into the conventional breaks in the steady rhythm of the *dhol*, "a double-headed barrel-shaped drum played with sticks" (SPARK in Education 2009, 4). Modern *bhangra*, however, was invented after the partition of India in 1947, which also resulted in the division of the Panjab region into Indian and Pakistani sections. Modern *bhangra* is the creation of a small group of hereditary performers of traditional Panjabi drumming and dance who received royal support; it has since become incorporated into representations of regional Panjabi identity by the post-colonial Indian state (Schreffler 2006). In still more contemporary terms, *bhangra* also refers to a popular music genre that emerged in the 1980s as Indians both in India and the diaspora-amalgamated traditional rhythms used by Panjabi *dhol* players with western pop, reggae, hip-hop, and rap rhythms. In that decade, Panjabipop and British *Bhangra*—both located under the overarching regional, linguistic, and ideological umbrella of *bhangra*—entered both the Indian and British mainstreams. *Bhangra*'s popularity, in both its modern, "traditional," postcolonial form and its more contemporary globalized form, led to its incorporation in commercial Hindi cinema—which led to further transformations that moved in parallel to *bhangra*'s already dual identity as a contemporary popular music form throughout global Indian communities (and beyond) and as a traditional symbol of Panjabi identity.

Sangita Shresthova uses the term "Bollywood dance" to allude to certain "costume choices, deployment of facial expressions, gestures (as interpretations of a song's lyrics), and movements like 'jhatkas and matkas' [pelvic thrusts], wrist whirls, hand gestures and turns all set to film music" (2003, 3). Peter Manuel suggests that "much of the movement" of this dance "cannot be said to derive from any style at all" (1988, 161); it has therefore been aptly described as "a lot of unknown jerky calisthenics" (Sarkar 1975, 110).

The Bollywoodization of *bhangra* can be understood to refer to a process that incorporated the dance moves and musical features of postcolonial *bhangra*, along with other Panjabi dance styles, into the visual grammar and style associated with Hindi cinema in the 1950s. Ashish Rajadhyaksha (2003) coined the term "Bollywoodization" to describe a process in which non-cinematic content is transformed by the adoption of content, address, and style encountered in the Hindi cinema. The process has been well underway following the liberalization of the Indian economy in the 1990s and has continued through the present. But I argue that *bhangra* has been at the musical core of a reciprocal process: While *bhangra* has become ever more *filmi*, the broader content of Bollywood dance has been strongly influenced by Panjabi culture. *Bhangra*-style dance now frequently appears in Bollywood films, even in contexts that do not directly refer to the Panjab. The Bollywoodization of *bhangra* performance and the "Panjabification" of Bollywood illustrate the forms and processes of intermediality that have characterized Indian popular genres through the penetration of its commercial cinema into Indian secular and sacred spaces. By unpacking the production of Hindi song and dance through the Hindi film's incorporation of regional folk traditions and the extent to which these traditions have been transformed by Hindi cinema, this chapter examines the intermedial relationships between *bhangra* and Bollywood song and dance.

Intermediality has been defined as "the interconnectedness of modern media of communication. As means of expression and exchange, the different media depend on and refer to each other, both explicitly and implicitly; they interact as elements of particular communicative strategies; and they are constituents of a wider cultural environment" (Jensen 2008). After elucidating *bhangra* and Bollywood dance, this chapter traces the history of *bhangra* on film beginning in the 1950s and the transformation of its grammar following its Bollywood sojourn, followed by the emergence of the *bhangra* music video in the 1990s, and finally, at the beginning of the 21st century, by the effective merger of *bhangra* with Bollywood song and dance.

Sidhu Brard suggests that *bhangra* was a male dance of the rural tribes of western Panjab, but in the eastern Panjab, "men considered it unmanly to dance, and dancing was considered as an effeminate activity" (2007, 312). He adds that the only time they saw a man dancing was "when *nachar* [traditional male dancers whose art consists in cross-gendered representation], dressed in female clothes with lipstick, face powder, long skirts, and artificial pigtails and veils, entertained in the shows" (ibid). This was corroborated by Laaj Bedi, the first director of the Song and Drama Division, Ministry of Information and Broadcasting (established in 1954), who had no recollection of *bhangra* being performed in her village near Amritsar before partition (pers. comm. 2008). Conceding that *bhangra* was historically a marginalized dance practice compared to the more popular *jhumar* dance, Schreffler argues that "the modern style of staged dance that is called *bhangra*, while sharing the same name, contains very few of the dance actions believed to have been performed in communal *bhangra*" (2006, 209).

One of the earliest performance groups associated with modern *bhangra* was an ensemble of hereditary entertainers (singers, dancers, drummers) called *bāzīgars* [literally, one who performs "*bāzī*" or "play"] from the Panjab village of Sunam that was supported by the Patiala and East Panjab States Union (PEPSU) (figure 7.1). Citing Iqbal Singh Dhillon ("Panjāb de Lok

Figure 7.1
The Patiala and East Panjab States Union *bhangra* troupe at India's Republic Day performance, January 1954.

Nāchāṅ vich Maulikta," 1992, 20 and *Folk Dances of Panjab*, 1998, 116), Schreffler contends that the PEPSU group's initial performance routine represented "Men's Panjabi Dance" with no pretext to representing any one dance wholly or authentically. Instead, it combined elements of various dances. Consequently, Schreffler regards the modern staged *bhangra* as an invented tradition, "consciously constructed by request of the Maharaja of Patiala in 1953, to include brief displays of actions culled from several Panjabi dances [to which] up through the 1970s Panjabi performance artists gradually added new dance steps and rhythmic variants, [to] shape what is now a sort of staged enactment of Panjabi national identity" (2006, 209). In Schreffler's opinion, modern *bhangra* was "reified in films and canonized in the colleges of Panjab, where *bhangra* dance groups function much like sports teams" (2006, 209). In view of this understanding of the invented nature of post-independence *bhangra* and its continuous reconstruction through its incorporation of other dance idioms, the hybridization of *bhangra* with Hindi song and dance following its incorporation into Hindi cinema could be viewed as yet another transformation.

Figure 7.2
The famous *dhol* player Bhana Ram Sunami (circa 1955).

Leading to *bhangra*'s reinvention in Hindi cinema as a celebratory, exotic, and expressly Panjabi performance genre was an iconic performance by the PEPSU troupe that occurred during an Indian Republic Day parade in New Delhi in January 1954, where they were one of the featured regional "folk" groups included to represent regional identity (Schreffler 2010, 20; Ballantyne 2006, 128–129). By the time of this performance, their dance style had been dubbed *bhangra*, "to evoke the regional Vaisakhi [spring]-time dance of North-Central Punjab" (2011, 237). This group from Patiala included the legendary *dhol* player Bhana Ram Sunami (pictured in figure 7.2), the Deepak brothers (Manohar, Avtar, and Gurbachan, pictured in figure 7.3), as well as students from Mohindra College in Patiala. As a result of this performance, the group was apparently invited to perform a featured song and dance scene in a Hindi film, where they provided a flavor of regionalized exotica and reinforced images of folk or village culture, albeit with no specific reference to the Panjab.

Accounts of *bhangra*'s early appearances in Hindi films center around 1956, though there is no agreement on which actually came first. Filmmaker and lyricist Gulzar considers the song scene "Main Koi Jhooth Boliya" ["Did I Tell a Lie?"] (video 7.4) from *Jagte Raho* (1956) "one of the earliest hit *bhangra* numbers" (2003, 275). According to Leante, "the leader of the [PEPSU] team, Manohar Deepak, took his group to Mumbai and in 1956

Figure 7.3
Bhangra pioneers, the Deepak brothers (Manohar, Avtar, and Gurbachan), with students from Mohindra College in Patiala (circa 1955).

bhangra made its first appearance in Bollywood movies such as *Jagte Raho* and, a few months later, *Naya Daur* (1956)" (2009, 191). Vyjayantimala, however, Bollywood actress and dancing star of the 1950s, recalled having performed a *bhangra* in the film *New Delhi* (1956), and that the song in question, "Tum Sang Preet Lagai Rasiya" ["I've Become Involved with You"] was a big success (Pradeep 2011).

Given *bhangra*'s rather unformed nature in the mid-1950s, there is an extent to which the "firstness" of these examples must remain in the minds of the performers (or beholders). For many Panjabis and musicologists, the dance performed by Manohar Deepak in *Jagte Raho* is a *jhumar*, another West Panjabi dance form that was more popular than *bhangra*. Vyjayantimala's performance, on the other hand, includes musical and gestural signs that have since come to be associated with *bhangra*, and she does take care to include the original *bhangra* call or *boli*: "*Bareen barsi khatan giya si*" [I was away for a dozen years in search of a living] toward the close of her performance. Given *bhangra*'s early association with masculine dance forms, however, Vyjayantimala's assignation of the label *bhangra* to this song scene may be a retrospective one. Many of her gestures, such as the gentle, sensuous gliding steps she and her accompanists demonstrate, are more closely connected to a women's dance form called *giddha* than to the vigorous, energetic gestures of the male *bhangra* dance. In this context, Vyjayantimala (who was of South Indian heritage, after all, and not overly familiar with Panjabi culture) may have confused *bhangra* with *giddha*. Despite the undoubted Panjabi nature of these two Hindi song scenes, the dance accompanying the song "Yeh Desh Hai Veer Jawanon Ka" ["This Is the Land of Brave Young Men"] (video 7.5) in *Naya Daur* (1956) has come to be regarded as the authoritative version and first cinematic vision of "traditional" *bhangra*.

BOLLYWOOD DANCE, *BHANGRA*, AND THE TRANSFORMATION OF CULTURE IN HINDI FILM SONG AND DANCE SCENES

"Bollywoodized" folk traditions, deterritorialized and decontextualized, have been used to represent rustic exotica for the urban Bollywood viewer for decades. Panjabi folk tunes and dances—such as the hit song "Saawan Ke Nazaare Hain" ["The Freshness of the Rains is Here"], composed by Panjabi music director Ghulam Haider, that appeared in the 1941 landmark film *Khazanchi*—have been the basis for many 'hit' songs since the 1940s. Arnold (1988), Manuel (1988), and Sarkar (1975) all agree that music director Haidar first introduced Panjabi folk rhythms and an effervescent musical style in the early 1940s. Manuel argues that Haider's combination of popular *ragas* with distinctive Panjabi tunes permanently altered the nature of, and perhaps defined, the Hindi film song (1988, 164), whereas Arnold avers that traditional Panjabi music style's "characteristics have become synonymous with those of the mainstream Hindi film genre" (1988, 181). Thus, the "Panjabification" of Bollywood began not in the 1990s, as Dwyer (2002) argues in her book, but as early as the 1940s.

Vikrant Kishore argues that "Bollywood films tend to alter the choreography, costumes, accessories, staging, musical instrumentation and context of the performance of folk dance forms when appropriating them for their song and dance sequences" (2011, 70). But he also notes (with some surprise) the reciprocal influence of film culture on folk practitioners, who negotiate and incorporate elements of Bollywood song and dance sequences into their practice. "Traditional" *bhangra* performers, such as Pammi Bai, admit that *bhangra* costumes, presentation, and choreography were all inflected by the grammar of the Hindi cinema following the cinema's appropriation of it (pers. comm. March 2006). Bai pointed out to me that the initial 1956 cinematic appearance of the PEPSU team encouraged a certain visual excess and spectacle in traditional *bhangra*. *Bhangra* costumes, choreography, and presentation thereafter appear to be inscribed by *filmi* spectacle that often serves to enhance stereotypical Panjabi flamboyance. Film dance movements also appear to be structured by a symmetry that is dictated by the needs of Hindi film style choreography and cinematography, an effect that might have previously been seen in the staging of *bhangra*.

The performance of *bhangra* represented in "Yeh Desh Hai" illustrates the transformation of the Panjabi dance in its early cinematic sojourns. The short traditional *boli* [call or catchphrase] is expanded into a three-and-a-half-minute song. The co-option of Manohar Deepak as one of the choreographers definitely contributed to the "Panjabi-ness" of the scene and to the imagined "authenticity" of the *bhangra* performance; but the entire sequence is structured by a style of choreography that is typically associated with Hindi cinema. The film not only reflects the classic management of identities by the postcolonial Indian state through the subsumption of regional *bhangra* dancers into a nationalized culture, but also subjects it to the contingencies of the film trade. Despite its well-intentioned attempt to exhibit Panjabi folk dance, this dance's placement in a Hindi film song and dance sequence subjects it to box office logic.

Although it must be conceded that "Yeh Desh Hai" does a wonderful job of showcasing Panjabi dance, it is nonetheless integrated into the format of the Hindi film song and dance. The "multicultural" nature of the scene in fact acts to homogenize Indian folk culture, a process that Srivastava (2006) and Shresthova (2003) have noted in Hindi film song and dance. In traditional *bhangra*, "men dance in a circular manner around a drummer playing the *dhol*," and it is the drummer who "dictates the tempo and intensity of the dance" (SPARK in Education, 3–4). In "Yeh Desh Hai," the focus is shifted as the regional Panjabi dancers lend exotic color to accentuate the "star power" of the actor Dilip Kumar. The song opens with a close-up of the *dholi* (*dhol* player) performing his introductory flourish. The camera then pans out to female dancers dressed in Rajasthani *lehnga choli* [long skirts and blouses] who are then followed by male dancers carrying the staves that have become increasingly stereotypical symbols of rural Panjabi identity before closing in on the lead actor Dilip Kumar. Not only is the traditionally male *bhangra* space desegregated through the presence of female dancers in "Yeh Desh Hai," Bollywood actors Dilip Kumar and Ajit arrogate the *dholi*'s function. Similarly, in the dance style practiced in the Sialkot region of western Panjab (now in Pakistan) whose movements dominated the dances of the original PEPSU team, the singer calls out to the dancers holding one hand to the ear and has the other arm stretching out in front of him. In "Yeh Desh Hai," other than a token jump and the *bhangra*-style speech, the two Hindi film actors predominantly use hand gestures to interpret the song lyrics, a practice commonly encountered in classical and cinematic dance traditions, but not in *bhangra*. After almost three minutes, the PEPSU *dhol* player Sunami and his *bhangra* dancers are finally permitted space to present the final two minutes of pure *bhangra* dance.

Noting the PEPSU group's cameo appearance in the film, Schreffler points out that it "is full of tumbling, along with their oft-pictured signature stunt of one man standing upon a pot that is balanced atop another man's head" (2011, 237–38). Yet the visual and musical images of *bhangra* established by the group in the *Naya Daur* dance set the basic pattern for all later appearances of dances understood to be *bhangra* (if not always Panjabi).

The film *Kashmir Ki Kali* (1964) included a mid-'60s example of *bhangra*'s incorporation in the star-centered mainstream in the form of the song "Meri Jaan, Balle Balle" ["My Love, Balle, Balle"] (video 7.6). The scene reveals several continuities with the *Naya Daur* dance (as well as some ruptures). In its retention of a real *dholi*, the presence of some of the PEPSU team dancers, and its use of movements that remain lithe rather than forceful or jerky, "Meri Jaan Balle Balle" appears to maintain the aesthetics developed in the *Naya Daur* sequence. The dancers also appear to be dressed or groomed in the fashion of what the PEPSU team must have looked like. Its major departure is the featured star (and lead dancer) Shammi Kapoor, who was already widely perceived as the "Elvis Presley of Hindi cinema" and who was strongly associated with Indian youth culture and globalized popular music, rather than with the traditional/folk ideologies of *bhangra*.

Unlike *Naya Daur*, in which the original PEPSU team leader Manohar Deepak was entrusted with choreographing the dance, the 1960s actor Shammi Kapoor allegedly "never worked with a choreographer and created every step spontaneously for the camera" (*Zeenews.com* 2010, online). The film did have an official choreographer, Surya Kumar (aka Robert Master), trained in North Indian classical dance and also adept at rock and roll; but Kapoor's unique and personal dance style is apparent. In addition, the gestures and facial expressions that highlight the meanings of the song's lyrics, visible in *Naya Daur*, become more pronounced in *Kashmir Ki Kali* as Kapoor holds the heroine Sharmila Tagore's hands while singing the words *"tere hath mein mera hath"* ["my hand in yours"]. Kapoor's facial expressions and flirtatious glances, with his head cocked to one side and shoulders thrown back, became the star's signature style over the years; they are clearly exploited in this sequence to give the song the character of a couple's dialogue, thus ending the gendered segregation of the male dance that was partially maintained in *Naya Daur*.

In the ongoing process of homogenizing folk content for the Hindi cinema's consumption, "Meri Jaan Balle Balle" appears to blend the teasing banter permissible in traditional *bolis* with the *giddha* form of women's song and dance to produce a new courtship dance suitable to Kapoor's film persona and Bollywood's needs. Further, if *Naya Daur* articulated a pan-Indian look by blending Rajasthani folk costumes with Panjabi, the Kashmiri character of *Kashmir Ki Kali*'s heroine makes possible the mixing of Kashmiri outfits and dance with Panjabi *bhangra*. Despite mouthing the *bolis* in the *sialkoti* fashion [the style common in Sialkot, a city in western Panjab], Sharmila Tagore and the other female dancers appear to be executing a mix of Kashmiri folk dances.

Until the 1980s, the Hindi film's co-option of ethnic musics usually proceeded by way of their exoticization. Exotic ethnicity was *bhangra*'s prime appeal in the Bollywood code of signification; but it was hybridized with other musics for the construction of a "Bollywoodized" ethnic music. In

Bollywood *bhangra*, actors danced to choreography by Bollywood dance trainers who mixed *bhangra* movements with disco and break-dance while leaving room for actors to improvise their own signature movements.

Familiar with *bhangra* as Panjabi folk dance since the "Yeh Desh Hai" number in *Naya Daur*, the audience of Bombay cinema was reintroduced to *bhangra* as Bollywood music in some of the increasingly sophisticated Hindi films in the 1990s; in conjunction with other developments in these years, *bhangra* in the Hindi cinema became part of a much more pervasive Panjabification of Hindi film culture. By the end of the millennium, almost no Bollywood film could be complete without a *bhangra* dance scene. Although the Panjabi setting of some of these films might explain the required *bhangra* presence, films with no fixed location also banked on *bhangra*'s popularity to produce musical hits. Films such as *Mohra* (1994), *Karan Arjun* (1995), and other Hindi films of the early 1990s included *bhangra* numbers, but *bhangra* became naturalized as an inherently Bollywood style as a result of its presence in the blockbuster *Dilwale Dulhania Le Jayenge (DDLJ)* (1995), as I discuss below.

DDLJ achieved the integration of the Indian diaspora into the aesthetic economy of Hindi cinema, as Mishra (2002) suggests; but it was also responsible in part for the late 1990s Panjabi wave in the new Bollywood film. That wave appears to have been equally triggered by the emergence of Panjabipop in India and *bhangra* in the U.K., both of which offered popular music alternatives to Hindi film song and its cultural dominance. Daler Mehndi, the "king of *bhangra*" (as he was widely known), and Bally Sagoo, India's most successful DJ of the 1990s, were the most prominent figures in these developments.

Daler Mehndi's Panjabipop first emerged from one of India's new non-film, cassette-based popular music companies to challenge the Hindi film song monopoly with the song "Bolo Ta Ra Ra" ["Shout Ta Ra Ra"], which sold 20 million copies throughout India. Mehndi primarily recorded and performed songs in Panjabi, for which he improvised a few simple, repetitive steps and hand gestures to accompany his lyrics; these have often been confused with *bhangra* and have been imitated in subsequent cinematic representations. Hindi filmmakers neutralized the threat that Mehndi and the Magnasound music company constituted by simply integrating *bhangra*, Panjabipop, and ultimately Mehndi as well, into the cinema's song and dance sequences. Atul Churamani was employed by the newly opened Magnasound and part of the team that launched Mehndi and other Indipop sensations in the 1990s. He points out that "by the late '90s, the music channels had opened up to Bollywood music and Bollywood, in turn, began to draw on the immense popularity of pop stars like Sonu Nigam,

Shaan and Daler Mehendi" (Raj and Khanna 2010). The popularity of new pop music videos, produced by Indian companies featuring Indian pop stars and disseminated by music channels MTV Asia and Channel V, represented a serious challenge to the Hindi cinema's song and dance sequences. The threat ultimately led to the incorporation of the *bhangra* music video in the song and dance idiom of Bollywood cinema.

It was Amitabh Bachchan, whose decades-long reign as India's most famous actor continued into the 1990s, who ushered in the *bhangra* wave in Bollywood in 1997, in one of his many "comeback" films, *Mrityudaata*, when he and Mehndi danced together in the song scene commonly known as "Na Na Na Re" ["No, No, No"] (video 7.7), for which Mehndi provided the song. While the film itself was a box-office flop, the song became a hit, and *bhangra* invaded Bollywood cinema on the back of Mehndi's unprecedented success. Although earlier Bachchan films had him dancing to quasi-*bhangra* numbers, such as "Disco *Bhangra*" from *Gangaa Jamunaa Saraswathi* (1988), it was the joint performance of Bachchan and Mehndi that embodied *bhangra*'s incorporation into the Bollywood mainstream and fostered the new trend. That trend, however, also received impetus from a new, simultaneous development in Indian popular music culture, the music video.

ENTER THE MUSIC VIDEO

Carol Vernallis makes a distinction between two kinds of music videos, narrative and non-narrative, and points out that most music videos in the West tend to be non-narrative (2004, 3). Pointing to the difference between film and the music video, Vernallis argues that the music video is unable to weave a coherent narrative in the same way as film does because it must follow the song, which is repetitive and cyclic rather than sequential; draw attention to the lyrics; and showcase the star (2004, 3). In contrast, the "thrust in Indian music videos is on storytelling" (Joshi 2000). Dwelling on the aesthetic differences between the Indipop music video and the Hindi film, Kvetko points out that while Bollywood album covers feature loud graphics and star actors, Indipop covers are devoid of sensationalism or theatrics (2005, 120). He argues that "the sounds of Indipop conjure private spaces and personal intimacy, but video and album covers go further to enhance this atmosphere of neoliberal individualism" (120).

The first *bhangra* videos were produced in the 1990s when music companies such as Magnasound signed up artists, produced their music, and came up with music videos employing young filmmakers whose professional experience was largely in the production of television commercials, such as Ken Ghosh, Pradeep Sarkar, and Radhika Rao. *Bhangra* music videos appear to have borrowed liberally from three distinct genres: the rock video, the country music video, and the Hindi film song and dance sequence. However, despite the availability of such models, early *bhangra* videos developed an aesthetic that remained partially connected to *bhangra*'s dance and performance traditions, and representations of Panjabi culture. At the same time, early *bhangra* video producers were, in part, oriented toward the values, aesthetic conventions, and media outlets of global music television and its rock and pop videos. Later *bhangra* videos, however, display a newly distinctive form of popular music and video culture that does lean strongly toward the Bollywood style. Unlike Western music videos, contemporary *bhangra* videos have a strong narrative orientation that presents lyrical content visually, as is so commonly seen in the song and dance sequences in Hindi films. Similarly, although *bhangra* emerged on the Indian popular scene in the wake of the liberalization of the Indian economy in the 1990s, the *bhangra* album does not conjure images of individual fulfillment produced by the shift to isolated places in Indipop albums; instead, bhangra continues to focus on collective conviviality (as in the Bollywood song scene) by featuring large gatherings.

Early Indian music videos such as Baba Sehgal's "Thanda Thanda Pani" ["Cold, Cold Water"] (1992; see chapter 8) reflected the industry's hesitancy toward *bhangra* as a pop genre. Largely shot on videotape rather than the more costly 35 mm film, the video's stylistic qualities were as limited as its production values. Daler Mehndi's first music video, "Bolo Ta Ra Ra," on the other hand, is a wonderful example of the gradual emergence of the *bhangra* video as a distinct genre. Former Magnasound executive Madhav Das, who produced the album, maintains that they "got... Daler to do a completely Indian *bhangra* that was fresh compared to the British *bhangra* coming in" (Kamath 2010, online). "Bolo Ta Ra Ra" borrows the performance concept from country music videos produced in the West   (i.e., a filmed performance intercut with narrative segments that illustrate the meaning of the lyrics). The video appears to be a straightforward recording of a young, pot-bellied Daler dancing with his characteristic insouciance, which alternates with a conceptual action that visually transliterates the song's lyrics.

> *Gadde te na chardi*
> *Gaddi te na chardi*
> She does not mount the ass
> Nor does she mount the jeep

The video shows Daler mounting an ass and a jeep in turns before repeating the performance shot to the refrain *"bolo ta ra ra ra,"* which has Daler dancing by himself. The performance shots have the effect of blunting the narrative drive, a result similar to that found in Hindi films. But this structure of combining live performance and conceptual iconographic or narrative elements represented an important step in the emergence of the *bhangra* video aesthetic.

It was Mehndi's 1997 film foray and the popularity achieved by "Na Na Na Re" that enabled Mehndi's later videos to reach an industrial and aesthetic maturity. When "Na Na Na Re" became an instant hit, it began the transformation of the *bhangra* music video. The larger-than-life *bhangra* figure, the robe and the turban, and the trademark gestures that came to define the Mehndi persona first appeared in this song sequence. The change from videotape to the more professional look of film and from existing film footage and still photographs to elaborately photographed and dressed sets, as well as the shift toward the flashy, glittering appeal that has become the dominant look of many contemporary *bhangra* videos, all began here. The newer videos also revealed a seamless glide from the performance to the narrative sections through improved editing qualities and a better conceptualization.

At the same time, *bhangra*'s visual image was being refined by its diasporic artists, who had had a longer exposure to the MTV aesthetic and sometimes had earlier access to more sophisticated production technology. This is clearly demonstrated by some of the *bhangra* videos featuring Gurdas Maan, the U.K.'s most famous *bhangra*/pop performer. His "Apna Panjab Hove" ["If I Were in My Panjab"] (video 7.8) (1996) music video shows a more advanced position both in terms of production quality and management of the narrative. It is marked by its professional film-quality look, but it also constructs a narrative based on the motif of the soldier's nostalgia for home. The video follows Maan's character, dressed in military uniform, expressing his yearnings for his home village in Panjab at his distant army outpost. If the images of soldiers bonding with one another away from home present a credible setting for nostalgia, the journey into the Panjabi homeland through the eyes of the returning soldier helps the narrative make a smooth transition into the Panjabi hinterland. With its superior production quality, carefully handled narrative, and star presence, the video is interchangeable with song clips from Bollywood films featuring soldiers, such as *Border* (1997) and *Soldier* (1998). The *filmi* look of the music video foregrounds Maan's evolution into singer-dancer-actor that Yash Chopra later capitalized on in the song "Aisa Desh Hai Mera" ["My Country Is Just this Way"] in *Veer-Zaara* (2004), which reproduces the ambience of the Panjabi village by borrowing the imagery of several of Maan's music videos.

Two music videos, both produced by the Birmingham-based Bally Sagoo, illustrate the growing sophistication of the *bhangra* video and the emergence of a narrative trope that was created with an eye to its crossover from the largely Panjabi viewer to a younger, mainstream audience. Both videos, "Gur Nalon Ishq Mitha" ["Love Is Sweeter than Jaggery"] (video 7.9) (1993) and "Aaja Nachle" ["Come On, Let's Dance"] (video 7.10) (1999), show a journey that ends in Panjab, naturalizing the performance context. The introduction of the Westernized outsider to the beauty and culture of Panjab forms the narrative of "Gur Nalon Ishq Mitha," in the context of a family wedding. The video begins with a Westernized girlfriend flying to Panjab to attend the wedding, the hero teaching her to dance the *bhangra*, and her domestication into the Panjabi space, which is signified through a change of clothing. "Aaja Nachle" begins with a luxury bus cruising through the Panjabi countryside and focuses on a young Westernized couple seated side by side. When the bus crosses a bend in the river, the camera pans to a group of rustic youths dancing the *bhangra* by the river. This becomes the cue for the young couple to hop off the bus and join the dancers.

Significantly, the music video ends with the girl returning to her roots, which is signified through the sartorial shift from a miniskirt to a traditional *salwar kameez*. A similar introduction of the Westernized outsider to the beauty and culture of Panjab forms the narrative of "Gur Nalon Ishq Mitha," though the setting now changes to a family wedding. The video begins with a Westernized girlfriend flying to Panjab to attend the wedding, the hero teaching her to dance the *bhangra*, and her domestication into the Panjabi space, which is again signified through a change of clothing.

Unlike many of their other music videos that alternate between episodes consisting of performance shots and narrative, the videos produced in support of Bally Sagoo's remixes of *bhangra* hits, like Malkit Singh's "Gur Nalon Ishq Mitha" and Hans Raj Hans's "Aaja Nachle," are purely narrative. Furthermore, they do not include images of the original performers, who are thereby reduced to a role similar to that of the film playback singer. Both of these videos privilege the narrative over the song's form. "Gur Nalon Ishq Mitha," starring Malaika Arora and produced by Polygram Multimedia's Radhika Rao, is "a simple tale of a girlfriend finding acceptance from the boy's family, set against the backdrop of a colourful wedding"; the video "immediately hit the number one slot on the music channels" (Joshi 2000, online). Rao, who is a film school graduate, infused a strong narrativity into the music video that has become a hallmark of Indian music videos. The video even manages to add tension to the narrative of family happiness at their daughter's wedding as the father chides his son for going to the airport to pick up his girlfriend: "*oye bhain da viyah hai, airport jan di koi zaroorat naheen*" ["It's your sister's wedding; you don't need to go to the airport"].

In the narrative world of the *bhangra* music video, the recurring narrative trope of the protagonist's journey from the cosmopolitan city to the Panjab (aligned with "Panjabi-ness" in major Hindi films from *DDLJ* to *Tanu Weds Manu* [2011]) has become an important intermedial feature. By the end of the millennium, the *bhangra* video had visually and aesthetically advanced to such an extent that it could afford to break free of the *filmi* influence to evolve as a distinctive genre that was, in turn, incorporated into Bollywood dance. Bally Sagoo's remixes of traditional *bhangra* not only ushered in the *bhangra* revolution in the U.K., but also set the trend for a new genre of music in the Hindi film industry.

BHANGRA IN BOLLYWOOD

While the music videos of Bally Sagoo's remixes of popular *bhangra* songs by Panjabi singers Malkit Singh, Hans Raj Hans, and Nusrat Fateh Ali Khan provided an alternative to the albums of Panjabi pop stars like Daler Mehndi and Gurdas Maan, Bollywood *bhangra*, choreographed by Bollywood choreographers such as Saroj Khan, Shiamak Davar, Farah Khan, and others, also evolved into an independent genre that intersected with the *bhangra* music video. A comparison of the music video with *bhangra* in film exhibits the intermediality between the *bhangra* music video and the *filmi* song and dance sequence through the music video's borrowing of film's narrative orientation and the film song's borrowing of music video editing style.

A comparison of Bally Sagoo's "Gur Nalon Ishq Mitha" with "Mehndi Laga Ke Rakhna" (video 7.11) in *DDLJ* demonstrates the strong intermediality that eventually resulted in the *bhangra* music video and Bollywood song and dance overlapping with one another. Both songs were picturized as *mehndi* ceremonies, in which the hands of the seated bride-to-be are decorated with elaborate designs by her female family members and friends. Traditionally, such rituals were gender-segregated, as shown in "Gur Nalon Ishq Mitha," which might thus be thought to display a greater fidelity to the Panjabi ritual. In practice, of course, both the actual ritual and these filmed representations seek to manage male presence in the *mehndi* ceremony and thus acknowledge "tradition." In addition, the film sequence begins with a playful gendered repartee that is part of many pre-wedding rituals and retains the Panjabi touch by segregating male and female dancers with the occasional breach by the Raj character played by Bollywood actor Shah Rukh Khan. If at all, the Bollywood sequence attempts to produce the Panjabi ambience more faithfully by its rooftop setting, ethnic costumes, *dhol* players, and so on, whereas the Bally Sagoo video, probably shot in one of the newly proliferating wedding halls, is more eclectic in its East-West borrowings.

The music video is Bollywoodized through the incorporation of dance gestures and movements associated with Hindi cinema. But the stylized choreography of the Bollywood song and dance is disrupted by the improvised and open movements of the music video. Another film song and dance sequence, the Bally Sagoo remix "Aaja Nachle" in Mira Nair's film *Monsoon Wedding* (2001), is structured by the same chaos and spontaneity characteristic of Panjabi weddings; the use of a handheld camera both enhances this sense of spontaneity and replicates the look and feel of the ubiquitous Indian wedding video. All the three sequences are marked by the presence of several generations of family members and the performance of rituals associated with Panjabi weddings. The crossing over of actors, musicians, and choreographers in these three sequences of *Monsoon Wedding* foregrounds the intersections among this crossover film, the conventional film, and the *bhangra* music video.

Bally Sagoo, in the meanwhile, has more recently moved on to remix film songs, further collapsing the boundaries between *bhangra* and Bollywood. The similarity of sets, the presence of model-turned-Bollywood actors, the costumes, the choreography, and the gestures and facial expressions that accompany the lyrics make the music video a perfect model for the *bhangra* in Bollywood weddings, from "Mehndi Laga Ke Rakhna" to "Ainvayi Ainvayi" in *Band Baaja Baaraat* (2010). From *Kuch Kuch Hota Hai* (1998) to *Patiala House* (2011), the *bhangra* in the wedding setting points to the heroine's affirmation of traditional values and integration into the family. With *Major Saab* (1998), the *bhangra* was inserted in the wedding procession instead of the preparatory rituals, with Amitabh Bachchan responding playfully to the traditional Panjabi women's song in an improvised *boli* "Ik Panjaban Kudi Panjaban," and *bhangra* became a must in all Bollywood wedding rituals.

While *bhangra* became ubiquitous in the wedding sequences in the films that followed, Subhash Ghai's *Taal* (1999) borrowed Bally Sagoo's sartorial style and mannerisms in the character played by Anil Kapoor, along with traditional Panjabi tunes and lyrics in a reverse case of homage, and the club-style *bhangra* featured in Sagoo's albums became a staple in Bollywood films in the new millennium. Beginning with *Kabhi Khushi Kabhie Gham* (2001), the club *bhangra* in "Everybody Say Shava Shava" has become as much a part of Bollywood song and dance as the wedding *bhangra*, albeit as it is interpreted by Bollywood choreographers such as Farah Khan, Shiamak Davar, and so on. The music videos of U.K.-based *bhangra* singers form the template that Bollywood choreographers play with in the club sequences while lending their distinctive Bollywood touch. The mutual implication of the *bhangra* video with the Bollywood song and dance has become so pronounced in the settings, sartorial choices, gestures, body movements, and facial expressions that the two have become almost indistinguishable from one another. "Nach Balliye" ["Dance, My Girl"] (video 7.12) in *Bunty Aur Babli* (2005) makes clear the extent to which U.K. *bhangra* structures the gait, mannerisms, and styles of urban youth in India through Bollywood's borrowing of British Asian youth idioms in a number of club-style *bhangra* videos like "Ma Da Ladla" (*Dostana* 2008) and "Maujan Hi Maujan" (*Jab We Met* 2007).

The intersection of the music video with Bollywood song and dance is certified by the presence of *bhangra* stars such as Mika Singh or Hard Kaur appearing in Hindi films (*Tanu Weds Manu*, 2011, and *Johnny Gaddaar*, 2007, respectively) and by the appearance of Bollywood stars in *bhangra* videos (e.g., Celina Jaitley in Jazzy B's "Oh Kedi" and Priyanka Chopra in Daler Mehndi's "Sajan Mera"). Bollywood audiences were so familiarized with British *bhangra* that *Singh is Kinng* (2008) could afford to feature Snoop Dogg in its title song; it was similarly so for Akon in the "Chammak Challo" number in *Ra.One* (2011).

CONCLUSION

Bhangra has been simultaneously "Bollywoodized" and naturalized as Bollywood song and dance since the 1950s. The two dance genres were further implicated into one another with the emergence of the *bhangra* music video in the 1990s. The presence of Bollywood in *bhangra* and *bhangra* in Bollywood illustrates the strong forms of intermediality that have characterized Indian popular genres through the penetration of Bollywood into the Indian secular and sacred space. By examining the intermediality between the bhangra music video and the Bollywood song and dance, this chapter unpacked the production of Hindi song and dance through its incorporation of regional folk traditions and the extent to which these traditions have been transformed by Hindi cinema.

For some who are aware of divergence in the Bollywood version from the realities and diversity of Panjabi cultural performance, Bollywood *bhangra* may indeed be a travesty. But its overwriting of traditional *bhangra* with a Bollywood semiotics of dress, appearance, gesture, bodily movement, and sound helps to re-inscribe this culturally coded Panjabi genre into a decontextualized Bollywood ethnic rite. *Bhangra*'s decontextualization and hybridization, while its exoticized ethnicity is retained, enables it to perform ethnic celebration in Bollywood blockbusters even in non-Panjabi contexts; this lends itself to decoding by all Indian ethnicities.

CHAPTER 8

Mimesis and Authenticity

The Case of "Thanda Thanda Pani" and Questions of
Versioning in North Indian Popular Music

PETER KVETKO

> We live constantly in the shadow of history's incompleteness, in the aftertaste of
> the sound bite's rolling echo.
>
> Taussig, 1993, 27

In *Mimesis and Alterity*, a meditation on the work of the German critical theorist Walter Benjamin, Michael Taussig explores sensory experience in relation to histories of representation. Living within a tangled dance of sameness and otherness, he argues, humans instinctively create meaning through appropriation. Yet appropriation is impossible without the imagination of difference. Drawing on Benjamin, Taussig emphasizes that the "mimetic faculty" and the experience of otherness are not merely visual, but also tactile, embodied, and, most interesting to me, aural. Thus the work of these theorists provides fertile ground for thinking about musical creativity. In what ways is the music with which we identify really ours? What roles do borrowed sounds play in our habits of self-making? In the age of samples, loops, and mechanically reproduced grooves, how are appropriation and otherness felt within the rolling echo of pop music?

In 1993, the same year that Taussig published *Mimesis and Alterity*, the first Hindi pop music video was broadcast on MTV Asia. The song, recorded by the then recently discovered singer Baba Sehgal, did not feature the classical sitar or the folk *dholak*, nor did the vocal quality resemble the timbre of a Bollywood singer. Instead, the rhythm was in step with the house music on international charts in the late 1980s and early 1990s (such as "Pump Up the Volume," 1987, by MARRS and "The Power," 1990, by Snap!). As female dancers with cut-off jean shorts thrust their hips and the actress Puja Bedi writhed under a shower of water, Sehgal bobbed his do-rag-covered head and rapped in Hindi as a gust of wind blew open his untucked white shirt.[1] From one perspective, this video artlessly imitates top 40 trends; it might be dismissed quickly by subaltern theorists as a manifestation of false consciousness or evidence of cultural imperialism. Yet as Benjamin (2005), Taussig (1993), and others have shown, and as I argue here, copying has the potential to be constructive; versioning can sometimes be productive; and appropriation often can lead to innovation.

Throughout the more than ten years that I have been interviewing musicians, fans, journalists, and record executives in Mumbai's popular music industry, the issues of mimesis and authenticity have been ever-present. This is certainly the case within the Bollywood music world, where music directors have always borrowed liberally from a variety of sources (from domestic folk and devotional music to the latest international hits) to create the eclectic sound (Arnold 1988) that is both celebrated for its affective power and derided for its lack of originality. But the majority of my own work has been on Hindi-language popular music independent of cinema, music that in the 1990s came to be known as "Indipop." Even more so than Bollywood, the Indipop world has faced severe criticism for being derivative, lacking originality, and promoting Indian "versions" that don't stand up to their "original" Western counterparts. Why, asked more than one record store shopper in Mumbai, would I want to buy an *Indian* Madonna when I can go out and get the *real* thing?

Comparisons and their underlying essentialisms are natural products of the human experience. In my own work, I habitually compare Indipop with American rock 'n' roll. Indeed, there are many compelling reasons to look at India in the 1990s by way of the United States in the 1950s. In both contexts, new technologies, emerging consumer groups, and sociopolitical transformations paved the way for significant changes in popular music. For the emergence of rock 'n' roll in the 1950s, it was television and vinyl records, teenagers, and post-WWII prosperity cast against the instabilities of the Cold War and the Civil Rights movement. In the case of Indipop in the 1990s, the entry of satellite television, especially music networks like MTV India and Channel V, led to a demand for domestic content. The liberalizing of the Indian economy propelled the country's expanding middle classes to seek new forms of consumerist pleasure and entrepreneurial opportunities. And the 50th anniversary of Indian independence, the violence of Hindu-Muslim rioting, and the escalating danger in Kashmir led to a heightened state of reflection and self-analysis.

Yet while the emergence of rock 'n' roll in the U.S. carried unquestioned historical significance, the impact of Indipop has been portrayed as minimal. Even between 1998, when I first went to India and encountered newspapers and shopkeepers lavishing praise on Indipop artists like Silk Route and Lucky Ali, and 2000, when I returned for a year of dissertation research on non-film music in Mumbai, enthusiasm about the Indipop movement had all but disappeared. Yet even today, well into the 21st century and amid the hype over India's rapidly expanding economy and consumerist possibilities, one is still tempted to ask, Why did Indipop fail? How was it that Indipop could not overwhelm the established formulae of Bollywood in the same way that rock 'n' roll overthrew the conventions of Tin Pan Alley? Although Bollywood had its "Elvis Presley" (see chapter 11), would a popular musician outside of cinema ever inspire a youth culture revolution?

Quick and easy explanations abound: India has too much cultural diversity to expect a single person, genre, or fashion to take hold nationwide. The country has neither the venues for widespread tours by bands nor the pervasive consumerist lifestyle required to devote expendable income on recordings, T-shirts, and concert tickets. The non-film music industry shot itself in the foot by releasing inferior music and was simultaneously weakened by piracy and the Internet. Film songs take on extraordinary lives independent of cinema and thus already fulfill many of the same desires as would a pop singer or rock band. And the list goes on.

None of these factors, however, prevented artists and music executives from pushing for "real music," as they might describe a popular music in which the song adheres to the identity of the performer rather than the actor on whom it is "picturized." Magazines such as *The Score* and webzines such as *Split*, *NH7*, and Tehelka's *The Music Project* are the latest publications to emphasize India's non-film music scenes. Reality shows like "Sa Re Ga Ma Pa," "Voice of India," "Fame Gurukul," "Indian Idol," and "Coke Studio" have been heavily promoted by the media industry, ostensibly emphasizing the unique talent, charisma, and physical appearance of the artist. These efforts have been directly related to the changing relationship between public and private, between intimacy and distance in a mass-mediated and increasingly globalized field of experience (Kvetko 2008). Unfortunately, marketing a pop star as a "real person" is inevitably more complicated when his or her sounds and styles are appropriated from elsewhere. The resulting tension between mimesis and authenticity animates much contemporary popular music, and the story of Baba Sehgal, northern India's first superstar of rap music, is a particularly compelling example.

Sehgal was among the first wave of Indipop stars in the 1990s. His cassettes, such as *Dilruba* (1990) and *Alibaba* (1991), released on the Magnasound label, appeared alongside Magnasound's other Indipop releases by Goan rocker Remo Fernandes, pop diva Alisha Chinai, fusion crooners Colonial Cousins, and *bhangra* star Daler Mehndi. Issues of appropriation and authenticity, however, are thrown into sharp relief in Sehgal's Hindi rap songs, especially the title track from his most successful album to date, *Thanda Thanda Pani* [*Cold Cold Water*] (1992), which owes its conception to the 1990 chart-topper "Ice Ice Baby" performed by Vanilla Ice.

As I suggest above, many commentators would argue that Indipop crashed shortly after takeoff and that a Hindi version of "Ice Ice Baby" might not merit a close academic study. Indeed, *Thanda Thanda Pani* and Sehgal's follow-up release *Main Bhi Madonna* [*I Am Also Madonna*] (1993) seem to be little more than stunts, novelty albums without enduring value. I argue here, however, that such recordings offer important insights into the analysis of musical meaning, a central concern for ethnomusicology and popular music studies. They reflect on the power of metaphor in everyday life, the practice of mimetic re-signification, and the utility of appropriating the "Other" in order to express one's self. Examples of this practice abound, from Gilbert and Sullivan's *Mikado*, to the appropriation of four-part choral harmony by Chinese nationalists, to Malian superstar Salif Keita mimicking the sounds of the Spanish language. Rather than dismissing acts of appropriation, sampling, or remediation, scholars such as Monson (1999), Born and Hesmondhalgh (2000), and Auslander (2008) have brought these issues to the forefront.

Appropriation and parody exist in a myriad of forms in Indian popular music (cf. Beaster-Jones and Marshall 2012; Booth 1993; Manuel 1993; Marcus 1992). Certainly, some instances of these processes are the work of subaltern subjects who mimic those who oppress them. Focusing on Baba Sehgal's biggest hit and basing my work on Taussig (1993), however, I argue that mimesis is a product of agency, not evidence of its absence. After exploring the story of Baba Sehgal, I propose four levels at which versioning in Indipop can be constructive, productive, and creative: as a template for innovation, as a cache of cultural capital, as a prelude to face-to-face collaborations, and as a form of meta-commentary on narratives of cultural purity.

"THANDA THANDA PANI" AND THE EMERGENCE OF
BABA SEHGAL

When compared to other stars of non-film pop in Mumbai during the 1990s, Baba Sehgal was somewhat of an outlier. Many of the early Indipop artists, such as Sharon Prabhakar, Suneeta Rao, and Alisha Chinai, were attractive women who came from an Anglophone background in Mumbai, had experience in drama and musical theater, and evoked the imagery of pop divas. The rapper Sehgal, on the other hand, was raised in Lucknow in the Hindi-Urdu heartland, far from the glamour of Mumbai. Yet this upbringing gave him a level of credibility with "the masses," and his fluency with vernacular linguistic idioms put him in step with a broader range of listeners.

During his years of university study (in engineering), Sehgal enjoyed playing drums and was particularly fond of American country music. After graduating in 1987, he returned to his native Lucknow, but the lure of fame called his name. He procured his first keyboard and began writing songs. He then met music producer Jawahar Wattal (who later produced Daler Mehndi's "Bolo Ta Ra Ra"; see chapter 7). The two worked on developing his songs and recording a demo album consisting of eight tracks. Sehgal took the demo to Atul Churamani at the Delhi branch of Magnasound, who was impressed enough to send him to the company's Mumbai headquarters. This was not an easy move for Sehgal. In a 2001 interview at his office in Mumbai, he told me that he was nervous about taking such a big risk:

> I said, "Mom, I'm going to Bombay." She said, "Beta, this is very tricky. We're from North. Lucknow." Anyway, I managed to reach Bombay. I had to start working on the second product, because I had to survive, because I knew nobody here.

Sehgal fortunately found a place among Magnasound's growing stable of non-film music artists. After releasing his first demo recordings as the album *Dilruba*, Sehgal recorded a follow-up album, *Alibaba*, although neither of these was a major success. Then, a chance moment at a music industry party led to a breakthrough for both Sehgal and Magnasound. Here is the story, as Churamani recalled during an interview with me nearly a decade later:

> In 1992 we were at a party and there was a girl singing "Ice Ice Baby," and Baba said, "Hey hey! Hang on a sec! Just play the track again; I've got some lyrics here." And I said, "We have something!" So I said, "Off to the office!" So next morning, bleary-eyed and hung over, we dragged ourselves into the office and

to [Magnasound head Shashi Gopal] we said, "Listen, here's something." And he said, "Yeah, if you think it'll work, go with it." And that's how I think "Thanda Thanda Pani" got off the ground.

Sehgal's appropriation of Vanilla Ice's "Ice Ice Baby" was entitled "Thanda Thanda Pani," which translates from Hindi literally as "Cold Cold Water." As Churamani states, the album was the first major breakthrough for the emerging Indipop music industry. According to Sehgal, the album sold 100,000 copies in its first three and a half months and brought Indipop music to the headlines of India's newspapers.[2]

Like "Ice Ice Baby," the recording of "Thanda Thanda Pani" begins quietly with shakers subdividing the beat before the entry of the bouncing bass line. Listeners familiar with the Vanilla Ice version might notice that in Sehgal's recording the tempo is slightly faster, the shaker intro only lasts for one measure, and the synthesized bass line is foregrounded by the disappearance of the shakers. The lyrics of "Thanda Thanda Pani" are framed as a story, and Sehgal enters by addressing the audience directly:

aap sab mere dost, my friends	All of you friends of mine,
jab bhi kisi five star hotel	whenever you go to some
jaate hain	five-star hotel
ya to khaane ke liye	either to eat,
ya kisi se milne ke liye	or to meet someone,
aur ya kisi aur kaam ke liye	or for some other matter
jo aap hi beheter jaante hain.	that you know better.
lekin mere doston	But my friends
main aaj aap ko apna anubhav	today I will narrate to you
sunaata huun	an experience of mine
jisse sun kar	which, after hearing it,
aap bhi goongoonaenge	will make you too hum along.
thanda thanda pani	Cold, cold water

In this opening section, Sehgal recites the lyrics at a conversational pace, inviting the audience to enter his world. He speaks directly to the listeners as a collective group of friends, creating a type of intimacy that is often cultivated in the marketing of pop music stars. Speaking over a repeating breakbeat, Sehgal preempts the listener's suspension of disbelief by implicating the audience in a dialogue. Sehgal also discards the barrier between the small number of people who frequent five-star hotels and the majority of his audience, implying that everyone can share this experience.

We then hear the refrain *"thanda thanda pani"* harmonized in soft, almost whispered voices, invoking an intimacy between recording and listener (cf. Kvetko 2004, 2008). After a break that features the sound of water being poured into a glass, the next section begins suddenly as Sehgal raps quickly and rhythmically in the first person. Sehgal explained to me that in the Indian context of the 1990s, the word "rap" primarily meant *fast* music.

main five star hotel	I went to a five-star
pehli baar gayaa.	hotel for the first time.
main ne dekha	I saw a swimming pool
paani se bhara swimming pool.	filled with water.
aaya manager bola	A manager came and said
baithiye please sir, sir, sir.	"Please sit, sir.
aap ki seva mein main haazir hoon	I am here to serve you.
kuch farmaiye boliye	Please tell me
kya aap ko chaahiye?	Do you need anything?"

In this section, Sehgal evokes the pleasures of urban consumerism. The setting is a five-star hotel complete with swimming pool, at which our hero is graciously attended to by the manager himself. According to the story, this is Baba's first time at such an extravagant place, and he seems a little overwhelmed by the environment. Thus, he reaches out to the imagination of listeners who, like himself, are just making the transition to being on their own in such a massive city. Although it is clearly a novelty song, one can already argue that the piece is also autobiographical of Sehgal's real-life journey to from Lucknow to Bombay.

And while he may be a novice in a five-star hotel environment, Sehgal confidently states that, no matter the context, the consumer should get what he/she pays for. Stepping out of the story and resuming his direct conversation with the listener, he casts the experience of visiting a luxury hotel as a universal act of individual consumerism by proclaiming:

jab aap itna rupyaa	When you are spending
kharch kar rahe hai to	so much money, then
aapko uski vasuli milni hi chaahiye	you ought to get your money's worth.

The shifting of voice continues, and Sehgal's rapper persona returns, spitting out a fast-paced sequence in which the plot thickens at the five-star hotel. He develops a headache and fever, yet instead of getting the *thanda pani* (cold water) he requests, the hard-of-hearing manager brings Sehgal a meal. As Sehgal voices his frustration more confidently, a waiter arrives.

Yet he too has failed to fulfill the simple request for water and brings a soft drink instead. Switching to English for perhaps an added level of authority, Sehgal growls, "Call the president!" Then:

staff ghabraya	The staff worried
jab president aaya	when the president came.
mera man machla	My mind was blown.
dekha soni soni kudi	I saw a hot babe
laal saariwaali aage khardi hai	in a red sari standing before me.

From this, the midpoint of the song, the narrative takes center stage and Sehgal's direct conversation with the audience ends. Although the song contains commonly used Hindi words that are unmarked by any regional inflections, Sehgal's description of the president as a *"soni kudi"* is a slight Panjabi reference and a nod to the broad influence of *bhangra* and Panjabi folk music on North Indian popular culture.

In contrast to the cool swagger of Vanilla Ice's character, Baba Sehgal is undone by the beautiful woman. After finally getting his cold water, thanking the president, and leaving the hotel, he scolds himself for forgetting to ask for her name. He imagines that his friends will mock him for being a coward, and in an act of desperation, he storms into her office demanding to know her name:

madam aapka naam kya hai	Madam, what's your name?
madam ne bhi dekha	She noticed that there was
mere maathe ka paseena	sweat on my brow and said,
boli naam bhi bataoongi	"I'll tell you my name, but first
pehle kuch lenge aap	would you like anything?"

As a city built upon ambition and the desire for *naam banaana* (making a name for oneself), Mumbai as the backdrop for this story is not incidental. Just as in reality, Sehgal went to the city eager to make a name for himself; his lyrics center around the struggle to become known to the city (embodied in the person of the five-star hotel's president). We have come full circle to another moment in which Sehgal finds himself anxiously encountering a new environment yet being served as a prototypical consumer.

"Thanda Thanda Pani" cannot be described as a translation or cover version of "Ice Ice Baby." The recording is based on local realities, culture-specific and class-specific ideologies, and individual modes of creative expression, transforming even the meaning of the song's title. Yet the two recordings share more than superficial similarities. For example, both recordings revolve around two common themes: place and miscommunication. Vanilla Ice describes cruising around Miami, eventually getting trapped in a shoot-out; but even though Vanilla Ice's character is armed and presumably firing shots as well, the police pass him by because he doesn't fit the racial profile. In "Thanda Thanda Pani," instead of the swaggering machismo of Vanilla Ice who entices women to abandon their jealous men, Sehgal offers nervous miscommunication in an Indian five-star hotel—an environment with which many of his listeners would have been as unfamiliar as his fictional hero—where he encounters authority and desire in the person of the female president.

Sehgal presents a character who navigates the urban landscape of aspiration and anxiety in a way that might have felt realistic to a non-elite Indian audience of the 1990s. Such realism, however tentative, stands in sharp contrast to Bollywood's fantastic spectacles. Sehgal's anxiety can be read as a metaphor for the experiences and feelings of India's aspiring middle class in their first forays into consumer capitalism following economic liberalization in 1991. This structural transformation was essential for Sehgal, Magnasound, and indeed Indipop as a whole. Before the new sound of Bollywood emerged along with multiplex theaters at the end of the millennium, Indipop was a soundtrack to economic liberalization in India.

"Thanda Thanda Pani" also demonstrates the layered nature of global pop music, in which musical materials are increasingly separated from their sources and circulate across time and space. This phenomenon, described by R. Murray Schafer (1969) as "schizophonia," has been taken up by Feld, who emphasizes the relationship between mimesis and domination: "The appropriation born of mimesis is both the official bastard of social hierarchy and the living mark that every relationship of copy to copied is an icon of unequal power relations" (1996, 16). For example, the underlying groove of "Thanda Thanda Pani" originally comes from the song "Under Pressure" by David Bowie and the band Queen, whose lead singer was a Parsi from Bombay (Farrokh Bulsara, later Freddie Mercury). But before the riff is recycled in India, it must first travel via a white American artist (Vanilla Ice) who frames the groove in an emerging African American performance style of the 1980s, adding the metaphor of ice to symbolize both his coolness under pressure and his prowess as a rapper, while also playing on the double meaning of ice as diamonds, the acme of consumerist desire. The re-contextualized groove and rap style eventually arrive in Mumbai via Baba Sehgal, an engineer turned pop singer, who transforms the rap from one of chauvinist posturing and racialized desire to a story of innocence and experience.

At the time Sehgal was recording "Thanda Thanda Pani," the offices of his music label, Magnasound, were bustling with activity. Thrilled by their burgeoning success, Magnasound chief executive Shashi Gopal and his associates forged ahead with more research into the expectations and preferences of Indian consumers. Gopal's overall model was based on a rather straightforward assumption: Because the public sphere was totally dominated by film music for so long, it was only natural that film music should be the dominant popular music genre. The emergence of pop music videos on MTV India, however, had the potential to change the media environment to which consumers were now being exposed. Music videos might gradually lead to a new cultural orientation. According to Shashi Gopal, Baba Sehgal's success was part of the process of cultural transformation taking place in urban India following economic liberalization. In my 2001 interview with Gopal at Magnasound's former headquarters in central Mumbai, he reflected back on the context for Sehgal's rise to stardom:

> It was a time when India was going through the demonstration effect in terms of rap. Meaning that it was always an exhibition of a potential country following a bigger potential country, and imbibing from them some styles. The first style that comes through is fashion. The second style that comes through is music. Then there's food. And then there's a quantum change.

Gopal feels that in the global realm of cultural appropriation, fashion is at the vanguard, followed closely by music (cf. Attali 1985). The combination of these two forces played an important role in Magnasound's marketing of Sehgal, Alisha Chinai, Daler Mehndi, and its other pop stars. At the same time, Gopal recognizes that cultural influences can also flow from a smaller "potential country" to a larger one, as is the case with bindis and mehndi becoming popular among suburban American teens. Competing in the global marketplace, Gopal was aware of the dynamic and often competitive environment in which culture can be packaged as tradition, commodity, and practice. It was no coincidence that many of Magnasound's biggest music videos, including Sehgal's "Dil Dhadke" featured occasional shots of classical dance and costume clearly recognizable as markers of traditional Indian identity.

From Baba Sehgal's perspective, the presence of his video in the global arena of MTV gave him a legitimacy that most local pop artists were unable to achieve. At the same time, he witnessed firsthand the illusory power that Western pop culture can have over those described by Wallis and Malm

(1984) as "small peoples." Sehgal takes pride in the great talent of local musicians in India. He complains, however, that Indian audiences are often not impressed with talent unless it comes with foreign credentials. While sipping coffee in his Andheri office, Sehgal offered the idiomatic Hindi version of the English saying "the grass is always greener on the other side," explaining to me that a talented Indian artist would garner more attention if coming from abroad rather than from India itself:

> You know, there's a saying in Hindi: *ghar ki murgi, daal barabar* [lit. a chicken at home is equivalent to lentils]. If you do something in India, suppose I sing like Michael Jackson and the arrangements are like Madonna's album, like it's amazing. People will say [unimpressed], "He's Baba Sehgal." Now same deal, if I settle in America, if I settle in Singapore, come back and promote it, Baba Sehgal coming from New York, it's like "Oh wow!"

In many ways, this anxiety encapsulates the challenges faced by many early Indipop stars. They were caught in an interstitial cultural zone. Like the Indian rock bands singing in English during the same period (Rock Machine/Indus Creed, for example; see chapter 11), the early Indipop stars performed music that often was understood to be "foreign" by the mass audience. In the late 1980s, India's reigning pop diva Sharon Prabhakar complained, "Pop music will die for lack of exposure. In India, we don't get time on TV and radio. There is a lot of talent. Why do they treat us as aliens? We are as important to Indian culture as the Qutub Minar. We are as national as anybody else" (Chopra 1988, 77). Thus, even if Indian pop stars were highly proficient and successful, they would always be suspect and would never be fully recognized for their talent.

As Baba Sehgal states, his entry into the MTV world dictated an increased attention to self-differentiation. Now that he was a pop star Sehgal told me, he needed to stake out his own space in the landscape of Indian popular culture:

> After my video was released, "Dil Dhadke," people started watching a singer on TV. Playback singers, basically they are backstage, they don't come on television. So people started showing interest, and then I started working out, because I was the only singer who was different from other playback singers, you know, with an image, with an attitude, with a style, and with different costumes.

Although differentiation between artists is the norm for many music genres throughout the world, it articulates a unique cultural statement in the context of Indian popular music. Not only does Sehgal need to find his place among pop singers, but his very presence challenges the expected role of the singer in Mumbai's music industry. Indipop artists such as Sehgal demand recognition as unique and creative individuals, something that they feel is especially difficult with Bollywood, the perpetual elephant in the room, whose presence is most keenly felt in Mumbai. The vastly more influential film music industry socializes its audience to experience the pleasures of voice (provided by the playback singer) and vision (provided by intensely scrutinized actors and their wardrobes) as separate, yet intertwined, texts (Majumdar 2001, 164). Reintegrating this "disembodied voice," I argue, is at the core of how Indipop performers and marketers have understood their work from the 1990s to the present.

One can clearly recognize this objective in the words of Sehgal's A&R man at Magnasound, Atul Churamani, who in 2001 described to me the challenges for record labels to promote sounds and artists that could challenge the hegemony of Bollywood:

> Everybody [in Indipop] is trying to be mass market, so they're creating stuff that sounds a lot like film. Film used to sound different. Pop came and sounded hip and Western. Film copied it. And they copied it better than pop could do it. Plus they have bigger stars to sell it. You know, they have a Shah Rukh Khan, a Hrithik Roshan, an Amir Khan, a Salman Khan, whereas you don't. And what's happened is that the budgets [for films] are enormous. You know, the production, the marketing, the promotion. Everything is on a gigantic scale. You're still, you know, bloody small people. So you don't have much chance of competing with those guys. So you've got to go out and create more stars. You've got to create people who will stand out on their own.

Churamani uses the words "stars" and "people" to emphasize that his business is to create a unified whole that will contrast with the division of labor between inventive minds, beautiful voices, and attractive bodies in the mainstream film industry.

Baba Sehgal continues to be a known celebrity in India, primarily because of his pioneering work in Indian rap but also because of a handful of songs he went on to record for films. He has appeared on televised talent shows and sung for South Indian films as well. But for Sehgal, Magnasound, and the many artists and executives who emerged during the 1990s amid the transformative years of economic liberalization, the Indipop boom quickly turned to bust. Though it initially took little interest in film songs, MTV India "went *filmi*" and largely abandoned non-film pop. Bollywood swallowed up and absorbed many of the voices and musical styles that were created in the Indipop realm, powerfully reinventing itself for the multiplex market. Other Indipop stars like Sonu Nigam, Alisha Chinai, Shaan, Mohit Chauhan, and KK have become important voices in film music, but Baba Sehgal has been left behind. While hip-hop culture grows more and more fashionable in India and performers with unique and compelling personalities are being sought from across the subcontinent, India's first Hindi-language music video star walks an uneasy line between authenticity and fraud, between innovator and poser. In concluding this chapter, I examine the ways in which mimesis and authenticity play out in the specific context of urban North India in the past two decades.

PRODUCTIVE VERSIONS, CREATIVE COPIES

Appropriations, simulations, and other forms of mimetic practice have long and important histories within Indian and South Asian diasporic music cultures. As I mentioned before, ethnomusicologists have increasingly emphasized that such acts of "borrowing" from external sources are fundamental to human musical creativity and that, while the Internet and digital technology have sped this process along, there is little that is new about this. In fact, rather than seeing it as an aberration, we might understand Baba Sehgal's song "Thanda Thanda Pani" as a natural form of cultural expression.

As it does with many issues in the study of North Indian popular music, Peter Manuel's book *Cassette Culture* (1993) grapples with this theme; Manuel even devotes an entire chapter to "the politics of parody." Although many of Manuel's concerns, rooted in his Marxist critique of commercial music, focus on the damage that centralized control over music production can do to the vitality of local music cultures, he nevertheless argues that "the setting of new texts to borrowed melodies is one of the most common and fundamental features of most forms of Indian music, from stock folk tunes to classical compositions" (1993, 114). In this light, hip-hop might appeal to South Asian music-makers like Sehgal because, like local folk traditions, it is rooted in practices of oral transmission, innovation built from stock material, and an emphasis on creativity in story-crafting rather than novel melodic innovation.

Before I turn to the specific case of mimesis in Indipop, I should mention the significant role of mimesis within Bollywood—again to highlight that an Indian version of "Ice Ice Baby" is not as farfetched as it may seem. First, film songs themselves are inherently mimetic (and schizophonic) in the sense that the musical recording is made at a prior time and is then played back during shooting while actors and dancers move and sometimes lip-synch to the prerecorded audio. Second, film song sequences and dance moves are reenacted for weddings and college culture shows throughout India and the South Asian diaspora. Such sequences are also professionally reenacted by both the original actors and others in lavish touring shows and as part of the growing number of televised awards ceremonies in India, where audiences revel in the live, mimetic recreation of familiar movie scenes. Third, film songs form the basis for televised singing contests in which current voices are measured against each other and the original recordings.

Despite the extent to which Bollywood producers remix, quote, and recycle intertextual references and the growth of mimetic recreation in contemporary film song sequences, Bollywood retains an inherent cultural validity that Indipop has struggled to achieve.[3] Mimetic practices play an equally important role within Mumbai's pop music scene, however (as they do in most global pop musics); but when pop musicians such as Baba Sehgal draw their musical inspiration from foreign sources, the seeds for rejection are already sown. In the spirit of a defense of "Thanda Thanda Pani," I conclude by discussing four ways in which acts of versioning and appropriation can play productive roles for non-film pop artists.

Versioning as a Template for Improvisation and Self-Making

In Mumbai, or anywhere else for that matter, most musical activity starts with the appropriation of preexisting material. Musicians begin with the familiar as a template from which new meanings can be constructed. As I have shown, "Thanda Thanda Pani," begins with appropriation, but it is transformed by Sehgal into a personal and socio-historic exploration of the social dynamics of urbanization in modern India. The autobiographical nature of Sehgal's music is equally clear in other recordings. For example, in the machine-like staccato rhythms of "Bombay City ka Sapna" ["The Dream of Bombay City"], Sehgal again speaks directly to his audience: "You too have seen the dream of Bombay" [*bombay city ka sapna dekha tu ne*]. Again he appears to share their feelings of alienation and their struggle for success: "The destination isn't far away/Don't despair" [*manzil door nahin hai/ maayus na hona*]. Another song from the same album features a chorus of female singers scrutinizing the Ludhiana *jat* [a Panjabi cultural identity widely and humorously essentialized in India as rural, rustic, unsophisticated, and so on], who has come to Mumbai to try to become an actor. What is particularly notable about the self-revealing nature of these two recordings is that they appear on a 1993 album entitled *Main Bhi Madonna* [*I Am Also Madonna*]. After borrowing from Vanilla Ice and introducing rap to the Indian mainstream, Sehgal's next move was to become Madonna, going so far as to appear on the album cover both as his established rapper persona and dressed in drag as the pop diva wearing a wig, jewels, and lace gloves. Baba Sehgal as Madonna may seem even more improbable than his appropriation of "Ice Ice Baby." However, Seghal does not imitate Vanilla Ice or Madonna so much as he uses their iconic images in a self-reflexive manner, in order to reinvent himself perhaps, but also to take playful jabs at the proclivity of Indian pop singers for the appropriation of the foreign. In this case, his primary target was Indipop superstar Alisha Chinai, who gained notoriety as "the Indian Madonna." In fact, the closer Sehgal gets to mimicking western pop stars, the more his own individuality emerges, as fantasy and reality are viewed side by side.

Versioning as a Tool for Building Brand Equity

As Indipop expanded during the 1990s, artists and executives were well aware of the challenges in unseating the hegemony of film music. One strategy employed by Magnasound was to borrow from established practices and experiences in a strategic effort to produce a sense of familiarity for consumers. The familiarity, therefore, becomes yet another tool to be employed by marketers in order to build brand equity in the domestic music market. I mention three examples here: (1) fan mania as set by the precedent of Elvis, the Beatles, and others; (2) Bollywood songs, images, and dialogue that are part of the everyday vernacular in North India; and (3) the proven popularity of cover versions and remixes, such as "Ice Ice Baby" itself.

One of the most popular simulations in Bollywood song sequences and, consequently, in Indipop music videos is the "live" concert for a crowd of adoring fans. The simulation of fan mania might seem obvious and trite, but for Indipop, it was a central form of mimetic activity that connected artist identity and status to those of established music industry stars. In the video for "Oh Meri Munni" ["Oh My Baby"] (1998), Remo Fernandes arrives for a concert and is met by throngs of fans and television reporters, projecting a model for behavior that his label, Magnasound, would hope to see materialize in the future. The Colonial Cousins video "Sa Ni Dha Pa" ["Do Ti La Sol"] features mock newspaper headlines that foretell a success story starting from their debut release, to sweeping the Grammys, to collaborating with Eric Clapton, and eventually vacationing with Whitney

Houston! Finally, Indipop songs such as Sehgal's "Dil Dhadke" (1992) include lyrical "callouts" to world cities to evoke the sense that his fan base has reached global proportions.

At the same time that Indipop recordings routinely indexed an international audience, they also demonstrated their entrenchment in North Indian popular culture by producing versions and responses to the Hindi film industry. For as much as they sought to distance themselves from Bollywood, Indipop artists inevitably were, and continue to be, understood in relation to film music. In "Jat Ludhiane Ka" ["I'm a Jat from Ludhiana"], for example, Baba Sehgal references two of India's most famous cinematic villains, first rapping one of the widely known monologues delivered by Amjad Khan (in his most famous role as the evil Gabbar Singh in *Sholay*, 1975), and later impersonating the voice of the evil mastermind known as Lion in *Kalicharan* (1976). Indeed, more than other Indipop stars, Sehgal's lyrics draw more directly from Hindi films because of both his non-Anglophone roots and the acceptance of quotations and sampling in the broader hip-hop aesthetic.

By the early 1990s, the proven success of sample-based hip-hop had demonstrated to Sehgal that a version of "Ice Ice Baby" could work. After all, Vanilla Ice's hit itself was a remake. For an aspiring Indian rapper, seeing a white rapper transforming an earlier popular song into the first hip-hop single to top the *Billboard* charts was an inspiration. As a double outsider (an *Indian* rapper and a *non-film* pop star in Bombay), Sehgal had much to gain by following the same path as Vanilla Ice.

Version Songs in Preparation for Future Collaborations

In my interviews with Indipop artists and executives, many noted the importance and desirability of collaborations with international singers, studio musicians, and engineers. In this sense, musical versioning appears not as appropriation but as an illusory collaboration that anticipates more desired face-to-face collaborations. For example, it was because of the success of "Thanda Thanda Pani" and the establishment of his pop persona as a fun-loving and playful character that Baba Sehgal was chosen for one of the first tie-ins between Hollywood and the Indian music industry: the re-recording of the soundtrack for Disney's *The Lion King* in Hindi. This mid-1990s project also featured Indipop diva Anaida in a duet for the song "Hakuna Matata"; it contributed to the global visibility of Indian artists in international projects and anticipated future international collaborations, such as Asha Bhosle's work with the Kronos Quartet or A. R. Rahman's Oscar-winning soundtrack for *Slumdog Millionaire* (2008). In another landmark of international collaboration, the Colonial Cousins—who had fictitiously projected a successful career defined by interactions with celebrities like Michael Jackson and Elizabeth Taylor—went on to be the first Asian artists to perform on the then-coveted MTV Unplugged series, on the same platform as the international stars Eric Clapton, Nirvana, and Bruce Springsteen.

In rock music history, of course, bands such as the Beatles and the Rolling Stones began their careers playing covers, hoping one day to be able to be on the same stage as their idols. Hip-hop culture too has moved from symbolic relationships (in the form of interactions with recorded samples) to a robust practice of guest appearances and collaborations of every possible variety. "Thanda Thanda Pani" becomes even more compelling as an example of this process when one recognizes that Vanilla Ice built his recording upon an established example of successful collaboration, that of David Bowie and Queen. An archeological dig into the layers of popular music history reveals the thread of versioning and collaboration as ever-present.

Versions that Explode Myths of Cultural Authenticity

Although they may be ubiquitous in popular music, we should not assume that the meanings and representational practices of versions are universal. Rather, we must take into account the specific socio-historical contexts in which versions are created and presented. This study has focused primarily on urban North India during the 1990s, the period of Indipop's brief rise to prominence and a time of enormous social change, especially in India's urban centers where the effects of liberalization and globalization were first and most apparent.

Along with economic and technological changes, a "culture war" gripped the country during the 1990s, symptoms of which were readily apparent in Mumbai. The 1992 demolition of the Babri Masjid, a symbol of Hindu-Muslim tensions in the country, was followed by two months of inter-religious rioting in the city and, subsequently, by a series of retaliatory bombings in 1993 and a broad-based hardening of the extreme fundamentalist positions of both Hindus and Muslims. Rajagopal (2001) has argued insightfully that the rise of religious fundamentalism in India was in part an outcome of the proliferation of new media and the expansion of a privatized market economy; but fundamentalist developments, which clearly sought to roll back India's growing cosmopolitanism, were an obvious threat to the makers of Indipop music.

The seeming absurdity of Baba Sehgal appropriating the identity of Vanilla Ice or Madonna can be read as a rejoinder to the absurdity of the escalating forms of religious nationalism and violent movements to promote cultural purity that gripped Mumbai during the early 1990s. Indeed, Sehgal's playful claim that even *he* could be called "Madonna," when set against the then-impending move to rename Bombay after the local goddess Mumba Devi, offers critique through a dialectical relationship. The more intense the effort to rename the city became, the more powerful was Sehgal's lampoon and its inherent critique of any "authentic" identity.

This dynamic evokes Lipsitz's (1994) ideas of "strategic anti-essentialism," which have been influential in my own work and in many other studies on popular music and the politics of identity. Nitasha Sharma's analysis of hip-hop culture among South Asian Americans, for example, devotes a chapter to the issues of appropriation and authenticity, though in the case of American *desi* youth, Sharma argues that they "identify with hip-hop in explicitly racialized ways by recasting constructed divisions of race" (2010, 271). Although my reading of Baba Sehgal is not based as clearly on explicit or strategic elements, amid the backdrop of mass social movements of cultural and religious nationalism, and reflected against the essentialist, family-values fare of mainstream Bollywood during that era, Sehgal's hip-hop identity indexes creative freedom and undermines narratives of both racial purity and multiculturalism in the form of cultures being *separate* but equal (cf. Prasad 2008).

CONCLUSION

In this chapter, I explored the "rolling echo" of one particular sound bite. From a groove born in a collaboration between a Parsi from Bombay and a British glam rock superstar, to a white rapper in Miami searching for a break, and finally to an engineer from Lucknow with a playful personality and dreams of stardom, the story of "Thanda Thanda Pani" can illuminate the complex ways in which mimesis and authenticity operate in globalized popular culture. Crude binaries of original/copy or authentic/counterfeit can have discursive value for local artists and culture brokers, and indeed even for scholars such as myself. But at the same time, such binaries impede our understanding of the unpredictable and wide-ranging circulation of musical ideas and practices in contemporary mass-mediated popular musics. The story of Indipop in the 1990s, as embodied in Sehgal's career, offers a useful lens for looking at this theme. It engages with a discourse of East versus West, *filmi* versus non-*filmi*, authentic versus copy, and real versus fantasy. In doing so, it carves out a place for Indipop itself that reveals a significance for this music—based on a multilayered network of exchanges and influences and a willingness to contest the very binaries that defined it—that exceeds Indipop's popular but thus far faltering history.

For a brief moment in the 1990s, journalists and music executives in India imagined that Indipop stars like Baba Sehgal would render the playback system in Bollywood obsolete. While this has yet to happen, Mumbai's film music world has indeed been transformed by a new generation of singers and music directors with non-film roots. Thus Indipop can only be understood *in relation to* Bollywood. In describing a similar dynamic in punk rock, Dick Hebdige borrows the semiotic term "present absence" to describe the way genres can be defined dialectically: "Punk includes reggae as a *present absence*—a black hole around which punk composes itself" (1979, 68). Likewise, attempts to define Indipop as a legitimate popular music genre must confront the "present absence" of Bollywood. Although some professional musicians no longer see a distinction between the two, attempts to stake out a separate ground for non-film Hindi-language music with a mainstream appeal do continue. Baba Sehgal, two decades removed from his biggest solo album, continues to release new recordings independent of films, such as "Mumbai City" and "Snoop Baba." As the "*baap* [father] of rap" in India, Baba Sehgal has roots in a middle ground of experience that more and more of us find ourselves in, thanks to the Internet and other digital media. In one way, we are living in the tangible realities of the ethnographic present, and in another, we are browsing, sampling, downloading, and networking beyond the limitations of time or space; but as we still gather deeply personal experiences and feelings, we sense the rolling echo of pop music while traversing the musical past, present, and future.

NOTES

1. The video for Baba Sehgal's "Dil Dhadke" can be found on YouTube.
2. Accurate data on album sales are difficult to find for this period of Indian popular music. This figure comes from a piece published about Sehgal in *The New York Times*. See Gargan (1992).
3. As seen in song scenes such as "Woh Ladki Hai Kahaan" ["Where Is that Girl?"] (*Dil Chahta Hai*, 2001) or "Bahara Bahara" ["The Spring Season"] (*I Hate Luv Storys*, 2010).

CHAPTER 9

Making Music Regional in a Delhi Studio

STEFAN FIOL

This chapter offers an ethnographic account of a single Garhwali album being produced within a Delhi studio.[1] The recording studio is a unique ethnographic space: It is bland, without windows, and completely unlike the kinds of spaces in which consumers will listen to the music created in it. Ethnographies of the recording studio have revealed how the recording process can be otherworldly, one step outside of real time and space (Meintjes 2003, 9). With multitrack digital recording, this experience is exaggerated: Sounds are recorded in fragments before being electronically manipulated and mixed together only in the final stages. Hennion suggests that in the recording studio, "the world as a whole is excluded and then reconstituted locally, in a series of punctuated relationships between the actors" (1989, 415).

In the densely packed migrant communities of East Delhi, between Noida to Ghaziabad along the Yamuna River, several hundred recording studios have emerged since the late 1990s. These studios mainly cater to the musicians and small-scale music companies that represent one of northern India's many linguistic and political regions. Despite, or perhaps because of, the intense competition in the music industry, producers, music directors, sound engineers, accompanists, and singers from particular regions tend to form tightly organized, mutually supportive networks. This chapter focuses on one such network and offers an ethnographically grounded narrative of the studio production of Garhwali *geet*, a genre of commercial song produced in the Garhwali language (cf. Alter 1998; Fiol 2008).

In order to create Garhwali *geet*, studio participants transgress the geographic, cultural, and stylistic boundaries of the region. Because the vast majority of recording happens in Delhi, 150 miles from the southern border of Garhwal (in Uttarakhand State), many of the musicians producing Garhwali *geet* hail from other parts of northern India, while others may identify as Garhwali without having visited the region or without speaking the language. It is thus unsurprising that many sonic conventions used in Garhwali *geet* are not part of the traditional soundscape of the Garhwal hills, even if they have come to be accepted as part of the style of the genre. Many of the studio participants who are involved in the production of Garhwali *geet* have also been involved in producing Hindi, Bhojpuri, Maithili, Panjabi, Rajasthani, and other vernacular language albums. Thus, an important question to consider is to what extent Garhwali *geet* actually represents the people and music of Garhwal, and to what extent it replicates more generic "regional folk" or even "*filmi*" styles that resonate across North India. Nonetheless, as I discuss below, certain aspects of Garhwali *geet* recordings are considered essential for sonically evoking "Garhwaliness": for example, *bansuri* (bamboo flute) introductions, pentatonic melodies, nasal and reedy vocal timbres, and particular rhythmic patterns deriving from indigenous drumming styles. Many studio insiders also conceptualize Garhwali *geet* as different from other styles of regional music in more general terms, contrasting the wholesomeness of Garhwali *geet* with the lewdness of Bhojpuri *geet*, the quaintness and sentimentality of Garhwali *geet* with the overt commercialism of Panjabi *geet*, or the cheapness of Garhwali *geet* with the polished professionalism of Hindi film music.

Although a handful of singers have become commercially successful through recordings, the vast majority of singers pay out of pocket to have their music recorded in the hope that an album can help them obtain invitations for stage programs. For people living in the Garhwal hills, the music industry is symptomatic of a broader regional experience of cultural and economic marginalization: The cultural "raw materials" of mountain villages—music, dance, dress, poetry, ritual—are exported to plains-based recording studios to be edited, packaged, and distributed back to consumers in the mountains and in urban migrant communities in the form of commodities that primarily benefit plains-based companies. Yet the centralization of this vernacular industry in Delhi has also been advantageous to many Garhwali artists, who discover support networks of other Garhwali migrants and who often find employment opportunities beyond the Garhwali music industry. Moreover, the distance that separates studio participants from their mountain communities lends emotional potency to the recording process and intensifies the sentiments of longing, nostalgia, frustration, and spirituality found in much of this music. Garhwali singers' experiences of traveling between Garhwal and Delhi—between an outlying region and the urban center of the nation—allow them to serve as cultural intermediaries, crafting the sounds and themes that may be understood as authentically regional, and articulating the desires of regional and national belonging. Ultimately, Garhwali *geet* has become an important mediator for cultural regionalism precisely because it transgresses geographic, cultural, and aesthetic categories.

As many ethnographic studies of studio production have demonstrated, the recording studio also privileges a distinct type of social discourse and a unique set of social roles (e.g., producer, music director, sound engineer, singer, session musician) predicated upon specific kinds of knowledge and behavior (Booth 2008; Greene 2001b, 2003; Manuel 1993, 163–166; Meintjes 2003; Porcello 1996; Scales 2004). If such roles are unique to studio spaces, they nevertheless correlate with social hierarchies of residence, class, caste, and gender that participants negotiate in their everyday lives. In the Garhwali industry, producers, music directors, and engineers are almost exclusively high-caste men; increasingly, they are Garhwali migrants settled in Delhi, but many come from other parts of North India and produce Garhwali *geet* in addition to other regional styles. Some male singers come from one of the two high-caste divisions (Brahmin and Rajput) found throughout Garhwal, but most come directly from the hills and thus have a lower-class status in the urban setting. Female singers and male instrumental accompanists are most often Garhwali migrants settled in Delhi; many of them come from one of the minority lower-caste communities of musical professionals found in the hills. Thus an uneasy demographic split exists between the dominant and unmarked categories of high castes, plains-dwellers, and men in supervisory roles in the studio (producer, music director, engineer) on the one hand, and the marked categories of hill-dwellers, low castes, and women in performance-centered roles on the other. The studio production of Garhwali *geet* is thus a distinctive social field in which power and different kinds of capital are negotiated between participants who occupy positions of relative dominance and subordination (Bourdieu 1977; Scales 2004). Whereas most singers in the Garhwali industry primarily value the recording as a way to enhance social prestige (cultural capital), studio professionals generally value the recording as an emblem of the locality or region that will appeal to the broadest possible consumer base (financial capital).

Below, I describe a recording session that took place in Delhi's Surbhi Studio in March 2005.[2] Surbhi opened in 2003, and it is one of dozens of recording studios that have opened over the past two decades in the alleys of East Delhi. Although specializing in Garhwali *geet*, the studio is rented out to a variety of production companies to create advertisements and a variety of vernacular music albums.

Dramatis Personae

Ajay, the producer of the project being described, is a Panjabi man who came to Delhi in his childhood during partition in 1947 and worked various jobs before opening the music company Himalaya Cassettes in 2001. Since then, he has released 18 cassettes and 25 video compact discs of Himachali and Garhwali *geet*. Vipin is the engineer and owner of Surbhi Studio, but he also happens to be Ajay's nephew; as a result of this relationship, Ajay has recorded the majority of his projects there (see Figure 9.1).

Rakesh is a Garhwali man in his 40s, and is one of only half a dozen well-reputed music directors in the industry. He trained in Hindustani vocal music for two years at the Bhatkhande Music Institute in Dehradun, and he has been the lead singer on seven albums of Garhwali *geet*. Over the last seven years, he has worked as a freelance music director, overseeing

Figure 9.1
Rakesh and Ajay with the author in front of Surbhi Recording Studio. (Photo courtesy of Stefan Fiol.)

the production of albums for both experienced and novice singers. Rakesh has typically worked in a lump-sum payment system whereby producers offer him a contract to oversee the album of a particular artist, and he subsequently subcontracts his own preferred group of accompanists.

This was the first recording project for Biju, a 22-year-old who worked as a lorry driver between Panjab, Garhwal, and Uttar Pradesh. His work had allowed him ample time to listen to cassettes and practice singing inside his cab. Although Biju did not anticipate fame or wealth to result from this recording experience, he had long harbored the dream to make a cassette and share it with friends along his driving route and in his village in Pauri Garhwal. Ajay had earlier told me about the craze for recording commercial albums in Garhwal:

> These [singers] cannot afford [much]. Most of them are, you know, selling vegetables. Some are cleaning residences, and they want to come up with an album. What these people do is, they get together a couple of friends, and just pool their money, say 1,500 or 2,000 bucks [rupees] each. And they're out with the album. You know, that's so damn cheap. [Garhwalis] have that passion for music. It's a desire from inside, "I want to burn an album," and that's the kind of happiness they get. It's their hobby, you know? They don't mind spending, going into losses, because these are not people who are businessmen...[but] they have their need...for fame, recognition. When I'm walking down the street, up in the hills, in Chakrota, and people can recognize [that] he has burned that album, he's that singer. This is why they want music companies, to become popular, not for money. Money is OK; if they've invested [20], and they'll get [20] back, they'll be quite happy. But this is his hobby. So this is why, everyday, new faces are coming. Everyday in the market, two-two-three cassettes are being launched...that's more than Indipop, in such a small region (Ajay Naithani, pers. comm. March 1, 2005).

For Biju, as for most novice Uttarakhandi singers, there were no easy avenues into the regional music industry. Getting the backing of a music director, producer, or studio is nearly impossible without either considerable savings or contacts within the industry. In deciding where and with whom to record, Biju relied upon a friend in his village who had recorded an album at Surbhi Studio and who provided him with the name of a trusted producer, Ajay. When Biju phoned Ajay, Ajay explained that he would try to help him, but he needed to have an idea of Biju's voice. So Biju sang a few lines over the phone, and Ajay told him he liked the "folk tone" of his voice. He agreed to support the project on two conditions: First, Biju would need to prepare the tunes and texts for a minimum of eight songs and then come to Delhi; and second, Biju would have to pay 50 percent of the production cost, or 15,000 rupees ($325), to cover a minimum offset production of 1,200 cassettes. Ajay later told me that he was skeptical about whether Biju would be able to come up with the money, and he showed me a handful of completed masters of first-time singers that had not been released because the singers had not yet come up with the remaining balances owed to the studio. Yet three months later, Biju was on a 12-hour bus journey from Pauri Garhwal to East Delhi with the money from his own savings and a loan from an uncle in Chandigarh.

Preproduction

This was Biju's first trip to the Lakshminagar neighborhood in East Delhi, and he had difficulty tracking down the studio's location in the maze of alleys. When he finally arrived, another Garhwali project was being recorded, and he took his seat on a bench in the small console room. Across from him was a large digital mixer and two computer monitors, taking up nearly half of the room's area; six other people were crammed inside the space, including the music director Rakesh seated behind the keyboard, a young man playing octapad, and several instrumentalists and visitors sipping chai. Through a large double-paned glass window, Biju saw two percussionists with headphones on, playing rhythmic variations in synch with a click track, as shown in Figure 9.2).

Figure 9.2
Biju, Vipin, and Rakesh in the production room. (Photo courtesy of Stefan Fiol.)

The mood of all the participants was relaxed and friendly, and Rakesh immediately made Biju feel welcome, cracking jokes in Garhwali and quizzing him on the details of his village. They moved into the soundproof studio chamber where the percussionists were sitting. Seated at the harmonium, Rakesh proceeded to find Biju's optimal "*Sa*" or tonal center, leading him up and down the scale by half-steps to explore his range. Biju was clearly nervous while singing; he later admitted to me that this was the first time he had sung before an audience since playing a role in the village Ramlila performance as an adolescent. He showed me his notebook of song lyrics, some of which he had composed during his long journeys as a lorry driver, and a few stanzas that he had solicited from a poet in his village. Although Biju prized the originality of his poetic compositions, he was comfortable recycling melodic material from the preexisting tunes commonly used in Garhwali recordings.

Rakesh later explained to me that he thought Biju had a decent sense of pitch and rhythm, but that he was limited by his folk style and a lack of technical knowledge about how an album is made: "The singers from Uttarakhand stay in 'folk,' but those who live [in Delhi] will have the chords in the melody. They have more consciousness about chords, and they don't follow the main melody but the chords. This is the influence of film music, of living in Delhi. They realize what chords are used. But the singer from the hills [like Biju], he will sing exactly in the folk style. He won't leave the line, even if you say cut it off here, he'll keep singing that right to the end." As Biju rehearsed the refrain [*asthai*] of each composition, Rakesh accompanied on the harmonium, stopping to make alterations to a word or a melodic phrase. The percussionists seated nearby began to play a series of variations on the *dholak* and *tabla* synchronized with the melodic rhythm of the refrain (video 9.3). Rakesh then signaled for Biju to continue with the second melodic phrase in the higher tessitura [*antara*], and the percussionists again found a new rhythm. Rakesh taught Biju to sing the antecedent phrase and then pause, leaving a gap for the accompanying instrument(s) to repeat the phrase, before repeating both the antecedent and consequent phrases. Because of the perceived redundancy in the two-phrase structure of most Garhwali *geet*, one of Rakesh's primary tasks as music director was to add variety by extending melodic sections, adding breaks between sections for choral or instrumental passages (often in the form of antecedent-consequent phrases between alternating instruments), and creating innovative intros and codas. According to Rakesh, the use of breaks also provided opportunities for the insertion of coordinated frame sequences in the video format. While Biju's album was going to be released first on cassette and only later in the video CD format (if it proved its value on the market), the comment revealed that music directors arrange sonic elements keeping in mind the potential for visual expression.

Ajay, the producer, was seated to the side, watching their interaction and reading Rakesh's cues. Only once did he speak up, suggesting that Biju's opening track, an invocatory hymn in the style of a *jagar* [possession ritual], be eliminated. "You should leave this for your next album," he explained, "people don't want to hear a *jagar* at the beginning, but something more upbeat, something to get them dancing." Biju protested mildly, admitting that he was personally invested in keeping this song. Ajay thus asked for a compromise, suggesting that they position the song at the beginning of side B. Ajay articulated the need for a diversity of themes and musical elements to attract different kinds of consumers, based largely on his experience of knowing what albums had sold well in the past. Yet he later explained to me that there was no need to alter Biju's list of songs because they conformed rather well to a successful formula. Biju had prepared two romantic duets—one about lovers from the Jaunsar region of western Garhwal, and one traditional dance song describing the flirtatious relationship between a brother-in-law and sister-in-law—a song about the sadness of migration, a song about the beauty of the Himalayas, an education song about environmental preservation, a devotional song (*bhajan*), and a *jagar* invocation in free rhythm.

Production

Once each song on the album had been roughly conceptualized, all the participants moved to the mixing room for a chai break. Biju offered everyone sweets to mark the auspicious occasion of his first recording session. Then Rakesh lit a lamp, recited a few inaudible prayers, and yelled "*Jai Badri Vishal ki...Jai*" ["Victory to Badri Vishal," or Lord Badrinath, a form of Vishnu worshipped in Garhwal], with everyone in the room voicing the syllable "*Jai*" together.

Following this abbreviated ritual, Biju sang a demo track of the first song while Rakesh accompanied him on the Casio keyboard. Then the two percussionists returned to the studio to record the rhythmic variations for this song on *dholak* and *tabla* while listening through headphones to a click track and the demo tracks of the keyboard and singing parts, as shown in Figure 9.4.[3] The most striking aspect of these drumming patterns was the resemblance they bore to indigenous *dhol-damaun* rhythms played in the Garhwal hills.[4] The percussionists from this session were Garhwali but grew up in Delhi and learned classical and light-classical styles of *tabla*

Figure 9.4
Vipin editing and recording percussion patterns. (Photo courtesy of Stefan Fiol.)

accompaniment. One of them explained to me how he had adapted indigenous rhythms to the *tabla/dholak*:

> This was about ten years ago. No, six, seven years ago, when all this folk [craze] started. There were no artists from the hills here in Delhi, they were all from Delhi. So [we] didn't understand [mountain rhythms]. And when these people came from the hills . . . we listened to the patterns of the *dhol-damaun* and adapted it to our drums. And today when we play on stage, we perform Panjabi, Haryani, Bhojpuri. Everything isn't the same to us; we are concerned with [matching] the tune, the composition. And the playing is related to [classical music]: *dadra* [six-beat cycle], *kaherva* [eight-beat cycle], *rupak* [seven-beat cycle]. We can also play classical (Subash Pande, pers. comm. 2005).

This percussionist admitted that the rhythms played by lower-caste, hereditary musicians in the village on the *dhol* were not identical to what he played on the *tabla*, but he also claimed that hill-dwelling drummers lacked the technical know-how and the clarity of playing for studio recording. This was reiterated by Ajay, who started out using rhythmic accompanists from the hills but later switched to more expensive Delhi-based accompanists. "They [from Delhi] are more professional. They'll do things fast. They'll go with the metronome, with the beat—the proper way, in fact" (Ajay Nichani, February 7, 2005). He explained that village drummers have difficulty playing with the metronome, playing indoors, and playing with a defined beginning and ending.

The process of recording the vocal demo track followed by the rhythm tracks was repeated for each song. Three of the eight songs used *kemta tala* (six-beat rhythmic cycle), three songs used *kaherva tala* (eight-beat rhythmic cycle), one song used *deepchandi tala* (14-beat rhythmic cycle), and the *jagar* invocation was in free rhythm. The percussionists were so practiced with these variations that on most of the tracks, they moved continuously through the song form—intro, *asthai*, instrumental interludes (called "music" sections), *antara*, and coda—without the need for verbal instructions or a second take. When there was any discrepancy between their interlocking parts, or with the click track, the percussionists immediately stopped playing. Vipin, the engineer sitting at the console on the other side of the glass (see figure 9.6), dragged the cursor on his computer screen back several bars and with a hand motion and eye contact, he cued the percussionists to "punch" or overdub the head or tail of the track (video 9.5). In order to maintain the flow of the recording, Vipin and the percussionists demonstrated considerable skill at punching, and the process was completed with little to no verbal communication (cf. Porcello 1996, 232).

During the dubbing of the traditional dance song, Rakesh felt that the words of the song conveyed an emotion that would be more appropriate in a slower tempo. Biju countered that this song needed to be presented in a moderately fast tempo because it was a *caunfla* dance song, and he hoped that people in his village would incorporate the song into their dancing at festivals (see Fiol 2011). After some discussion, Rakesh deferred to Biju's

Figure 9.6
Percussionist playing patterns on the *dholak*. (Photo courtesy of Stefan Fiol.)

judgment, admitting that it was important for the song to fit the local conception of what a *caunfla* dance song should sound like. Biju's modest victory reminded me of Meintjes's discussion of the ways that the subordinate artist is often able to challenge the views of the dominant music director, either by playing brilliantly and obfuscating the need for alteration, or by resorting to "cultural authority" in certain matters (2003, 105). Although this was a mild and short-lived dispute, it illuminated entirely different ways of thinking about the functions of the musical commodity. For full-time studio professionals, the album should stand for the diversity of sentiments and practices in Garhwal, and it should appeal to Garhwalis as a commodity that can be appreciated through listening alone. Biju, in contrast, hoped that songs from his album would become locally meaningful in Pauri Garhwal and would be incorporated into festival dance settings. Ultimately, Biju got his way in part because he was a paying client, and in part because Ajay and Rakesh did not expect the cassette to have a wide distribution throughout Garhwal in any case. Biju would be the primary distributor of his own cassette, and thus it was important for him to create an album that was locally, rather than pan-regionally, meaningful.

After lunch, a number of melodic accompanists arrived in the studio and recorded mandolin, bamboo flute, and sitar in succession. The order of recording was largely determined by the accompanists' schedules; many studio accompanists recorded four albums in a single day and spent most of their time running from one studio to another. Ajay and Rakesh selected the instruments for dubbing largely on the basis of the project's budget. When Biju asked whether they couldn't add more instrumental accompaniment to the album, Ajay responded, "We have limitations too. We can't use sitar in every song. If there's just a mandolin there, then we have to use it. If we use the mandolin for four songs, and the sitar for four songs, then our cost doubles. So we try to use the same instruments in all the songs. Expenditure is the main thing" (pers. comm. March 1, 2005). Rakesh also explained to me that when he arranges the music for an album, he thinks about the preferences of the rural consumer and tries to follow the characteristics of each locality within the region. Through trial and error, he has found that Garhwali and Kumaoni consumers responded better to rhythmic innovations, while Jaunsari consumers responded better to variations in instrumentation.

For this recording, Rakesh called in several non-Garhwali accompanists, although this was not his preference. He explained that percussion and flute accompanists should ideally be from the hills because of the need to produce the right "folk feeling":

SF: Is there a difference in the style of playing, in the feeling produced by the accompanists from the hills and elsewhere?

RAKESH: Yes, the musicians should be from the hills (*pahari*). The music director who plays Casio may or may not be from the hills, but the accompanist definitely [should] be, because the "pattern" must be taken from the hills. The flute also will be played by a hill person. The Casio doesn't give that "feel" like the flute and rhythm do. The Casio you might want to play in a "Hindi" style, or an outside style, but the best rhythm will be Uttarakhandi. The proper Uttarakhandi "feeling" should come; if instead of the Uttarakhandi person some foreign one is used the album will be a failure, because the "folk" [sound] doesn't come (pers. comm. March 1, 2005).

A *bansuri* (bamboo flute) performer from Varanasi was present during this conversation, and he agreed with Rakesh's sentiments. Although he had studied all styles of folk and classical music, he claimed that until one lived in a particular region for a long time, it was close to impossible to play with the necessary "feeling." Yet he did feel that one could come close to imitating a regional sound without being brought up there: After living in Bihar for some years, for example, he claimed to be able to play *bansuri* in a "Bhojpuri dialect." But without having visited Uttarakhand or Himachal Pradesh, he admitted that he still needed time to learn the *pahari* (mountain) dialect of flute playing.

This attitude was again put on display in an interaction with the mandolin accompanist who was having difficulty following the rhythm used in one of the tracks. Rakesh played a series of melodic motives on the keyboard and waited for the mandolin player to reproduce the phrase before continuing with the recording. During the dubbing of the interludes, Rakesh interrupted his playing numerous times, asking him to repeat takes. The rhythmic phrasing for this particular song was in a typical Jaunsari pattern that is rhythmically dense and hesitates slightly before each downbeat, making it difficult for this performer to improvise freely. After overdubbing the interlude twice, Rakesh said it was fine and moved on to the next song. But later he decided not to use the mandolin part for this song, explaining that the problems in this performer's playing were not due to any lack of training or experience—it was because he was not Garhwali. "This rhythm is in our blood," Rakesh explained, indicating that one should be born in Garhwal to be comfortable improvising within it. I pointed out that Rakesh (and Biju) were from Pauri (central Garhwal), and that the song in question was from Jaunsar (west Garhwal). Rakesh admitted that his own exposure to Jaunsari rhythms had primarily been through musical recordings, but he maintained that there was a biological basis to a musician's ability to feel the folk rhythms from their region (i.e., state). This is an example of how regionalist discourse has permeated the studio environment in Delhi, naturalizing the relationship among political boundaries, cultural belonging, and biological inheritance.

As per convention on Garhwali *geet* albums, *bansuri* was used liberally on the album (on five of eight songs) and particularly during the free rhythm introductions, the interludes between verses, and the codas. Most of the dubbing was executed in a single take, showing off this performer's facility in expanding or truncating phrases to fit a fixed unit of time. The flautist credited his training in Hindustani music for the accurate pitch placement (here he used the classical term *svara prastara*) of his performance. Despite never having visited Garhwal, the dubbing of the *bansuri* player was quick and smooth.

During spare moments in the day, Rakesh added keyboard parts to the mix, doubling melodies at the octave, adding passing tones and ornamented figures, and creating subtle countermelodies. Rakesh demonstrated how he primarily utilized common harmonic progressions of I-IV-V or i-iv-v in the bass lines and chordal parts, and at the end of phrases, he frequently used ascending arpeggios following the progression I-III-IV, which he termed the "mountain touch." He explained that the keyboard should be used to complement the mood and the acoustic mix of each song. In some places, it was necessary to play more legato chordal passages on the strings sample, while in others he played staccato arpeggios on musette, oboe, bagpipe, or accordion samples. Rakesh occasionally recorded indigenous Garhwali instruments like the *shenai* (oboe) and *mashakbaja* (bagpipe), but because of limited funding and the time needed to tune these instruments precisely to match the other instruments, he decided to substitute keyboard parts on this album.

The next day, after all of the rhythm and instrumental tracks had been recorded, Biju was asked to record his songs along with the female vocalist Rekha. Rekha was a full-time vocalist with considerable classical training; she estimated that she had sung on no less than 5,000 Garhwali albums. The participation of a first-rate female singer such as Rekha is considered essential to the success of a Garhwali album and is often enough to launch the career of an inexperienced male singer. Ajay later explained, "What happens is that when some of these poor people come down from the hills, they have their dream, you know? To have one song with Rekha. It's as if I have done vocals with Lata Mangeshkar. She and I, we have done the same project together. You know, they brag about this kind of stuff" (pers. comm. March 3, 2005). Although the success of this album was directly connected to Rekha's participation, she (and the other handful of regular female vocalists in this regional industry) did not enjoy equal status in this male-dominated industry. Except for one solo album, Rekha had always sung duets with (usually inexperienced) male singers who wrote the lyrics and whose names appeared first on the album cover, while her name appeared second, third, or not at all. Financially, Rekha was remunerated at a fixed rate per song (between 500 and 2,000 rupees), irrespective of the commercial success of the album.

Rekha and Biju stood together in a soundproof chamber with headphones on, each holding up the lyrics on sheets of paper. Biju was clearly nervous about singing with Rekha, but everyone encouraged him. As Ajay had done previously, Rekha commended Biju on the folk tone of his voice, by which she meant the enunciation of the text and the nasal quality of his vocal timbre. Rekha's voice, in contrast, was bright, mellifluous, and extremely high—a thin replica of Lata Mangeshkar's upper range. In this recording, as in others I witnessed, there was an unspoken equivalence of the female voice with sonorous melody, and of the male voice with folk authenticity in timbre, diction, and lyrics. Rekha sang through her part quickly, rehearsing several of Biju's lyrics where she wanted to produce vocal embellishments. All the other participants sat inside the console room, huddled around the computer monitor watching Vipin cut, paste, and re-record parts (video 9.7).

In total, it had taken one full day to dub the percussion and melodic accompanists, and one full day to record the vocal parts for all the songs. Rakesh and Vipin were the only people involved in the production from start to finish, as Ajay was only intermittently present. The process of multitrack recording ensured disjuncture, with rhythmic accompaniment providing the base upon which keyboard fill-ins, keyboard bass, flute, mandolin, sitar, and finally voice were subsequently and independently layered.

Postproduction

Several days later, Biju returned to Garhwal on a bus, leaving Rakesh and the engineer Vipin to finish postproduction. Rakesh was familiar with the Nuendo editing software, but he let Vipin run the controls. Using a form of studio discourse blending Hindi with technical English vocabulary derived from the software program's control menu—cutting, pasting, effects, cloning—they explained the process to me as they went through each song. The first thing Vipin did was to mute the head and tail of each track in the recording, cutting out all extraneous sounds. Then he normalized each track in order to maximize the wave form without exceeding zero decibels, thereby eliminating any distortion. The next step was to equalize each track; this controlled the sharpness or dullness of the timbre. Vipin made only a few adjustments, he said, because he had equalized each track on the console during the dubbing process.

Vipin and Rakesh then listened to each track in its entirety, to ensure that the form of the song was complete. Sections were cut and pasted to elongate or shorten tracks as needed. The lack of clarity in one section of *dholak*-playing led Vipin to seamlessly "drag and drop" from another section of the track. Sound effects such as echo and reverb, common in mainstream Hindi music and higher budget recordings of Garhwali *geet*, were not added in this case because of the low budget, but also because, according to Ajay, "mountain [*pahari*] listeners do not appreciate many effects." In one of the upbeat dance tunes, they added an electronically generated modulation effect to the vocals called D-Tune (also known as Auto-Tune). The use of D-Tune has become popular in Garhwali *geet*, and it is one of the cosmopolitan features that appear to divide the musical tastes of young and old. Although it may be considered an imitation of Western, Indipop, or Bollywood musical practice, I believe it also corresponds to an indigenous preference for nasal and strident timbres.

The final stage of postproduction was the mixing process that engineers consider the most difficult and time-consuming aspect of studio production. Vipin explained that in high- budget productions, many aspects would need to be taken into account during mixing, such as the intention of the song, the flexibility of form, and the diversity of melodic and rhythmic tracks. In most Garhwali recordings, however, there were only a few of rules to follow: "wet and dry" sounds should be balanced, the intensity of vocal and instrumental tracks should be balanced, and percussion should be in the foreground of the mix without dimming the clarity of the lyrics. In tracks that used the sitar, Vipin wanted to increase the overall sound without increasing the wave amplification; the sitar track was thus "cloned," doubling its volume output by pasting it into another track. The average number of tracks used in these recordings was about ten, including *dholak*, *tabla*, octapad, *sitar* (twice), male vocals, female vocals, bass, sustained chords, and in some of the songs, male/female chorus, mandolin, and flute. After a few hours, the tracks of all eight songs were finalized, and each song was "mixed down" or mastered onto a file. Rakesh gave a copy of the master to Ajay, who sometimes suggested changes in terms of a song's overall volume, speed, and balance; in this case, however, he did not suggest any changes, preferring to trust Rakesh's decisions.

CONCLUSION

I focused on this one studio recording session in order to ethnographically document how sound recording is mediated by the diversity of social and musical identities in the studio, and vice versa. I chose this narrative for its ordinariness, in the sense that the majority of Garhwali albums are the result of inexperienced male singers traveling to East Delhi and working with studio professionals of both Garhwali and non-Garhwali backgrounds. Nevertheless, the social and musical processes I described cannot be projected to stand for all recording sessions. Scales reminds us that the studio "is not in itself a site of any one particular kind of social formation or process and that there are a vast number of possible relationships and outcomes within any recording context" (2004, 268). For example, had I focused on the recording process of an established singer in the Garhwali music industry (of which there are no more than a dozen), there would have been a more equal power dynamic between participants in the studio, with less time devoted to preproduction and more to postproduction.

This narrative is in many ways consistent with the conventions of popular music production under market capitalism: There is the conception of an ideal consumer market that guides production decisions; there is geographic and cultural distance between the sites of production in the metropole and the sites of consumption in the village or regional enclave; there is a strict division of labor within the recording studio; there is a goal of producing a musical commodity consisting of approximately eight five-minute tracks; and there is a corpus of musical elements that have come to mark the Garhwali *geet* genre as distinct from other vernacular popular musics (see below). In many other ways, however, this narrative exposes an alternative model of popular music production that relies heavily upon non-market influences. Significantly, because there is no guaranteed return on the investment, music producers demand that inexperienced male singers like Biju fund their albums upfront. This financial arrangement results in a cottage-industry approach to musical production whereby loose networks of artists and producers from distinct sub-regions create albums and distribute them to particular sub-regions of Garhwal. Singers and producers stylistically shape the albums according to the desires and expectations of local constituencies, in addition to their own preconceived ideas about indigenous folk culture. Although personal profit is certainly a motivation for most of the individuals involved in studio recording, there are also other motivations at play, such as the desire for upward social mobility, local prestige, cultural preservation, the pleasure of community and creativity, and the novelty of making a commercial studio album. Only through detailed ethnographies of vernacular musical production can we begin to understand how the principles of market-based capitalism are being subtly adapted to local forms of sociality, knowledge, and value.

Extrapolating from this narrative, it may be possible to identify several sonic features (in addition to the obvious element of language) that are essential to signifying "Garhwaliness." Although some of these sonic features were articulated as important during the studio session, others have become conventional over time and are to some extent unreflexively replicated in one studio production after another. First, several participants commended Biju for the constricted, nasal timbre of his voice, which was referred to as his "folk tone." This is a preferred quality in a great deal of Garhwali singing, and I believe it extends to a preference for the strident, reedy keyboard effects (bagpipe, oboe, or accordion) sampled by music directors. Second, studio participants were generally insistent that the *bansuri* (bamboo flute) should be used on nearly every track of Garhwali *geet*. The ubiquity of the *bansuri* is somewhat strange, as this instrument is seldom played in Garhwal today, though it was prevalent in the past (Petshali 2002).[5]

Third, the use of melodies in pentatonic modes (corresponding roughly with *ragas* like Durga, Bhupali, and Malkauns) is a regular feature of Garhwali *geet* that is rooted in almost all categories of indigenous song. Except for Rakesh and several accompanists, most studio participants I met did not have knowledge of Hindustani musical theory, but they freely borrowed pentatonic melodies from rural song traditions and earlier recordings of Garhwali *geet*. Fourth, Rakesh cited rhythm as probably the single most important and distinguishing feature of Garhwali *geet*. Vipin tended to foreground percussion in the overall mix; no fewer than 4 percussion tracks, and often as many as 15, were layered to produce a full, "wet" sound. While preferring *tabla* and *dholak* to indigenous instrumentation, studio percussionists stressed the importance of rhythmic patterns that had been adapted from indigenous drumming styles in Garhwal (although they also played patterns that could be used on other regional folk recordings). As the example of the mandolin player illustrated, rhythmic aptitude is conceived in biological or ethnic terms; non-Garhwalis are thought to be unable to play certain rhythms correctly because they have not inherited this ability. This discourse is similar to the South African studio context that Meintjes describes in which rhythmic discrepancies were explained as a product of essentialized biological (racial) inheritance, whereas melodic discrepancies were primarily understood as a sign of a lack of musical education (2003, 116–117).

If there are many ways that Garhwali *geet* sounds like other forms of North Indian vernacular popular song (e.g., *asthai/antara* form, monophonic, *raga*-inspired melodies, gendered singing parts, *tabla/dholak* accompaniment), there is also a predictable corpus of melodies, instrumental samples, rhythms, and timbres that uniquely characterize contemporary Garhwali *geet*. But to answer the question "what makes this music Garhwali?" I have stressed an ethnographic approach that goes beyond an examination of discrete, decontextualized sonic attributes, and instead traces the processes of negotiating sound and social position within the studio context. When we learn, for example, that Biju has taken out a loan and traveled 150 miles to fulfill his dream of making an album; that Rakesh has substituted keyboard parts for acoustic instruments because of the lack of a production budget; that Biju has argued for increasing the tempo of a track so that it would be more suitable for communal dancing in his village; that Rakesh conceives of the ability to play with "folk feeling" as a matter of biological inheritance; or that accompanists model many of their *tabla* and *dholak* rhythms on indigenous *dhol-damaun* patterns—such examples expose the multiple motivations and subject positions that are negotiated to produce Garhwali *geet*.

POSTSCRIPT

I caught up with Biju a few months later, long after his album had been released, and I asked him what he thought of the result. "It turned out OK, I guess, but I would have done everything differently in retrospect. I didn't know anything about the studio, and I trusted their judgment. But they didn't really show me how to sing, and they didn't work with my lyrics at all. . . . I wanted a chorus to be used in the romantic duet, and I wanted to have real folk drums on the *jagar* recording . . . my family liked this track best, and said it should have been longer." Biju indicated that he would like to make another album someday, but he didn't think it would be possible anytime soon. He got back about 10,000 of the 15,000 rupees he spent on the album, selling them by hand along his driving route through the hills. Although he was happy to have made the recording, he appeared somewhat disillusioned with the entire process, but he did say, "One thing made it feel worth it, though—when I boarded a bus in Pauri one day and I suddenly heard my cassette being played! That made me feel pretty special."

NOTES

1. I am profoundly grateful to all the producers, sound engineers, and artists who shared their creative processes with me; also to the editors of this volume for their thoughtful guidance. Research for this article was generously supported by fellowships from Fulbright-Hays and the Wenner-Gren Foundation.
2. Names and personal details have been altered in this description, and I have combined observations from several studio sessions observed in 2005 in order to form a more cohesive narrative.
3. The advantage of using a click track is the precision for interlocking multiple percussion parts, allowing the engineer to cut and paste patterns between any sections of a song. A few music directors and accompanists I met preferred not to use it, however, claiming that it takes away from the spontaneity and live sound of the playing by covering up what Keil termed the "participatory discrepancies" in the music.
4. The *dhol-damaun* pair is the heart of musical life in Uttarakhand. The *dhol* is a double-headed barrel drum played on one drumhead with an open hand and on the other drumhead with a stick. The *damaun*, a shallow kettledrum played with two thin sticks, fills in the strong beats of the *dhol* with more regular pulsations.
5. Shepherds in Himachal Pradesh often play small bamboo flutes (*murli*) on extended, high-altitude treks. The cousin of the *bansuri*, the twin flute (*algoja*) was once popularly performed by *Baddi* (or *Beda*) performers, but is now largely obsolete. Although I have not yet conducted research on this topic, the popularity of the *bansuri* in Garhwali *geet* may be related to the longstanding use of the *bansuri* in the dance-song sequences from Hindi films that are shot in mountain landscapes.

PART THREE

Live Music, Performance Cultures, and Re-mediation

Latin American Music in Moving Pictures and Jazzy Cabarets in Mumbai, 1930s–1950s

BRADLEY SHOPE

This chapter explores Latin American popular music production and consumption in the first half of the 20th century in Mumbai. It focuses on the period between the mid-1930s and the early 1950s, when Latin American music in Hollywood films influenced the entertainment approach of jazzy cabarets that targeted specialized audiences of Europeans, British, and elite or minority Indians (predominately Christian Goans, Anglo-Indians, and Parsis). To begin, this chapter traces the popularity of the Carioca—a dance introduced to the world in the 1933 release *Flying Down to Rio* starring Fred Astaire, Ginger Rogers, and Dolores del Rio—in Mumbai, and explores the relationship between this film and the development of local Carioca cabarets. The second half of this chapter uncovers the relationship between live cabarets in Mumbai and the development of Hindi film songs containing Latin American sounds and images. To expound, this chapter investigates the song-dance sequence "Deewana Yeh Parwana" ["An Intoxicated Moth to the Flame"], composed by C. Ramchandra, from the 1951 film *Albela*, which drew inspiration from Latin American cabaret themes in Mumbai and Hollywood films starring Carmen Miranda, such as *Down Argentine Way* (1940) and *That Night in Rio* (1941). Carmen Miranda was a famous Hollywood whose films were screened in India starting from the early 1940s.

From the late 1930s to the late 1940s, Hollywood films with Latin American themes flooded American and international markets. By 1945, 84 films with Latin American subjects had been produced in the United States (Shaw and Dennison 2007, 183), and many were products of the "good neighbor policy" aimed at securing cooperation and understanding between North and South America. These imaginative films, including those starring Carmen Miranda and Dolores del Rio, made use of colorful Latin American stereotypes. Their representations of Latin America showcased non-threatening, welcoming, and high-spirited characters (López 1993, 70–71) that, in India, appealed to select audiences interested in Western music and film. Entrepreneurs and dancehall proprietors in Mumbai designed jazzy cabarets with Latin American themes to target these consumers. At the end of this chapter, I suggest that Hollywood films and Latin themed cabarets in Mumbai inspired a number of enterprising Hindi film song composers and arrangers, including C. Ramchandra, the composer duo Shankar-Jaikishan, O. P. Nayyar, and Naushad Ali. I focus on C. Ramchandra and his trumpet-playing music assistant Chic Chocolate, who were especially influenced by the Latin American music they heard in Hollywood films. The cabaret industry enabled Ramchandra to witness and engage live Latin American music, and supported his strategy of incorporating musical material from a diversity of sources. These (and other) composers wrote in a uniquely identifiable Indian film style through creative use of Western modes and harmonic systems interconnected with Indian musical structures, and through their compositions demonstrated a depth of knowledge of globalized music from across the world that is hard to overestimate.

SCOPE AND ORIENTATION

In the decades leading up to the mid-20th century, international and domestic entertainment groups performed in cabarets, variety shows, and staged revues in live venues throughout Mumbai. Mumbai was a commercial center with busy ports and efficient transportation links to Europe and the Commonwealth, and its doors were open to foreigners and international flows of commodities. To profit from its cosmopolitan character, entrepreneurs opened for-profit theaters and other staged performance spaces in elite hotels, restaurants, and clubs. By the mid-20th century, the colonial administration had built members-only dancehalls in military cantonments, railway institutes, and hill stations throughout India. A wide variety of amateur and professional performers made use of these venues. Dancehall proprietors in Mumbai organized cabarets as early as the late 1910s that included formal dining, alcohol consumption, and designated dancing spaces adjacent to a stage for a floorshow or dance band. Cabarets were often inspired by subject material from Hollywood or European films, and many venues boasted jazz bands composed of foreign musicians, including African Americans. By the late 1940s, Mumbai cabarets and Hollywood cinema influenced a small number of early Hindi film music composers, including those listed above.

As Booth and I explain in the introduction to this volume, most of the studies presented here focus on musical developments during and after India's period of economic and regulatory liberalization. In chapter 2, Natalie Sarrazin suggests that extraordinary changes in technology and media extended the creative possibilities of Hindi film music in the 1990s, which resulted in expanded patterns of film song consumption across the globe. In chapter 5, Jayson Beaster-Jones suggests that the defining characteristics of film music became somewhat more ambiguous beginning in the 1990s in part because new production techniques and digital technologies expanded the scope and character of film songs. Finally, Niko Higgins in chapter 12 claims that changes in dissemination media, especially the Internet, have shaped the development of new fusion music in urban centers throughout South Asia. These and other studies of contemporary music suggest that the character of popular music in India—and indeed popular music anywhere in the world—changes because of shifts in technologies and media, including its production, dissemination, and consumption. Studying past trends in globalization, as I do here, expands our understanding of this process and informs our analysis of contemporary music in India.[1] The approach of this chapter gives historical depth to current developments in transnational music and media, and reinforces the notion that globalization impacted popular music in India during much earlier eras.

HISTORICAL CONTEXT

After the turn of the 20th century, new media and sound technologies supported access to global sounds and broadened the consumer base for Latin American music in jazzy cabarets in North India. But encounters with transnational popular music influenced the entertainment practices of select audiences from at least the mid-1800s, when an emerging performance infrastructure supported international traveling entertainers and early networks of global artistic exchange. The institutional and economic infrastructures of colonialism supported many of these exchanges. For example, British (and Portuguese) military or regimental bands created a demand for instruments and sheet music, and the music curricula of European schools spread knowledge about European music and broadened the scope of its production and consumption. Music stores such as Furtado & Company and Rose & Company sold sheet music and instruments by mail order. From the mid-1800s, retail establishments even sold black minstrel paraphernalia such as banjos, bones, and tambourines. These commodities supported the black minstrel circuit in India. Entertainment entrepreneurs and colonial administrators built new venue spaces to accommodate circuits of traveling performance troupes, and stores sold instruments, sheet music and other music paraphernalia through efficient distribution networks.

By the turn of the 20th century, gramophone recordings disseminated both Indian and Western music, and facilitated increased engagement with commercialized music from around the world in the privacy of the home (Amanda Weidman 2010). Gerry Farrell (1997) claims that the gramophone in India represented "the acme of Western inventiveness, the almost miraculous purveyor of sound on small black discs, a commodity loaded with potent technological and cultural power" (110). From the 1910s, the latest popular music and dance styles from the Americas were available on gramophones, including tangos, maxixes, Sambas, Gaucho dances, ragtimes, and early jazz. But consumers of gramophone discs and other media were far from being exclusively associated with the colonial body. Nor were the products of these entertainment industries solely European or North American origin. The Gramophone and Typewriter Company (GTC) opened its Indian branch in 1901 and by 1908 had opened India's first record pressing plant in Calcutta, gaining a clear market advantage at the time. Indian musicians and artists constituted the primary artistic pool for their recordings, including performers from the theater and drama industries. Thus, soon after gramophone players and discs became established import commodities, local producers began recording Indian content. India boasted a vibrant market for both locally-produced and imported gramophone discs.

The turn of the 20th century witnessed the proliferation of gramophones, radio broadcasting, and moving picture exhibitions, and in the 1920s, entrepreneurs took advantage of business opportunities in the for-profit jazz entertainment industry and built new clubs and hotel dance spaces to support a growing demand for dance bands. The pervasive dissemination of foreign cinema influenced the content and character of performances of live music, and jazzy cabarets often featured thematic material from British and Hollywood films. Ballroom dancehalls began to accommodate American-style cabarets that featured dinner and dance bands with reserved seating in an intimate setting.[2] Latin American popular music was one part of the development of this cabaret industry and supported a tripartite creative cross-pollination between musicians, audiences, and entertainment entrepreneurs. By the time *Flying Down to Rio* was screened in North India in 1934, innovative entertainment commerce and reconfigured artistic (and economic) dissemination patterns circulated jazz and Latin American music in specialized venues throughout the country.

FLYING DOWN TO RIO

A taste for Latin American popular music was shaped by its distant geographic origins, exotic underpinnings, and its capacity to musically embody cosmopolitan awareness of the wider world. Musicologists and ethnomusicologists have addressed cosmopolitanism in a variety of contexts and have offered a number of definitions. Paul Greene, following Pollock et al. (2000) and others, straightforwardly suggests that cosmopolitanism involves "various ways of thinking and feeling beyond the local" (Greene 2011, 92). Martin Stokes (2007) defines musical cosmopolitanism as the "located ambitions, desires and dreams that situate the music we make and listen to in a 'world'" (6; see also Largey 2006). Audiences listening to Latin American music in India clearly sought out a sense of shared cosmopolitanism, and skillfully embraced the wider world through detailed knowledge of music and popular culture on a global scale.

Foreign cinema enthusiasts in India flocked to Hollywood films that showcased Latin American themes. The film *Flying Down to* Rio (1933) (figure 10.1) is a useful example to consider. This successful Hollywood film was screened for weeks in urban centers throughout India in 1934. Hollywood icons Fred Astaire and Ginger Rogers danced the Carioca in an elaborate cabaret scene and promoted it as a new style of dance from Rio de Janeiro. For months, audiences attended Carioca dances and theme shows in Mumbai in nightclubs, restaurants, hotel ballrooms, social clubs, and dancehalls.

Newspaper reviews were overwhelmingly positive. The *Times of India* wrote in June 1934 that the Carioca was a "New Exotic Dance," complete with a "Brazilian native orchestra."[3] Some articles claimed the Carioca was edgy, using terms such as "bizarrerie." One review argued that the film was uniquely exceptional and asserted that it was "well on the way to breaking all records for a film of this type in Bombay."[4] Another claimed that the film

Figure 10.1
Advertisement for *Flying Down to Rio*, *Times of India*, 1934.

had "conquered all Bombay crowds [who] clamour[ed] to see it in spite of the terrific rains."[5]

The Carioca dance scene is set in a cabaret, complete with a large stage and elaborate decor. It begins with Astaire and Rogers sitting at a dinner table commenting on the curious and complex nature of the dance, including the fast footwork and sexually charged touching of foreheads, a primary defining characteristics of the dance. Astaire, in a moment of inspiration, tells Rogers, "I'd like to try this thing just once. C'mon, Honey." Rogers confidently responds, "We'll show 'em a thing or three." They then try the dance and quickly become the focus of attention because of their fancy, percussive foot moves and stylized dancing (video 10.2). Astaire and Rogers take control of the choreography and openly enjoy its unique character and style, which give the dance legitimacy and acceptability in the face of its strong sexual overtones. Rogers and Astaire then leave the cabaret stage, and a choreographed performance takes over that includes close-up shots of couples dancing. Rogers and Astaire then rejoin the group and demonstrate confidence at completing a successful crossover into a dance from Brazil.

This scene points to larger ideas about South America typical of Hollywood films that emphasized expressions of Latinized exoticism through music and dance (see Swanson 2010, 73). *Flying Down to Rio* in many ways characterized North Americans as uninhibited and South Americans at the mercy of conservative social values. This stereotype is somewhat atypical in Hollywood films with Latin American themes. Brazilians were typically represented more animated and boundless than their North American counterparts. The topsy-turvy stereotype in *Flying Down to Rio* offered justification for audiences in India and elsewhere to accept the questionable exotic dance moves of the Carioca. Further, the music in this song and dance scene incorporated a diversity of stylistic elements from Hollywood show tunes and tap routines, and audiences were treated to tempered sexual behavior through dancing performed by well-known Hollywood stars. The film conflated Brazil with the origins of the Carioca, tempered it with a safe and exotic appeal through the routines of Astaire and Rogers, and successfully juxtaposed Rio de Janeiro with the familiar character of Hollywood, thus making it available to mass audiences.

Live-venue cabarets in Mumbai boasted Carioca dancing for months after the initial screening of *Flying Down to Rio*, spearheaded by local jazz orchestras and traveling troupes from cruise ships. Sometimes these cabarets boasted elaborately choreographed representations of the Carioca, and other times orchestras simply programmed the song itself into an evening's repertoire. Audiences learned the dance by watching the film or through lessons at local dance schools, including the Alpha School of Dancing in Mumbai.[6] Joseph Ghisleri's Symphonians, a dance band in residency at the ballroom of the Taj Mahal Palace Hotel, situated along the shore of Mumbai's inner harbor, regularly performed the Carioca in 1934. According to the *Times of India*:

> The Carioca tune from "Flying Down to Rio" is extremely intriguing. It has a rhythm peculiarly it's [*sic*] own. One trace of a little of the Tango, a little of the rumba, and more than a spice of the Brazilian maxixe. The mixture makes it fascinating, so much so that Jos[eph] Ghisleri has already included it in the repertoire of the Symphonians.[7]

Ghisleri's orchestra was composed of an impressive mix of foreign and local musicians, which increased their popularity among audiences who desired to witness the most up-to-date sounds performed by international professional orchestras. Ghisleri's orchestra also included African American musicians who by their very presence in India infused live performances of the Carioca with exotic intrigue. Cabaret program booklets and newspaper advertisements marketed African American musicians living in India using racial iconographies such as balloon-like heads, exaggerated red lips, and cartoonish body postures. During this summer, Joseph Ghisleri aggressively promoted his trumpeter Crickett Smith, an African American musician from New York City, in his Carioca events.[8] As a black musician, Smith added a nebulous layer of African American authenticity to the Carioca and he fit neatly into localized representations of Afro-Brazilian performance practices and stereotypes.

Crickett Smith was one of a number of African American jazz musicians to arrive in India in the 1930s. Teddy Weatherford, Roy Butler, Rudy Jackson, Creighton Thompson, Bill Coleman, Leon Abby, and others came from the Chicago and New York jazz scenes of the early 20th century and offered a layer of legitimacy to jazz and Latin American performances in India (Shope 2007). These musicians were considered innovative and exemplary jazz artists and commanded authority in jazz connoisseurship.

The proprietors of a number of expensive hotels designed thematic shows in 1934 to benefit from the increased attention to the Carioca and *Flying Down to Rio*, and entertainers often choreographed elaborate cabaret performances. For example, the cabaret duo Iwe and Iwe, in residency at the Taj Mahal Palace Hotel, designed two shows that included a Carioca dance competition.[9] Joseph Ghislerie performed the music for Iwe and Iwe, and the show received critical acclaim. Other cabarets boasted Carioca themes even in 1935, months after the first screening of *Flying Down to Rio*. Shows were not limited to the Taj Mahal Palace Hotel. The Excelsior Theatre, for years a venue for variety entertainment, organized regular Carioca events.[10] The Capitol in Mumbai boasted Carioca or Brazil cabarets performed by the Tropical Express Review, a Latin-themed variety troupe that received a "Wild Reception" among audiences.[11]

Throughout the first half of the 20th century in India, Latin American popular music was partially defined through the manufactured exotics and black primitivism associated with its assumed African origins. A 1921 article in the *Times of India* that addressed the popularity of Latin American music in dancehalls around the world suggested that the "first inventors of the Argentine tango, the Brazilian maxixe, and the numberless dances of Cuba were all negros.... The negro has a great sense of cadence."[12] This newspaper article proposes that musicians of African ancestry carried innate musical abilities that helped define the untamed, exotic nature of the Carioca, which might have appealed to British and European audiences in India. The mixed background of the "native" orchestra in *Flying Down to Rio*, the nebulous Afro-Brazilian origins of the Carioca, and the Hollywood authenticity of Astaire and Rogers created exotic appeal through knowledge of distant geographies. The *Times of India* claims that Latin American music originated in Africa not only to suggest it had primitive appeal, but also to hint at a transnational depth that was attractive to audiences. Latin American music brought the wider world and all of its racial, musical, and cultural associations into the domestic entertainment industry.

LATIN AMERICAN CABARETS

Attention to Latin American dance began two decades before the arrival of *Flying Down to Rio* in 1934. Though this film brought Latin American music to audiences in India efficiently and expansively, gramophones mediated Latin music's initial presence in India years earlier. Gramophone companies imported discs of the maxixe in 1914 in Mumbai.[13] The origins of this dance in its ballroom manifestation are ambiguous and contentious, but it was typically considered to be a combination of the tango, the *lundu*, and the habanera, among other styles. It was sometimes referred to as the Brazilian tango or South American tango in advertisements in India. Elite venues such as the Excelsior, the Taj Mahal Palace Hotel, and the Gaiety promoted maxixe dance lessons and cabaret performances. That year, gramophone discs of the South American tango, which many listeners in India believed was similar to the maxixe, were easily available in stores and by mail order, and were widely advertised by "His Master's Voice" in large newspaper spreads.[14] The gramophone medium itself increased taste for the maxixe, and gramophone advertisements helped disseminate knowledge about its popularity. The popularity of the maxixe in 1914 in India followed the maxixe fad that swept the United States the same year. Seigel (2005) suggests that the global reception of the maxixe represented a series of Afro-diasporic encounters popular in the 1910s (94), echoed two decades later by the Carioca (96).

Sill another maxixe revival occurred in Mumbai in 1933. One reviewer in March of that year wrote that "[f]rom Brazil comes a very fascinating dance, called the Maxixe ... being of Gaucho origin, it is of a quite different expression and preferred by many people."[15] The terms "maxixe" and "samba" seemed to have been used interchangeably, and nebulousness in definition and scope was apparent. The samba was labeled in one cabaret that year in Mumbai as a "clever Burlesque" and a "a very clever and graceful dance of the maxixe type."[16] In early 1934, the Taj Mahal Palace Hotel ballroom boasted a cabaret theme that focused on revivals of old dances, and reviews suggest that these included the "Mattchiche" or the "Maxixe Bresilienne," again nebulously defined styles of Latin American tango or samba.

Newspaper advertisements and reviews often labeled this renewed interest in the Latin American tango and maxixe in 1933 and early 1934 as gaucho music and dance revivals. One cabaret review at the Taj Mahal Palace Hotel in 1933 described the maxixe as "a dance of South America full of the traditional Gaucho movements."[17] The term "gaucho" at the time loosely referred to a cowboy, cattleman, or herdsman of South America, particularly southern Brazil, Chile, Argentina, Paraguay, or Uruguay. Gaucho branding added an additional element of exotic appeal. Select audiences were introduced to films that included gaucho characters or lifestyles beginning in the 1920s. Rudoph Valentino dressed in typical gaucho clothing and danced the Argentine tango in *A Sainted Devil*, which was screened in India in 1926. *The Gaucho*, starring Douglas Fairbanks, was screened in Mumbai in 1928. Additionally, the BBC broadcast "Danza de Gaucho" ["Gaucho's Dance"] to audiences in Mumbai occasionally throughout the 1930s. By this time, film and cabaret audiences in India conflated the tango and maxixe with romantic notions of gaucho lifestyles featured in foreign cinema.

By the 1940s, many jazz orchestras understood that learning Latin American repertoire could help secure more jobs performing in a larger scope of venues. Many venues hired orchestras that promoted a Latin American brand. The Taj Mahal Palace Hotel in Mumbai hired José Gadimbas and His Latin American Band in November 1948 to perform in the main air-conditioned ballroom. Gadimbas's orchestra came directly from high-end establishments in France, and their image and repertoire reflected a taste for manufactured Latin American music and images; they were labeled a Latin American group even though they were largely European. They performed nightly through 1949 at the Taj Mahal Palace Hotel and the adjacent Green's Hotel. The Gadimbas Orchestra was one of the first well-publicized foreign groups to regularly promote Latin American themes.

Latin American popular music entered the repertoire of most jazz orchestras in Mumbai after the success of the Gadimbas Orchestra. The June 4, 1949 edition of the serial brochure of the Federation of Musicians (India) stressed that "Latin American numbers go over big with the audience[s]...bands all over the country would do well to study the trend and stock up." A review of the Mumbai Swing Club concert on March 13, 1949, suggested that a section of the program titled "Latin American

Rhapsody" was the highlight of the evening. This portion of the program featured a "fast samba" titled "Tico Tico,"[18] which is a traditional Brazilian *chorinho* piece popularized by Carmen Miranda in her 1947 film *Copacabana*. This piece featured accordionist Goody Seervai, who later recorded for Hindi film composers Shankar-Jaikishan, and a "slower samba" section titled "Veni-Veni" led by timbales player Eddie Jones. Meanwhile, on February 4, 1949, a concert at the Swing Club boasted a samba written by local dance band leader Hal Green titled "Latin Americana" that was a big hit, and one review claimed that "to say it was well received would be putting it mildly."[19] These and other Latin American-themed events in 1949 were sometimes supported by elaborately decorated cabarets, complete with amateur dancers solicited through classified ads.[20] It is no coincidence that 1949 was the year that C. Ramchandra composed the music for *Samadhi*, which was his initial foray into Latin American (and jazz) music. The song "Gore, Gore, O Banke Chore" ["O Fair One, Pass by My Neighborhood"] from this film borrows heavily from the song "Chico, Chico from Puerto Rico" performed by Carmen Miranda in *Doll Face* (1945). Ramchandra was heavily influenced by cabarets and live music events similar to the ones described above.

Carmen Miranda's Hollywood films of the 1940s increased the popularity of Hollywood representations of Latin America in India. Films such as *That Night in Rio* and *Down Argentine Way* were screened beginning in 1941 and occasionally reappeared throughout the decade into the 1950s. The Ritz, a popular cabaret venue in the late 1940s, boasted a "South American Nights" cabaret act influenced by Miranda's films and performed by local dance band Johnny Baptist and His Rhumba Orchestra. Audiences were urged to dress "South Americano."[21] These trends occurred in smaller urban centers as well. On Friday, May 4, 1945, at the Mayfair Ballroom in Lucknow (an interior city in Uttar Pradesh), the cabaret artist Ramonde impersonated Carmen Miranda, accompanied by a 14-piece American swing band[22] composed of U.S. military personnel stationed in the city.[23] Carmen Miranda impersonators were booked through the late 1940s in Lucknow and other urban centers in North India.

HINDI FILMS

Hollywood cinema, cabaret productions, and local jazz musicians influenced some of the core Hindi film song composers and arrangers of the 1940s and 1950s. These composers were highly adept at integrating commercialized music into their compositional approach and practice. The use of jazzy elements in films, especially early on, was restrained and subtle, and composers did not necessarily secure the talents of local musicians in Mumbai. Latin characteristics are heard as early as 1943 in scores composed by Naushad Ali. His 1943 film *Kanoon*, the song "Ek Tu Ho, Ek Main Hoon" ["It's You and Me"] showcases a prominent Latin American three+two clave rhythmic pattern that is preceded by a busy piano introduction that hints at early piano rags, perhaps "The Entertainer" by Scott Joplin. We also hear a busy muted trumpet. Another early film, *Anmol Ghadi* (1946), also uses jazz-like elements, but in this film, the influences are unobtrusive and cautious. The song "Man Leta Hai Angdai" ["I am Overcome with Apathy"] (video 10.3) carries a pronounced Latin American clave throughout and begins with a solo muted trumpet fanfare, a technique seen in many early pieces as a way to signal to the listener that they will be treated to a lively orchestrated jazzy piece.

By 1950, a handful of composers and arrangers continued to heavily infuse songs with Latin American elements. C. Ramchandra attended jazzy cabarets and interacted with a number of Mumbai jazz performers, including Chic Chocolate. Chocolate and other local cabaret musicians provided the talent to produce many of his compositions. The staged cabaret sequence "Deewana Yeh Parwana" from the 1951 film *Albela* perhaps most explicitly showcases the collaborative accomplishments of Chocolate and Ramchandra. Chocolate performed Latin American music in dance bands as early as 1941 with his group, Chic and His Music Makers. They recorded 20 tracks between 1943 and 1945 with Columbia Records, some of which showcased Latin American sounds. Most were covers of songs appearing in Hollywood films, including a few rumbas like "She's a Bombshell from Brooklyn" and "You Discover You're in New York," both performed by Carmen Miranda. C. Ramchandra frequented Green's Hotel in Mumbai to hear Chic Chocolate's band in the 1940s and 1950s. In fact, a number of cabaret program booklets from the 1950s thank Ramchandra, who often attended original swing competitions "by special courtesy of Filmistan Limited."[24] Ramchandra actively sought out dance band musicians to record, arrange, and compose for his films, and he made use of Chocolate's experience performing jazz and Latin American music in live venues.

C. Ramchandra is the credited composer of *Albela*. Before his work with Chocolate, early Ramchandra works such as *Nirala* (1950), *Namoona* (1949), *Sargam* (1950), and *Samadhi* (1950) also made use of Latin American sounds, and many display dance band-style orchestras in the background like the ones that he would have seen in cabarets, often complete with European or American musicians.

Chocolate and his orchestra are dressed in stylized Latin American costumes in "Deewana Yeh Parwana" (video 10.4), and they perform instruments associated with Latin American popular music such as the shekeré, the cylindrical shaker, and the bongos. The opening shot focuses on the hero Bhagwan playing a conga drum, which puts down a rhythmic foundation that is then layered by the bongos and the shaker. The camera slowly zooms out, and the entire band is visible just as a muted trumpet fanfare begins, fully establishing a Latin American jazz orchestra sound. The orchestra is not on a bandstand; the musicians are positioned individually on an elaborately designed inclining stage. The heroine Geeta Bali then appears at the top of the stage posed with hands in the air, and slowly makes her way down to the front to meet Bhagwan. Muted trumpet solos and breaks by Chocolate are frequent. The dancing contains a mixture of Spanish, Indian, and Carmen Miranda-flavored moves interspersed with some swing dancing.

The song-dance sequence "Week-End in Havana" from the 1941 Carmen Miranda film of the same name bears noticeable similarities to the *Albela* song-dance scene. *Week-End in Havana* was screened to enthusiastic crowds in India throughout the 1940s and 1950s, and local music stores sold imported recordings of songs from this film. The "Week-End in Havana" scene starts with a rhythmic foundation on a low conga-style drum, followed by a roll on smaller bongo drums, shakers, and then an entrance of the entire band, led by a muted trumpet performed with the bell positioned upward, curiously similar to Chocolate's stance at the beginning of "Deewana Yeh Parwaana." The costumes of Miranda's orchestra bear a striking resemblance to those worn by Chic Chocolate and his band.

The striking resemblance of the music, dance, stage proxemics, and costume in *Albela* to the staged musical material of Carmen Miranda films is hard to ignore. The introductory materials of many of Carmen Miranda's musical segments often begin with her posed at the top of an elaborately designed structure from which she descends. She is often hidden in darkness while the band plays introductory material, and then begins her descent as the lights come on. Frequently, the band is not on a formal bandstand, but informally positioned to her side. Many variations of such scenes begin by focusing on an instrument, perhaps a drum or a shekeré, from which the camera expands outward as the introductory material ends and Miranda enters. Many of these formulaic elements are seen in the musical segment "I like To Be Loved by You" from the film *Greenwich Village* (1944), the segment "Batucada" from the film *If I'm Lucky* (1946), and the song "Tico Tico no Fubá" from the film *Copacabana* (1947).

Other scenes in *Albela* mirror the Latin American music of Carmen Miranda films. The song sequence "Dil Dhadke Nazar Sharmaye" ["Fearful Heart Is Embarrassed"] incorporates an implied three + two clave. The pickup into the second beat of this song and another titled "Mere Dil Ki Ghadi Kare Tik Tik Tik" ["The Watch in My Heart Goes Tick Tick Tick] is emphasized by a rolling piano, which gives a Latin American feel, and is a technique prominently featured in some musical segments of Miranda's films *Copacabana* and *That Night in Rio*. Further, many of Geeta Bali's dance solos in *Albela* include brief yet pronounced moves that mirror those of Carmen Miranda, including quick samba-style footwork.

Hindi film audiences were not typically exposed to Hollywood cinema. The overwhelming majority of the film audience for *Albela* would not have been directly involved in the regular consumption of Miranda's images or would not have known of her at all. Borrowing material from Miranda's song sequences infused "Deewana Yeh Parwaana" with a fantasy of an unaccompanied female dominating the highest point of an upwardly tiered stage descending to her unsupervised lover amid images of elaborately dressed musicians. The producers of "Deewana Yeh Parwaana" followed a strategy of creating exotic appeal through the use of foreign material that rose above real-life limitations and restrictions in India.

CONCLUSION

Latin American popular music is one example of the dissemination and commercialization of thematic ideas in both cabarets and early films, and is one part of a long and complex history of popular music development in India that enabled musical exchanges between live and recorded performance mediums. Similar exchanges existed for decades prior to the early 20th century, influenced by advances in commodity distribution networks and sound technologies. In the end, artistic exchange within the domain of Latin American music operated effectively between Hindi films and local music economies, facilitated exposure to performance practices that were both global and local in scope and orientation, and contributed in one small part to the complex development of early Hindi film music. To be sure, other thematic materials, such as Hawaiian, Island, Spanish, Arab, and French, were infused into cabaret themes, so my case study of Latin American popular music is just one example. Audiences embraced a wide variety of music because of its capacity to access the wider world beyond India, and my exploration of Latin American popular music illustrates that a complex set of exchanges between multiple styles of foreign and domestic sounds has occurred throughout the history of popular music development in India.

NOTES

1. See Cristina Magaldi (2009) and Derek Scott (2008) for discussions of earlier examples of the globalization of music.
2. The first documented evidence I found of a cabaret in India was in 1916. See *Times of India*, November 25, 1916.
3. *Times of India*, June 16, 1934.
4. *Times of India*, June 30, 1934.
5. *Times of India*, June 18, 1934.
6. *Times of India*, February 3, 1935.
7. *Times of India*, June 29, 1934.
8. As an African American, he joined the group to critical acclaim, with reviews claiming he displayed the most "unusual and striking effects" in his playing style. *Times of India*, Mumbai edition, July 6, 1934.
9. *Times of India*, July 6, 1934.
10. *Times of India*, October 1, 1934.
11. *Times of India*, February 3, 1935.
12. *Times of India*, May 6, 1921.
13. The gramophone was available in stores in large urban centers beginning in the 1890s.
14. *Times of India*, February 21, 1914.
15. *Times of India*, March 24, 1933.
16. *Times of India*, October 23, 1933.
17. *Times of India*, February 3, 1933.
18. From a Federation of Musicians (India) publication printed on June 4, 1949.
19. Ibid.
20. *Times of India*, July 13, 1948.
21. *Times of India*, July 22, 1948.
22. Many military units, both British and American, started ad hoc swing bands, and this band was likely composed of U.S. servicemen stationed in Lucknow or the nearby city of Kanpur. They were in high demand. The orchestra was led by Lee Connelly.
23. See *Pioneer*, Lucknow edition, May 3, 1944.
24. See *Times of India*, June 15, 1950.

CHAPTER 11

The Beat Comes to India

The Incorporation of Rock Music into the

Indian Soundscape

GREGORY D. BOOTH

This chapter offers three case studies on music that has variously been
identified as rock 'n' roll, beat, and/or rock music.[1] In the United
States, the first and last of these terms had relatively distinct generic
and historical implications; the same implications applied in Britain,
although the term "rock 'n' roll" was often replaced by the term "beat
music." The Indian press generally followed the British practice, referring to guitar bands as "beat groups" well after the term (and the music)
had been replaced by the rock music of the later 1960s and onward (see
below). Musicians themselves adopted the new shorter American term
more quickly, calling themselves rock musicians, sometimes applying
the term retroactively and sometimes ignoring any possible genre distinctions. In a conversation with me in 2011, Suresh Bhojwani, a member of one of India's earliest guitar bands (and proud owner of the first
Fender Stratocaster guitar in Mumbai), used all three terms in less than
a minute. Speaking of 1963, Bhojwani recalled that "there was no real
music scene, no rock and roll scene, what we used to call beat groups."
Bhojwani was 15 years old at the time. "I used to go to Bangalore a lot,
like for school holidays and those things. Bangalore had a more thriving
rock scene at that time, more than Bombay. They were much more up on
what's happening." Because these distinctions are ambiguously used in

many contexts, I report usages as recorded, but otherwise use the term "rock" to refer to all guitar band music of the 1950s–1990s.

India's first, tentative engagement with rock music was more visual than musical. Nasir Hussain's 1957 film *Tumsa Nahin Dekha* represented "the Hindi cinema's first consistent attempt to address a Westernized teenage audience" (Rajadhyaksha and Willemen 1995, 113). That attempt centered around actor Shammi Kapoor, who developed his resemblance to Elvis Presley and his aptitude for dancing in the song scenes of subsequent films such as *Dil Deke Dekho* (1959), *China Town* (1962), and *Kashmir ki Kali* (1964). Most of the songs to which Kapoor danced, however, bore little resemblance to rock 'n' roll. They offered listeners a highly arranged, light pop style that had been composed (for the most part) and performed by the same older generation of multipurpose composers and studio musicians who produced everything else in the Hindi film music industry. Although the song scenes found in these films were unquestionably attempts to address Westernized teenagers in India, no teenagers were involved in the creation or performance of this music.

The first actual attempts by young Indian rock fans to address their peers through the performance of rock began around 1960 and had coalesced into identifiable bands by 1963. From that time, rock music—in a diverse range of stylistic, linguistic, and industrial forms—has continued to form a part of India's popular music soundscape. The careers of those who created India's rock 'n' roll, however, and the options for those who sought to listen to it, were consistently vulnerable to the effects of rock's transplantation to an environment in which rock musicians and their music struggled to fit into the musical and industrial mainstream, both of which focused on film song. At the broadest level of culture and in the context of India's culture industry, rock was almost invisible.

This chapter does not offer a comprehensive history of rock in India, or even in Mumbai. Those topics require more extensive treatment and research. Here, I examine the factors and conditions defining specific moments in the careers of three specific rock bands from Mumbai: the Jets in the mid-1960s, Waterfront in the mid-1970s, and Rock Machine (later renamed Indus Creed) in the late 1980s. These choices offer unique perspectives on the rock scenes of these years, while simultaneously providing a basis for understanding broader, systemic changes in rock and popular music over the entire period from the mid-1960s to the mid-1990s. These bands illustrate rock's changing cultural and industrial place in the Indian soundscape. These careers also illustrate rock's cultural, linguistic, stylistic, and industrial vulnerability in that soundscape.

Rock's place in the Indian soundscape and music industry was affected by three interconnected conditions: (1) India's postcolonial identity vis-à-vis the cultural practices and content of the former colonial culture (Great Britain) and the hegemonic influences of the U.S. music industry; (2) the economic and regulatory structures of an essentially socialist Indian government; and (3) the unique nature of India's culture industries and the almost nonexistent market for recorded music as a standalone commodity between 1950 and 1980.

India's postcolonial identity affected the attitudes of both the Indian government and large portions of the Indian public who responded variously to the newly, if only partially, "foreign" nature of Western-style nightlife: social dancing, nightclubs, dance clubs, and the consumption of alcohol. These responses problematized the already limited market for the equally foreign music that was economically supported by that nightlife culture. The sometimes-negative attitude toward British/American cultural forms and practices, however tentative or unspoken it may have been, was especially important (and sometimes problematic) for Indians whose cultural heritages connected them directly to the biological and/or cultural heredities of colonialism. Indians in these categories—Goan Christian, Parsi, Anglo-Indian, and other minority groups with similar associations—were major leaders in the production of early Indian rock.

Until the mid-1990s, Indian rockers sang in English. Thus, listening to or playing rock inevitably aligned its proponents with the ideals, fashions, and behaviors of Western youth, at least to some extent. English was also important for the *Junior Statesman* [hereafter *JS*], a new weekly culture magazine that highlighted the music, fashion, and ideologies of Western popular culture from the late 1960s through the 1970s. Journalist and commentator Dubby Bhagat said that *JS*'s target market were "those people who talked English, thought English and went on to do jobs where English was essential" (pers. comm. via e-mail, 2006). Bhagat also argued, however, that rock fans used their preferred music to reinforce two quite distinct ideological positions: "Young [people] were divided into the people who could afford the whole Carnaby Street apparel and those who deliberately (while listening to rock music) made it a point to be very, very Indian by wearing *khadi* [traditional handloom cloth, with nationalist, Gandhian ideological implications]. The *khadi* lot talked Hindi and the others English" (ibid.).

Rock's ambiguity was part of a deeper Indian ambivalence regarding the place and the value of Western popular culture in a postcolonial nation, even for those Bhagat might have called the "Carnaby Street lot." A 1971

JS editorial makes clear what might indeed be described as the "love-hate" nature of that ambivalence: "Your best friend might tell you if you've got it...they call it 'American Culture,' and anyone who has it...is considered a cross between a moron, an anti-people person and a social subversive" (Supriya 1971, 4). The editorial continued by noting that characteristic "symptoms" of this condition included "long hair, tight trousers, sports shirts, and a passion for pop music." It is clear that many young Indians were seeking to engage with, if not emulate, Western culture; but it appears they wished to do so on terms that suited their own sense of Indian identity and (perhaps) nationalism.

Even for those committed fans of Western culture, the economic and regulatory structures that were imposed by the Indian government effectively restricted access to both physical products (music players, musical instruments, performance equipment, etc.) and cultural commodities (such as recordings, films, and print material) of the West. The "License Raj" (see the volume's introduction) and its consequences kept many transnational music companies from distributing their products in India or made those products that were distributed prohibitively expensive. Together with the concomitant concerns over the potential influences of foreign (and largely Western) corporate capitalism and over earlier phases of what would later be called globalization, this environment limited audience exposure and access to Western content. It also retarded the incorporation of the Indian audience into a globalized economy and market for cultural commodities produced in the West (films, music, and so on). These conditions, together with the relatively low levels of English comprehension outside the main cities in these years, enforced a relatively small market for direct imitations of foreign styles. The market that did exist consisted largely of those urban youth who were wealthy enough to overcome the substantial obstacles to music and musical instrument acquisition.

Finally, India's culture industries were dominated by an almost total orientation toward the production of commercial films and film songs (Booth 2011). The popularity and accessibility of film songs, via films themselves and radio, left little industrial or economic scope for rock or other non-film popular styles, especially songs sung in English. The alignment of the sounds of popular Indian-language film songs with the cultural and emotional images of the stories and stars of the commercial cinema made for a unique process of genre and meaning construction that was further exacerbated by the institution of playback singers (Majumdar 2001) and that prevented the development of stylistically distinct Indian music stars.

Indian approaches to the production (or reproduction) of American youth culture reflected similar responses in the late 1950s and early 1960s by the global and hegemonic music industries, located in the U.S. and in Britain. Those industries were struggling with their own confusions about popular music, culture, and generations. Many early venues and audiences for rock were constructed as part of, or as youthful adjuncts to, an "adult" popular culture that had developed in the U.S. in the later 1950s and that combined the more commercial (and often more sedate) elements of R&B, jazz, and early rock, as embodied in such artists as Sam Cooke, Nat "King" Cole, Frank Sinatra, and the post-1959 recordings of Elvis Presley, among others. An assumption that rock was going to "grow up" and that popular music would somehow maintain a primary allegiance to the ideologies of the adult world of the 1950s continued to afflict the music industry and was expressed in the ways that early rock and pop acts were constructed with regard to image, lyrics, and performing behaviors.

These factors had an impact on rock's early development in India where they interacted with purely national developments that curtailed the development of consumerism and "youth culture." Following Indian independence, Indian attitudes toward the West and Western culture varied widely across region and socioeconomic class. Although nationalist concerns for identity operated against the consumption of popular Western culture, postcolonial elitism often supported that consumption. Cultural forms and behaviors whose origins were explicitly Western, such as jazz, may have been discouraged in some contexts, as Fernandes (2012) reports; but by the middle of the 1960s, there was also a perceptible "move away from the overwhelming Nehruvian paradigm" of relatively austere Indian nationalism (Mazumdar 2011, 130). Consequently, nightlife continued in some urban centers, albeit in a sometimes limited (and sometimes nonalcoholic) fashion; the elite hotels of India's major cities, which had a relatively large foreign clientele, were important places that provided some of the earliest venues for India's early rock bands, such as the Jets.

The Jets Rock Mumbai

The Ambassador was one of Mumbai's most prestigious hotels in the 1960s. It featured an equally elite nightclub called the Other Room. As figure 11.1 shows, in 1965, the club was featuring "Asia's Swinging Sensations" on Saturday nights. Three aspiring rock guitarists, Malcolm Mazumdar, Mike

Figure 11.1
The Jets in a newspaper publicity advertisement for the Other Room nightclub at the Ambassador Hotel, Mumbai (L-R standing: Malcolm Mazumdar, Mike Kirby, Suresh Bhojwani; seated: Napoleon Braganza, circa 1965). (Courtesy of Mike Kirby.)

Kirby, and Suresh Bhojwani, who attended the same Jesuit all-boys high school in South Mumbai, recruited drummer Napoleon Braganza in 1964 to form the Jets' lineup. Three of the four were raised in predominantly Christian contexts, and all were raised by parents who spoke English and who listened to global popular musics.

The Jets' repertoire was based primarily on British interpretations of late 1950s and early 1960s American rock 'n' roll songs, initially those of Cliff Richard and the Shadows, as well as Tony Sheridan, although they regularly performed at least one song by Bill Haley and the Comets. As their impact and recordings reached India, songs by the Beatles and the Rolling Stones came to dominate the Jets' repertoire.

Although their performances (initially at school functions, charity events, Christmas dances, and church fairs) were both well rehearsed and well received, the Jets were a school-boy hobby rather than a professional band. Viewing the band as a mildly productive and otherwise harmless hobby, the Jets' parents (especially the Kirbys, but also the Bhojwanis) were quite supportive of their sons' enthusiasms. And, as teenage boys, the Jets learned what so many popular musicians before them had also learned: Beyond the enjoyment they derived directly from performing on stage, the new popular music was a good way to meet girls and to participate in the larger adult world in way that would have normally been quite difficult.

In mid-1960s India, rock was at least as much a novelty item as it was dance music. By and large, jazz/dance bands played the more standard fare, to which some elite Indians danced. In a conversation with me in 2012, Mike Kirby recalled, "We provided a kind of side show. It was rather like the older generation saying, 'Oh here is what the mad younger generation is up to, and here are these four guys, they're going to play some songs for you.'" Kirby's band-mate, Suresh Bhojwani, explained to me that the manager of the Ambassador's Other Room was "a friend of my father's. So he said 'why don't you come do a cabaret act here.' That meant they had a regular band and all that, but we came on during the break and did a 30-minute rock and roll act" (pers. comm. 2011). Although the music the Jets were playing was dance music in the rest of the world, dance music in India was provided by "dance bands" playing a largely non-improvisational and codified form of swing.

Figure 11.2 shows the program for a holiday dance evening organized by a distinctive immigrant community with strong global connections, at which the dance music was provided by Goan band leader Maurice Concessio. The Jets were invited to play "Special Items." Similar programs show the Jets playing music during intervals, before events began, or as special or featured items while the "real" bands were taking their breaks. In many cases (especially charity events), the band played for free. For their Saturday night performances at the Ambassador, they were given dinner; during their engagement at the prestigious Grand Hotel in Kolkata, they received accommodation as well.

The Jets began playing on homemade instruments. Guitarist Mike Kirby's father had an engineering background; he embarked on his second career as an instrument maker when he repaired a badly broken instrument he and his son had found in Mumbai's famous "Chor Bazaar" [lit. thieves market], where many secondhand items are sold. "We bought it for five rupees and took it home. My dad fixed it up and we electrified that guitar" (Mike Kirby, pers. comm. 2012). The elder Kirby subsequently built many instruments for local students and enthusiasts in the mid-1960s. Foreign-made instruments were not regularly imported at this time and were made extremely expensive by the Indian government tax and foreign exchange regulations. Foreign-made musical instruments and amplifiers,

THE JEWISH CLUB

PRESENTS ITS

ANNUAL PURIM DANCE

WITH

MUSIC BY: **MAURICE CONCESSIO AND HIS BAND**

NOVELTY ITEMS PRIZES

SPECIAL ITEMS BY: **THE 'JETS'**

THE MENU

CHICKEN CHATURNI
ROAST CHICKEN
ALOO MUKALA
MUTTON PANROLLS
VEG : SAMOOSAS
ICE CREAM OR COFFEE

GUESTS OF HONOUR : Mr. and Mrs. M. E. HASKELL

Figure 11.2
The program card for the Purim Dance organized by the Jewish Club of Mumbai, 1964.
(Courtesy of Mike Kirby.)

however, gave their owners an enormous advantage. Bhojwani explained to me that he increased his and his band's prestige when he talked his parents into importing "a Fender Strat[ocaster] and Super Reverb amp in 1963; I managed to pressure my parents into [buying] it. And that one amp was our sound. Everybody was so impressed because the Jets had reverb! There was no PA or anything.... Bass, vocal, rhythm all were in that [one amplifier]. But instruments were very hard; the import rules were horrendous" (pers. comm. 2011).

Oral accounts of this period suggest that the Jets were the first organized rock band in Mumbai, if not India; but that distinction did not last long. By 1965, the Jets were able to participate in one of India's earliest "beat contests," in which a number of bands competed for a range of prizes and/or titles (e.g., cash awards or recording sessions, titles such as "best band," "best singer," etc.). A number of these contests awarded recording sessions as prizes, but in the absence of a functioning music industry, such sessions amounted to very little:

We won a contest [held in Green's Hotel]; that was 1964 or '65. And with the contest came a recording contract with HMV. And HMV was a very old staid company; but they saw this thing was happening, so they said, "OK, let's try." And so we went into their studio and recorded an original song. We came up with this rock and roll number, I think it was called "Go Away Girl," or something. And we recorded it, it came out and nothing happened (Suresh Bhojwani, pers. comm. 2011).

"Beat Nite" (figure 11.3) featured the best of Mumbai's rapidly burgeoning population of rock bands, including the original version of a band called the Savages, who became one of Mumbai's most active and popular bands through the 1970s.

Beat events became formalized (if not precisely commodified) in 1968 when this format was adopted by the Simla Tobacco Company. The Simla Beat Contests grew into a national event, with preliminary, regional rounds in Mumbai, Chennai, Kolkata, and Delhi; the winners then competed in a national contest that was held in a different city each year (although Mumbai seems to have been the most popular choice). *JS* also sponsored "beat nites," "freak outs," and their own contest, in conjunction with their own sponsor, the Cordel Fabric Company.

Despite the increasingly anachronistic label, beat contests continued well into the 1980s, by which time all of India's original beat groups were long disbanded. A 1988 article in *Playback & Fast Forward* (a relatively short-lived popular music and technology magazine) reported on a beat contest called "Conga" that took place at Mumbai's drive-in theater that

Figure 11.3
The program for Beat Nite (Mumbai), one of India's earliest beat contests. (Courtesy of Mike Kirby.)

year. Although the article's anonymous author noted the "paucity of bands and good performers" at this contest, bands from Mumbai, Hyderabad, Chennai, and Pune all took part (n.a. 1988, 42).

The Jets disbanded in 1966, not long after winning the early Beat Nite depicted in figure 11.3; but their example had an impact on their juniors: In a post on his "Nandu Bhende Blog" dated August 28, 2009, Bhende recalled, "the numerous beat shows in Bombay at that time, with bands like the Reaction, The Jets, Beat 4, The Savages etc. had got me hooked and I was ripe to join the Rockers of the world." Nandu Bhende's blogged recollections demonstrate the beginnings of the kinds of localized role modeling through which popular music culture has frequently been transmitted.

THE EXPANSION OF ROCK AND ITS ACCEPTANCE AS DANCE MUSIC

Mumbai's (and, indeed, India's) rock scene continued to expand through the late 1960s and 1970s. The Jets were joined and succeeded by the Mystics, Riot Squad, Velvette Fogg, People, Brief Encounter, and many others (some involved in the rock scene suggest Mumbai may, at times, have been home to as many as 200 bands), almost all of which were relatively short-lived and "part-time." The rapid appearance and disappearance of bands was caused both by the logistic difficulties of playing rock in Mumbai in the 1960s and 1970s (relatively few venues, little economic support) and no access to a viable recording industry. "Western pop music is not a money spinner [in India]. And why should it be? After all, pop, or popular music is for the people by the people and in the language of the people" (Bhagat 1974, 30). Dubby Bhagat here identifies one of the significant dilemmas for India's rockers. In India of the 1960s and 1970s, "the people" spoke Hindi, Telugu, Malayalam, and other Indian languages, but not English. They listened to traditional musics and to the songs of India's film industries, not to globalized English-language pop or rock. Interestingly, Bhagat offered (an admittedly unspecified) support for anyone producing Hindi-language rock: "If anyone starts a Hindi pop group, *JS* and I will give them our full support. Who says that English...must be the language of rock music?" (ibid.). Despite the apparent logic of this rhetorical question, it would be nearly 20 years before rock would appear in Indian languages.

In the 1970s, rock remained a temporary hobby for most musicians. Ardeshir Damania was a guitarist in a briefly functioning band called the Gnats; in a blog post published on the Garage Hangover blog on April 25, 2011, he reflected on the challenges he and his colleagues faced at the time:

After 1968, I decided to take my studies a little more seriously and sold my guitar to a college friend…and the Gnats disbanded. Most of the boys of our generation grew up and had to earn a living, which was not possible in India through playing in rock bands.

Although the bands kept changing, venues that featured rock bands and catered to a younger audience (both Indian and international) did multiply in Mumbai as the 1960s progressed. Western rock and pop bands gradually replaced the jazz/dance bands as the dance music of choice for the Indian elite. In 1967, the Taj Mahal Palace Hotel, Mumbai's landmark luxury hotel, opened a new venue, no longer a nightclub but a discotheque called "Blow Up." Soon, the major hotels of the Indian metropolises were all opening new discotheques for the dancing pleasure of the country's urban elites and its international visitors. Bashir Sheikh, drummer for the highly successful Mumbai band the Savages, told me, "If people wanted to dance they came to our gigs. And they appreciated it very much. They loved it" (pers. comm. 2011).

The Savages, like almost all the other bands in Mumbai (and in India), played covers. Like many amateur rock bands globally, Indian bands performed their versions of songs recorded by more professional recording stars. "People wanted to hear those songs which were hit songs from the West. And we were happy to play that. There was very little impetus for us to play originals" (Suresh Bhojwani, pers. comm. 2011). When the Savages wanted to play their own compositions, they needed to slip them in: "What we used to do, we'd play three to four covers, then play one of our own. But not that many bands used to write their own music. It was all covers" (Bashir Sheikh, pers. comm. 2011).

Although playing covers was a common global practice, the particular conditions of Indian public culture made originals even less common (and less viable) than they were abroad. Those who came to hear local bands in the new rock venues wanted to hear the hits of the Rolling Stones, the Kinks, Jimi Hendrix, the Doors, and others. They wanted the *experience* of listening and dancing to rock 'n' roll, of participating in a '60s (and '70s) youth culture that they perceived, however vaguely, through the print media and the accounts of friends overseas. Nandu Bhende, who may have been Mumbai's most active and successful rock vocalist in the 1970s, was aware that he and his friends were searching for a different kind of cultural experience: "We, as people who listened to this kind of music, were very different from mainstream India. Very, very different. We dressed differently, and acted differently" (pers. comm. 2010). Bhende realized even then, however, that these young, "different" Indians were, in effect, recreating in Indian terms a youth culture about which they had relatively little information. "There was very little media around that would have given us the idea. There was no television. So I don't know how we got it. It came largely through the music. There were pictures, album covers, these things, but that's about all" (ibid.).

No foreign rock bands toured India in the 1960s or 1970s (it was only in the 1980s that the economic, technical, and regulatory viability of foreign rock acts in India was to gradually begin to improve). Recordings of foreign rock were expensive and not widely available. American or British films were relatively limited and routinely censored. Performances by local bands were literally the only way young Indians could approximate the cultural experiences that they were reading and/or hearing about. The rock concerts and clubs provided an ersatz experience for young Indians. Shashi Gopal, who was part of that generation, proposed that "we were the Woodstock generation. We were passionate about music. We were into rock music and all that. And nothing was available" (pers. comm. 2008). Gopal moved from being part of the Woodstock generation to being part of the music industry in the 1980s when he led the development of Hindi-language pop.

Waterfront and "Originals"

The practice of playing cover versions of British and American hits was enabled, in part, by India's practical estrangement from the global network of international copyright law. India acceded to the international treaty on intellectual property (commonly the Berne Convention) in 1958. Nevertheless, there being hardly any Indian export industry in mediated cultural goods, there was little economic incentive for the Indian government to make intensive efforts to enforce international copyright laws or treaties during most of the 20th century. Bands and hotels could feature live performances of hit songs with little or no concern that copyright holders would even be aware of these infringements, let alone respond to them. In Mumbai, with one notable exception, bands continued to play covers until the later 1980s and beyond. A band that appeared in the 1970s, Waterfront, did indeed make the transition from being a cover band to being a band that played only originals; but the effect of this transformation on Waterfront's career demonstrated the economic futility of playing original rock songs in India.

In 1972, guitarist Derek Julien, a South Mumbai musician and neighbor of the Jets' Mike Kirby, had a choice to make: He could join a band that was about to depart to Kuwait on a six-month performance contract or he could remain in Mumbai and join Waterfront, which then consisted of Adil Batiwala (keyboards), Soli Dastur (guitar), Roger Dragonette (bass), and Trilok Gurtu (drums). Jobs in the Persian Gulf, on the East Coast of Africa, or on local cruise ships were not uncommon opportunities for Mumbai's pop bands. Such jobs often paid better than work in India; furthermore, cruise ships offered musicians additional incentives with opportunities to purchase musical instruments or equipment in ports such as Singapore, where the selection was larger and the prices lower.

Instead of going to Kuwait, Julien—who had already had an extensive career playing rock in Mumbai and Delhi—joined Waterfront, which thus became a quintet. In 1970, the band was playing in a discotheque called Hell in the basement of the Hilltop Hotel in the Worli area of Mumbai. Although Waterfront was playing covers when he joined, Julien explains the band's subsequent transformation to an originals band as the result of their own musical interests:

> Soli [Dastur] had written this song and we said, "Let's try it," because we were all into the idea of playing originals. So we tried this one song and it sounded so good you know, that we were sold. And it turned out Roger [Dragonette] had composed a whole bunch of songs—he was a big Dylan fan—so Roger started bringing his songs, and they sounded good. Within six months, our entire repertoire changed to only originals (pers. comm. 2012).

The problem with this transformation, however, was that it imperiled the group's financial survival:

> There was no market for originals; it was the worst situation to be in financially. We got the reputation for being very difficult. And we really only existed because Soli was sinking so much money into the band (ibid.).

Dastur had family resources that he was willing and able to devote to the provision of the group's day-to-day needs.

Keyboardist Adil Batiwala had learned keyboard playing with his mother's dance band (Nelly and Her Band, figure 11.3) and was instrumental in founding Waterfront, but gradually withdrew after the mid-1970s due to health reasons, only occasionally performing with the band. Figure 11.4 shows him playing at a corporate gig circa 1977 for Air India.

In 1974, the rest of the group, with new drummer Ranjit Barot, moved into a house owned by Dastur. The group became somewhat

Figure 11.4
Waterfront: a corporate gig for Air India, circa 1977, L-R: Adil Batiwala (keyboard), Roger Dragonette (bass guitar), Soli Dastur (guitar), Ranjit Barot (drums), Derek Julien (guitar). (Photo courtesy of Derek Julien.)

reclusive, playing—by Julien's reckoning—"six concerts a year." As Barot has recounted, however, they rehearsed and recorded their music consistently:

> We were just obsessed; we were like social suicide cases. We had no life except wake up in the morning, get stoned and play and then get stoned and sleep and wake up, and do the same thing in the next day, every day (pers. comm. 2012).

Like other bands in India and the world, rock culture in the 1970s almost inevitably included considerable recreational drug use.

Perhaps because they were playing originals, the band recorded a great deal of their rehearsals and many of their rare performances.

> We started recording practically everything we played. We set up a regular Sony cassette [2-track] recorder which had the facility to record a mix of the two direct inputs and the two mic inputs simultaneously, each input having its own fader. By putting together some really stone-age splitter boxes, we managed to have very basic control of the channels (Derek Julien, e-mail comm., 2012).

These recordings of Waterfront's rehearsals and performances, although not professionally produced, are some of the only audio material extant from this entire period of India's rock history.

Dastur's composition "Flowers of Silence" (video 11.5) has three sec-⊙ tions: (A) an introductory riff in a six-beat metrical structures (four beat groups total); (B) a verse section in a four-beat structure (eight beat groups, repeated three times); and (C) a slower bridge section also in four-beat structure (eight beat groups). The resulting structure, with repeated sections, is A-B-A-B-A-C. This structure is itself repeated twice; after each of the two repetitions, Julien plays an extended guitar solo. The performance combines the sounds of later 1960s "psychedelic" rock with the technical creativity of some of the 1970s progressive rock that was being recorded by bands such as King Crimson and the Mahavishnu Orchestra, with virtuosic and elaborate instrumentals, unusual meters, and approaches to mode and harmony that were more sophisticated than in the majority of rock being produced. Drummer Ranjit Barot specifically refers to the influence of the Mahavishnu Orchestra at this time: "And then of course, Mahavishnu Orchestra just screwed it all up you know. It was all so thick. I think I stopped playing for a week when I heard [Mahavishnu drummer Billy] Cobham. 'How do you play drums like this?' And it was hard because we did not have any visual reference, so you just copied it really badly, tried to figure out" (pers. comm. 2012). It is ironic, of course, that at least some of the musicians in the Mahavishnu Orchestra (such as John McLaughlin) were being influenced by the modal and rhythmic features of Indian classical music at this time. It is also worth noting in this context that both of Waterfront's drummers had been trained in the classical drumming traditions of North India and thus had the ability to deal with rhythmic structures that most rock musicians would have considered challenging.

Barot's drumming on "Flowers of Silence" is intricate and very dense and certainly in the style of Billy Cobham. His textural and rhythmic intensity is matched by the bass and guitar interjections that respond, in call-and-response fashion, to many of vocal phrases. Julien's guitar solos show the influence of Jimi Hendrix, as well as John McLaughlin (among many others); his inventive approach and his use of electronic effects, such as phase-shift and distortion, were distinctive for the time. The relatively unusual harmonic sequence moves the performance well out of the realm of the standard pop song (regardless of place of origin). Similarly, the changing meters and speeds make it clear that this music was not meant for dancing.[2]

Despite their "obsession" and access to some financial support, by 1980, Waterfront succumbed to the same pressures that affected other Indian bands (marriage, the desire for financial stability, etc.). Band members opened recording studios, became involved in film music production, continued with the hotel music scene, or left professional music altogether.

CASSETTES, MTV, AND THE BEGINNINGS OF MUSICAL GLOBALIZATION

By the mid-1980s, there was good news and bad news for rock musicians who sought to make a career out of music. In the former category was the advent of audiocassette technology in the late 1970s. This new format significantly reduced the cost of music production and consumption and exponentially increased the size of the Indian market for sound recordings. By the 1980s, the possibility of a recording career in popular music outside the context of the Indian film industries was becoming a reality for the first time since Indian independence. The first stirrings of economic liberalization were slowly increasing Indian access to Western musical sounds, technology, and instruments. Furthermore, as the decade progressed, Indian fans finally began to gain direct access to live performances by Western rock and pop musicians (e.g., early tours by bands such as Wishbone Ash, Boney M., and the Police in the early 1980s, and the 1988 Human Rights Now! concert held in New Delhi, which featured Bruce Springsteen, Peter Gabriel, Sting, and others).

The bad news, however, included the global success of Michael Jackson (*Off the Wall*, 1979, and *Thriller*, 1982) and disco that redirected much Indian (and global) attention away from rock. As "Ali," a journalist apparently working under a pseudonym, wrote in a short article published in *Screen*, India's English-language film (and music) trade journal, "Disco also worked its magic in Gandhi-ji's India. Within a short while it was disco, disco everywhere" (1981, 8).

To add to rock's challenges, the pop vocalist and the pop song format that disco emphasized, together with disco's less socially confrontational ideology and more fashion-conscious visual iconography, resonated more closely with broader levels of Indian taste (and with its indigenous popular film-song culture) than did the often unkempt and sometime aggressive images of guitar-band rock. Much of the increased economic and audience capacity that cassettes created in India in the 1980s was absorbed by recordings of pop vocalists, such as Shweta Shetty, Daler Mehndi, Alisha Chinai, and others, who offered stylistically syncretic (and often Hindi-language) versions of original popular music, and who could be promoted via the new cassette format that fans could actually afford. Pop vocalists also took over many of the remaining live performance nightlife venues (that had formerly offered work to rock bands) even as these venues began to disappear: "[Pop vocalist] Sharon [Prabhakar] was soon singing in all kinds of places, in all the five-star hotels" (John 1981, 8).

Rock Machine, I-Rock, and New Possibilities

Rock remained the preferred music of a relatively small, largely urban, and in some ways marginal audience that was concentrated primarily in India's more elite secondary and tertiary English-medium institutions. Colleges (which are secondary institutions in India) had always been centers of rock fandom, as music entrepreneur Shashi Gopal recalled of the 1970s: "Every college campus, every dorm, every club attached to a dorm always had English music" (pers. comm. 2008). As the public presence of rock began to decline, student support continued in the form of annual school dances and festivals and specially organized rock concerts in hired venues.

One important college festival in Mumbai was (and still is) Malhar, sponsored by St. Xavier's College, one of India's most prestigious English-medium colleges. In 1986, two of Mumbai's most popular rock bands, Mirage and Rock Machine, were scheduled to appear at Malhar. The musicians who constituted Rock Machine had begun playing together in 1984. By 1986, the band had changed somewhat, but still had the usual mix of community backgrounds. Like most Indian bands, they played covers of Western hits, primarily songs that were found on LPs by British and North American bands like Led Zeppelin, Thin Lizzy, Van Halen, Nazareth, Rush, and others belonging to what was increasingly being called the "heavy metal" genre of rock. The importance of the ideological distinctions between rock and pop, however, was brought home to Rock Machine and their friends in another rock band, Mirage, as they were rehearsing for their scheduled appearance at Malhar.

> Farhad Wadia: Someone went and told him [St. Xavier's principal], "How can you permit this? This rock music is the music of the devil, and it promotes, sex and drugs and all those things." So overnight, two or maybe three weeks before, he announced this: "Sorry, at Malhar, no more rock." They were OK with a pop act or some such thing.
>
> Now, Malhar was the biggest festival in the country; so playing there meant you were at the top of your profession, or you were the biggest band. So we were all very disappointed, because we had been rehearsing for three to four weeks already for this. So when we went to the meeting—it was the student council that ran this festival—one of the guys there, he was a very entrepreneurial and he saw opportunity where others saw adversity. So he said, "Ok, I'll take this on, and I'll find the venue and I'll pay you the same" (Farhad Wadia, pers. comm. 2012).

Although the student organizer disappeared at the last minute, the two bands, led by Mirage's guitarist/vocalist Farhad Wadia and Rock Machine's Mark Selwyn, decided to carry on, ultimately performing to a crowd of 4,000 enthusiastic students. The event, held at Rang Bhavan, a large auditorium adjacent to the college, came to be called Independence Rock (and

Figure 11.6
Young Indian rock fans at an unidentified concert by Rock Machine at the popular Rang
Bhavan Auditorium, Mumbai, circa 1987. (Photo courtesy of Mark Pinto de Menezes.)

subsequently I-Rock). Mumbai has had an I-Rock festival almost every year
since 1986; the event has spread to other cities as well. As the 1980s progressed, college shows like Malhar became the primary remaining venues
available for the live consumption of rock music. Figure 11.6 shows an
enthusiastic Mumbai audience at a concert by the band Rock Machine at
the Rang Bhavan auditorium.

Rock Machine's career, however, was coincident with a range of changes
in India's musical, regulatory, and media environments, and with the perceived beginnings of globalization in the country that began under the lead-
ership of the young Prime Minister Rajiv Gandhi. Drummer Mark Pinto
de Menezes had spent a year in a technical institute in the United States
studying music, and he joined the band arguing for more professionalism
and a full-time commitment to music (pers. comm. 2011). Rock Machine
(figure 11.7) was subsequently chosen to represent rock's national face and
sound on the Russian tour (1987–88) of the Indian government's enormous international public relations exercise of the late 1980s, the Festival
of India. For this event, intended by the Indian government to "re-brand"
India on a global level, the band needed original compositions (although
still sung in English). The songs composed for the Festival of India became
the basis of the first full-length album of original rock songs sung in English
and recorded and released in India, called *Rock 'n' Roll Renegade*.

Figure 11.7
Rock Machine: a publicity photo during the recording of "Rock 'n' Roll Renegade."
L-R: Jayesh Gandhi (guitar), Mark Selwyn (bass guitar), Mahesh Tinaikar (guitar), Mark
Pinto de Menezes (drums), Uday Benegal (vocal), Zubin Balaporia (keyboard). (Photo cour-
tesy of Mark Pinto de Menezes.)

Rock 'n' Roll Renegade embodied a host of innovations. In addition to
being the first of its kind, it provided the motivation for the first national
tour by an Indian rock band and served as the basis for India's first rock
music video, filmed (appropriately enough) in the band's old haunt, the
Rang Bhavan Auditorium, in the early 1990s. The video itself demonstrates
India's rapid mastery of the conventions of MTV: the choreographed duel-
ing guitars, smoke machines, torn jeans, "big hair," and aggressive gestures
of 1980s hard rock are all present.
Rock 'n' Roll Renegade was released in 1988 by CBS Records, which was
only the second transnational music company to have established itself
in India during the first 35 years of Indian independence. Having arrived
in India in 1982 and built a new record and tape production facility, the
company was still struggling to find its footing in the confusing film-song
oriented Indian market. Following standard American industrial practice,
the company released *Rock 'n' Roll Renegade* and sent the band out to tour
the country promoting their release. Following standard practice in India
at the time, however, the recording was promptly and intensively pirated.
Drummer Mark Pinto de Menezes recalls the band's frustrations at not
finding any copies of their cassette as they toured the country, supposedly

to support sales of the album. When the band reached northeastern India, however, a region with a large Christian population and a widely reported enthusiasm for rock, they found more than fans. Walking down the street in Aizawl (the capital of Mizoram state), they discovered their cassette:

> They're showing us our cassette. And even we hadn't seen it. And we said, "Where did you get this?" And they said, "Oh it's just here in the shop." So we went there, and it was all pirated. And the owner was so nice: "Oh, you're the guys on the cassette!" And we said, how did you get this? And he told us, "We managed to get one copy from somebody in Delhi and one from Bombay" (Mark Pinto de Menezes, pers. comm. 2012).

Despite the cassette pirating, *Rock 'n' Roll Renegade* managed to sell 10,000 legitimate copies in its first six months (Hazarika 1989). In 1990, the band released a second album, *Second Coming*. But this time, their music company was an Indian one, Magnasound. Registered in 1986 by Shashi Gopal, a veteran of the music industry who had worked for both the Gramophone Company of India and CBS, Magnasound focused on both Indian-produced and foreign rock and pop. The company led the development of India's earliest music videos, including those by Rock Machine. Following personnel changes in 1992, Rock Machine renamed itself Indus Creed in 1993.

As important as I-Rock and the cassette revolution were for Rock Machine, much of their impact came from their engagement with the music video format and their fortuitous, coincident emergence just as music video (as a format) and music television (as a medium) were becoming possible in India. In 1991, satellite television was introduced in India, which could then boast more than 12 million television sets, in the form of Star Television based in Hong Kong. Star offered five channels, one of which introduced Indian viewers to the joys of the increasingly global MTV. The locally produced music television channel Zee TV was introduced in 1992. Seeking local Indian rock and pop acts for its new market, MTV naturally focused on India's most commercially successful band.

"Rock 'n' Roll Renegade"—filmed, appropriately enough, as a concert performance at Rang Bhavan Auditorium—was the band's first music video and one of the very first in India. In a development that has increasingly come to characterize the economics of Indian rock, the video's production (including a re-recording of the song itself) was sponsored by an Indian corporation. The images of Indian musicians playing and performing in the global styles and fashions of international rock were enormously popular with many young Indians.

Rock Machine/Indus Creed produced two further music videos between 1992 and 1994 to support songs from *Second Coming*. The first of these, "Top of the Rock," was so widely in demand that MTV put it in heavy rotation in 1992. The second video from *Second Coming*, "Pretty Child," was released in 1993 (by which time the group had changed its name). "Pretty Child" was a more reflective ballad for which the band recruited a classical Indian *tabla* drummer. Viewers/listeners appeared to perceive that additional—and "traditional"—timbre as an "Indianization" of the band's sound. Partially in response to this development, the video won the MTV award for Best Asian Music Video (Viewers' Choice) in 1993.

Satellite television transformed the position that rock music occupied in the country. By the time Indus Creed stopped performing in 1997, India and its music industry were well on the way to becoming integrated into a musical (or media) world economy. The need for local rockers to replicate foreign hits had vanished with the appearance of MTV; further moves toward economic liberalization meant that the struggles first-generation Indian rockers had experienced (to acquire Western music and instruments) were no longer part of anyone's musical experience. Although they were not the first rock band to concentrate on the production of original songs (as I have shown), Rock Machine/Indus Creed were the first to be able to make something of a career out of that process.

CONCLUSION

At the beginning of this chapter, I argued that three interconnected conditions were responsible for the unique history and nature of rock music in India. India's postcolonial identity and its cultural and political relations to the colonial (and hegemonic) West, the remarkable License Raj that was created by the Indian government, and the almost unbreakable commitment to film song on the part of India's music producers all affected the careers of the bands I examined here, as both collective units and individual musicians. When rock music began in the 1960s, India was still fighting wars, both physical and political, to fully establish its postcolonial identity, the regulatory structures of the License Raj were less than 10 years old, and the founding generation of India's post-independence film industry was in its prime. Rock music, as early bands like the Jets experienced it, fit neatly (and almost unquestioningly) into this environment; it was a pastime, a pleasant novelty, a fad of the younger generation, and a music largely associated with India's Christian, English-speaking, and mixed-culture world.

Central themes in rock's subsequent history are highlighted in the three case studies presented here. It is also clear from this discussion that the reason for rock bands' existence in the 1960s, '70s, and early '80s was the reproduction of local versions of a global music and of local forms of popular culture experiences that were equally global. While the License Raj lasted, the direct experience of foreign culture was otherwise unobtainable for many Indians.

Indian rock's industrial and mediated highpoint came in the 1990s, with the professional recordings, national tours, and music video successes of Rock Machine/Indus Creed and vocalist Gary Lawyer. But, as Rock Machine guitarist Mahesh Tinaikar recalled to me, the early 1990s witnessed the end of media interest in English-language, Western-style rock.

> Then it slowed down, because MTV and Channel [V] decided this was a very niche market. They wanted to expand; so they started promoting Hindi pop, and that became very big. By 1995 it was huge, and they also started promoting Bollywood (Mahesh Tinaikar, pers. comm. 2012).

Moving into the 21st century, rock, primarily in its "metal" forms, has continued as a semi-professional niche music, as part of the culture of young, elite (and mostly male) Indians, sung and performed in English, Hindi, and (quite noticeably) Bengali. In the context of the new globalized India, however, rock is no more remarkable than any of the other global forms (most significantly, hip-hop) that are part of the contemporary Indian soundscape.

NOTES

1. Sincere thanks to the musicians and others who contributed time and documentary materials to this chapter: Ranjit Barot, Dubby Bhagat, Nandu Bhende, Suresh Bhojwani, Soli Dastur, Shashi Gopal, Derek Julien, Mike Kirby, Mark Pinto de Menezes, Bashir Sheikh, Mahesh Tinaikar, and Farhad Wadia.
2. Julien has recently begun re-recording many Waterfront songs for posting on the Internet via YouTube, for example: http://www.youtube.com/watch?v=6PNJo1zYpIA and http://www.youtube.com/watch?v=9Pj38CkOh0w.

CHAPTER 12

"Be True to Yourself"

Violin Ganesh, Fusion, and Contradictions in
Contemporary Urban India

NIKO HIGGINS

In 2007, an anonymous writer reflected on the confluence and integration of cultures in South India. This reflection appeared in a program for a concert by the celebrated violin duo, brothers Ganesh and Kumaresh.

> The link between tradition and modernity comes when the *sampradaya* [tradition] of music reflects itself through the modern vision of each musician. In our society we generally see conflicting elements getting together almost like a confluence. It is like wearing a *jibba* [also a *kurta*, or a collarless long men's shirt] with jeans or having *idli-vada-sambar* [South Indian cuisine] and pizza-noodles on the same day or maybe talking Tanglish [Tamil and English hybrid]....It is also like using the electronic *tampura* with the traditional *tampura* on the same stage (concert flyer: Ganesh and Kumaresh, February 10, 2007 at Narada Gana Sabha).

There has been a widespread acknowledgment among journalists and scholars about the transformative changes in urban India over the course of the last two decades. Because of sweeping economic reform in the early 1990s, an economic optimism and concomitant new class of consumers have led to the projection of a "new" India that represents a break from the past. In print, recent titles such as *India Rising* (Zakaria 2006), *India*

Becoming: A Portrait of Life in Modern India (Kapur 2012), *India Arriving: How This Economic Powerhouse is Redefining Global Business* (Dossani 2008), *The Indian Renaissance: India's Rise After a Thousand Years of Decline* (Sanyal 2008), and *India Booms: The Breathtaking Development and Influence of Modern India* (Farndon 2009) proclaimed this transformation with unambiguous confidence. Although each author occupied a different position on a wide continuum of responses to these changes, they all agreed that the "new" India is indeed new.

How can we *hear* these transformations, including people's reactions to such a period of change? The *jibba* and jeans metaphor from the concert flyer quoted above brings together several themes that I address in this chapter using the cultural practice of music: tradition, modernity, cosmopolitanism, and to a less apparent extent that I develop later on, the Indian middle class. This flyer asserts the visions of musicians as crucial strategies for making sense of these recent changes, an assertion that I pursue in this chapter.

CARNATIC CHILLS

On February 10, 2007, violinists Ganesh and Kumaresh performed at their CD release event in Chennai, India. They titled their recording *Carnatic Chills* and subtitled it "Ganesh-Kumaresh newage violin exotica"; it was the latest recording by this well-known duo. The event took place in Narada Gana Sabha, one of the largest auditoriums in the city, and was packed to capacity, with scores of people waiting outside and unable to enter. The brothers have been musical celebrities in Chennai for a few decades. They were child prodigies, and they currently spend much of the year touring India, Europe, and North America. They are musical virtuosos trained in Carnatic, or South Indian classical music; but while most of their yearly performances are recitals of Carnatic music, they also perform what they refer to as "contemporary classical music."[1]

Carnatic Chills features the brothers' compositions and improvisations of contemporary classical music, which for this project included musicians performing on instruments common to the Carnatic repertoire, such as a bamboo flute, *mrdangam* (a barrel-headed drum), and *ghatam* (a clay-pot percussion instrument), as well as Western instruments like a keyboard, bass guitar, and drum set.[2] During the release event, they played a short concert, about an hour long, and beforehand they partook in a ritual familiar to South Indians in which guests were invited to help publicize the event and formally launch the recording.

The guests did not speak during the event, but their attendance helped to heighten the formality of the occasion. The guests included a member of an Indian record company, Saregama, and two chief guests: percussion master T. H. "Vikku" Vinayakram and renowned film composer A. R. Rahman. These guests were well chosen because of the ways in which their music has united multiple musical practices. Vikku Vinayakram was trained as a Carnatic percussionist and in the mid-1970s performed with the extremely popular group Shakti, which featured British guitarist John McLaughlin, Carnatic violinist L. Shankar, and *tabla* virtuoso Zakir Hussain. The music of Shakti fused together jazz and Indian classical music, but also the two different classical traditions in India, northern Hindustani and southern Carnatic musical practices. A. R. Rahman has been an internationally known film composer of Hindi- and Tamil-language films, and has more recently composed for British and Hollywood films as well, winning two Grammy Awards for his music in the film *Slumdog Millionaire* (2008). While Vinayakram represented the tradition of Carnatic music and Rahman has been a popular music celebrity, they both have forged their own unique musical paths and are symbols of pushing the boundaries of their respected musical practices.

In a press release titled "Chilling Out with Ragas" published a few days later in *The Hindu*, the widely read English daily newspaper, journalist Chitra Swaminathan mentioned Ganesh and Kumaresh's motivation for the project: "according to the brothers, though they wanted the album to have a contemporary appeal, they ensured that their experiments with sounds were based on traditional *ragams*. 'We wanted it to reflect the contradictions in today's life,' they said during the launch of the album" (Swaminathan 2007).

The attempt to bring traditional *ragams* together with contemporary appeal in this statement took on a more complicated meaning when the musicians said that this would "reflect the contradictions in today's life." Rather than asserting any kind of seamless unity, they instead chose to point toward a potential tension in their music that would mirror the tensions or contradictions of everyday life in urban South India. This tension, a recurrent theme in which musicians negotiate tradition and modernity, is an important dimension of South Asian performance in general:

> In South Asia, performers and listeners continually rearticulate a tension, common to many performance traditions, between faithfulness to received versions of the past and aspirations to create something recognizably new.... Performers disagree about what innovations are superficial or substantial, but they all strive to keep their arts alive, keep them new (Wolf 2009, 18).

This tension between faithfulness to the past and creative aspiration to innovate has been built into the ways in which musicians absorb the lessons of their teachers, remain attuned to their listening publics, and express their individual creative agency.

Still, Swaminathan's article and Ganesh and Kumaresh's assertions left important questions unanswered: What is contradictory about contemporary appeal and traditional *ragas*? How does music mediate these contradictions in today's life? How do these contradictions help us understand more about contemporary urban Indian culture? In this chapter, I describe how musicians combine musical practices often represented as discrete and separate, and analyze how music reveals some of the tensions of urban 21st-century India. In Chennai, musicians combine elements of Western jazz, rock, and classical music with South Indian classical and film music. Musicians and audiences often refer to this hybrid popular music practice as "fusion." With this term, musicians highlight musical mixing and situate fusion as a form of popular music that overlaps a series of politicized boundaries of popular, classical, Indian, and Western. It is therefore a contested musical practice with some champions and many naysayers, and it presents a unique opportunity to learn how music making and contemporary urban South India are linked through a relationship of irresolution.

Carnatic Chills helps clarify the role of fusion in contemporary urban South India in the way it negotiates "the contradictions in today's life." By explicitly avoiding the term "fusion," Ganesh and Kumaresh also pointed to the ways that fusion in the South Indian city of Chennai is a contested musical practice that creates tensions when bringing together multiple musical practices as it attempts to unite them. But by describing their music as "contemporary classical music," they strategically attempted to elide the criticism of pandering to the masses when they were, in essence, creating music with a greater popular appeal than their Carnatic music, as was also evident from the subtitle of their recording, "newage violin exotica." As I describe later, *Carnatic Chills* overall has much more in common with the nebulous practice of fusion than with Carnatic music.[3]

In this chapter, I take a close look at Violin Ganesh (as he is commonly called in South India) in order to describe and analyze one example of a form of popular music known in urban South India as fusion. I describe some of the tensions that characterize his approach to and understandings of the practice of fusion in order to show how musicians synthesize the categories of Western and Indian music. Rather than conceiving of fusion as musicians' responses to generalized systems of globalization and a series of forces acted upon them (Stokes 2007, 2–6), I understand fusion as integrated with a cosmopolitanism that is both local and trans-local

(Turino 2000), as well as observable in a specific place and time (Stokes 2007, 6). Bringing together ethnographic description with literature about cosmopolitanism and studies of the "new" Indian middle class, I reveal how fusion is contested by showing how music sounds the tensions that constitute debates about the new India. The ambivalence of many musicians and audiences to embrace fusion demonstrates some ways in which music and contemporary urban India are continually intertwined with issues that surround the new India. Overall, I show how the practice of fusion in Chennai reveals a transitional moment in Indian history that uses new materials to express old desires: Musicians use a range of musical instruments and sounds understood as non-local and "new" to expand and maintain Indian tradition, celebrate distinctive local Indian identity, and also embody a global cosmopolitan savvy. I draw from my ethnographic fieldwork on fusion in Chennai, my experiences as a musician, my observations living in Chennai, and an extended interview with Violin Ganesh in January 2008.

DIFFERENCES BETWEEN FUSION AND CARNATIC MUSIC

Many of the tensions surrounding fusion stemmed from its overlapping relationship with Carnatic music. One way of discovering the differences was by asking musicians about their performances. When I spoke with Ganesh, I learned that he characterized performances of fusion and Carnatic music in different but related ways. He said that when he plays a *kalyanam kacceri* (a wedding concert), he could play Carnatic music "with more abandon" but that he still had to play to his patrons' expectations. He said he "could try out things, but not too much, because they expect you to do justice to what you always do" (Violin Ganesh, pers. comm. 2008). He compared this to *sabha kacceris* (a concert of Carnatic music in a private musical organization run by enthusiasts and the most prevalent form of musical patronage for Carnatic music in Chennai), saying that "*sabhas* are more serious" and require "a certain kind of music" (Violin Ganesh, pers. comm. 2008).

At that point, I told Ganesh that I had heard him and his brother give a Carnatic *kacceri* (concert or recital) near a temple in Thiruvanmiyur, a neighborhood in the southern part of Chennai. I mentioned that near the end, he and his brother harmonized a certain melody, with one violin playing the melody and the other playing harmonic tones from the same *raga*. All melody in Carnatic music is strictly monophonic, and their rendition of the composition was clearly a prearranged departure from their usual Carnatic *kacceris*. After they finished the piece, someone in the audience asked the brothers what they had just performed. I recounted how Ganesh explained to the audience that if his brother started on *sa* (the root note of the *raga*), Ganesh would start on *dha* (an interval of a sixth above), and if his brother moved to *ri* (the second step of the *raga* scale) Ganesh would play a *ni* (the seventh step of the raga scale). This clearly differed from standard practice in a *sabha kacceri*. Ganesh responded:

> That's very new to these people because we've been doing this for a long time. But only now we are bringing it into *sabhas*. Because we didn't know how these people would take it. And in the end, we thought it doesn't really matter [laughter]. Because we have to be very comfortable with ourselves, and play what we want to play because that's why people come. You have to be true to yourself. Then we started playing these things in *sabhas* and I think it's very positive. I myself am surprised that the feedback has been very positive (Violin Ganesh, pers. comm. 2008).

This statement shows how Ganesh conceived of his Carnatic and contemporary classical music as separate, but that in being true to himself, he wanted to introduce this kind of arrangement to *sabha* audiences and, as a result, bring these different practices closer together. When they started introducing some of their original arrangements, Ganesh enjoyed these changes to their usual program, as well as the positive feedback. It also shows that as professional musicians with a clear understanding of the differences between various patrons, they adapted their programs to fit specific performance contexts while also gently pushing some of their audience's expectations. But "being true to yourself" also reveals a gap between the expectations of his audiences and his individual creative choices. By asserting his own creative agency, he not only maintained established standards of musical performance, but also carved out a place for himself among a broad field of musicians in Chennai.

IS EVERYTHING FUSION?

Many Carnatic musicians who perform fusion in addition to their Carnatic music marked clear boundaries between the different practices: Carnatic music was Carnatic music, and fusion was fusion. Depending on what they were hired to play, they would get different musicians to accompany them, and perhaps perform in a different space with a different repertoire. But Ganesh's boundaries were more complicated. He clearly disapproved of the word "fusion" to describe his non-Carnatic music, and he also called into question whether distinguishing between Carnatic music and contemporary classical music is necessary. Later in our interview, Ganesh posed the problem of the word "fusion" by calling attention to the ways it presupposes an imagined purity that never existed. Here he identified the implicit assumptions of fusion as a hybrid music that obscures the hybridity of its sources. In the context of music-making in South India, the concept of musical hybridity is associated with popular music (fusion and film, for example), and the concept of musical purity is associated with Indian classical music, in which many musicians and audience members invest in the idea of a pure Indian tradition unchanged by outside cultural influences. Ganesh's position was in distinct contrast to the ubiquitous construction of Indian classical music as an unchanging essence of Indian tradition; but Ganesh avoided any potential criticism by grounding his contemporary classical music in what he privileged as the essence of Indian tradition—the systematized practices of *raga* and *tala*:

> So many things have come here and we've adapted. I'm playing a violin. It's a violin I bought in America. So do you mean to say that . . . I'm playing fusion music? Because I'm playing the violin? And Muttuswamy Dikshitar [1775–1835, a celebrated composer of the canonical Carnatic repertoire] also composed small, small songs, taking a melody from British anthem, taking some other march, and put in some *sahityam* [text, lyrics]. He did a lot of songs. Do you mean to say that Dikshitar himself was a fused guy? [Laughter] . . . Where do you start it and where do you end it? Music is all about adaptability and that's why the music is great. Because you adapt so much, and even then, the core is there, which is the *raga* and *tala* (Violin Ganesh, pers. comm. 2008).

Ganesh's experience shaped his understanding that musicians need to be flexible to accommodate the many changes around them, while still remaining moored to those elements that he prioritized as the key principles of his musical background and identity. As a result, he laid out a model of music-making in which he navigated a distinct set of rigid guidelines with individual agency. When he named the principles of *raga* and *tala* as the core, he rooted his music in the highly systematized practice of Indian classical music. By mentioning his adaptability as a musician, he also showed how his contemporary classical music is a kind of reframing of these core principles or practices of Indian classical music. His understanding of *raga* and *tala*, then, was flexible enough to apply it to different musical contexts with different accompanists, themes, and composers, and also a secularizing of the music, but not so flexible as to lose its Indian classical roots.

The adaptability Ganesh mentioned could be seen as a response to India's recent period of economic growth and prosperity attributed to such ideas as globalization, liberalization, or the new India, but this adaptability has been a historically continuous part of musicians' experiences in the 20th century. The changes afforded by technologies such as the radio, gramophone, microphone, and cassette have been well documented as having a significant impact on practices of Indian classical musicians (Bakhle 2005; Farrell 1997; Higgins 1976; Lelyveld 1995; Manuel 1993; Neuman 1990 [1980]; and Weidman 2006). Since the 1950s, the long-playing record also dramatically influenced Indian classical music by enabling its global circulation. The global encounter with Indian classical music was therefore most widely mediated through the mass circulation of LP's, in addition to some landmark performances at the Monterey Jazz Festival and Woodstock. Indian classical music was catapulted onto a more global stage by a few musicians who, despite their interpretation by the West as Indian traditionalists, also incorporated fusion into their careers.

One generation of Indian musicians gave a particularly public face to this encounter. These musicians were instrumentalists, and most of them came from North India. They forged a new role for the Indian classical musician who performed around the world *and* performed fusion. Ravi Shankar, Ali Akbar Khan, Alla Rakha, Zakir Hussain (son of Alla Rakha and therefore representative of the younger generation), and from the South, L. Shankar and L. Subramaniam are the best-known senior musicians who have redefined the role of the Indian classical musician as a globally relevant disseminator of Indian classical tradition—in the West, they are synonymous with Indian music. One substantial reason for their success in forging such pathways in the West was their openness, however measured and varied, to fusion. Ironically, Westerners often held these musicians up as symbols of Indian tradition, but it was their openness to fusion that made these these encounters possible in the first place.

These musicians provide unique and important inspiration for the practice of fusion in Chennai because of the models of successful musicianship they have given in both India and the West. As a result, they also forged a new patronage infrastructure that opened up performance opportunities for both classical music and fusion. Violinist L. Subramaniam gave evidence of this new form of patronage in his textbook that summarizes the theory and practice of Carnatic music (Subramaniam and Subramaniam 1995). Co-authored with his late wife Viji, the book focuses exclusively on making Carnatic music accessible to uninitiated listeners and contains a brief history, summarized biographies of composers, descriptions of the concert format, Carnatic systems of *raga* and *tala*, and forms of composition and improvisation. The book contains two brief biographical summaries of L. Subramaniam's career. Both celebrate his professional musicianship by mentioning his acceptance in the West and his accomplishments in fusion. The longer one describes his Western classical music studies, numerous commissions, and collaborations with conductor Zubin Mehta and violinists Stéphane Grappelli and Yehudi Menuhin. It is likely that his extensive Carnatic background is an assumed set of prerequisites for an even more extensive—and therefore remarkable—list of accomplishments in the West with fusion. But the biographical summaries contrast with the content of the book and almost undermine its purpose. What is required to become a professional Indian musician? The book's gap between its exclusively Carnatic subject matter and the multi-genre careers of the authors leaves this question unresolved, except for the following excerpt:

> Due to mass media communication and increasing global travel, the public has a greater opportunity to be exposed to different cultures and performing arts. This is also due to advanced technology and the availability of music from different parts of the world in the form of cassettes, compact discs, videos, etc. Because of these factors, it is possible for an Indian performer to establish himself internationally, provided he understands the perceptions, expectations, and the understanding of the international audience and meets the resultant challenges with innovation, creativity and musicianship. He has to compete with several great international performers from other cultures (Subramaniam and Subramaniam 1995, 17).

International acclaim for Subramaniam has doubtlessly resulted from his astonishing musicianship, but it has also hinged on his openness and desire to perform fusion. Nestled in the first chapter and never developed or addressed again, this programmatic statement of what international musical success demands of Indian musicians emphasizes creative innovation, openness to adjusting to audiences' alternate modes of listening to Indian music, and savvy entrepreneurship for staying competitive in a limited but exceptional field of musicians. Therefore, although historical precedents for fusion did exist, they were often embedded in a discourse that obscured their relationship to Indian classical music. But whether acknowledged by Ganesh or not, the life and music of musicians like L. Subramaniam opened up a range of possibilities both in India and abroad for performing music that is "true to yourself" while also asserting themselves as original, creative, *and* "traditional" musicians with a taste for self promotion.

Savvy entrepreneurship was a distinctly important part of the *Carnatic Chills* release. On a printed flyer I received, which also served as a VIP ticket to the event a seat near the front, the text on the back described the motivation for this project:

> Music is not just an expression of the musician's thoughts or ideas, but is also a
> reflection of his or her own contemporary social life. These thoughts and ideas
> are presented through *Ragam* and *Talam* which are the greatest contributions
> of Indian music to the world of music. It is based on these aspects that the core
> idea of every concert is built[.] Thus is born "Carnatic chills" another thematic
> production (concert flyer: February 10, 2007, at Narada Gana Sabha).

This first paragraph of the flyer highlights Ganesh and Kumaresh's creative agency as a tool to mediate their experiences in contemporary Indian society, and it also very strategically situates this agency within the systems of *raga* and *tala*. The last sentence states that every concert of theirs is built on these fundamentally Indian contributions, but then describes *Carnatic Chills* as a "thematic production" to depict the recording and the release as an important event, not just a CD. Certainly Vinayakram and Rahman's presence contributed to making the event a "production." Here the brothers were at once stating the affinity of their contemporary classical music to Carnatic music and Indian tradition while also distinguishing it as a thematic production in order to assert this release as a special event, unlike a Carnatic *kacceri*. Carnatic recordings often have release events as well, but to my knowledge, rarely with the kind of pomp and circumstance that even come close to the spectacle of this event. As it turns out, Ganesh had a specific influence for the style of marketing for this release:

VG: So we need to do something about that, how we market Carnatic music. Because everything has to be marketed.

NH: Definitely.... But with your CD release I noticed that especially because you had Rahman there. You had...

VG: Vikkuji.

NH: ... of course. And then you had someone from the studio there, from the record company, Saregama. So it was a nice assembly....

VG: We had to do it because once you do a CD, by itself it cannot reach the people. Whatever we do, unless it's done in a proper way, it's become like the West where you have to do the whole thing. Like even play a concert.... When we went to Paris, I think in 1998 or 1999... John

McLaughlin was releasing his CD with Hariji, Hariprasad Chaurasia. We went to the launch. It was in the big Virgin store....

NH: That's where the release was?

VG: Yeah. And he played.

NH: There?

VG: There, he played. He there, Vikkuji there, Zakirbhai there, so all of them. Because we were touring with Zakirbhai at that time. So I saw that, and then I realized how we have to market music.... How a CD function could be. How you reach the people. What kind of things you have to do to get the CD popular for the people, to the press. Everything. So those things, we have to do it here too. And if we have some friends here like Rahman, that helps! [Laughter] (Violin Ganesh, pers. comm. 2008).

Making their CD release a thematic production, rather than just a recording, was an idea borrowed from guitarist John McLaughlin. This influence underscores the links between the practice of fusion in Chennai and the new India. For better or worse, the idea of a CD release by Carnatic musicians who are asserting *their* Carnatic-influenced contemporary music seemed to be part of a trend in aggressive advertising. This was part of the ammunition for critics of fusion in Chennai, arguing that it is all marketing hype, artless virtuosity, and under-rehearsed jam sessions. But those advocates of fusion saw events like the *Carnatic Chills* release as an assertion of India's global relevance in the way it united those aspects of distinctly and essentially Indian culture (the *ragas* and *talas* of Carnatic music) with the flair of a production that displayed India's economic prosperity by way of the record label's investment in the event. In this way, the practice of fusion was a node of contestation as it attempted to "reconcile Indianness with globality" (Mazzarella 2003).

ENGLISH AND THE INDIAN MIDDLE CLASS

In the next paragraph, the concert flyer continued to assert Ganesh and Kumaresh's contemporary relevance with a comparison between the English language and changing styles of music:

Musicians, patrons, *rasikas*, the educators all live in a society where the whole world is become one beyond boundaries, one without languages but...English has become the language of the educated. It is but natural that music also changes lanes and gets into a mode of expression which can communicate to a newer breed of audiences of the world. Therefore the personal expressions of musicians if accepted by the music loving audiences also tend to change the style of performances (concert flyer: February 10, 2007, at Narada Gana Sabha).

This assertion of English as the language of the educated was consistent with the event's presentation. The organizers hired an English-speaking master of ceremonies to introduce the musicians and narrate some of the text on the flyer. He spoke English with an overtly dramatic and exaggerated British accent—not the pervasive and more subtle British-influenced Indian English—which invoked a formality that seemed more European than Indian. Although Tamil is the main language in Chennai and in the state of Tamil Nadu, English is on most Chennai street signs and in many movie theaters, and most high-school-educated people, particularly in South India, speak and understand basic conversational English. In Chennai, English remains pervasive. It has also inevitably crept into what many refer to as "Chennai Tamil," or even Tanglish, as opposed to "*sen*" Tamil, or "pure" Tamil. Because of years of contentious pre- and post-independence language politics, English has also served as the lingua franca of India, a communicative bridge between the dominant languages associated with particular states and regions, though this has diminished in the past few decades, particularly in North India. Since 1965, however, English has nationally been the "subsidiary official language" to Hindi.[4]

English has persevered in Chennai as a local "Indian" language through consecutive periods of colonial rule and national independence, so it's noteworthy that it is the language of cosmopolitanism. Ganesh and Kumaresh used English as a metaphor for the widespread relevance of their contemporary classical music, a comparison they would likely not make with their Carnatic music; just as English circulates as the predominant language of the educated cosmopolitans, so should their contemporary classical music sound the experiences of this group. This subtly highlights the inverse and more critical position as well—that Tamil is just as locally Indian and globally inaccessible as Carnatic music.

In Chennai, the English language also provides one of the most recognizable attributes of a particular segment of India's middle class—the same segment that attended this event. Leela Fernandes has written about the relationship between the Indian middle class and the English language:

The term *middle class* itself does not have a precise indigenous linguistic equivalence; there is thus an in-built linguistic connotation to middle class identity that privileges English-educated segments of the middle class as the elite tier that defines middle class identity (Fernandes 2006, 226).

In addition to Ganesh and Kumaresh's music, the sounds of English helped to invoke a contemporary cosmopolitan relevance in which the audience members were encouraged to feel that they were a part of these musicians' lives, and feel, like the musicians themselves, comfortable traveling the world, playing fusion, and speaking English. This middle-class audience was united by the idea of linking a symbol of Indian traditional essence (classical music) with a more global, contemporary, and cosmopolitan aura, thereby combining their projection of how the Indian nation sounds with their imaginations of what was global about this event. Based on the energy in the auditorium that day, my perception was that the audience participated in this performance of cosmopolitanism because the professional musicians presented a contemporary Indian music "of the world":

> The growing visibility of this new Indian middle class embodies the emergence of a wider national political culture, one that has shifted from older ideologies of a state-managed economy to a middle class-based culture of consumption. While in the early years of independence, large dams and mass-based factories were the national symbols of progress and development, cell phones, washing machines, and color televisions—goods that were not easily available during earlier decades of state-controlled markets—now seem to serve as the symbols of the liberalizing Indian nation. While earlier state socialist ideologies tended to depict workers or rural villagers as the archetypical objects of development, such ideologies now compete with mainstream national political discourses that increasingly portray urban middle class consumers as the representative citizens of liberalizing India (Fernandes 2006, xv).

Fernandes and also Mazzarella (2005) showed how the discourse of the middle class as representative of a national aspirational dream with which most people identify—while previously not a feature of Indian society—has become more commonplace.[5] India's economic liberalization (1991–present) has been a period in which these changes have become more obvious. Prior to 1991, Nehruvian socialist nationalism (named after India's first prime minister, Jawarharlal Nehru) arguably created a middle class of government workers devoted to a more Gandhian model of restraint and local productivity. Mazzarella argued that this older Indian middle class sharply contrasts with the post-1991 new middle class of entrepreneurs, cosmopolitans, and consumers, who "might be brash and vulgar" and who

"have transcended both 'traditional scruples' and 'colonial hang-ups'"
(Mazzarella 2005, 7).

CONFLICTING ELEMENTS

Although cell phones and washing machines provide obvious examples of recent changes in the material culture of India, fusion provides a window into the performative and imaginary domains of "liberalizing India" that create an opening for the newer middle class in which cosmopolitanism is a defining feature. A Chennai resident attending the CD release event could feel part of the trans-local habitus of cosmopolitanism because of the ways Ganesh and Kumaresh's music combined Indian traditional music with a contemporary, and potentially global, relevance. The last paragraph of the concert flyer (the prologue for this chapter) explicitly spelled this out with its references to how the musicians link tradition and modernity and create a confluence of conflicting elements.

Ganesh and Kumaresh wanted to link tradition and modernity in a way that is direct, obvious, and also faithful to the *sampradaya* of music and to their own creative energies. But this attempt at resolution opened up a series of questions that their music can help answer: Do the sounds of Carnatic-trained violinists with a keyboard, bass guitar, and drum set constitute "conflicting elements?" If so, is their music a confluence? Does describing these elements as "conflicted" accomplish the opposite intention and actually reinforce their potential incompatibility? Also, does merely stating a resolution as a confluence actually resolve this potential conflict? A close listening to one track on *Carnatic Chills* helps address these questions.

"FLIGHTS OF FANTASY"

The third track, "Flights of Fantasy—based on *raga janaranjani*" (video 12.1), begins with a violin sounding a slow unaccompanied phrase without a *tamboura*, the stringed instrument that provides the omnipresent drone in Indian classical music. An added reverb fills out the solo violin sound that is soon joined by the other violin. Both violinists play with limited *gamakas*—the slides, oscillations, mordents, and other subtle manipulations of pitch that are so crucially important for the identity of any given *raga*—but with enough *gamakas* so that the violins are still identifiable as Indian, and to the more familiar ear, Carnatic. A keyboard enters soon after, and its sounds of synthesized strings outline a chordal progression that supports the two violins, which constitute the prominent foreground. After this, one of the violins harmonizes with the other in parallel intervals. The piece continues to feature the entrances and exits of the accompanying instruments, always featuring the violins as the sonic foreground, as well as alternations between unison and harmonized melodic lines. Throughout the piece, sections never last too long and always lead into the next, usually linked by rhythmic similarity and increasing melodic activity.

The short excerpt from "Flights of Fantasy" effectively demonstrates this continual progression through a series of short sections, and more importantly, the sonic attributes of this piece's Carnatic structures. The excerpt begins right before the entrance of the percussion instruments, which accompany the Carnatic rhythmic cadence played by both violins in unison. The end of the cadence marks a significant change; a repetitive and decaying electronic effect resolves the mounting tension and transitions the piece from an eight-beat meter (unaccompanied by percussion) into a four-beat meter that features the violinists trading short solos over a drum machine and keyboard texture. Soon after, another texture emerges with more forceful drum accents. The excerpt ends with one of the violinists completing a phrase with a Carnatic *gamaka*.

The compositional organization and progression of these sections and the repetition of the eight- and then four-beat phrases demonstrate that the composers of this piece are clearly Carnatic musicians accustomed to the kind of theme-and-variations structure of the South Indian *kriti* song form. As a result, the piece's development is a gradual and continual melodic variation with increasing rhythmic activity in which the violins always hold the textural foreground. Apart from the harmonizing voices of violins and keyboards, the central logic of the compositional approach to this piece was derived from Carnatic music. The keyboard has an almost constant presence in much of the fusion performed in Chennai and is the most direct link to the "newage" label they gave this project. As a result, *Carnatic Chills* is effectively a Carnatic interpretation of New Age music.

This excerpt shows that the oft-mentioned contradictions are extremely subjective and nowhere obviously located in musical sound, but still clearly an important part of the interpretation of this music from the perspective of Chennai in the 21st century. If, as the flyer described, this is the sonic equivalent of wearing a *jibba* and jeans, then *Carnatic Chills* is as normalized as a man wearing a *jibba* and jeans, which happens pretty frequently, particularly among the younger generations.

So the most salient message of this track, of the language during the CD release, of the event itself, and also of Ganesh's thoughts during our interview is not so much determining whether these musical elements, instruments, *ragas*, and harmonies are all contradictions, but rather the ways that Ganesh, the record company, and the press constructed these features as contradictions. Ganesh and Kumaresh's strategy of naming the contradictions and then offering the solution of their music, which would "reflect the contradictions in today's life" (Swaminathan 2007) has a way of underscoring these elements as contradictions that perpetuate them as irreconcilable, mismatched, and incommensurable. But their strategy also coexists with this irresolution, as if to argue that the tensions and incongruencies of everyday life can be heard, interpreted, and made to coexist through musical sound.

COSMOPOLITANISM AND THE NEW MIDDLE CLASS

Those who spent their evening attending a concert of contemporary classical music that presented and attempted to resolve some of the contradictions of being both Indian and global partook in a performative, musicalized, and distinctly privileged kind of problem. India's recent economic prosperity has led to dramatic changes in India's metropoles in the last two decades, and as mentioned above, changing class dynamics have been a defining feature of this period. Different segments of the middle class have arisen in contrast to one another, creating a complex Indian middle class with competing interests. Craig Calhoun identified how an elite tier of the middle class uses cosmopolitanism to distinguish its elite status from the rest of the middle class:

> Contemporary cosmopolitanism commonly reflects the experience and perspective of elites and obscures the social foundations on which that experience and perspective rests.... Cosmopolitanism alone commonly focuses attention away from...political, economic, and social questions and towards apparently free-floating ethics and culture (Calhoun 2008, 441).

Calhoun warned of the dangers of focusing too much attention on the superficial signs of cosmopolitanism, of which music-making could be seen to be a part, but the *Carnatic Chills* release event and my conversation with Violin Ganesh provide clear evidence that the practice of fusion addresses serious political, economic, and social questions about the conditions of middle-class contemporary Indian culture. Calhoun's point that the *Carnatic Chills* event could have been interpreted by other Chennai classes as the privileged and exclusive games of middle-class elites is also helpful because it questions the elitist foundations on which the practices of fusion rest. It reminds us that with sheer numbers, the world of classical music is small compared to the national and international reach of film music. If those numbers are comparatively small, the number of people interested in fusion or contemporary classical music is even smaller. But regardless of the size of a fan base, the issues that Ganesh and Kumaresh have synthesized into their creative output show that this fused combination of classical, popular, and Western music encapsulates experiences that are relevant to an increasing number of Indian citizens.

CONCLUSION

Ganesh and Kumaresh's music demonstrates how fusion causes problems as much as it resolves them, and understood as part of a continuum of fusion in the latter half of the 20th century, it also shows that the problems have been present and unresolved all along. At the release event, they wanted to publicize and market their hard work in a way that would reward them, and the chief guests that night were a key to the night's success. Both are titans of the Chennai music scene in completely different but complementary ways: Rahman as film music composer celebrity has obvious ties to fusion sounds from all around the world, and Vikku Vinayakram's former trailblazing in fusion and present status as an institution for learning and inspiration were equally powerful. The inclusion of these two guests also provided a subtle message that connected Ganesh and Kumaresh's music with the international reach of Rahman's film music and the historical lineage of Vinayakram's classical music. In the press release a few days later, Chitra Swaminathan wrote, "The chief guests also reflected the cool and the classical, which is what 'Carnatic chills' is all about" (Swaminathan 2007).

However, the central tension that remained unresolved during my conversation with Ganesh was his perspective on the differences between his contemporary classical music and his Carnatic music. He made several descriptions of his music that, on the one hand, elided both practices into one, saying that he was just playing what he naturally was. On the other hand, he clearly separated Carnatic *kacceris* and his contemporary classical concerts, estimating that if he plays about 100 concerts a year, roughly 10 percent of them will be contemporary classical music (Violin Ganesh, pers. comm. 2008). His ambivalence about whether or not to combine them or keep them separate in the way he talked about them is indicative of the tensions that surround the practice of fusion in Chennai. There was a general uncertainty among musicians and audience members in Chennai about fusion, which endowed this musical practice with contestation. The ways that the CD release event of *Carnatic Chills* both reified and resolved the musical and social contradictions of contemporary Chennai also show how fusion sounds the many tensions and irresolutions of present-day urban India. This example of contemporary music-making demonstrates the ways that overlapping ideologies of Indian tradition, economic and cultural change, shifting class formations, and cosmopolitanism can all be heard as a sign of the multiply constituted experience of urban India.

NOTES

1. There are multiple ways of spelling "Carnatic." I chose this particular spelling here because it was the choice of Ganesh and Kumaresh on their album.
2. The release event featured Keith Peters, bass guitar; Ravichandra, flute; Dhanashekar, keyboard; Arun Kumar, drums and percussion; Mannargudi Easwaran, *mrdangam*; and S. V. Ramani, *ghatam*. These are the same musicians as on the recording.
3. Rather than understanding fusion as a genre, I purposefully avoid the concept of genre in favor of fusion as a musical practice. Although seminal and recent work on genre has shown the processual ways genres are shaped by various individuals and social consensuses (Briggs and Bauman 1992; Scott 2008; Holt 2007; and Fellezs 2011), these writers form a concept of genre that is too cohesive for fusion in Chennai. See Higgins (2013) for a more in-depth explanation about the difference between genre and practice for fusion in Chennai.
4. See the Indian government document "Notification No. 2/8/60-O.L." Ministry of Home Affairs, dated April 27, 1960.
5. William Mazzarella and Leela Fernandes both offer more in-depth descriptions and discussions of India's middle-class history and present manifestations. In India, the model of a pyramid best illustrates class distribution—the upper classes are comparatively much smaller than in the United States and the lower classes are comparatively much larger.

CHAPTER 13

At Home in the Studio

The Sound of Manganiyar Music Going Popular

SHALINI AYYAGARI

INTRODUCTION

In January 2008, while conducting research in western Rajasthan, I was invited to attend a recording session that one of my research collaborators, Gazi Khan Barna, a well-known musician from the region, was to conduct in Jaipur, Rajasthan. I eagerly accepted the invitation, seeing it as an opportunity to observe these musicians outside their familiar village performance settings. Many questions as to what would happen in the recording studio came to mind: How would the Manganiyar musicians adjust their music to this new context? What would be lost or gained through the experience for the musicians? How would the resultant recordings be utilized? How would the musicians respond to the increasingly widespread shift from traditional to mediated and often popular music among the Manganiyar?

It was only after the recording session in Jaipur that it became apparent to me what an increasingly important and innovative role such recording studios have in contemporary musical creativity, innovation, genre-making, preservation, and marketing of the Manganiyar community among its musicians, record producers, and music consumers (Beaster-Jones 2009; Booth 1993; and Chanan 1995). This chapter examines the recent usage of recording studios by musicians from the Manganiyar community, delving into four integral facets of the recording studio experience: (1) innovative performance practice in the recording studio and the musical freedoms that the technology of the studio affords the musicians; (2) the ways in which recordings made in recording studios are utilized, accessed, and distributed by musicians; (3) the tension between preservation and innovation that plays out during the recording process; and (4) a larger phenomenon whereby many Manganiyar musicians are now transitioning from more customary, localized performance practices and contexts to diverse practices and popular settings. The recording studio ultimately plays a large part in this phenomenon.

The Manganiyar

The Manganiyar are a community of hereditary, professional musicians hailing from the Thar Desert region of western Rajasthan (Ayyagari 2012). Customarily, they have provided family genealogies and ceremonial music for their hereditary patrons for remuneration in kind for at least the past three centuries. With modernization in the past 50 years, however, the importance of these age-old patronage relationships has waned for both the musicians and their patrons. Although these relationships still exist, they now complement other economic relationships and practices, such as development initiatives, cultural tourism, and more modern modes of musical production and consumption. Manganiyar musicians routinely tour abroad, some six months out of the year, performing predominantly in Australia, Europe, and North America. Inherent in performances in these new contexts are musical innovation, novel performance practice, and more musical freedoms and creativity, to be discussed throughout this chapter.[1] Manganiyars have adapted their art to modern tourism and the global arts economy; participation in recording studio culture and media is an integral part of this adaptation.

In the Studio

The number of recording studios in Rajasthan has grown in the past decade. Many have catered to Manganiyar musicians by nurturing business relationships and musical collaborations. While the majority of Rajasthani recording studios are located in larger metropolitan areas like Jaipur, Jodhpur, and even the more provincial Jaisalmer, what was intriguing to me was the impressive number of recording studios popping up not in cities, but throughout the remote desert landscape of western Rajasthan. With increasing access to electricity and the affordability of recording equipment, there have been a number of small do-it-yourself style studios on the outskirts of villages and along seemingly deserted dusty roads in western Rajasthan. Although many of these studios have been ephemeral in nature—here one day and gone the next—the fact that they were there at all indicates that there is at least some demand and desire for them to exist in the first place.

This chapter examines the Manganiyars' experiences as they engaged in two specific recording studio/project initiatives, both part of a trend in informal do-it-yourself studios. The first and larger case study focuses on Morchang Studios, built in 2005, as the brainchild of Jaipur-based entrepreneurs John and Faith Singh. "Morchang" refers to an instrument played prevalently in western Rajasthan, also known as the jaw harp or Jew's harp. Morchang's founders are better known for their more established business endeavor, Anokhi, an artisan-based woodblock printing and natural dye business, which they founded in Jaipur over 30 years ago. In 2002, they expanded their entrepreneurship to the founding of a charitable trust, the Jaipur Virasat Foundation (hereafter JVF). As an extension of their foundation efforts, the Singhs later founded Morchang Studios, a recording studio with the goal of promoting and preserving regional music traditions of Rajasthan. Morchang Studios was at its recording peak between 2007 and 2010 under the direction of producer Aditya Bhasin and sound engineer Nick Atkins. The JVF-studio connection served as a platform for musicians to visit the studio, learn about recording technology, conduct a recording session free of charge, and then have free access to those recordings to distribute and sell as they pleased. Many musicians from the Manganiyar community took advantage of this opportunity and became the musical face of Morchang Studios. The studio was not functioning during my field visit in 2010, but it has since been revived and renamed Studio Roots, serving as a platform for the music group collective Rajasthan Roots.

The second recording studio/project on which I focus is Amarrass Records, established by Ashutosh Sharma and Ankur Malhotra in 2009, to deliver what Malhotra has described as "a contemporary world music experience." The first record put out by the label was a live recording of "Manganiyar Seduction," a dramatic interpretation of Manganiyar traditional performance repertoire staged in the metaphorical space of the Red Light District of Amsterdam, Netherlands, by the Indian theatrical director Roysten Abel. According to the label's website,

> We often listen to music in flashes and fleeting moments, but its impact is long lasting. What stays with us are everlasting melodies, the glorious beats, an essence of the moment captured in rhythm. Built on a shared vision, passion

and love for music, Amarrass Records is our attempt at finding and creating new solutions to address old issues and find a sustainable way forward to preserve, promote and enhance music that matters.[2]

After experimenting with many different kinds of music and various ways of promotion, Sharma and Malhotra came to the conclusion that the most interesting music for them to promote was in their own backyard in India, and that this music was worth preserving. Over the past two years, Amarrass Records has released four records of Manganiyar music and a number of videos on YouTube documenting the music Sharma and Malhotra saw and heard while touring western Rajasthan. Amarrass has also hosted what they hope will become an annual Amarrass Desert Music Festival.[3]

INNOVATIVE PERFORMANCE AND MUSICAL FREEDOM

The Manganiyar recording session that I witnessed at Morchang Studios in 2008 involved a large number of musicians under the supervision of their director and Manganiyar musician Gazi Khan Barna and demonstrated considerably more innovation and musical freedom than I had imagined. I had assumed that Gazi Khan Barna would have invited a few musicians to accompany him for a more customary and intimate small ensemble session, and that the session would consist of various audio recording takes with each instrument and voice recorded in parts separately, followed by a thorough editing and mixing process by the studio's engineers. But this recording session would not be what I had expected because of the large number of musicians involved.

The ambience of the recording studio first struck me as being unique. The ethnomusicologist Louise Meintjes theorizes the importance of studio spaces a becoming "non-places" and losing their connections with the "local." In this way, Meintjes has argued, musical identities can be re-imagined, processed, and projected out into the global marketplace (2003). Contrastingly, despite Morchang Studios' recording equipment acquired from the U.K. and its British sound engineer, the studio harnessed the ability to invoke the local through created space. At the time of my visit in 2008, Morchang Studios was a small and cozy studio outside of the hubbub of the old, walled Pink City of Jaipur in eastern Rajasthan. The studio itself was conducive to interaction and musical conversation between performers, featuring large, open, and inviting spaces for recording. The decor was very typical in its associations with Rajasthan—the walls painted in vivid but warm hues of saffron with details in gold, traditional Rajasthani art and handiwork decorating the walls, and beautiful and inviting carpets lining the floors. The track lighting throughout the studio space is something not often seen in Rajasthan, and it provided a warm, natural light, rather than the more typical florescent lighting found indoors in Rajasthan; this gave the feeling of being outdoors, an environment very familiar for more customary Manganiyar performance contexts. The studio space, then, invoked the space of Rajasthan in an effort to make local musicians feel more comfortable and produce a "Rajasthani" sound. I hypothesize that JVF and Morchang Studios' original intention of preservation of Rajasthani music traditions led to the creation of a studio space that nurtured a sense of home rather than envisioning a "non-place" as theorized by Meintjes.

Beyond this visually stunning studio space, what was most distinctive about this recording session was the choice of ensemble for the recording. Instead of a small, intimate group of three or four musicians, which is generally what comprises a customary Manganiyar performance, there were 20 musicians who performed together in the recording session. In customary Manganiyar performance, instrumentation typically consists of a lead singer accompanied by the kamaicha (a bowed lute), with rhythmic accompaniment of the dholak (a double-headed hand drum), and rhythmic flourishes by the khartal (two pairs of wooden castanets), usually four musicians in all.[4] The ensemble used in this recording session, however, featured multiple performers on the same instrument, creating the equivalent of orchestral sections. Gazi Khan Barna served as the lead singer and conductor of the various instrumental sections of kamaichas, sarangis (a bowed lute similar to the kamaicha), harmonium, child singers, khartal, dholak, and murli (a double-reed instrument).[5] The most unique addition to the instrumentation in the recordings was that of the dautara, a plucked lute with two to five strings (Barthakur 2003).[6] This instrument was not present during the initial recording session, but appears to have been added later during the editing process and can easily be heard in the finished recording. The juxtaposition of this instrument (with its standout twangy musical timbre) with other, more customary Manganiyar instruments creates an interesting timbral contrast. The dautara fills in short melodic interludes between sung verses with a distinctive syncopated rhythm and fades in and out almost unnoticed throughout the performance. An electric bass was also added during the editing process, creating an implicit sense of harmony under the Manganiyar melodic lines.

Another difference between the Manganiyar customary practice and this recording session was Gazi Khan Barna's role within the ensemble and the unusual preparation that he carried out before the session. This preparation included actively choosing the repertoire to be performed in the recording session ahead of time during the bus journey from Jaisalmer to Jaipur. Typically, Manganiyar musicians depend on real-time improvisation and setting to dictate performance repertoire; performances are thus occasion-driven. For example, at a patron's wedding, Manganiyar musicians have a fixed repertoire of wedding songs to choose from. The improvisation lies in the songs that are chosen from that fixed repertoire, melodic and rhythmic improvisation within the performance of each song, and choosing lyrics based on those people in attendance and the mood of the performance. For the Morchang Studios recording session, Gazi Khan Barna not only chose the repertoire ahead of time, but he also wrote down (during the bus journey) an arrangement of song lyrics and musical forms, dictating what musicians would play and when. Gazi Khan Barna, having previously participated in many recording projects and having performed worldwide for the past three decades, is well aware of the contextual demands of the recording studio as opposed to live, ritual-based performance. However, in a community of musicians that prides itself on oral tradition and memorization (some musicians brag that they have over 100 generations of patrons' names memorized), and whose musicians are for the most part illiterate, this act can be seen as innovative.[7] Throughout the recording session, older Manganiyar songs were rendered in new and innovative ways, and Gazi Khan stood before the group of musicians, earphones on his head, with a microphone in one hand and his pages of notes in the other, literally conducting the musicians, both practices well beyond the norms of Manganiyar musical traditions, where smaller groups of musicians are able to rely on musical and physical cues to guide and keep performances together.[8] Within this large group, the performance was also unique because of its form, which included calculated solos, fade-ins and fade-outs, and the use of Panjabi-language song lyrics for one number, "Vari Jaon."

The priorities of the musicians during the recording session at Morchang Studios were atypical of other recording sessions I have witnessed. The musicians seemed to prioritize social interaction and live performance. The musicians did not assume, as other musicians perhaps more familiar with the nature of studio sessions might, that music in this context can consist of different parts that can be recorded in separate takes and mixed together later. These musicians were still very much working within a live performance mentality, depending on interactions, cues, and playing off of each other to make the music into a coherent performance. In addition, the musicians were dressed in their colorful public performance outfits, which are especially worn in performance contexts involving foreigners. Their facial expressions, interactions with each other, and general demeanor were equally typical of "live" public performance contexts, rather than the various jam and practice sessions they have in their villages. At times during the session, it almost seemed like the musicians might stop paying attention to the director at any moment, to carry on in a style of improvisatory playing more familiar to them. Thus, while Gazi Khan Barna was working in a different performance mentality than is customarily done, the musicians were not. Gazi Khan's performance mentality was most likely due in part to his prior experiences in recording studios and decades of performing in non-customary performance contexts outside of India. In this way, Gazi Khan served as a conduit between the traditional world of musical patronage in western Rajasthan and the global, technologically advanced recording studio.

The presence of a video camera documenting the entire session to be uploaded to Morchang Studios' YouTube page inevitably played a part in the musicians' presentation, adding another complicated dynamic into the mix. The various videos presented on that YouTube page (including the recording session I witnessed) were produced by Nick Atkins and Aditya Bhasin between 2006 and 2010. They serve as an online account of the recordings in sound and vision. According to the page, "Much of the work has been recorded live (albeit with 'one take' overdubs)...as this represents the reality of the performance."[9] Morchang Studios producers' ideas of what fidelity to live performance meant were of the utmost importance. In the case of this particular session, while the reality that this quote cites did indeed take place during the session, it was a reality inherently mediated by the musicians' awareness that they were being recorded and were thus performing for the camera, treating it more as a live performance than a recording session.

Influenced by both the symbolic and actual freedoms that the recording studio technology provided, Gazi Khan Barna took this opportunity to think outside of the box and deliver a musical product unlike other Manganiyar performances. Although the musicians were not necessarily thinking about recording technology as part of the collaborative creative process, the music itself was freed from the constraints normally adhered to in the ways described above. Their understanding of what they could do and their experience of what actually happened differed greatly. Thus, the creativity in this context was not so much about the technology itself, but about the musical freedoms that the technology afforded to the musical creative process.

RECORDINGS AND RIGHTS IN AND OUT OF THE STUDIO

The year after the recording session discussed above, I attended a concert in Berkeley, California, by a group of five Manganiyar musicians on tour in the United States. After the concert, the musicians sold CDs. Upon a closer look at the CDs, I noticed a number of interesting features. None of the musicians featured on the album cover, superimposed onto a barren Rajasthani desert background of sand dunes, were the musicians who had just performed in the concert. When I got home and listened to the CD, I was struck by a moment of déjà vu. I had heard this song performed before, but not at the concert that night. After a moment of contemplation, I realized the song was one of the performances I had watched being recorded the previous year at Morchang Studios in Jaipur during the Gazi Khan Barna recording session. The implicit expectation of a CD being sold at a concert was that it would consist of recordings made by the group of performers seen that night in live performance. This was not the case.

These contemporary circumstances of Manganiyar music happening on a global circuit facilitated by recording studios raise a host of questions: How is intellectual property conceptualized in these conditions, and how do assertions of authorship and creativity occur in and out of the recording studio? How does a collectively produced cultural product, like an album made in a recording studio, highlight issues of technology, space, power, aesthetics, and authorship? And how then do these issues take shape in the production and recording of a CD, which is then distributed internationally in contexts radically different from those in which it was produced (cf. Greene 1999, 2001a, and 2003).

In 2010, I spoke with one of the musicians from the Berkeley performance the year before and asked him about the CD they had sold that night. The musician at first did not even recall the CD; but on further explanation, he chuckled and told me that he had been given a copy of the recording not long before that U.S. tour, had a local studio duplicate it, and proceeded to sell and make enough money from the proceeds to provide pocket money while on tour and buy souvenirs to take home with him. The musician did not explain to me any rights or permissions he received to duplicate the recordings, and although he knew the musicians who were involved in the Morchang Studios recording project, his relationship with them was not made clear to me.

I do not imply here that Manganiyar musicians are unaware of or unconcerned with issues of authorship. Instead, this example highlights the freedom that the musicians performing in Berkeley felt in selling CDs that were not their own.[10] For the Manganiyar, the same authorship constraints that are present in performance practice do not apply when it comes to recording technology. For example, during the live performance in Berkeley, these same musicians were very careful to tell the audience when they were performing a non-Manganiyar song, or to name a Manganiyar musician who originally made a particular song well known. It is clear then that technology does not simply or necessarily overpower or Westernize musical life or thought concerning authorship and appropriation. Rather, technology provides new possibilities for a range of behaviors, as scholars such as Hughes (2002), McCann (2005), Riley (2004), Schur (2009), Vaidhyanathan (2001), and Young (2010), have suggested. It is the people, after all, who use the technologies, and it is they who dictate the morals surrounding the uses of that technology.

Manganiyar music, like other types of contemporary and popular music, cannot be adequately modeled as something that happens only in a local context, employing only the expressive means specific to a locality, group, or community (Marcus 1992). In this case, a specific group of Manganiyar musicians was selling recordings of other Manganiyar musicians—for their own personal profit—while performing in a very non-customary context. Even Manganiyar music, considered by many in and outside of India to be the epitome of "authentic folk music," happens along a global circuit of rapid communication, complicated technology, and varying influence as an accelerating and disjunct global cultural flow. In this way, contemporary Manganiyar music is not so different from other types of popular music. Manganiyar music takes its "place" wherever and in whatever context it is heard. The recording studio, then, serves as a nerve center where sounds are quickly absorbed, reworked, reincorporated into new music, and spread to new contexts (Porcello 1996; Rasmussen 1996; Sharma 2007; and Théberge 1997). Clearly, Rajasthan's new recording studios have had an impact on Manganiyar musicians' control of production, duplication, and distribution of their own music, albeit on a very small-scale level and sometimes not necessarily in accordance with more general understandings of music ownership and authorship etiquette.

Simon Frith has observed that "... electrical recording (and amplification) broke the previously necessary relationship between a musical object in space and a musical object in time. Recording perfection ceased to refer to a specific performance (a faithful sound). The 'original' in short, ceased to be an event and became an idea" (1996, 234). Although Frith is referring more to the fidelity of the sound, it is clear that the same kinds of transformations result as the recording studio process alters Manganiyar musicians' ideas about ownership and about the studio itself. The ways in which the studio process alters Manganiyar musicians' ideas about ownership gives them the freedom to think about their music not as a specific performance by specific performers, but as a technological tool for innovation and livelihood. Thus, the issues and anecdotes recounted here speak to what I foresee as being a more expansive trend in the years to come of Manganiyars' musical lives intertwining with technology in new and innovative ways to produce novel images, sounds, and ideas, where authorship is secondarily important.[11]

THE TENSIONS BETWEEN PRESERVATION AND INNOVATION

Next, I focus on the two particular recording studios and their associated record labels that Manganiyar musicians have been closely associated with: Jaipur's Morchang Studios (discussed above) and Amarrass Records, which was founded in 2009 as both a recording studio and record label; the label has released many albums featuring Rajasthani (mainly Manganiyar) musicians. Both of these companies seem to struggle with their goals of putting out marketable, popular, and innovative music while also encouraging Manganiyar musicians to maintain their traditional repertoire, instrumentation, and ways of making music. In these cases, then, what are the tensions between preservation and innovation in musical production, and how are these enterprises grappling with this balancing act? In what ways do these recording companies shape Manganiyar musicians to make them more popular, and in what ways do they hold them back?

Morchang Studios

The Jaipur Virasat Foundation (JVF), which has a controlling interest in Morchang Studios, originally saw the studio as part of their mission to preserve Rajasthani traditions in collaboration with UNESCO; they thus had one foot in the recording industry and one foot in the cultural preservation sector. According to their general mission statement, JVF has "pioneered a holistic, culture-based and cross-sector approach to livelihood through its various activities, events, advocacy forums, and networks, always employing artisan and specialist skills."[12] JVF produces a number of annual festivals in Rajasthan that they claim act to reify tradition and sustain customary cultural performance among the many hereditary communities of musicians, dancers, and artists of Rajasthan, including the Manganiyar. Speaking specifically of Morchang Studios, the project's founder John Singh said that the studio was "a developmental music project which aimed to preserve, nurture, and share, to a national and international audience the folk music of Rajasthan" (pers. comm. 2007).

As of June 2011, however, Morchang Studios had been closed down due to financial hardship. The facility, renamed Studio Roots, was subsequently revived through the efforts of Aditya Bhasin. The studio's mission was no longer to simply provide a recording platform for Rajasthani regional artists, but was now centered on the goal of cross-cultural collaboration through music. Many of the photographs uploaded to the studio's website, its YouTube page, and Bhasin's personal Facebook and MySpace pages focus on foreign (mainly American and European) musicians jamming with Rajasthani regional artists, most prominently younger musicians from the Manganiyar community. In our e-mail correspondence, Bhasin described to me his beginnings with JVF and Morchang Studios: "After one meeting with John Singh, discussing the possibilities of working with thousands of artists from different communities of Rajasthan, the scope for experimentation, production, freedom of expression, and thus empowering them and providing a stable livelihood seemed like a mission and a vision that I just couldn't walk away from" (pers. comm. 2010).

An integral part of Bhasin's involvement with Morchang Studios is Rajasthan Roots, which he founded in 2004 and which he prefers to call a "collective of folk musicians" rather than a band or a group.[13] This ever-changing group of musicians produces a type of fusion music that Bhasin believes is marketable to a wide range of audiences both in and out of India. According to Bhasin, "We stayed away from the typical fusion—either with [W]estern drums or drumbeats and allowed for the sound to evolve on its own. By introducing instruments which made the music and tone warmer such as the bass guitar and other melodic instruments such as the bamboo flute, guitar and saxophone, the outcome was an easily palatable sound to people all around the world across all age groups" (e-mail comm., 2010). Here, Bhasin describes "typical fusion" as non-Western music that includes Western drums or drumbeats. Instead, I argue that, while Rajasthan Roots' sound may not be "typical," it appeals to a more popular listening base by using familiar instrumentation like the bass guitar, guitar, and saxophone.[14] By fusing these Western instruments with more customary Manganiyar instruments like the morchang, kamaicha, and dholak, the music is able to reach larger audiences and enables Rajasthan Roots to ultimately be more popular (see Feld 1994).

But at the same time as Bhasin chooses to speak about the Manganiyar influence in Rajasthan Roots' music in terms of a contemporary sound appealing to a popular audience, he also chooses to mystify it as something traditional, customary, rare, untainted, and worth preserving as it is. In a piece he coauthored for the online Indian music magazine The Big M, Bhasin describes the first few years working with Morchang Studios as a "crash course for [him] in every sense":

> Vinod and I would jump into John [Singh]'s SUV and drive off into the country-side. Sometimes it would be all night *Jagrans* [all-night Hindu religious ceremonies], an opportunity to meet Jasnath Ke Bhope [a well-known Rajasthani priest and singer]—dancing barefoot on burning embers of coal, or a whole village of *Tejaji ke Bhope* [Rajasthani priest-singers who worship *Tejaji*, the Rajasthani Hindu diety]—dancing with hundreds of defanged cobras and sometimes it would be Momasar [a small Rajasthani village in Bikaner District]—where on every *Holi*, for three days everyone dresses up in drag, in unimaginable characters and they dance, act and perform street theatre.[15]

Thus, although Bhasin performs as a key member of Rajasthan Roots, he is also able to step back and construct an exotic mysticism around the Manganiyar as an outsider would, providing, as the group's director and visionary, a view of the Manganiyar as something mystical, traditional, and worth preserving. In this case, the group's marketability and promotion are integrally tied to the act of preservation. Ultimately, Bhasin believes that

> [t]he need to have a contemporary interpretation of the folk music of Rajasthan was required to evolve the age old traditions of the region and bring it to international standards of production. By keeping its essence intact, emphasis was made to introduce warmth and depth—bass, vocal harmonies, effects, etc. to the music, and also to produce the electrifying percussion of Rajasthan into a pulsative groove, also allowing space for all of the nuances of the traditional instruments to be heard....By encouraging the musicians to write their own songs they leave behind their own legacy for future generations to follow, and creating the new sounds of Rajasthan![16]

Here, Bhasin speaks about the "essence" of Manganiyar music. However, it is implied in his comments that this essence does not necessarily appeal to a more popular audience, be it in India or outside of India. Therefore, in order to make this essence palatable to non-specialist audiences, Bhasin introduces "warmth and depth" through instrumentation and studio effects. He also adds what he calls a "pulsative groove" to the already intricate and dynamic customary Manganiyar percussion (dholak and khartal). Although Bhasin was not clear what he meant by "pulsative," the foregrounding of Manganiyar percussion instruments in the group leads me to believe he is referring to a Manganiyar conception of rhythm, but one that is made more explicit and prominent. These changes appeal to a more popular audience and are ultimately what allows Rajasthan Roots to sell concert tickets and CDs, and become more popular.

Morchang Studios/Studio Roots, with its present, revitalized focus on Rajasthan Roots, is thus a place for musical hybridization to take place. According to Bhasin, "[The studio] serves as a platform for creativity and expression, encouraging the musicians to experiment, to create the new sounds of Rajasthan" (e-mail comm., 2010). Such experimentation seems to rarely be carried out for its own sake. The collaboration among various musicians then takes the place that the studio sound engineering practices did in Morchang Studios' earlier formation and specifically in the previously discussed Gazi Khan Barna recording session. Both forms of the studio seek to create inspired hybrids that are capable of attracting new and lucrative audiences.

Amarrass Records

> In December last, after our hugely successful Manganiyar Seduction show at Purana Qila, we embarked on a series of ambitious journeys. Fascinated by the music of the Manganiyars, a 400-year-old community of Muslim musicians, we cris-crossed Rajasthan to look for the finest among them. We wanted to research and document their rich musical heritage, and most of all, we wanted to record their music in its purest form: with traditional instruments—all in one take and acoustic.[17]

Taken from Amarrass Records' website, this statement resonates with that of Aditya Bhasin above in describing his life-changing field trips throughout western Rajasthan absorbing the local colors and flavors of music, with the same foregrounded exotic and essentialist discourse. Amarrass Records' interest in fidelity, analog faithfulness, the LP format, and acoustic sound is at once innovative (in a region where recorded sound quality has not been the most important feature of recordings) and retro (by using an older recording format) at the same time. Yet, their rhetoric of "rich musical heritage," purity, and tradition in the above quote points to a desire to represent their work as primarily concerned with preservation, in a parallel fashion to Morchang Studios. In this way, Amarrass Records is attempting to preserve Manganiyar music by changing it through the uses of recording technology.

Part of this attention to preservation can be seen in one facet of Amarrass Records' project, the Amarrass Society for Performing Arts. Through the creation of a database of folk artists organized state by state, the goal of the society is to allow musicians to interface directly with their listening audience, without the intervention of a third party—be it a record label or a tour organizer. They call this their "Amarrass fair trade model."[18] Through the medium of a website, visitors will be able to book artists directly for events and buy recordings, using "fair trade policies regarding payment for services and support mechanisms to fund artists, their families, and the heritage that inspires the creation of their music."[19] However, the society's founders do not define what they actually mean by fair trade; the phrase comes across more as catchy lingo than a transparent financial system to free musicians like the Manganiyar from outside parties. In addition, they do not take into consideration that the number of Manganiyars able and willing to use the Internet is still relatively small; many Manganiyars live in villages with little electricity and a lack of computers, and are sometimes illiterate. "Fair trade," as defined by the European Fair Trade Association, then, is not so fair or evenly accessed by the Manganiyar.

Another goal of the Amarrass Society for Performing Arts is to promote music education among professional folk musician communities in order to help Manganiyar children sustain their musical traditions instead of having to turn to other professions to make a living. The preservation role that the Amarrass Society is taking on in the lives of the Manganiyar (at least in the rhetoric of the website) is a large one, not to be taken lightly, with a potentially heavy impact on the community. Interestingly, in order to fund such an ambitious education project, Amarrass Records has made a portal on their website where visitors can order and purchase an authentic instrument from the community. According to the website, "Lakha Khan [referring to a well-known virtuosic Manganiyar sarangi player] has four *sarangis*, each from a previous generation in his family. This instrument is in his blood. Contact us to find out how you can get a *sarangi* handcrafted by the master."[20] Although the demand for such an instrument—the masters of which are in India and possess a highly specialized playing and tuning technique very difficult to learn—is not likely to be very high, such a marketing idea apparently aims to democratize music-making of such communities like the Manganiyar. Such sales, however, bring into question the goals of selling traditional Manganiyar instruments: Is the goal of such sales spreading the playing of the instrument internationally, turning these instruments into inanimate artifacts for foreigners, economically supporting musicians and instrument makers to continue their trade, or a combination of all of the above? These questions are not answered on the studio's website, and the possible positive results of such an initiative are questionable.[21] This practice demonstrates Amarrass Records' intentions but also the clear impact therein of the tensions between preservation and innovation.

While Amarrass Records' series of field recordings aim at preservation of musical repertoire that is in danger of being lost, according to their website, "This music isn't only for the purist, however, as anyone who hears it will know. We also believe it has the power to move people from all age groups and cultures. This is world music, and it deserves a world audience."[22] What then is the difference between "purist music" and "world music" in such a context? This quote points to the marketability and the broad audience that this music has the potential to attract. Amarrass Records aims to accomplish this goal through the uses of technology—in the recording studio, through easy access to the music through Internet downloads, through watching YouTube clips of their fieldtrips to rural Rajasthan, and through online commodification of traditional Manganiyar instruments.

Amarrass Records has put out five albums on LP (and also CD and downloadable MP3). According to Ankur Malhotra, "What the LP essentially does is bring back the art of listening to music. It's a process that requires some amount of time and patience. You take the vinyl out of its cover, dust it, place it on the turntable and gently drop the needle on the track you want to play. It's an experience, and it needs listening to" (pers. comm. 2011). In addition, their third album, *Banko Ghodo* (2012), was only able to be made with funds partly raised through Kickstarter.com, a crowd-sourcing website.

Although one of Amarrass Records' goals is to give an empowering voice to those musicians who have not been recognized, all of the artists on Amarrass Records' albums are those few Manganiyar musicians who are the most well known in the community, having traveled many times on tour outside of Rajasthan and India, and they tend to be the wealthiest in the community. Thus, while Amarrass Records' practices are innovative in the use of the Internet for promotion and fundraising, recording media, and festival organizing, they also aim at cultural and musical preservation, albeit in a problematic way that points to a lack of knowledge about the community, their culture, and the economic impact that such endeavors have on local music-making.

MANGANIYAR MUSIC GOES POPULAR?

While there are indeed many deep-seated changes currently happening among the Manganiyar musician community in terms of performance practice, instrumentation, patronage, and visibility, their music style and repertoire have not drastically changed. Instead, their popularity is shifting from a more insular network of long-held patrons and a somewhat more recent local tourism market (since the 1980s) to international touring, diverse audiences, new venues, and active recording lives.

The musical influences that the two recording initiatives, Morchang Studios/Rajasthan Roots and Amarrass Records, bring to Manganiyar music are indeed those of the world of popular music. According to Aditya Bhasin, "Since my upbringing was mostly in American schools in Europe and my influences in music were all the classic bands such as the Beatles, Rolling Stones, Creedence Clearwater Revival, Jimi Hendrix, etc., most of the music and lyrics that I wrote were in English and of [W]estern style" (e-mail comm., 2010). Likewise, Amarrass Records' founders were deeply influenced by Western popular music. Ankur Malhotra is based both in Madison, Wisconsin, and New Delhi. In Madison, he is a DJ and popular music radio host. He also runs the online Madison Music Review, which is a community-based forum promoting local live music, festivals, and active discussions and reviews of music, with a focus on popular and electronic music. In addition, Malhotra is the producer of Musique Electronique, an electronic dance music (EDM) festival. The sensibilities of the two recording initiatives in terms of repertoire, sound, editing, and promotion stem from a popular music background, evident in their recordings, studio/recording practices, and Internet presence.

The question then arises, are these two initiatives turning Manganiyar music into popular music? While Bhasin calls Rajasthan Roots' genre "folktronica" and the founders of Amarrass Records call it "world music," it is still at its essence Manganiyar music. Perhaps the number of instruments and arrangement have changed (as in the case of Gazi Khan Barna's Morchang Studios session), but the essence of their music remains the same. The dautara stringed instrument addition to the Morchang Studios recording of "Vari Jaon," discussed above, is an example of this, having been recorded after the session and the track laid over the original Manganiyar track. In the musical collaborations between Manganiyar musicians and Malian musicians during the Amarrass Desert Festival 2011, each musician essentially took turns performing instead of improvising together. As technology becomes more accessible, so too does Manganiyar music and culture, with Manganiyar music and even their instruments available for purchase with the click of a computer mouse. What was innovative in this context was the changing audience and broadening interest in Manganiyar music. Although the music has not essentially changed, the contexts and genres in which Manganiyar music is considered are changing very rapidly.

Even in collaboration with Western artists at Studio Roots, the Manganiyar musicians continue to perform the same music they always have, depending on the Western artists and studio engineers to bend, change, and improvise in accordance with the Manganiyar practices. The ethnomusicologist Stefan Fiol has argued in his study of recording distribution among Himalayan musicians that, while many believe that the recording process dilutes regional culture and threatens the survival of village traditions, such recordings actually serve to reinvigorate and popularize regional and rural festivals (2011). This appears to be the case with regard to the Manganiyar, their recording studio practices, and performances with non-Manganiyar musicians. An online reviewer of a Rajasthan Roots concert from February 2011 from The Times of India agrees with this:

> But it was when they made collective music that they won hearts. Kusumakar Pandya played the flute, Aditya Das played the *dautara* and sang, Kutle Khan dexterously switched between the *kartal*, the *bhapang*, *morchang* and also sang, while a bevy of other musicians also accompanied them on the bass guitar, the drums and the *dholak*. And for whoever may have thought folk music could be boring, here was history being rewritten.[23]

Bhasin put it succinctly in an interview with The Times of India in 2010: "Rajasthani music has everything going for it. It has trance, rhythms, vocals. We aim at taking folk beyond tourist lodges by bringing folk to a multicultural platform and creating contemporary music that appeals to varied musical tastes and age groups. We want to see it evolve on its own. Why can't Rajasthani folk win the Grammys?"[24]

CONCLUSION

The success of, for example, the musical hybrids produced by Rajasthan Roots is based on commercial viability, not on whether their provocative juxtapositions add up to a coherent resolution of the identity issues and power politics they raise in the first place. At the same time, while Bhasin is the initiator and outsider (to some degree) in the musical process, his calling the group a "collective" speaks to the input of all the musicians involved, namely the Manganiyar. By treating such music more as "folk" sonic and visual source materials for new recordings and performance/

collaboration opportunities, Manganiyar musicians are showing that their customary music can indeed fit within the multitracked syntax of a global music circuit.

The extension of the recording industry into Rajasthan in recent years has not been achieved as only an external imposition (although there is external intervention). Instead, it has been a process of collaboration and mutual need between the studios and the musicians. Therein lies the innovation. These projects are successful only through increased involvement, demand, and collaboration by Manganiyar musicians. At first many of the studios found in Rajasthan in the last few decades were temporary—they used rented equipment often operated by sound engineers not necessarily concerned with fidelity, sound quality, or the musicians themselves. Things have changed. Permanent sound studios have been established throughout Rajasthan, and innovative projects like Morchang Studios/Studio Roots and Amarrass Records are paving the way for new, technical, and innovative ways to work with recorded sound while also promoting the livelihood of musicians as they continue to transition from an insular world of local patronage to more popular music venues, studios, and stages all over the globe.

Contextual linkages to participatory and community-based music-making are manifest and highly meaningful, but they are continually challenged and redefined through interaction with recording technology and commercial popular market forces. Manganiyar musicians thus actively make choices and employ recording technologies in accord with their own needs and sensibilities, often resulting in refunctionings of musical practices that expand their popularity beyond their local patronage and tourism markets.

NOTES

1. The Manganiyar were originally promoted by the Jodhpur-based folklorist Komal Kothari, beginning in the 1960s. Kothari produced the first international concerts for Manganiyar musicians, many of whom have now become savvy concert tour organizers in their own right.
2. http://www.amarrass.com/label/label, accessed June 2012.
3. http://www.amarrass.com/amarrass-desert-music-festival/artists/the-thar-meets-the-sahara-a-report-from-the-amarrass-desert-music-festival June 2012.
4. The term "customary" in describing Manganiyar live performance practice is relative. Chanan Khan Manganiyar has told me that this instrumentation, although it is considered more traditional, is a fairly recent phenomenon. Prior to the 1960s, when Manganiyar musicians began performing outside of their villages, the dholak was not typically used, and the khartal had a much less integral role in the performance.

5. All of the musicians with the exception of the three sarangi players were from the Manganiyar community. The sarangi players were from the Langa community, a community of hereditary musicians structured similarly to the Manganiyar.

6. The dautara (also known as dotara or dotar) is more commonly found in north-eastern India, especially in Assam.

7. Gazi Khan Barna stands out from many Manganiyar musicians in his higher level of education (10th standard), his determination to educate his five children (both boys and girls), and his efforts beginning in 2003 to found a non-governmental organization to educate Manganiyar children in both standard education and music.

8. Gazi Khan Barna's behavior and role during the recording session are uncommon among Manganiyars generally, but they do reflect his wider musical experience. He debuted his innovative Desert Symphony ensemble at the Jaisalmer Desert Festival 2003; the performance involved sections of multiple musicians playing the same instruments. The Desert Symphony revolutionized Manganiyar festival performances and at the same time turned them into spectacles. Other musicians have subsequently emulated this type of large-scale performance.

9. http://www.youtube.com/user/morchangstudios, accessed June 2012.

10. The recordings that were being sold at the concert in Berkeley were recorded under Morchang Studios' simple agreement that allows them to use the recordings as they see fit for promotion and broadcast. In exchange, the studio provides the musicians with a CD of the recordings that they can duplicate and share as they like.

11. Manganiyar musicians for the most part tend to not prioritize authorship and copyright, because most of their music is considered community property. The appropriation of a Manganiyar song, "Nimbuda," in the soundtrack of the Hindi film *Hum Dil De Chuke Sanam* (1999) by the film's musical director, Ismail Durbar (who was listed as composer of all the film's songs), opened many Manganiyar musicians' eyes to the opportunities and pitfalls involved in issues of music ownership and property.

12. http://www.jaipurvirasatfoundation.org/index.php, accessed June 2012.

13. Since Rajasthan Roots gave its first concert in Jaipur in 2004, the collective has toured throughout India and abroad.

14. One example of this type of fusion stemmed from a 2007 collaborative acoustic recording project done at Morchang Studios between Rajasthan Roots and the British beatboxer of South Asian origin, Jason Singh. This session included an improvisatory song called "Jaipur Express," that demonstrates collaboration, interaction, and improvised musical conversations between the beatboxing and customary Manganiyar instrumentation.

15. http://thebigm.co.in/2010/03/preserving-their-roots/, accessed June 2012.

16. http://www.rajasthanroots.com/about_us.html, accessed June 2012.

17. http://www.amarrass.com/label/label, accessed June 2012.

18. http://www.amarrass.com/amarrass-society/amarrass-society, accessed June 2012.

19. Ibid.

20. http://www.amarrass.com/lakha-khan/amarrass-society/lakha-khan-sarangi-maker, accessed June 2012.

21. In 2008, a Manganiyar musician told me that he sold his family's kamaicha instrument to a tourist in order to make money to support the family. The kamaicha is an instrument that is becoming increasingly rare among the Manganiyar community for cultural, aesthetic, and economic reasons. For this reason, a musician

selling his instrument is frowned upon in the community. A few months later, the tourist sent the Manganiyar musician a photo of the *kamaicha* hanging on a wall in his home in Paris, not being played.

22. http://www.amarrass.com/artists/artists/mitha-bol-volume-1-of-the-amarrass-field-recordings, accessed June 2012.
23. http://articles.timesofindia.indiatimes.com/2011-02-04/lucknow/28355266_1_rajasthan-roots-folk-music-musicians, accessed June 2012.
24. http://articles.timesofindia.indiatimes.com/2010-01-28/news-and-interviews/28126085_1_rajasthani-internationally-palatable-sound-folk-beyond-tourist-lodges, accessed June 2012.

CHAPTER 14

The Livenesses of Pandit Bhimsen Joshi's Popular *Abhangas*

ANNA SCHULTZ

When Pandit Bhimsen Joshi passed away last January at the age of 89, I was among the countless people who, despite not knowing him personally, felt the loss. When I heard the news, I felt somehow comforted by interviews and stories of face-to-face encounters with Bhimsenji (as he is affectionately known by fans). The more ordinary and personal the stories, the more informal the interviews, the more they felt live. I particularly loved his Marathi interview with the late musicologist Dr. Ashok Ranade ("Pandit Bhimsen Joshi in conversation with Dr. Ashok Ranade," n.d.). Bhimsenji's responses were honest, to the point, insightful, and quite devoid of self-consciousness about his star status. My own memory of a brush with Bhimsenji at a performance by sitarist Usman Khan in Pune in 2000 echoes what others have written about the simplicity of his affect. Before the concert started, he sat quietly at the back of the temple performance venue, unassumingly greeting fans who touched his feet while he waited for attention to shift back to Khan Saheb. In some sense, this chapter on recorded liveness emerged from the desire to find residues of Bhimsenji's life in unexpected places.

Bhimsen Joshi was known as the supreme voice of the Kirana *gharana* (musical lineage) of Hindustani (North Indian classical) music. His voice was strong and resonant in every part of his register; he could improvise melodic phrases that seemed endless; and he thrilled audiences with his exciting use of dynamic contrast. His many live concert recordings attempt to capture some of the dramatic Bhimsenji, but what about the simple, everyday Pandit Bhimsenji? I propose that some of his most highly produced recordings, those featuring his popular *abhangas* (Marathi devotional songs by poet-saints of the *varkari* sect), convey a surprising range of "livenesses" that helped him to reach various listening publics, and indeed their mediation helped paradoxically to bring "life" to those performances. He addressed multiple audiences through a careful mixing of "mediatized" livenesses that lent them both a stylistic and quantifiable popularity.[1] Bhimsenji was loved throughout India as a singer of Hindustani classical music, but he holds a special place in the hearts of Marathi- and Kannada-speaking people because of his classical renderings of Marathi and Kannada devotional songs.

ABHANGAS AND THE *VARKARI* TRADITION

Abhangas became a part of Bhimsen Joshi's musical profile in 1972, when he first performed a *Santvani* [words of the saints] concert in Pune, a practice that he continued on a regular basis through 2005.[2] His renderings of *abhanga* were so popular that his versions and tunes became reabsorbed en masse into the folk music repertoire, and tickets for his *Santvani* concerts were even more expensive than for his classical ones (Nadkarni 1994, 105). As table 14.1 shows, I have counted 18 *abhanga* albums by Bhimsen Joshi, but there are surely others that I have not been able to find.

Bhimsenji's *abhanga* concerts and recordings were collaborative endeavors with his producers, with the composers Shrinivas Khale and Ram Phatak, and with his accompanists. The majority of his concert and recorded *abhangas* were composed by Shrinivas Khale (*Times of India* 2009), who is known primarily as a music director for Marathi and Hindi films, but who also composed songs for non-film recordings of playback singers Lata Mangeshkar, Asha Bhosle, and Kavita Krishnamurti, and classical singers including Ulhas Kashalkar and Veena Sahasrabuddhe. Most of his remaining *abhangas* were composed by Ram Phatak, a Marathi singer-composer.

Marathi *abhangas* are songs of devotion to Lord Vitthala with lyrics by Marathi saints. *Abhanga* is a couplet poetic form comprised most often of four lines, but sometimes as many as 24, with about eight stressed syllables (Chitre 1991, 207; Jones 2009, 126; and Schultz 2004, 55). In *abhanga* performance, two melodic phrases called *dhrupad* and *pad* are usually used, the former as a refrain and the other for the verses, as in the *sthāi-antarā* structure of North Indian vocal music or the *mukhda-antara* structure of Hindi film song.[3] The last line contains the signature of the saint who composed

Table 14.1. BHIMSEN JOSHI *ABHANGA* ALBUMS

Year	Title	Cover Image	Song Times	Company	Medium
1971	Tirth Vithal	None	Approximately 8 minutes	Gramophone Company of India, HMV	7 inch 45
2002	Gavoo Konate Geet [Marathi abhangas and Hindi bhajans]	Marathi cover	1:59–3:34	Saregama	CD
2010	Lokpriya Abhang (with Lata Mangeshkar, Music director: Shrinivas Khale)	Cover in Marathi with images of Bhimsenji and Lataji	3:13–8:00	Saregama	2 CDs
2001	Lokpriya Abhang (with Jitendra Abhisheki)	Larger letters in Marathi, smaller in English. Photos of artists plus an image of Vitthala.	4:38–9:14	Saregama	CD
1980–1981 (vol. 1 re-released in 1996 by Gramophone Company of India, HMV)	Abhangvani. Music dir. Ram Phatak.	Cover in English for vol. 1, Marathi for vols. 2 and 3. In all three, he shares the cover with Vitthala. (1996 releases)	6–7:02	EMI	Cassette (1980) CD (1996)
1999 (2006)	Maze Maher Pandhari	Marathi cover	6–7:03	Saregama	CD
1990	Tuka Jhalase Kalas	Cover in Marathi, with Bhimsenji's image the same size as Tukaram, plus a small image of Vitthala and Rakhumai.	6:35–12:25	T-Series	CD
2000	Golden Hour, vol. 12 - Devotional	Cover in English with only Bhimsen Joshi's face.	5:54–6:35	Saregama	CD

Year	Title	Cover description	Duration	Label	Format
2001 (mp3 release in 2011)	Indrayani Kathi - Abhangavani	Cover in Marathi with small transliteration of title and artist in English. Images of Saint Jnaneshvar, Vitthala, and varkaris, with Bhimsen Joshi's face in lower right-hand corner.	5:54–7:54	Saregama	CD
2001	The Versatile: Natyageet & Abhang, vol. 1	Cover in English. Part of a series that includes other artists. Only Bhimsenji's image on cover.	9:14–11:36	Music Today	CD
2004	Pt. Bhimsen Joshi's Bhajans	Cover in English, with large image of Bhimsenji and smaller images of saints and Vitthala.	14:23–10:17	Sea	CD
2005	Abhang	English cover with large photo of Bhimsenji.	9:15–11:35	Music Today	CD
2006	Santjan Yeti Ghara	Cover entirely in Marathi, with image of Bhimsenji and the composer.	9:50–12:16	T-Series	CD
2006	Mantra (other CDs in series are jantra and tantra)	English cover; large image of elderly Bhimsenji looking heavenward.	32:16–32:17	Times Music	CD
1984	Sanjivani Gatha	unknown	unknown	Svarupa Enterprises	Cassette
1987	Sant vani/Marathi bhajana	unknown	unknown	Universal Cassettes	Cassette
unknown	Bajans, vols. 1 and 2		unknown	Shankar & Co.	CD
2006	Akshaya Gani		unknown	Saregama	2 CDs

the *abhanga*. For example, the final line of *abhangas* by Tukaram begins with *"Tuka mhane"* (Tuka says).

The *abhanga* song genre emerged from the *varkari sampradaya*, a thriving Marathi devotional sect with roots in the works of the 13th-century poet Jnaneshvar (also called Jnandev). Jnaneshvar's writings are the earliest extant examples of devotional poetry for Lord Vitthala, the dark Krishna for whom a temple was built in Pandharpur in southern Maharashtra during the early part of the 13th century and who is visited each year by hundreds of thousands of pilgrims (*varkari*) (Deleury 1994, 1–21). The Marathi *abhangas* of Jnaneshvar and the saints who followed him—Namdev, Janabai, Eknath, Cokhamela, Tukaram, and others—comprise the primary literature and song texts of today's *varkari* tradition. The *varkari* saints shared a belief that religious experience should be accessible to all devotees, and they promoted expressive devotional practices that require no special training or knowledge.

The egalitarian ideals of the *varkari* tradition are expressed in the performance structure, movement, and themes of *abhangas*. In non-studio contexts, these songs are sung collectively during *kirtan*, while walking on the pilgrimage, and in informal song sessions. In Maharashtra, unlike in most other parts of India, *kirtan* refers to a type of devotional performance led by a vocal soloist known as a *kirtankar*, most often in a temple. A *kirtan* usually lasts two to three hours and consists of a variety of song genres, storytelling, and religious discourse. *Varkari* singers in *kirtan* and on pilgrimage are accompanied by a *mrdang* (double-headed barrel drum), Several of the singers play *tal*[4] (small, thick, concave brass cymbals) while dancing and singing. The collectively performed songs of the *varkari* tradition have simple, repetitive melodies and, when performed during *kirtan* or in *bhajan* (Hindu devotional song) sessions, are characterized by musical structures of increasing intensity that create powerful devotional responses. These structures include a quickening of tempo, a shortening of melodic phrases, and an increase in the height of the dance steps. Saint Namdev (13th–14th century) described the heightened experience of devotional communion achieved through simple collective songs like these:

> The temple resounds with *kirtan*,
> The beautiful *rasa* [taste, sentiment] of *mrdang*, *tal*, and *vina*
> [stringed instrument used as a quiet drone].
> The servants of Hari sing joyously,
> *Reaching the limits of bliss* (Inamdar 1979, 129, #207, my translation).

Bhimsen Joshi was not a *varkari*, that is, he did not make the annual pilgrimage to Pandharpur; but his *abhangas* evoke and interpret *varkari* aesthetics. *Abhanga* poetry can be sung in any style, using any tune that fits the prosody, so Bhimsenji is not alone in singing *abhangas* in a non-*varkari* style.

LIVENESS AND POPULAR MUSIC

It may seem a bit odd to include works of one of India's greatest classical singers in a volume on popular music. If anything, one might argue, his *abhangas* belong to the genre of "devotional songs"—so how are they popular? In the most literal sense, these songs are popular because millions of people know and love them, but this does not distinguish popular music from other styles of well-circulated recorded music. I argue that there are specific stylistic markers that render many of Bhimsen Joshi's *abhangas* "popular" even though the songs belong to a devotional repertoire and Bhimsenji was a classical musician. Bhimsenji's *abhangas* are devotional by genre (with a given set of meanings and extra-musical associations), but as style (with empirically identifiable sonic features), they are a mixture of popular, classical, and devotional. Following popular music scholars, I define popular music as a music commodity that is mass-produced and marketed for a "heterogeneous audience" (Beaster-Jones 2007, 5) and that has sonic features emerging from its association with the mass media (ibid.; Manuel 1993, xvi; and Shuker 2005, xiii). The process of becoming stylistically touched by mass media is what Philip Auslander has called "mediatization," and it is a characteristic of recorded *abhangas* and of the concert performances of those same *abhangas*.

This project addresses liveness in Bhimsenji's mediatized *abhangas*—they may not all belong to the *genre* of popular music, but through their mediated evocation of liveness, they are stylistically adapted to mass media in ways that sound "popular." Though I did not know Bhimsen Joshi, his composers, or his arrangers personally, I have conducted ethnographic research with *varkaris* and other Marathi devotional performers, which has given me a sense of the performance contexts that are evoked in his songs. This chapter is primarily about the production rather than the reception of these songs; for my purposes, production includes engineering, composition, arranging, and performance.

Auslander introduced "liveness" as a corrective to the assumption that live and mediated performances occupy distinct domains (2006, 85–86). Music videos, "unplugged" concerts, and simulcasts all "exemplify the way mediatization is now explicitly and implicitly conjoined to live experience" (2006, 87). Auslander locates mediatized liveness squarely in a postmodern moment, in which (for example) Milli Vanilli's lip-synched "live" performances in 1989 were simulacra of studio recordings the duo never made (2006, 88). In contrast, Bhimsenji's concert performances existed in dialogue with his recordings, but the production value of his concerts was minimal compared with the light shows, choreographed dance scenes, and stage props of American pop concerts. The recorded devotional songs I discuss reference real performance contexts, and I find value in thinking about the blurred boundaries between liveness and mediatization in these more traditional recordings. By tracing the livenesses of these *abhangas*, I explore how different *abhangas* are directed toward particular listeners, but also how the same *abhangas* may address different listeners in different ways. By exploring the mosaic texture of livenesses in recorded music, we can begin to see beyond the simplification of a style or genre being associated with a single group of people.

Bhimsen Joshi's popular *abhangas* present a tension not only between liveness and mediatization, but also between different types of liveness. Louise Meintjes similarly identified multiple discourses of liveness in South African recording studios. She defines liveness as "an illusion of sounding live that is constructed through technological intervention in the studio and mediated symbolically through discourses on the natural and the artistic" (2003, 112). Meintjes argues that debates on the live are about consumer fantasies of participatory music and that the "physiological experience of the listener out there is imagined by music-makers in the studio when they succeed in creating the 'Sound of Africa! Africa!'" (2003, 115–116).[5] As Meintjes has shown through careful ethnographic research, the kinds and degrees of liveness are subjects of debate in recording studios, and those debates are situated within wider discourses of authenticity and African-ness. Similarly, a range of compositional, arranging, and studio techniques are used in Bhimsen Joshi's popular *abhangas* to evoke and hail audiences who occupy different sorts of subject positions. In Bhimsenji's recordings, we can hear the liveness of a classical concert, the liveness of *varkari* pilgrims, and the liveness of Bhimsenji's body. These recordings do not just mediate performance for repeated listening; they also mediate between the listening publics of farmers and urbanites, fans of folk music and fans of classical music, and between *varkari* pilgrims and those who idealize pilgrimage but are not themselves pilgrims. I rely on recordings, reviews, interviews, and my experiences with *abhanga* performances by traditional Marathi devotional singers to consider the multiple livenesses and potential "listener[s] out there" of Bhimsenji's *abhangas*.

By considering Bhimsen Joshi's *abhangas* as popular music, I am in some sense at odds with Bhimsenji's own assessment of his *abhangas*. According to biographer Mohan Nadkarni, "Bhimsen's view is that *Sant Vani* is not a type of popular or light music, but that it is expressed through the medium of *raga* music" (1994, 105). Indeed, when he performed *abhangas* in concert, he sang the *taans* (melodic runs) and *alap* (unmetered opening section) of *khayal* "[a] type of vocal composition in North Indian art music and the style in which such compositions are performed" (Widdess n.d.) and enunciated the *abhanga* texts less clearly than he did on most of his devotional recordings. Given Bhimsenji's insistence that *Santvani* is not popular or light, and given that his *Santvani* concerts were performed in a classical style, it is interesting that his 10- to-16-minute concert recordings that retain the liveness of classical music concerts represent only a minority of his recorded *abhanga* output. Much more common are the three-to-eight-minute short *abhangas*, which convey livenesses of an entirely different order to reach other audiences.

IMAGE AND MARKETING IN BHIMSENJI'S *ABHANGAS*

Both Jacqueline (Jaime) Jones and Jayson Beaster-Jones show how labeling on devotional CDs and in record stores in India suggest intended audiences (Jones 2009, 145; Beaster-Jones 2007, 213), and Jones notes that the labels are meant to reach non-*varkari* audiences. Although "these labels don't always clarify precisely what it is that one gets on a CD of *varkari abhangas*, they do bear some of the strategies used in the marketing of this repertoire" (Jones 2009, 145).

Jones argues that Bhimsen Joshi's canonical status positions his devotional songs in their own style category, and suggests that the spare covers with images only of Joshi and with writing in English indicate that they're marketed toward elite consumers, though she mentions—and I have also observed—that these recordings are also consumed and appreciated by *varkaris* (Jones 2009, 147). She differentiates Bhimsenji's light classical recordings, which incorporate Hindustani classical instrumentation and techniques, from "popular collections" of *varkari* songs by other singers, which mix *varkari* instrumentation with synthesizer, temple bells, and flute (2009, 149–150). Generally speaking, classical vocalists are accompanied by *tabla, tanpura,* and often harmonium (less commonly *sarangi*); *varkari* singers are accompanied by *mrdang* and *tal*; and popular orchestrations can include a mixture of Indian and Western classical instruments plus a variety of synthesized sounds. My survey of Bhimsen Joshi's recordings affirms that, while many—if not most—are light classical in the ways that Jones describes, they draw enough from techniques of the popular to muddy these classificatory waters significantly. I also address the iconography of Bhimsenji's less (light) classical album covers, which are in Marathi and trade in regional religious imagery.

LIVING IN-BETWEEN

Bhimsen Joshi transcended and transgressed borders. He was born on the border between Karnataka and Maharashtra, a border that shifted and was renamed multiple times during his life in a way that contributed to his identity as a person of Kannada descent who made his home in Maharashtra and who was equally comfortable in Kannada and Marathi. Not only did the borders shift around him; he also shifted around the borders, seeking guidance in numerous North Indian cities. When Bhimsenji was born, his native town of Gadag was in British Bombay state (Majumdar 2004, 10), which became independent Indian Bombay state after independence, was assigned to Mysore state after the linguistic reorganization of states in 1956, and was renamed Karnataka in 1973. He moved back and forth between the stylistic borders of classical music and popular theatrical, film, and devotional music, and he moved between the colonial world in which Hindustani music was an elite pursuit and the postcolonial world in which Hindustani music became a mass phenomenon.

In Kundgol, Karnataka, Bhimsenji began studying with his primary guru, Sawai Gandharva of the Kirana *gharana*, who guided his young disciple to the highest levels of artistry and introduced him to the people of Pune, Maharashtra in 1946 (*Indian Express* 2011). Gandharva had a penchant for drama music, and he passed his taste for classical and light musical styles on to his disciples Bhimsen Joshi and Gangubai Hangal (Nadkarni 1994, 39–42). Joshi's guru helped him to hone his skill with devotional songs, but his first experiences with *kirtan* and *abhanga* came from his grandfather Bhimacharya. In a televised interview, musicologist Ashok Ranade asked Bhimsenji if his family somehow knew that he would have such a strong singing voice since they named him Bhim, the Pandava of the Mahabharata known for his large stature and immense strength. Bhimsenji laughed and told him no, that he was named after his grandfather ("Pandit Bhimsen Joshi in conversation with Dr. Ashok Ranade," n.d.). His grandfather Bhimacharya was a well-known *kirtankar* (singer of *kirtan*) in the region, and it's been reported that Bhimsen borrowed his grandfather's *tanpura* (string instrument that produces a drone) to practice singing classical music long before he began his formal training in music (Bannerjee 2011; Majumdar 2004, 10; and Nadkarni 1994, 45). The young Bhimsen was also an avid listener of the *kirtans* of Chinappa Kurtakoti, a *kirtankar* who performed at a nearby temple and taught Bhimsen devotional songs and harmonium playing (Bannerjee 2011).

MANY LIVENESSES

Bhimsen Joshi's *abhangas* are difficult to place generically because they use a wide range of production, arranging, composition, and performance techniques to index various musico-cultural practices and multiple styles of mediatization. That said, there is something uniquely "Bhimsenian" about all of them that extends beyond the raw sound of his voice. In what follows, I address two categories of musical play in Bhimsen's *abhangas*: varieties of liveness, including those of the classical *mehfil*, *varkari* performance, and Bhimsen Joshi's performing body; and varieties of mediatization that draw these *abhangas* into proximity with regional folk and light classical idioms. The parameters through which I chart the interplay of liveness and mediatization include dynamic range, bodily movement, vocal range, song length, ornamentation, improvisation, adherence to *raga*, ambient and audience sounds, instrumentation, chant, and production techniques.

Bhimsen Joshi's "Corporeal Liveness"

Paul Sanden introduced "corporeal liveness," or "liveness invoked by music's connection to an acoustic sounding body, usually that of a human performer" as a corrective to the notion of recordings as "disembodied sound" (2009, 3). His study of Glenn Gould's recorded humming voice and creaking piano stool helps rectify understandings of Gould as a "cerebral" musician (2009). In an audiovisual age, musicians don't need to perform their bodies as audibly as Glenn Gould did to carry resonances of those bodily images into sound recordings. Artists with particularly striking stage images or bodily comportment can evoke visual images for listeners in audio recordings. I find it difficult to hear Lady Gaga without imagining her elaborate costumes or to hear Pandit Bhimsen Joshi without imagining his famous dramatic arm movements and facial expressions. A Google image search for Bhimsen Joshi produces an array of photographs of his striking facial expressions from live performances, suggesting that the expressiveness of Bhimsenji's singing—metonymically represented through his face—is a key aspect of how his music is marketed and remembered. Most reviews and tributes mention the dramatic ways in which Bhimsenji's physicality became sound. This obituary in *The Economist* is typical:

> Music seemed to require him to use every part of his body. From a slow, mes-merised, almost motionless start his eyes would roll upwards, foreshadowing the ascent of the notes that emerged from his distended, gaping mouth. His hands flailed, as though reaching for some imagined object just out of his grasp. Perhaps Bhimsen Joshi was trying to bring back to earth a soaring note from one of his magnificent *taans*, the series of rapid melodic passages with which great classical singers in the Hindustani tradition of northern India demon-strate how skilled they are (*The Economist* 2011).

In concert performances, he turned his face and eyes skyward when he reached for higher notes, and he opened his mouth wider, raised his eye-brows, and scrunched one side of his face as he sang the fluid *taans* for which he was known. He moved his face and sometimes his body close to and away from the microphone to look at accompanists or to provide a spa-tial difference for repeated passages that was heard as musical variation. In moments of intensity, he actually moved his face closer to the microphone to make the sound louder. A video concert recording from 1975 illustrates this type of movement—in a performance of "Raga Bhairavi" (video 14.2), Bhimsenji began phrases by bending at the waist to bring him closer to the microphones, backing away to lessen dynamic tension toward the end of phrases.

In a recording of the *abhanga* "Teertha Vitthala, Kshetra Vitthala" ["The Holy Site of Vitthala, the Sacred Place of Vitthala"] from the same concert, he often produced a stream of quiet *taans* looking skyward (and away from the microphone) (video 14.3). The clearest way that this physical move-ment translates into audible sound is in his incredible dynamic range, a hallmark of his style that emerged partly through alterations in the force of air through his vocal cords, but also through his interaction with the microphone.

This sense of bodily movement is profoundly audible in Bhimsenji's *abhanga* recordings. His "Roopa Pahata Lochani" ["On Seeing the Form of Vitthala"] from the *Abhang* (2005) album features significant dynamic fluc-tuations within the first minute of the recording, and his voice on "Teertha Vitthala, Kshetra Vitthala" from the *Swaranand* (2004) album is louder toward the beginnings of phrases (refer to 00:35–00:40). In "Arambhi

Vandina" ["From the Beginning I Will Worship"] (*Abhangvani* Vol. 1, 1996), Bhimsenji sings the phrase "*Ramanama vani*" ["Saying Rama's name"] at a medium dynamic level and repeats it quietly between 1:28 and 2:32, a technique heard in many of his recordings (of multiple genres) and which may be related to his practice of turning to accompanists when he repeats phrases in concert performances. The flattening of vocal dynamic range is one of the major differences of his more mediatized recordings, such as *Abhangvani* Vol. 2 (2002), which also includes a reverb effect on Bhimsenji's voice. Phrases don't begin with a blast here, nor does his voice become much quieter for the refrains, as it does for "Teertha Vitthala, Kshetra Vitthala." When I played one of these recordings for a Stanford University radio program, the host couldn't recognize the voice as Bhimsen Joshi's, perhaps in part because dynamic range is such a critical aspect of his vocal signature.

Abhanga recordings also convey a corporeal, personal liveness by referencing the unique characteristics of Bhimsen Joshi's performance practice. Indeed, any recognizable voice can convey the liveness of an individual if we imagine not a generalized musician, but a specific musician singing into a microphone in a particular way. The key here is that the specificity of a unique vocal style can convince listeners that this is a real performance rather than a less marked simulation. Dynamic range is just one marker of Bhimsen Joshi's unique musical style. In addition to the characteristics he shares with other proponents of the Kirana *gharana*, he had a particularly large range of three octaves and the ability to move fluidly between lyricism and stunningly intricate *taans*. For many other singers, *taans* are something one works up to, but Bhimsenji could place them anywhere in a performance without sacrificing subtlety or catapulting the performance into pure virtuosity.

In my opinion, the compositions by Ram Phatak and Shrinivas Khale seem to be composed for Bhimsen Joshi's unique style and capabilities. Most of his *abhangas* by these two composers not only evoke *bhajan* style through use of *bhajani theka* (an eight-beat rhythmic cycle used with *bhajans*), *tal*, *mrdang*, and chorus, as I demonstrate below; they also share particular melodic contours and *taans*. Although the intensity of Bhimsenji's voice is felt most profoundly in his higher register, his lower register boasts a resonant sonority. Indeed, in a way that I think was meant to enhance these aspects of his voice and also to provide scope for his cascading *taans*, the majority of Bhimsenji's popular *abhangas* have very "catchy," singable melodies that nonetheless have a larger range than many folk *abhangas* and at least one *taan*.

The six-to-seven-minute songs on *Maze Maher Pandhari* (2006) exemplify these signature compositional features, particularly each song's opening phrase that returns as a refrain (see table 14.4). Three of the six songs on the album begin on the high *Sa* (tonic) and descend within just a couple of *tala* cycles to the middle *Sa*, and two begin on the sixth or seventh scale degree and ascend to the high tonic before descending. This contour provides a concise taste of Bhimsenji's bright higher register and resonant lower register. The octave range and descending melodic contour are not unusual for *abhangas*, but the regularity of this pattern is striking in Bhimsen Joshi's case. All of the songs include ornamentation on "ah" sounds in the opening phrase and some include *taans*. "Maze Maher Pandhari" ["Pandharpur Is My Mother's Home"], the first song on the recording, begins with a flourish of straight *aakar taans* (*taans* on "ah") outlining the pentatonic scale of *Raga Deshkar* in ascent before landing on the high *Sa* to begin the song (video 14.5). The melody then descends back down to the middle *Sa* and rests on the *Re* (second scale degree) before he repeats the phrase, now with ornaments on the "ma" and "r" of *maher* that become attached to the melody for the remainder of the song. "Dnyaniyancha Raja Guru Maharao" ["King and Guru among the Learned"] similarly begins on the high *Sa* and descends over the first phrase to the middle *Sa*, but not before singing an elaborate ornament on the high *Sa* and linking the two repetitions with a melismatic flourish on the "rao" of "*Maharao*" (video 14.6). These types of gestures are characteristic of Bhimsen Joshi's performance practice and are distilled in the refrains of his *abhangas*. In combination with his characteristically mobile performing style, they help us to hear Bhimsenji's unique body in recorded performance.

Classical Liveness

Moving outward from the idiosyncratic liveness of Bhimsen Joshi's body, we can hear the liveness of more general contexts. The classical concert is conveyed through particular production techniques, performance techniques, and non-musical "concert sounds." Although the more popular of Bhimsenji's *abhangas* are between three and eight minutes, the classicized ones are at least nine minutes long, which is about the length of his live *abhanga* performances heard in *abhanga* concerts or at the end of classical *khayal* concerts.[6] Improvisation is minimal for the shorter songs, while the ten-minute *abhangas* include ample improvisation.

Intended audience and genre are indicated to some extent through album imagery and song length (see table 14.1). Of the approximately 32 Bhimsen Joshi devotional albums that I have found, 18 are of Marathi *abhangas* (the rest are Hindi and Kannada *bhajans*), and of those 18, I located 13 covers

Table 14.4. PANDIT BHIMSEN JOSHI, *ABHANGAVANI*, VOL. 1
(EMI 1980). ALL SONGS COMPOSED BY RAM PHATAK

Song Title	Title Translation	Poet-Saint	Length	Opening phrase initial note	Range of opening phrase	Taans and ornaments
Maze Maher Pandhari	Pandharpur is my Mother's Home	Eknath	7:03	Sa (High Tonic)	1 octave	Ascending taans on "ah" to opening phrase; ornament on "Ma" (high tonic) and "r" (5th) of "Maher"
Mazha Bhav Tuze Charani	I Concentrate On Your Feet	Namdev	6:21	Dha (6th)	1 octave	ornament on "bhav" (7th)
Sukhache He Nam Avadjine Gave	Sing the Joyous Name with Love	Soyarabai	6:05	Ni (7th)	1 octave	ornament starting on "nam" (4th)
Kaya Hi Pandhari	My Body is Pandharpur	Eknath	6:47	High tonic	Interval of 9th	ornament on "ya" of "kaya" (high tonic)
Gyaniyancha Raja Guru Maharao	You are Guru and King amongst the Learned	Tukaram	6:18	High tonic	1 octave	ornament on "ra" of "raja" (high tonic); taan on "rao" of "Maharao"
Ata Kothe Dhave Man	How Can My Mind Be Elsewhere?	Tukaram	6:00	Ga (3rd)	Interval of 6th	Taan on "ta" of "ata," ornament on "n" of "man" (4th)

or online cover images. Of those 13 covers, eight are entirely in Marathi or in Marathi with a Roman transliteration of the title in small letters. All but one of the albums comprised of songs ranging in length from two to eight minutes have covers in Marathi with images of Bhimsen Joshi alongside those of Vitthala and/or *varkari* saints (figure 14.7, *Maze Maher*

Pandhari). Conversely, all but one of the albums of songs longer than nine minutes have English covers and include only Bhimsenji's face, without images of deities and saints (figure 14.8, *Abhang*, English). In other words, the albums of longer improvisatory songs are marketed as classical music with a focus on the artist, rather than as devotional music with a focus on religious content. The former are directed toward English-speaking, and thus middle-class, audiences rather than toward Marathi-speaking audiences that may or may not be middle class (Jones 2009, 147).

The *Abhang* (2005) album is comprised entirely of longer *abhanga* performances. The cover features a warmly colored photo of Bhimsenji that glows as though he's looking into the sun. Other than the word "*abhang*," there is no iconographic indication that this is a devotional music album, and indeed, the songs on the album can be appreciated in the ways one appreciates Hindustani improvisation as much as they can be appreciated as devotional music. We can identify the songs on this album as *abhangas* because the *tabla* player plays *bhajani theka* and because the text is by a Marathi saint, but the difference between these songs and Bhimsenji's other, less classical devotional *abhangas* is heard immediately in the instrumentation. Whereas most of his less classical *abhangas* include cymbals, some of the songs on *Abhang* are accompanied only by a *tanpura* drone, which is ubiquitous in North Indian classical music but is rarely heard in *varkari* performance contexts or in Marathi *kirtan*.

Figure 14.7
Compact disc cover: Bhimsen Joshi, *Maze Maher Pandhari*, Saregama, 2006 (Gramophone Company of India, Ltd., 1996).

Figure 14.8
Compact disc cover: Bhimsen Joshi, *Abhang*, Music Today, 2005.

The improvisations of Indian classical music are more varied and virtuosic than in *varkari* performance, and Bhimsenji's more classically oriented *abhangas* become increasingly abstracted from the original song melody with each repetition of text. This trend toward abstract melody over text is also heard in his enunciation, which is generally less clear than in his shorter *abhanga* recordings, and in the fact that he moves more freely and frequently into *aakaar* improvisation, that is, improvisation using only the "aa" syllable. There is also a stricter adherence to *raga* than in some of the shorter *abhangas*, and these *ragas* are elaborated with the form of *khayal*, that is, with initial statements of each line to be followed first by subtle variations with brief moments of *aakaar* and *sargam* (solfege) improvisation, working up to extended and elaborate *taans* within a given *raga*.

These classicizing elements don't necessarily mark liveness, but liveness *is* heard through production techniques and extra-musical sounds that suggest a live concert performance. Of course, there is applause at the end of the tracks on the *Abhang* album, but the audience is particularly palpable on "Zani Dhav Aata" ["People Now Run"] (video 14.9) with interjections of "*kyaa baat hai*" ["that's something!"] and "waa" ["wow"].

These acclamations occur when Bhimsenji performs elaborate *aakaar* *taans* and when he ventures outside of the set pitches of the *raga*. In this track, they happen so often and the audience voices are so audible that one has the impression not of a large concert auditorium, but of an intimate gathering of connoisseurs called a *mehfil*. In keeping with the liveness aesthetic, production effects are minimal, and we hear the tuning of the *tabla*. "Zani Dhav Aata" is in *Raga Jhinjhoti* (the lowered seventh appears on descent and is missing in ascent) and features accompaniment by harmonium, *tanpura*, and *tabla* rather than *mrdang* and *tal*.

Varkari liveness

The majority of Bhimsenji's *abhanga* albums are designed to transport listeners not to the concert hall but to the pilgrimage and collective performance of the *varkari* tradition. Unlike the concert liveness described above, though, these recordings are not meant to sound as though they were recorded live while on a pilgrimage or in a collectively performed *bhajan* session in a temple or home. Instead, they convey a mediatized and edited sense of liveness as oxymoronic as that may sound. There is no audible tuning, no applause, and no coughing; the arrangements are more varied than in collective *varkari* sung worship; and effects like reverb are clearly added in the studio. Although the tracks don't sound like field or concert recordings of *varkari* performances, I propose that certain sounds, gestures, and motifs index *varkari* liveness through production and arrangement. Bhimsenji was not a *varkari*, that is, he did not make the annual pilgrimage to Pandharpur and participate regularly in *varkari* activities. As a classical singer who performed in concert venues, it makes sense that the "livest" of his recordings evoke classical concerts rather than pilgrims' songs.

The Bhimsen Joshi *abhanga* recordings in which *varkari* liveness dominates share a particular instrumentation, aspects of form, meter, idiomatic phrases, tempo, and length. The recordings that I describe are between three and eight minutes long, and they are among some of his most popular pieces. Key markers of *varkari* practice in these *abhangas* are instrumentation and rhythm. All of Bhimsenji's *abhangas* evoking *varkari* liveness are set to the four- (or eight-) beat *bhajani* rhythmic cycle, which is expressed with the drum syllables *dhin—na dhin—dhin na ge / dhin—na tin tin na ge* that produce a distinctive (and widely recognized) three + three + two rhythmic feel. This is the main rhythmic cycle used in *varkari* performance, but in live performance, the singer or singers begin the song and the drum enters after a few repetitions of the opening melody. In these more popular *abhangas*, the rhythmic instruments set the tempo before Bhimsenji begins singing, an ordering more characteristic of *filmi* and "light music" arranging. The meter is evocative of *varkari* practice, but through this reordering, it has been adapted to give an exciting start for popular recording, and it is the first clue that these recordings are conceived in a linear, prearranged fashion rather than with the more predictable cyclical form of live *varkari* performance.

Varkari-ness is also evoked through the instruments that maintain the rhythmic drive: *mrdang* and *tal*. While *tabla* is used to accompany most non-*varkari* music in Maharashtra, singers in the *varkari* tradition are accompanied by the *mrdang* (also called *pakhwaj*). *Tal* are similarly evocative of *varkari* practice. While flat hand cymbals known as *jhanj* are used for other types of Hindu devotional music in Maharashtra, the thick, concave *tal* cymbals are associated almost exclusively with the *varkari* tradition. Again though, Bhimsenji's *tal* are adapted for popular recording. On pilgrimage and in *varkari kirtan*, *tal* are usually played by a group of people. *Tal* is incredibly difficult to record in live contexts because the intensity of sound often distorts recordings. If one *tal* is difficult to record, a group of 10 or 20 can be positively overwhelming. Rather than dealing with the recording headache of a large set of *tal*, most of Bhimsenji's recordings use only one or two, the minimum needed to provide a *varkari* feel. As can be heard in video 14.5 and 14.6, in most cases these traditional *varkari* instruments are supplemented by the *tanpura* and harmonium of Hindustani vocal music.

In addition to the *tal* and *mrdang* of *varkari* performance and the harmonium and *tanpura* of classical, light classical, and non-*varkari* devotional music, many of Bhimsenji's *abhangas* include *bansuri* (bamboo flute), violin, and sitar. Indeed, all of the songs on *Maze Maher Pandhari* include some combination of these extra-*varkari* instruments. *Bansuri*, violin, and sitar are staples of more "classical" Hindi film music, the dominant form of Indian popular music, and these instruments are indeed arranged in a *filmi* manner in many of Bhimsenji's *abhangas*. This is perhaps not surprising, given that Bhimsenji's primary music directors also composed music for films and film singers. "Maza Bhav Tuze Charani" ["My Feelings at Your Feet"] (video 14.10) from the *Maze Maher Pandhari* (2006) album (music director Ram Phatak) begins with *tanpura*, *mrdang*, and *tal* like most of Bhimsenji's *abhangas*, but rather than moving directly to the voice, we first hear an introduction with *bansuri*, then sitar, then sitar and *bansuri*. Once Bhimsenji begins to sing, the *bansuri* accompanies him quietly and heterophonically until sitar, harmonium, violin, and *bansuri* emerge to the foreground during the interludes between strophes. In her path-breaking study of Hindi film music, Alison Arnold notes that this trading of solos by an eclectic array of instruments is a key characteristic of Hindi film song style (Arnold 1988).

Varkaris believe that anyone can have access to the divine through profound experiences of devotion cultivated through collective song. Bhimsen

Joshi is a solo classical artist, but his use of a chorus on some songs is perhaps the most profound marker of his *varkari* liveness. *Varkari* instruments can be brought onto the concert stage without changing the solo dynamic, but a group of singers suggests a different kind of performance. Unlike in a *kirtan* or other *varkari* song event, though, the chorus in Bhimsen Joshi's popular *abhangas* is highly arranged and controlled, so they're not likely to take over the performance as they might during a *kirtan*. "Maze Maher Pandhari" begins with *tal* and *mrdang* but is quickly taken over by a chorus chanting "*Vitthala Vitthala Vitthala . . .*" (video 14.5). This chant is heard in every *varkari kirtan*—from time to time, a *kirtankar* takes a break from the narrative to lead the congregation in this chant, often seemingly losing himself in the name. In *kirtan*, this chant hovers on the tonic and is occasionally interrupted by a three-note downward scalar passage. The main difference between the two styles of chant is that Bhimsen Joshi's small chorus's chant is very "square," with the "Vi" coinciding with beats 1, 3, 5, and 7, and "tthala" with 2, 4, 6, and 8, while *varkari* chanting increases notably in tempo, with a simpler rhythmic pattern in which the loudest drum stroke coincides with an accented "tthala." That said, we have enough information in the Bhimsen Joshi arrangement to know that he is invoking *varkari* chant, though in stylized form.

In other songs, he improvises a "Vitthala" chant spontaneously when the *abhanga* text includes the name "Vitthala." In "Vitthala Geetin Gava" ["Sing Songs of Vitthala"] (video 14.11), he needs only three iterations on the same note to evoke this chant, a claim that I think can be made because this moment of stasis is striking, positioned as it is within a context of fluid melodic movement. At the end of "Teertha Vitthala Kshetra Vitthala" (video 14.12), he moves to a chanting of Vitthala with some melodic improvisation, but with rhythmic patterns that mirror what is heard in temples, and with the characteristic increase in tempo, leading to a fade-out, a gesture made possible by recording media but one that evokes a sense of a non-ending performance.

Perhaps Bhimsenji's devotional track that best makes use of this sense of collective worship with increasing structures of intensity is "Jai Jai Ram Krishna Hari" ["Praise to Ram Krishna Vishnu"] (video 14.13) from the *Mantra* album. This 29-minute track employs only this single line of text— a song type that in Marathi is called a *bhajan* or *gazar* and in North India is called a *kirtan*. Here, the chorus truly operates as it would during a *kirtan* or *bhajan* session, and the tempo increases as it would in *varkari* performance. This may be Bhimsenji's only *varkari*-esque performance with minimal mediatization. The *Mantra* album was recorded in 2006 and is to my knowledge his last new album of Marathi devotional music. His voice has lost none of its expressivity, flexibility, or accuracy, but it had lost a bit of its strength. This is to be expected for a man in his 80s, as perhaps is the very fact of this type of performance, which has neither the arranged folkish-ness of his shorter *abhangas* nor the pyrotechnics of his classically oriented *abhangas*.

So, how are these *abhangas* popular? The songs I've discussed so far, particularly those in the second category, are popular inasmuch as they are short pieces with catchy melodies and some sort of "hook." On a continuum of mediatization, the *abhangas* that evoke classical liveness are the least mediated, in the sense that they sound like they were recorded during a concert performance rather than in the studio. Most of the others that we have heard were clearly recorded in studios. They lack the audience interjections and applause of concert recordings, and they're arranged and through-composed in ways that are atypical for Indian classical, semi-classical, and folk concerts of unrehearsed improvisations. But "popular" has different resonances for different listening publics, and although many of the shorter *abhangas* are mediatized, they are stylistically distinct from the paradigmatic popular genre of India, Hindi film music. Even those songs produced with significant vocal reverb and mixed instrumentation, like the more classical film songs, lack synthesizer sounds and a crooning vocal delivery typical of *filmi* music.

FROM LIVENESS TO LIVE PERFORMANCE

The above description of mediatization and liveness in Bhimsen Joshi's *abhangas* suggests that those *abhangas* evoking the liveness of *varkari* pilgrimage are more popular, arranged, and mediatized than those associated with the liveness of classical performance. Based on my own ethnographic experience with Marathi *kirtan* and classical concerts in India, I offer a tentative interpretation. Concert-going is part of the experience of the urban middle-class people who patronize Indian classical music, so recordings tending toward classical liveness can activate personal memories. On the other hand, most middle-class people have never been on a pilgrimage to Pandharpur and may only have heard *varkari* pilgrims singing as they proceed through Pune on their way to Pandharpur. The *varkari* tradition has a significant presence in Maharashtrian cities, but most of the people who actually become dedicated *varkaris* and pledge to walk each year are from the countryside.[7] *Varkari kirtan* can be heard in Pune but is hugely popular in villages and pilgrimage towns like Pandharpur and Alandi. With this in mind, it makes more sense that the *varkari* liveness of Bhimsen Joshi's *abhangas* would be reformulated to make sense to audiences who have little actual exposure to *varkari* performance. Even those who have not experienced *varkari* performance firsthand, or have only minimal exposure to it, have seen classic films like *Sant Tukaram* (1936) and *Sant Dnyaneshwar* (1940), so they have a sense of what constitutes music of the *varkari* pilgrimage.

As a classical singer of *khayal* who only later in his career began performing *abhanga* concerts, it is not surprising that Bhimsenji's *abhanga* recordings would be oriented toward classical music audiences that have little experience with *varkari* performance. But that's not the entire story—although he classicizes all performances with his use of *raga* and his approach to improvisation, many of his *abhangas* are in short formats that share just as much with popular music genres. Moreover, although there is some distinction between the English-language CD covers geared toward urban cosmopolitans and the Marathi-language covers that are marketed toward non-English speakers, it is also true that in some cases, the same CD is sold with a Marathi cover and an English cover. Charting the listenership would be an almost impossible task, but during my fieldwork, I found several indications that Bhimsen Joshi is admired as much by devotional singers as he is by classical singers and audience members. Jaime Jones has noted that his *abhangas* have achieved some degree of canonicity within the *varkari* tradition, and I heard many urban, Brahmin *kirtankars* perform his melodies during the course of a *kirtan*. Although most *abhangas* are sung to many different tunes, there is less variation for the *abhangas* that Bhimsen Joshi has recorded.

My final example is a *rupace abhanga*, which is an *abhanga* on the form of the divine. These *abhangas* are performed at the beginning of *varkari kirtans* and are occasionally performed in the more urban *naradiya kirtan*. One of the commonly used *abhangas* of the divine form is "Rupa Pahata Lochani" (video 14.14) by Saint Jnaneshvar:

> *Rupa pahata lochani /*
> To see your form /
> *Sukha jhale ho sajani /*
> Gives me joy, my friend /
> *To haa Vitthala barva /*
> Vitthala is good /
> *To ha Madhava barva /*
> Vishnu is good /
> *Bahuta sukrutachi jodi /*

What a virtuous pair/
Mhanuni Vitthali avadi /
This is why I love Vitthala /
Sarva sukhace agara /
The source of all joy /
Bapa Rakhumaidevivar /
Is Father and Rakhumai /

Varkari kirtan versions of this *abhanga* (video 14.15) are usually in Raga Bhairavi, with audience members and a chorus singing while standing in a semicircle behind the *kirtankar*. The only instruments are *mrdang*, with its particular ringing resonance, and *tal*. The *mrdang* plays *bhajani theka*, with the *tal* accent pattern stressing the first and fifth beats of the eight-beat cycle by striking the center of the cymbals, becoming gradually faster and building in excitement.

Bhimsenji sings the same *bhajan* in the classical *raga* of Deshkar (pentatonic, omitting the fourth and seventh, with an orientation toward the upper tetrachord) and begins with a meditative solo that is adorned by his characteristically flexible *taans*. At 1:24, he is joined by *tal*, *mrdang*, *tabla*, quieter cymbals (*jhanj*), harmonium, and a quiet chorus. He sings the *abhanga* with clear enunciation to help listeners understand and reflect on the form of the divine. Moreover, while the *varkaris* sing an unadorned melody that can be repeated in call and response, Bhimsenji improvises melodic lines, but only introduces variations after the text and tune are firmly established.

I recently heard a young *naradiya kirtankar* from Pune named Shreeyas Badave perform "Rupa Pahata Lochani" (video 14.16). The core melody is identical to Bhimsenji's and is also in *Raga* Deshkar, but Badave has added some *kirtan*-isms (such as the cymbal pattern) and his own improvisations. The two main styles of Marathi *kirtan* are *varkari* and *naradiya*. *Naradiya kirtan* is usually performed by urban Brahmans and is more presentational than *varkari kirtan*. *Naradiya kirtankars* sing without a chorus. They choose a wide range of songs that audience members may not know, and they sing in a classically inspired style. Badave's performance was in the hall of a Pune housing society and—as is typical—he was accompanied by harmonium, *tabla*, and *jhanj* (flat hand cymbals) rather than *tal* and *mrdang*.

Here, we hear a progression from the original *varkari* recording, to Bhimsenji's *varkari*-esque performance, to the Bhimsenji-influenced classicized version in a *naradiya kirtan*. This process is one that I've encountered many times in *naradiya kirtan*. If *naradiya kirtankars* are devotional performers who have some contact with the more rural *varkari* tradition, but who also have training in North Indian classical music, then it's no surprise that these songs of Bhimsen Joshi are popular with them.

CONCLUSION

Through multiple recorded livenesses, Bhimsenji was able to evoke performance contexts outside of the recording studio. But the translation from live to liveness takes multiple paths, and we can't assume that the people evoked in the song are the same as the imagined audiences. Through Bhimsenji's *abhangas*, listeners may connect with their own musical memories, or they may tap into prosthetic memories of experiences they never had (Landsberg 2004). But markets are unruly: They can reach many audiences, intended and unintended, and the listenership cannot be contained. So what may be a prosthetic memory for urban middle-class audiences may be a stylized personal memory for rural *varkaris*. Through Bhimsenji's *abhangas*, classical audiences get a mediated glimpse of *varkari* experience, and *varkaris* gain access to classical music through a familiar repertoire.

The varied textures of liveness can teach us about how recordings produce listeners and how listeners produce music. Part of what interests me about Bhimsenji's *abhangas* is that they combine liveness and mediatization with such variety, but even more interesting is that they hail different audiences through a range of livenesses. But this is not exactly to say that he dabbled in different styles of music, an idea to which he would have objected. I purposefully use the term liveness because he was not performing *varkari* music when he referenced *varkari* experience, nor was he exactly performing *varkari* music in a classical style. When *varkari* liveness is filtered through Bhimsenji's corporeal and classical liveness, the result is electrifying. By evoking rich worlds of experience that lie beyond the recording studio, worlds that mean different things for different listeners, he managed to become perhaps the only singer who truly appealed to Maharashtrians of all backgrounds.

NOTES

1. "Mediatized" cultures and events are colored to varying degrees by processes and expectations of mass media. This differs from the on/off connotations of "mediation." As Philip Auslander (1999) argues, "live" performances can be heavily mediatized without being fully mediated. The concepts of "liveness" and "mediatization" are further developed in the rest of this chapter.

2. His son Shrinivas revived the *Santvani* concerts in 2009 (see *Indian Express* 2009, *Times of India* 2009).

3. Sometimes *abhangas* are sung verse by verse, without a refrain. Thank you to Gregory Booth for the *mukhda-antara* suggestion.

4. This word is pronounced with a retroflex "t" and "l." It is distinct from the word for rhythmic cycles (here transliterated as "*tala*"), which is pronounced with a dental "t" and "l."

5. This was an exclamation made in a recording studio when a musician captured a musical feel that his collaborators identified as sounding particularly "African."

6. Bhimsenji's live *abhanga* recordings available on YouTube are between 10 and 16 minutes in length.

7. My characterization here is a bit simplified. Jaime Jones's dissertation is an excellent study of *varkari* music as it is taught in the city of Pune.

CHAPTER 15

Bollywood in the Era of Film Song Avatars

DJing, Remixing, and Change in the Film Music Industry of North India

PAUL D. GREENE

Starting in the mid-1990s and accelerating in the 2000s, remixes of North Indian film songs have grown dramatically in popularity and preponderance in Indian marketplaces, soundscapes, and airwaves. Remixes are made of contemporary film songs, and also of film songs from the 1980s, '90s, and 2000s. A growing portion of the music that young Indians listen to is made not only by the film industry's music directors, but also by disc jockeys from India's mushrooming nightclub scene, who expand their inventories by crafting remixes of songs from popular Indian films, mostly from 20 to 30 years ago. Working with new technologies, DJ-remixers produce layers of film song vocal lines over house, trance, and hip-hop dance beats, juxtaposed with passages of Western and Indian musics. DJs spin their remixes at clubs, share them in DJ networks, and upload them to the Internet, where they are downloaded by other DJs, as well as listeners throughout the Indian world. The remix scene grows through a healthy synergy with diasporic Indian scenes, such as that of *bhangra* in Birmingham, U.K. (Huq 1996). DJs increasingly travel back and forth between the U.K., India, New York (Maira 2002), and other parts of Asia, sharing music and musical ideas. Most remixers are amateurs, who freely produce, spin, and distribute their remixes largely to spread their fame, with little or no direct monetary compensation, taking advantage of the Internet to do so. The North Indian film industry, Bollywood, has responded to all of this activity by hiring DJs to produce remixes of its own music, which are then marketed alongside the originals. Remixes are sold on CDs, played on FM radio, and aired with videos on television. Not infrequently, remixes outplay originals on the airwaves and in the lives of young people in cars, in college dorm rooms, at home, and elsewhere. Remixing has led to transformations in the politics of music production and marketing, in the social organization of the Bollywood film industry, and in the kinds of meanings and functions that Bollywood songs take on in social life.

There is little evidence that the rise of remixes has undermined or even significantly challenged the centrality of Bollywood in Indian popular music. The film industry has retained its dominant position in India's music market, but it has had to adjust. The rise of remixes has changed how much of India's popular music is made, the concerns that guide its production, and the sound of Indian music generally. It is a significant aesthetic shift in the Indian soundscape, growing out of and reflecting a rise in urban dance club culture, and it has brought about structural changes in the industry. It reflects a shift in emphasis toward a young, urban, pre-professional, and dance-loving music market. At the center of these new developments is the DJ-remixer, a significant new figure and role in India's popular music. The DJ-remixer has become a semi-established role in the contemporary music industry, alongside the film music director, the playback singer, and the session musician.

This chapter examines DJs and DJ discourse in Delhi and Mumbai as a way to understand the new concerns and practices that they bring to shaping the popular music of North India today. These new concerns reflect not only what is danceable, in terms of tempo and overall energy level, but also the values and aspirations of a recently enlarged class of young, cosmopolitan, pre-professional Indians, many of whom are cultivating careers in the economic sectors of Indian society that have exploded in the recent business process outsourcing boom. DJs understand that getting to know these people is part of their job. Another, perhaps equally important part of the job lies in acquiring a tremendous breadth of musical knowledge. In the DJ booth, DJs sense which tracks in their libraries and which mix practices inspire visible energy on the dance floor. The skills of beatmatching, scratching, turntabling, layering, and producing digital music—first imported into India as early as the 1980s—are subservient to the goal of getting this audience to dance.

This chapter draws on field research, which I conducted primarily in Delhi, together with the satellite communities of Noida and Gurgaon, and secondarily in Mumbai, during 2007–2009. I collected music and observed musical activity in the scenes in which it takes place. I interviewed record company managers and executives at Times Music, Sony Music India, and T-Series. I interviewed dozens of DJs, including some of North India's most popular figures: DJ Aqeel, DJ Jazzy Joe, DJ Rummy, DJ Akbar Sami, and DJ Megha.[1] For a few weeks, I took DJ lessons at DJ Rummy's nightclub Kuki in Delhi, where I learned how to beatmatch and layer tracks live. I also interviewed roughly 200 remix listeners in the Delhi area.

DJING, REMIXING, AND REMAKING

DJing and remixing are related activities, but not identical. And Bollywood remixes are a somewhat special case in the global remix trend, in that most Bollywood "remixes" are actually remakes, in terms of the way they are produced, but nevertheless they are believed by most listeners to be remixes and are invariably called remixes. This point is taken up below. DJing is a live practice of mixing, layering, and programming music recordings before a dancing audience using a DJ console. Most DJs in India today do not use vinyl LPs or LP turntables; instead, they mix using a console that includes two digital turntables that play CDs, but emulate the feel and capabilities of LP turntables. DJing involves skill in beatmatching, in which the DJ synchronizes two recordings so that their beats are aligned and in synchronization on the two CD players. The DJ then adjusts faders and controls to transition from one song to another, to layer the melody of one track over the bass of the other, and to dismantle, combine, and loop tracks or parts of tracks for creative effect. A Bollywood melody may be combined, for example, with Western house beats; a vocal line from one track may be combined with the rhythm section of another. Because the focus is on dancing and live mixing creativity, DJs tend to produce a continuous stream of music. A single track may be extended to 10 or 15 minutes or longer. Transitions from one track to another may be blurred or even undetectable.

Remixing, in contrast, is a music production practice that extracts elements of an original song and results in a new recording (cf. Tankel 1990). The recording bears many of the characteristics of live DJ mixing; however, it is typically not as long and has a more clearly discernible beginning and ending. Whereas live DJing is in many respects an impromptu process of musical creativity, remixing is more carefully planned and calculated in advance. DJs typically produce remixes for later use in their DJ booths, so that they have recordings that already combine many of the sound qualities and musical elements they want to use. And remixes have gained popularity well beyond the dance floor in India—they are played over the radio, distributed through the Internet, and enjoyed by listeners in cars, student dorms, and at parties.

Remixes sonically resemble live DJing in many respects, although the actual production techniques and technologies are distinct. Remixers in India work on personal computers that serve as digital audio workstations (DAWs). Since the early 2000s, music editing, mixing, and production software specifically designed for remixing have been available to young North Indians of the urban middle class. These software packages allow remixers to manipulate, loop, and layer tracks on a computer screen, performing many of the functions that can also be achieved through a DJ console. When remixing a song, a DJ lifts this vocal line and sometimes other distinctive elements, loops them, layers them on top of new dance beats, and juxtaposes this recognizable, old film-song material with new material. Software that is especially efficacious for making remixes is loop-based, such as Sony Acid, Logic, and Apple Loops. DAWs typically include instrument patches and sound samples, enabling the user to generate music entirely within the computer if desired. And DAWs also have built-in effects processors, to add to certain tracks of music any desired echo, reverberation, or flange effects. With a minor investment in software, a personal computer can be transformed into a remixing DAW, which in many respects obviates the need for a sound studio. Today in India, there are thousands of remixers sitting before computers, generating remixes, and publishing them on the Internet, or, if they have advantageous contracts, selling them to record companies.

In most cases, Bollywood remixes actually require the remixer to reconstitute the vocal line: hire either the original vocalist or a new vocalist with a similar voice, coach him or her, record the result, and copy the accompanying instrumentation. The reason for this is because pre-1990s Bollywood film songs were not recorded using a metronome, or a studio click track. As a result, with some exceptions, the only way to add Western electronic dance beats to a vocal line is to reproduce the vocal line from scratch, having the vocalist sing against a click track that is audible over headphones as they perform in the studio. There are a handful of remix vocalists who have built a reputation as copycat singers of famous playback singers. The fact that most Bollywood remixes are actually remakes is something that virtually all DJs are aware of, but very few listeners realize. Bollywood remixing can be considered a practice of song versioning—which takes many forms in India—but with the important qualification that there is a genuine effort to reproduce, as closely as possible, an original vocal line, in its original form, down to the timbre of the voice. Further, Indian listeners invariably believe that they are hearing the original vocal line reproduced electronically—that is, that the vocal line is not a version, but the original precisely reproduced. The fact that Bollywood remixers painstakingly work to reproduce vocal lines as closely as possible and then showcase them in clear, simple mixes further emphasizes the importance of the vocal line in Bollywood remixes.

Except for a tiny percentage, remixers are part-time musicians who produce and distribute their remixes primarily to spread their fame. Many hope that as their fame spreads, they may gain more opportunities to DJ and perhaps one day get the attention of the film and music industry. DJ-remixers hired by the film and music industry produce tracks to be sold along with original film songs, both on CD and through the Internet. The music industry also produces and sells collections of these remixes, also on CD and through the Internet. The nature of the business relationships between professional remixers and the rest of the industry is varied and evolving. I am aware of no standard pay scale or financial arrangement. Remixers are new additions to the industry, and they seem to be growing in standing.

In the sections that follow, I explore themes that came up in my interviews with DJs, remixers, and DJ-remixers. My approach is discourse analysis. As much as possible, I present my fieldwork findings in the actual words of Indian DJs and music producers. These professionals speak in quite articulate English, and I allow them to present themselves and what they are doing. I then elucidate broader patterns, meanings, and implications, drawing on the broader experience of my field research to date and pertinent background information. I organize the sections starting with musical topics and progressing to social topics, which mirrors how I organized my field interviews. That is, my ethnomusicological approach to conducting interviews and analyzing discourses was to start with questions pertaining to music, and then follow the discourse as it shifted toward cultural and social topics. In this way, I allowed my informants to shape my conclusions about the ways in which music is or can be a vehicle for shaping culture. I have selected a variety of interview quotations in order to adumbrate the range of positions I encountered in DJ discourse.

MUSICIANSHIP

DJs and remixers offer a variety of points of view on their own musicianship and on the musicianship required to be an effective DJ or remixer. Reflections on the value of musicianship and musical competencies reveal the social role that DJ-remixers see themselves as having, and that they aspire to.

> To be good at it, you need a sense of rhythm.... You don't need to be a musician. When we remix, we don't play around much with the keys and chords of the original song. That's not our job (DJ Suketu, in Shah 2003).

In contrast, DJ NYK believes,

> You need to be a musician to be a good remixer.... There is a formula I have in mind. It is hard to explain. First of all, I need a good bass line. That is the backbone of the track, not the drums. It gives that jumpy feel. Then obviously the groove. Then some effects...I keep it clean and simple. Yet groovy. I do change the chords. The focus is on the first melody, and I change the chords. You have to be a musician before you can be a good remixer.

DJing has only recently become a prevalent or central activity in Indian popular music, and it involves skills that are markedly different from those of music director, composer, playback singer, or session musician. DJs are not actually composing songs or performing on instruments, other than the DJ console or the personal computer. Perhaps as a result, there are various views on the musical competencies required. All DJs emphasize sensitivity to rhythm, but for many an understanding of harmony and chords is unimportant. This is evidently the position of DJ Suketu, one of the most popular remixers in North India. DJs like NYK, who emphasize skills in working with harmony and chords, tend to have great aspirations for the role of the DJ-remixer. Some DJs aspire to become music directors and play an even more active role in shaping India's popular music; this point is taken up below. One area of agreement is that DJs see themselves as bringing a different, non-traditional skill set to the popular music industry. For the most part, they view this as a strength, a reflection of the fact that music has changed and therefore new roles and skills are needed. They do not apologize for a lack of knowledge about harmony or chords, or a lack of facility with musical instruments.

MUSICAL KNOWLEDGE

By musical knowledge I am referring to the breadth of knowledge that DJs have of popular music recordings. This is a key selling point for a DJ, and it this knowledge that a DJ brings to bear as he or she tries to find and deliver the sounds that get an audience dancing. "Being a DJ is a tough task...one must have a knowledge of music" (DelhiDJs.com, accessed November 15, 2007). Other DJs emphasize the impact of their choices on their audiences:

> Personally, it is more like psychology. For the people who are there, give them the best at the start, and then educate them about what is there. Make them happy and then only will they listen to what you want to say. Some people want the same song over and over, even if just played. This pisses us off (DJ Vikram).

> Ninety percent, I entertain the crowd; ten percent, I give them something else they would get nowhere else. Maybe my own remixes. The crowd is not stupid. Hearing a mash-up inspires them, because they know the words. [It] makes them happy, inspires them for creativity. Oh, DJ has created something. They take away something they would not get anywhere else. I make sure I do that: ninety percent entertainment, ten percent education. Good sounds [that are] not on TV (DJ Jazzy Joe).

I find it noteworthy that DJs rail against people in the dance crowd who request the same songs over and over again. From their point of view, this is boring, and a preponderance of such requests results in a boring dance evening. It is even boring, they suggest, for the very people who make the requests. DJs speak most negatively about working at wedding receptions, where these requests happen most frequently. DJs insist that they know better than their dancing audience what will animate the dance floor. This conviction is based on their tremendous knowledge of music, an understanding of what kinds of people comprise the dancing crowd, their experience spinning at dance clubs, and a willingness to challenge or stretch their audiences a bit. Further, there is an "educational" aspect to DJing that DJs speak of: When an audience is being pushed slightly, DJs say a "click" happens. The audience feels inspired, and the DJ feels like the music just happens, or flows. This, at least to a DJ, characterizes a successful dance event, and given the popularity of DJing in India, it is arguable that dancing audiences have come to value the leading role of DJs, despite the fact that the DJ may resist some of their specific requests.

FUSION AND CONFUSION, REMIX AND CREATIVITY

In my 200 interviews with remix listeners, I was struck by an overwhelming negativity about the creativity of DJs. Even among listeners who avidly listened to remixes, there was a consensus that the DJ himself or herself was doing very little that could be called creative. Remixing is little more than "cut and paste" on a computer screen, as one listener put it, belying the actual technological and musical skills and effort that DJs must put into painstakingly remaking originals against a click track, experimenting with layering and juxtaposition, and so on.

Against this criticism, DJs are quite articulate about what constitutes a good mix, and the kind of effort and creativity that go into remixing. In a good remix, the elements must retain certain essential characteristics, and they must be audibly distinct in combination. I begin with quotes that reveal how DJ-remixers think about, value, and treat the original Bollywood song melody and words.

> Indians are still listening too much to melody and words. Don't get that anywhere else, so it is good, too. That is distinctively Indian (DJ Vikram).
>
> Indians listen to melody in a certain way. They are taking vocals and putting music on top (DJ Megha).
>
> The centrality of the singing voice is important. There is a fresh touch to Bollywood singing (DJ Akhtar).

In response to questions about the popularity of remixes in the first years of the 21st century, DJs and others often noted the pre-existing familiarity of the film songs that were being remixed. Anindya Banerjee, the A&R manager for Mumbai's Times Music argued, "first of all, the basic reason is that the song is already hit. The original song is already in [the] listener's mind." DJ Vikram agreed with Banerjee's assessment, but noted the combination of familiarity with novelty: "[T]hey have taken what is in [fashion] and fused it with what was famous, old."

Other DJs, however, have argued that remixes should simplify the musical complexities of film songs, and that this is what appealed to their listeners. "Bollywood remixes have to be short and spicy. As I said earlier: clean and simple. For a common man [listener], yes, it should be clean and straight. If you use all the tweaky sounds, people will not get into it" (DJ NYK). Similarly, DJ Jazzy Joe suggested that in the creation of remixes, "the challenge is to keep it simple. You're adding one song to the other, but you want both to keep their simplicity. Don't add too much in the way of scratches, extra samples, and so on."

Taken together, these interview quotes reveal a special emphasis and value on the vocal line, which leads to an aesthetic of simplicity and clarity. The vocal melody and words must be clearly presented, not clouded by other sounds. Although the unique contribution of the DJ-remixer is to mix and layer sounds and beats, that does not mean they should overdo it, or that they lack a sensitivity to the special value placed on the vocal line. I agree with DJs Vikram, Megha, and Akhtar: This special value of the vocal line is a common characteristic of much South Asian popular music (cf. Greene and Henderson 2000). But there is an added reason for emphasizing the vocal line in the case of Bollywood remixes. Retaining the vocal line clearly allows the remix to build on the popularity of the film song and to nostalgically invoke the world and mood of the original. DJs are quite conscious of guarding this "simple," clear sound; and DJs like NYK describe very different production practices when making other types of remixes, such as New Age ones.

Remix aesthetics have much to do with cultural identity. In the following quote, DJ Jazzy Joe compares remixes specifically to other kinds of fusion of Indian and Western elements, and raises the concern about how to combine styles while retaining a sense of Indian identity:

> Indian music is mixed with Western tunes. I'm not against it. But not at the cost of identity. I feel Indian music should be Indian music. Then you could travel, but from whom and to whom? You should not sell your home just because you are traveling. Ultimately, if you lose identity, you cannot contribute to the world music scene. I believe identity should remain and changes are welcome. There is room for both. My name is Jazzy Joe. Jazzy means funky. Joe is a most common English name. Average Joe. Joe balances the jazz. I am basically an easy-going guy. I am the Average Joe. It balances the two things. I maintained my identity as Average Joe plus added this jazzy thing to it. It's not lost, added, which is a remix. Be yourself and then add onto it. A remix should add onto the song. Not change the song. A core is there which does not change. Everything else adds onto it. There is a real distinction between a remix and a fusion. If you have ice cream with a cookie, the ice cream does not change with the addition of the cracker [cookie]. But in fusion, the core changes. You break up the biscuit [cookie] and mix it into the ice cream. You cannot separate later. The elements are there, but I have to eat both. In a good remix, mentally you can separate out the elements: ah, this is the instrumental of that song, and the words are of this song [smiles]. . . . These "remixes" are actually remakes. But fusion? No, that is confusion. I believe in remix because of the creativity. New things can come out. Experiments. This is the number one reason (DJ Jazzy Joe).

As much as possible, remixers seek to retain musical elements, such as a vocal melody, exactly as they were first heard. These quotes reveal that this is a matter of identity: For Bollywood remixers, the original film-song vocal line is a guarantor of Indian-ness. Whereas Bollywood music directors often seamlessly weave together elements of Western classical, Western popular, Indian, and other elements, producing integrated musical styles that blend the different elements together thoroughly and naturally, Bollywood remixers celebrate the patent distinctions and contrasts between the cultural elements juxtaposed in the mix. Moreover, remixers view musical fusions negatively: Artful fusions in which differences between musical elements are smoothed over actually compromise cultural identity. The remixers' position is evident in the effort they take to painstakingly reconstitute Bollywood vocal lines as accurately as possible, and then to place them in simple mix contexts in which they can be clearly heard. N. S. Padmanabhan hears in contemporary Bollywood remixes a new celebration of Indian identity within world music: India is not reduced to a musical sound bite or to a flavor added to other musical textures. Instead, India finds more full expression in extended vocal lines that are precisely retained and supplemented by Western dance beats. As DJ Jazzy Joe argues, remixing can not only retain cultural identity; it can also be an important basis for musical creativity. Remixing allows one to be creative without compromising who one is. The remixer is like a chef whose creativity lies more in brilliant and striking combinations than in recipes prepared in the slow cooker of musical fusion.

SOCIAL ORGANIZATION OF MUSIC PRODUCTION

DJs have a lot to say about their role in the overall production of music. They recognize and readily articulate their unique role and contribution to shaping the soundscapes of India today. They remember a past in which they were ignored, and they have regrets about being undervalued today. And they have aspirations for greater recognition and an even greater role: A few DJs see DJing and remixing as a stepping stone toward becoming music producers, or even music directors. They reflect on issues of musical copyright, are concerned about how to properly reward musical creativity, and generally think that their own creativity as mix artists is undervalued in the music market. Jazzy Joe is quite articulate about his vision for a board that would more equitably oversee rights and compensations for music directors, original artists, and DJ-remixers.

First, it is important to note that although remixing is based on the live, interactive dynamism between the DJ and dancers on the dance floor, the actual crafting of Bollywood remixes is a remarkably solitary activity:

The availability of software is such that there are so many people who are sitting at home and doing a good job. Much more than those in front [i.e., most famous]. Behind, they are doing a great job (DJ Vikram).

In India remixing is very, very studio based, very technology based. Elsewhere it is more live, playing, or in a garage.... Here, when you talk remix, the idea is in a studio. Getting someone to sing. Again, it is a remake, not remix. Very less live remix. No one wants to remix live. Which is actually prerogative of the DJ that can do that (DJ Jazzy Joe).

In a similar vein, DJ NYK, pointed out that there was no training available for his craft. "There are no institutions that teach music production software. It took me over one year to learn to use it."

Although DJ NYK may not be correct in his assertion that there are *no* institutions in India that teach music production software, I find his perception to be common among remixers: that learning to remix is a solitary activity. Jazzy Joe likewise talks of Indian remixing as very studio-based, and he contrasts this with remixing practices he believes take place elsewhere in the world, in which there is more interaction among musicians in the production of remixes and less emphasis on producing a polished product. In addition to the criteria of simplicity and clarity discussed above, this "studio" emphasis evidences a concern for a polished, professional sound; a remixer spends a considerable amount of time sitting in front of a computer, mostly alone, and crafts and refines the sounds and the mix. To some extent, this is necessitated by the fact that most Indian "remixes" are actually remakes, requiring the recording and manipulation of new music. This is one respect in which Bollywood remixes differ from the live mixes one hears in the dancehall, even if many of the live mixes are based on remixes. It also distinguishes Bollywood remixing from remix practices elsewhere in the world.

Remixers are quite articulate about the role they play in the production of India's popular music today, as well as the role they believe they should play:

> Now, we are able to get the original tracks from film song production. After 2002, whatever songs have come out, they give the original vocal and instrumental tracks. Originally they gave only the whole mix and asked us to layer on top of it. We need it in multitrack format. I might even want to keep a trumpet, not necessarily the vocal line. Some nice music parts, I can cut and paste parts. Maybe I just get four tracks of vocals and backup vocals. I may trash 45 tracks, and add one. I should have that ability (DJ Sunny Sarid).

DJ Sunny Sarid describes a central challenge in making Bollywood remixes. Unless the remixer receives the original multitrack recording, it is difficult to separate out the different elements in order to make mixes. If one wants to extract a vocal line fragment or a trumpet melody, one can use a high-pass filter to extract only the high frequencies, but this results in some distortion or change in sound quality. This challenge is in addition to the challenge of beatmatching Bollywood songs, which were not recorded using a click track. I consider his closing statement to be quite telling: "I *should* have that ability." Unlike studio musicians or music directors of the past, remixers consider it appropriate to have and *expect* to have direct access to original multitrack recording tracks. They argue that this should become the standard basis from which to make new music. Not surprisingly, along with this are certain expectations about ownership of music, and therewith about how DJs, artists, music directors, and music/film companies should be interrelated and organized.

> The Internet has happened, and music has gone far. It is very experimental now. You get recognition as an artist in [the] country. No longer do they say: oh, you don't have anything to do, so you are DJ (DJ Megha).

DJ Sunny Sarid contrasted the conditions and structures of copyright and royalty between India and elsewhere:

> In the U.S., the original artist gets a royalty. That is not the system here. The film director pays the music director outright for all the rights to the music. Here, it is initially the film director who pays the music director a one-time fee. Singers too. The rights go to the producer of the movie or the recording company. There are no royalties every time the film is aired; the music company gets them. This is a huge difference. Now, it is starting changing. [Music Director] A. R. Rahman now asks for a 33 percent share in music that is sold. He is not outrightly selling his work. It is all evolving right now. We are trying to follow the West, but it will take longer because India does not have a popular music industry [separate from the film industry]. . . . For this reason, the original artist complains. He's not paid (DJ Sunny Sarid).

DJ Sunny Sarid's position here is slightly overstated and simplified; historical examination reveals shifting complexities in the ways that musicians and music directors have been compensated over time, and that music directors have sometimes received royalties (Booth 2008, 207ff.).

> I believe in creative freedom. I feel DJs, artists, and companies should sit down together. They should submit a mix to a board, who contacts the artists. Ask each artist if the mix helps their song or hurts sales. Develop a unified format, a global music company. Let them give money to all involved. There should be a legal process, instead of shutting creativity down. One way or another it will happen. You can't stop DJs from experimenting. We need a legal solution rather than all these problems and issues. We have had music long enough.

The industry has been around long enough. Why can't we work out these small issues? (DJ Jazzy Joe)

Although music copyright lawsuits are considerably rarer in India than in the U.S., these quotes show that DJs are aware of concerns about musical ownership, and are also concerned about properly identifying and rewarding creativity. They consider their own activities to be creative and therefore call for financial reward. These quotes reveal how they see DJing and remixing as a valuable musical practice that calls for changes in the social organization and politics of music production. Jazzy Joe goes so far as to envision a new mechanism—a music board of some sort—to oversee the proper financial relationships, which are the relationships generated by processes of musical creativity.

Whereas most remix listeners in my interviews characterized DJs as technologically empowered but not musically skilled, remixers themselves evaluate their musical skills, as well as their contributions to the music production and distribution processes, quite highly. Many DJs visualize themselves playing a more central role in music production: "[P]ersonally, I feel for a producer, it helps if one is a DJ and then becomes a producer" (DJ Vikram). There are socio-industrial challenges to these kinds of transformations, however, as DJ Sumit Setil argues: "In Bollywood, we are restricted. DJs are becoming music producers but cannot become music director. That will change. We will become music director[s]." Although DJs and remixers express a desire to become music producers, most of them specify little about what being a music producer would actually be like. Instead, I find that quotes like this reveal a general desire to exercise more control over the creative process and the resources for making and distributing music. With a few exceptions, I am not aware of specific business plans or visions for the kind of producer a DJ would be.

One of the key roles DJs now play is in music promotion. As might be expected, this is especially important for music company personnel, as N. S. Padmanabhan, the product manager for Times Music has argued:

Popularity involves radio plus TV plus clubs. The DJs are in these clubs. Most prestigious clubs in Mumbai host DJs who play the song they have remixed. The club scene has become a key component of music promotion. Clubs have been there for a long time. But now it is a fad. For the last ten years they have been very famous. They actually had clubs in the 1980s, but they were visited by extremely rich and famous people. Now it is opened up and better known....In the 1980s normal people did not go. They would think it's too prestigious or expensive or upmarket to just walk in. The club scene has become popular largely because of the sheer number of clubs opening up recently (N. S. Padmanabhan).

The distribution of new music, especially outside the structures of Indian film song, has historically been a challenge in India. Padmanabhan noted that DJs could play a role in addressing this challenge:

Basically it is about the avenues in which stuff is played. All the clubs are play-ing it. All the TV channels play it. All radio [stations] play it. All three channels. In India the radio does not create hits. The [radio] channel policy is only to play hits. Only play songs if they have [already] become hits. So for original hits, you can't do it through radio. It's very difficult to break through with an original hit in India. If it's not popular on TV, or strong sales covered by newspapers, radio will not play it. Plus it helps to know the clubs play it (N. S. Padmanabhan).

DJs are also aware, however, of their importance to the music industry:

Not everyday, but I'm very much in touch with the vibe that is happening. What people are dancing to. I know the sound of the current moment. Someone who doesn't club just makes music for himself. Will it be popular? Just depends (DJ Aqeel).

DJ is the person who knows what the public wants. The connection is very direct. You see them dancing (DJ Jazzy Joe).

DJs are very interactive, not studious like you [referring to the author]. They also can tell quickly about people. Including whether a person is a scientist or whatever. You cannot be a normal human being. You have to be technological and know people very well. So when I meet someone I already know a little how to relate to them (DJ Vikram).

It is very hard to find sponsors to make [remix] music for the market. Mostly, remixers in Delhi give their remixes to DJs at clubs, only. Those DJs don't pay for this. They distribute the music for their response. When you get a good response, then you throw the music into the market.... People only remember your remixes when they come on TV or radio. Maybe through a website, but less so. It is very important to come on an album or TV (DJ Hemant).

What has happened with remixes is [that] a lot of people my age or younger would never [have] heard songs if not for this. Remixing has done really well for the industry. It has given people job opportunities. Before that there was just film music. Same old singers, same old. Remixes opened up avenues for job opportunities. So many people are getting employed to do so many things. Studios have helped everyone (DJ Aqeel).

These interview quotes from a music company executive (N. S. Padmanabhan), from one of India's most famous DJ-remixers (DJ Aqeel), and from a struggling and mostly unknown remixer (DJ Hemant) reveal the range of perspectives on the roles and challenges of DJs in their relationships with the music industry. From the music company's point of view, represented here by Padmanabhan, playing remixes in the now-popular club scene has become a vital means by which songs can become popular, and also by which the market potential of songs can be assessed. DJ Aqeel presents what he believes he has to offer to record companies and the reason he believes he should be well paid to produce remixes: that he is in touch with the vibe and knows how to remix in a way that taps into this mystical aspect of music's popularity. In fact, I conducted this interview at his dance club, Poison, one of the leading nightclubs in Mumbai. In my listener interviews in Delhi, I found DJ Aqeel to be one of the two most popular Bollywood remixers (the other is DJ Suketu). He embodies the potential that N. S. Padmanabhan speaks of and that DJ Hemant aspires to. He offers the music industry a hands-on understanding of the dance vibe of the moment, and the sales of his remixes effectively "prove" his self-presentation and reputation. DJ Hemant likewise sees the club scene as a means to popularize remixes and thereby become famous as a DJ-remixer, but he faces the challenges of a struggling musical professional who has not (yet) achieved the breakthrough and recognition that DJ Aqeel enjoys. The final quote from DJ Aqeel offers a perspective on how clubbing, DJing, and remixing have opened up the music industry, filling India's soundscapes with a greater variety of music and also creating new job opportunities in the industry. This is the potential that animates DJ Hemant's aspirations and dreams.

For some DJs and some music industry figures, DJs have become a permanent, established part of the music business. "They already are. Take Suketu, or Akbar Sami. They are established names. Once they grow up as DJs they go on to compose their own music. I don't think this is a temporary phase. DJing is in and will stay" (Anindya Banerjee). "DJs are a new, permanent part of the music industry. They cannot compose original songs. But they can remake them. Give [a song] a new application. You can hear it in a club, and dance, as well as hearing it while driving" (DJ Aqeel). Times Music's N. S. Padmanabhan emphasized the interactive relationship between DJs, remixes, music companies, and the film industry:

When they release a soundtrack of a film, they release five songs plus five remixes of the same songs. They release remixes before the film. Every time before the film. No way it can be released after. There is a six-week window before. They use songs and videos of songs to promote films. Film albums are now combined with remixes of the same songs. Sometimes they hire a DJ. Mostly they hire a famous DJ. Sometimes the music director does it himself (N. S. Padmanabhan).

Since the 1990s, Bollywood has entered a new era, an era in which film songs are heard in multiple versions, an era of clubbing, and an era of DJing. Despite negative characterizations of remixing even by its most ardent fans, it is clear that the industry respects the talents and contributions of DJs. The Bollywood music industry has come to terms with structural change in the areas of music marketing and musical production, with dance clubs serving as proving grounds for a song's popularity, and new mix aesthetics central to Bollywood music. And the DJ is, at least for now, a semi-established figure vital to both marketing and production.

As the remix era challenges time-honored notions of original ownership and authorship of Indian film songs, the industry has adapted to capitalize on the new dynamics, by hiring DJs and releasing remixes themselves. While a handful of DJs like Aqeel, Suketu, Akbar Sami, Whosane, and Megha find new avenues for employment, there are also many like DJs Hemant and NYK who continue to labor with little financial reward. It is unclear the extent to which DJing and remixing may have challenged the centrality or profitability of the Bollywood music industry. And it is unclear at best whether some of the aspirations of DJ-remixers will be fulfilled: to become Bollywood music directors, to be fully recognized as artists, to have their creativity valued and financially rewarded alongside that of other musical artists. But popular music aesthetics have been powerfully transformed; India's soundscapes have changed; and the structure of the music industry is altered. There are no signs that any of these musical trajectories will be reversed any time soon.

NOTES

1. Except where noted, all the quotations from Indian DJs in this chapter are personal communications that occurred between 2007 and 2009.

Afterword

Capitalisms and Cosmopolitanisms

TIMOTHY D. TAYLOR

As the American century settles more firmly into the dustbin of history, more and more people around the world are singing on the global stage. To be sure, cultural forms produced in the United States and Europe are still globally dominant, but they are less productive of global emulators than they once were and are now more productive as sources for styles and ideas for musicians around the world, who take these styles and ideas to make local and regional musics that are frequently local, regional, and cosmopolitan simultaneously, or connect themselves to their diaspora, or connect themselves to a global social movement.

The presentation of the local, regional, and cosmopolitan in Indian popular music is one of the welcome offerings of this illuminating collection, which provides a panoptic (though not comprehensive—this would clearly be impossible) view of various forms of popular music being produced in India. It's an astonishing variety, as one would expect: devotional music, rock music, DJ remixes, film songs, and much more.

Given India's longstanding connections to the West through colonial and later pathways, the editors claim in their introduction, "Meaning in India's popular music has been closely linked to historical patterns of the various forms of capitalism and semi-capitalism in Indian music production and to industrial frameworks that often...shadow the dynamic growth of the cinema...." Since, as some have argued, capitalism as we now know it began with merchant capitalism in the British East India Company in the early 17th century, India, capitalism, and thus cultural production have been intertwined for a very long time, perhaps longer than anywhere else.

In this volume, this complex relationship is clearest in the many chapters about the contemporary and recent past, during the process of the liberalization of the Indian economy, which acquired a new urgency in 1991. This new phase of the process, which grew out of a balance-of-payments crisis, prompted India to enter into a bailout agreement with the International Monetary Fund that required certain economic reforms. Although the Indian government didn't undertake all of these reforms, neoliberal policies were implemented that will sound familiar to many readers: opening India to trade and investment, deregulation, privatization, and the rise of consumption, at least among those who can afford it (see Sharma 2011). For me, as a longtime student of music used in advertising, the most emblematic sign of this shift to a liberalized, consumer economy was the ascendance of A. R. Rahman, an international superstar who figures prominently in these pages, from the world of advertising music to internationally successful film music composer[1] (such a leap has never occurred, to my knowledge, for musicians in the American advertising industry, though many composers have tried).

But, of course, there is more to neoliberalization than this. The many authors in this volume focus on a number of different aspects of this new economic universe, from the rise of a Western-style consumer culture to the introduction of new digital technologies in the production of music (and elsewhere, of course), to new forms of youth-oriented identity conceptions.

Let me consider some of these developments in some detail. Perhaps what occurs most frequently in these chapters are observations and discussions of new forms of Indian subjects, especially among younger, post-liberalization generations. The importance of youth (sub)cultures, new forms of identity conceptions, new forms of cosmopolitanism, the rise of the consumer, and new modes of femininity are discussed by many of these authors. For example, Natalie Sarrazin's chapter on digital technologies in 21st-century Hindi cinema examines several recent films that portray post-liberalization generations as cosmopolitan urbanites. Kaley Mason, in a fascinating chapter on femininity and music in the Malayalam-speaking state of Kerala, considers new forms of femininity brought about by liberalization, epitomized by the fashion show and dance talent contests, and, Mason writes, practices in popular music performance. Peter Kvetko's chapter on issues of "versioning" in North Indian popular music analyzes a recording by Baba Sehgal as registering anxiety over the middle-class Indians' increased engagement with consumption following liberalization.

But it is probably the new, post-liberalization cosmopolitan subject that receives the most attention from these authors. I have long been rather leery of making arguments about "new" cosmopolitan subjects, because most of the theoretical literature on the subject fails to historicize it: There have been cosmopolitans as long as there have been cities and travelers. In India, as in other postcolonial nations, the situation seems to me to be even more complex, even vexed. At what historical point does a colonialized subject who has been forced to learn the colonializer's language become a cosmopolitan subject simply because she happens to know that very same European language? Does such a historical point exist? Although it is clear that in today's India, knowing English is a form of cosmopolitan capital, as Niko Higgins discusses in his chapter (about which more later), one wonders about the complex historical, social, and cultural transformations that made it so. I still vividly remember reading, years ago, Ashis Nandy's vigorous defense of his employment of an older idiom of English because that was what he had been forced to learn, and his concomitant refusal to update that idiom to be more gender-inclusive (Nandy 1983).

As I was saying, the emergence of a recognizably new post-liberalization cosmopolitan subject is central to many of these chapters. Mason's contribution on women in the film music industry in Kerala shows their increasing cosmopolitanism, a "cosmopolitanism from below" as he calls it, that entails openness to the outside world combined with a sensitivity to their region. Co-editor Shope's chapter on the uses of Latin American musics in films from the 1930s to the 1950s—during the end of the British Raj, when one could argue that a different regime of cosmopolitanism was in effect, if it could be called cosmopolitanism at all—argues for a form of cosmopolitanism among some audiences in their increased knowledge of the world beyond their borders. At the other end of the historical spectrum, Niko Higgins's chapter examines Violin Ganesh, half of a brother duo of violinists in Chennai, who employs musical sounds that both retain and enlarge the tradition in the ears of his middle-class, cosmopolitan audience.

Many authors also discuss new digital technologies, which have had a profound effect on the production, distribution, and consumption of music in countries where these technologies are accessible. Other sorts of new digital technologies, of course, have played a crucial role in neoliberal economies around the world, facilitating nearly instant and complex bank transactions, lightning-speed communication, and much more. Sarrazin thematizes technology in her chapter and how it has affected creativity and the production of media, arguing that Hindi film music composition became more eclectic as a result of the creativity facilitated by new technologies. Joseph Getter discusses the modalities of the production of Tamil film music, which rely heavily on digital technologies, not only for production but also for distribution. Several authors tackle recording studios and their effects on musicians and recordings: Shalini Ayyagari's chapter on Manganiyar music from western Rajasthan follows Manganiyar musicians into the recording studio and observes how they learned and reacted to the technologies used in the recording process; and Stefan Fiol offers a chapter on Garhwali musicians in the recording studio. Jayson Beaster-Jones's article on style and genre in Indian film songs hears studio techniques in songs as markers of a non-film song aesthetic. Anna Schultz discusses questions of liveness and mediation in Pandit Bhimsen Joshi's popular *abhangas*, noting how his recordings are produced in such a way to reach different audiences. And Paul D. Greene discusses DJs who do remixes of North Indian film songs, musicians whose very art is dependent on recent digital technologies.

Remixes, of course, introduce, via sampling, musics from outside the world of the music being remixed, and musical hybridity (or whatever one wants to call it) is another recurring theme in these chapters. There has never been a time when different peoples and musics haven't mixed, but long-distance hybrids are now much more possible and easily produced since the advent of recording and, later, digital technologies. And they seem to be the musica franca of younger generations of post-liberalization Indians, as Mason notes.

Hybridity (a term I dislike—see Anjali Gera Roy's chapter for a critique, as well as Taylor (2007)—but continue to use because it enjoys greater currency than any other one) isn't just about music, of course; it is about a relationship to music. Its most recent iterations convey a good deal about the way peoples and musics move in today's world. Most illustrative of this point is Roy's chapter, which tackles the complex history of *bhangra* music, originating as Panjabi dance music, traveling to the U.K. with Panjabi immigrants, being revived in both the U.K. and India, and now used in Bollywood films.

All of the foregoing—new forms of subjecthood, the advent and use of new technologies, an increased movement of peoples and cultural forms—are part of today's neoliberal, globalized world, registered in sound all over the planet and in these chapters. A few of these chapters are historical (by editors Booth—including a fascinating chapter on early rock music in India—and Shope, as well as a chapter by Stephen Hughes on the gramophone and religion in colonial South India), providing a welcome historical introduction to the majority of the chapters (and in some cases offering thematic precursors to the chapters on more recent case studies, such as Shope's discussion of cosmopolitanism during the twilight of the Raj). Most of the chapters, however, concentrate on the present or recent past and offer a rich and multifaceted portrait of music production in the ongoing liberalizing of India. Taken as a whole, the chapters show an India still grappling with the now-old problem of how to be both Indian and modern in an increasingly fast-changing world, one that betrays no sign of slowing down.

NOTES

1. For a treatment of the role of advertising in liberalizing India, see Mazzarella (2003).

REFERENCES

Adorno, Theodor. 1976. *Introduction to the Sociology of Music*. New York: Seabury Press.

Ali. 1981. "Disco: A New Religion?" *Screen* 30 (52), September 11: 8.

Ali, Naushad. 2004a. The Magical Music of *Baiju Bawra*. In *Notes of Naushad*, Shashikant Kinikar, ed., 65–72. Mumbai: English Edition Publishers and Distributors.

——. 2004b. The Discovery of Lata Mangeshkar. In *Notes of Naushad*, Shashikant Kinikar, ed., 119–126. Mumbai: English Edition Publishers and Distributors.

Alter, Andrew. 1998. "Negotiating Identity in the Garhwali Popular Cassette Industry." *South Asia* 21 (1): 109–122.

Appadurai, Arjun, and Carol Breckenridge. 1995. "Public Modernity in India." In *Consuming Modernity: Public Culture in a South Asian World*, Carol Breckenridge, ed., 1–20. Minneapolis: University of Minnesota Press.

Arnold, Alison. 1988. "Popular Film Song in India: A Case of Mass-Market Musical Eclecticism." *Popular Music* 7 (2): 177–188.

——. 1991. *Hindi Filmi Git: On the History of Commercial Indian Popular Music*. Ph.D. thesis, University of Illinois at Urbana-Champaign.

Attali, Jacques. 1985. *Noise: The Political Economy of Music*. Manchester, UK: Manchester University Press.

Auslander, Philip. 2006. Liveness: Performance and the anxiety of simulation. In Andy Bennett, Barry Shank, and Jason Toynbee, eds., *The Popular Music Studies Reader*, pp. 85-91. New York: Routledge.

Auslander, Philip. 1999. *Liveness: Performance in a Mediatized Culture*. London: Routledge.

Ayyagari, Shalini. 2012. "Spaces Betwixt and Between: Musical Borderlands and the Manganiyar Musicians of Rajasthan." *Asian Music* 43 (1): 3–33.

Babb, Lawrence A., and Susan S. Wadley, eds. 1995. *Media and the Transformation of Religion in South Asia*. Philadelphia: University of Pennsylvania Press.

Bakhle, Janaki. 2005. *Two Men and Music: Nationalism in the Making of an Indian Classical Tradition*. Oxford, UK; New York: Oxford University Press.

Balasubramaniam, Balaji. 1999. "Muthalvan: A Movie Review by Balaji Balasubramaniam." *Balaji's Thots* blog. Accessed October 1, 2009. http://www.bbthots.com/reviews/1999/mudhalvan.html.

Ballantyne, Tony. 2006. *Between Colonialism and Diaspora: Sikh Cultural Formations in an Imperial World*. London; Durham, NC: Duke University Press.

Bannerjee, Meena. 2011. "Immortal Legacy." *The Statesman*. Accessed March 26, 2011. http://www.thestatesman.net/index.php?option=com_content&view=articl

e&show=archive&id=357106&catid=47&year=2011&month=1&day=28&Itemid=66.

Barthakur, Dilip. 2003. *The Music and Musical Instruments of North Eastern India*. New Delhi: Mittal Publications.

Baskaran, S. Theodore. 1981. *The Message Bearers: Nationalist Politics and the Entertainment Media in South India, 1880–1945*. Madras, IN: Cre-A.

BBC News South Asia. 2011. "Bollywood's 'most expensive' film Ra. One to hit cinemas." Accessed July 30, 2012. http://www.bbc.co.uk/news/world-south-asia-15442697.

Beaster-Jones, Jayson. 2007. "Selling Music in India: Commodity Genres, Performing Cosmopolitanism, and Accounting for Taste." Ph.D. diss., University of Chicago.

——. 2009. "Evergreens to Remixes: Hindi Film Songs and India's Popular Music Heritage." *Ethnomusicology* 53 (3): 425–448.

——. 2011. "Re-tuning the Past, Selling the Future: Tata-AIG and the Tree of Love." *Popular Music* 30(3): 351–370.

Beaster-Jones, Jayson, and Wayne Marshall. 2012. "It Takes a Little Lawsuit: The Flowering Garden of Bollywood Exoticism in the Age of Its Technological Reproducibility." *South Asian Popular Culture* 10 (3): 249–260.

Benjamin, Walter. 2005. *Walter Benjamin: Critical Evaluations in Cultural Theory*, P. Osborne, ed. London: Routledge.

Bhagat, Dubby. 1974. "In Search of an Indian Pop Scene." *Junior Statesman* 6 (January 12): 18, 30.

Bimbi, Rajendra. 2001. "Seeking a Style: *Meri Jaan*, Vasundhara Das's First Private Album, Shows Her Seaching for the Right Genre." *Music Magazine*. February. Accessed April 10, 2012. http://www.themusicmagazine.com/merijaan.html.

Booth, Gregory. 1993. "Traditional Practice and Mass Mediated Music in India." *International Review of the Aesthetics and Sociology of Music* 24 (2): 159–174.

——. 2008a. *Behind the Curtain: Making Music in Mumbai's Film Studios*. Oxford, UK: Oxford University Press.

——. 2008b. "That Bollywood Sound." In *Global Soundtracks: Worlds of Film Music*, Mark Slobin, ed., 155–198. Middletown, CT: Wesleyan University Press.

——. 2009. "'Burman-dada Was Total Indian': Issues of Style, Genre and Indigeneity in S. D. Burman's Film Songs." *Journal of the Indian Musicological Society* 40: 6–28.

——. 2011. "Preliminary Thoughts on Hindi Popular Music and Film Production: India's 'Culture Industry(ies),' 1970–2000." *South Asian Popular Culture* 9 (2): 215–221.

Born, Georgina, and David Hesmondhalgh, eds. 2000. *Western Music and Its Others: Difference, Representation, and Appropriation in Music*. Berkeley, CA: University of California Press.

Bose, Derek. 2008. "Reel Funk." *Spectrum—The Tribune* (online edition), May 18. Accessed August 3, 2012. http://www.tribuneindia.com/2008/20080518/spectrum/main7.htm.

Bourdieu, Pierre. 1977. *Outline of a Theory of Practice*. Cambridge, UK: Cambridge University Press.

Brard, Sidhu. 2007. Brard, Gurnam Singh Sidhu. 2007. *East of Indus: My Memories of Old Punjab*. New Delhi: Hemkunt Publishers.

Briggs, Charles L., and Richard Bauman. 1992. "Genre, Intertextuality, and Social Power." *Journal of Linguistic Anthropology* 2 (2): 131–172.

Burwick, Frederick. 1991. *Illusion and the Drama: Critical Theory of the Enlightenment and Romantic Era*. University Park, PA: Pennsylvania State University Press.

Calhoun, Craig. 2008. "Cosmopolitanism and Nationalism." *Nations and Nationalism* 14 (3): 427–448.

Carati. 1983. "Pon Makal Sarasvati" ["Golden Daughter Saraswati"]. *Bommai*, April: 13–17.

Cellini, Joe. 2009. "Scoring 'Slumdog Millionaire' with Logic: An Interview with A. R. Rahman." *Apple: Logic Pro*. Accessed September 4, 2012. http://www.apple.com/logicpro/in-action/arrahman.

Chakrabarty, Dipesh. 2000. *Provincializing Europe: Postcolonial Thought and Historical Difference*. Princeton, NJ: Princeton University Press.

Chakravarty, Sumita S. 1993. *National Identity in Indian Popular Cinema, 1947–1987*. Austin, TX: University of Texas Press.

Chanan, Michael. 1995. *Repeated Takes: A Short History of Recording and Its Effects on Music*. London: Verso.

Chatterjee, Gayatri. 1992. *Awara*. New Delhi: Wiley Eastern Limited.

Chatterjee, Partha. 1993. *The Nation and Its Fragments: Colonial and Postcolonial Histories*. Princeton, NJ: Princeton University Press.

Chitre, Dilip. 1991. *Says Tuka: Selected Poems of Tukaram*. New Delhi: Penguin Books.

Chopra, Anil. 1988. "The Power and the Glory." *Playback and Fastforward*, September: 74–77.

Clifford, James. 1997. *Routes: Travel and Translation in the Late Twentieth Century*. Cambridge, MA: Harvard University Press.

Columbia Records Catalogue. 1934. Chennai, IN: Orr's Columbia House.

Coomaraswamy, Ananda K. 1909. "Gramophones—And Why Not?" In *Essays in National Idealism*. Colombo, IN: Colombo Apothecaries Co. Ltd.

Cousins, Margaret. 1935. *The Music of Orient and Occident: Essays Towards Mutual Understanding*. Madras, IN: B. G. Paul & Co.

Daily News & Analysis India. 2008. "Shah Rukh Khan as popular as Pope: German media." February 10. Accessed September 17, 2011. http://www.dnaindia.com/entertainment/report_shah-rukh-khan-as-popular-as-pope-german-media_1150157.

Das Gupta, Amlan, ed. 2007. *Music and Modernity: North Indian Classical Music in an Age of Mechanical Reproduction*. Kolkata, IN: Thema.

Deckha, Nitin. 2007. "From Artist-as-Hero to the Creative Young Man: Bollywood and the Aestheticization of Indian Masculinity." In *Once Upon a Time in Bollywood: The Global Swing in Hindi Cinema*, Gurbir S. Jolly, Zenia B. Wadhwani, and Deborah Barretto, eds., 61–69. Toronto: Tsar Books.

Deleury, G. A. 1994 [1960]. *The Cult of Vithoba*. Pune, IN: Deccan College Postgraduate and Research Institute.

DeNora, Tia. 2000. *Music in Everyday Life*. Cambridge, UK: Cambridge University Press.

Derné, Steve. 2000. *Movies, Masculinity, and Modernity: An Ethnography of Men's Filmgoing in India*. New York: Praeger.

Devika, J. 2007. *En-gendering Individuals: The Language of Re-forming in Early Twentieth Century Keralam*. New Delhi: Orient Longman.

Dossani, Rafiq. 2008. *India Arriving: How This Economic Powerhouse is Redefining Global Business*. New York: AMACOM.

Dudrah, Rajinder Kumar. 2006. *Bollywood: Sociology Goes to the Movies*. New Delhi: Sage.

Dwyer, Rachel. 2002. *Yash Chopra*. London: British Film Institute.

Economist, The. 2011. "Bhimsen Joshi, singer of India, died on January 24th, aged 88." Obituaries, February 3. Accessed March 11, 2012. http://www.economist.com/node/18060826.

Farndon, John. 2009. *India Booms: The Breakthtaking Development and Influence of Modern India*. London: Virgin Books.

Farrell, Gerry. 1993. "The Early Days of the Gramophone Industry in India: Historical, Social and Musical Perspectives." *British Journal of Ethnomusicology* 2: 31–53.

———. 1997. *Indian Music and the West*. Oxford, UK; New York: Oxford University Press.

Feld, Steven. 1984. "Communication, Music, and Speech about Music." *Yearbook for Traditional Music* 16: 1–18.

———. 1994. "From Schizophonia to Schismogenesis: On the Discourses and Commodification Practices of 'World Music' and 'World Beat.'" In *Music Grooves: Essays and Dialogues*, Charles Keil and Steven Feld, eds., 257–289. Chicago: University of Chicago Press.

———. 1996. "Pygmy POP: A Genealogy of Schizophonic Mimesis." *Yearbook for Traditional Music* 28: 1–35.

Fellezs, Kevin. 2011. *Birds of Fire: Jazz, Rock, Funk, and the Creation of Fusion*. Durham, NC; London: Duke University Press.

Fernandes, Leela. 2006. *India's New Middle Class: Democratic Politics in an Era of Economic Reform*. Minneapolis; London: University of Minnesota Press.

Fernandes, Naresh. 2012. *Taj Mahal Foxtrot: The Story of Bombay's Jazz Age*. New Delhi: Roli Books.

Filmfare. 2001. "Interview, Best Playback (Male), Lucky Ali, Na tum jaano na hum—Kaho Naa...Pyaar Hai." April. Accessed May 1, 2012. http://downloads.movies.indiatimes.com/site/april2001/ivw7.html.

Fiol, Stefan. 2008. "Constructing Regionalism: Discourses of Spirituality and Cultural Poverty in the Popular Music of Uttarakhand, North India." Ph.D. diss., University of Illinois at Urbana-Champaign.

———. 2011. "From Folk to Popular and Back: Assessing Feedback between Studio Recordings and Festival Dance-Songs in Uttarakhand, North India." *Asian Music* 42 (1): 24–53.

Frith, Simon. 1996. *Performing Rites: On the Value of Popular Music*. Cambridge, MA: Harvard University Press.

Gargan, Edward. 1992. "The Many Accents of Rap around the World; India: Vanilla Ice in Hindi." *New York Times*. August 23, section 2, 22.

Gera Roy, Anjali. 2010. *Bhangra Moves: From Ludhiana to London and Beyond*. Aldershot, UK: Ashgate.

Getter, Joseph, and B. Balasubrahmaniyan. 2008. "Tamil Film Music: Sound and Significance." In *Global Soundtracks: Worlds of Film Music*, Mark Slobin, ed., 114–51. Middletown, CT: Wesleyan University Press.

Gopinath, Gayatri. 2005. *Impossible Desires: Queer Diasporas and South Asian Public Cultures*, 29–62. Durham, NC: Duke University Press.

Govil, Nitin. 2008. "Bollywood and the Frictions of Global Mobility." In *The Bollywood Reader*, Rajinder K. Dudrah and Jigna Desai, eds., 201–215. New York: McGraw-Hill/Open University Press.

Greene, Paul. 1999. "Sound Engineering in a Tamil Village: Playing Audio Cassettes as Devotional Performance." *Ethnomusicology* 43 (3): 459–489.

———. 2001a. "Authoring the Folk: The Crafting of a Rural Popular Music in South India." *Journal of Intercultural Studies* 22 (2): 161–72.

———. 2001b. "Mixed Messages: Unsettled Cosmopolitanisms in Nepali Pop." *Popular Music* 20(2): 169–87.

———. 2003. "Nepal's Lok Pop Music: Representations of the Folk, Tropes of Memory, and Studio Technologies." *Asian Music* 34 (1): 43–65.

——. 2011. "Musical Media and Cosmopolitanisms in Nepal's Popular Music, 1950–2006." In *South Asian Media Cultures: Audiences, Representations, Contexts*, Shakuntala Banaji, ed., 91–105. London: Anthem Press.

Greene, Paul D., and David R. Henderson. 2000. "At the Crossroads of Languages, Musics, and Emotions in Kathmandu." *Popular Music and Society* 24(3): 95–116. Reprinted in *Global Pop, Local Language*, Harris M. Berger and Michael Thomas Carroll, eds., 87–108 (University of Mississippi Press, 2003).

Grimaud, Emmanuel. 2003. *Bollywood Film Studio, ou, comment les films se font à Bombay*. Paris: CNRS Éditions.

Gronow, Pekka. 1981. "The Record Industry Comes to the Orient." *Ethnomusicology* 25 (2): 251–284.

Guha, Ramachandra. 2007. *India after Gandhi: The History of the World's Largest Democracy*. London: Picador.

Gulzar. 2003. "Music: In Tune with the Times." In *Encyclopaedia of Hindi Cinema*, Gulzar, Govind Nihalani, and Saibal Chateerjee, eds., 271–78. Delhi: Popular Prakashan.

Hansen, Kathryn. 1992. *Grounds for Play: The Nautanki Theatre of North India*. Berkeley, CA: University of California Press.

Hazarika, Sanjoy. 1989. "India Plays Its Own Rock-and-Roll." *New York Times*, September 5. Accessed June 2012. http://www.nytimes.com/1989/09/05/arts/india-plays-its-own-rock-and-roll.html.

Hebdige, Dick. 1979. *Subculture: The Meaning of Style*. London: Methuen.

Herzfeld, Michael. 2005. *Cultural Intimacy: Social Poetics in the Nation-State*. London: Routledge.

Higgins, Jon B. 1976. "From Prince to Populace: Patronage as a Determinant of Change in South Indian (Karnatak) Music." *Asian Music* 7 (2): 20–26.

Higgins, Niko. 2013. "Confusion in the Karnatic Capital: Fusion in Chennai, India." PhD Disseration, Columbia University.

Holt, Fabian. 2007. *Genre in Popular Music*. Chicago; London: University of Chicago Press.

Hughes, Stephen. 2002. "The 'Music Boom' in Tamil South India: Gramophone, Radio and the Making of Mass Culture." *Historical Journal of Film, Radio and Television* 22 (4): 445–473.

——. 2005. "Mythologicals and Modernity: Contesting Silent Cinema in South India." *Postscripts: The Journal of Scared Texts and Contemporary Worlds* 1 (2–3): 207–235.

——. 2007. "Music in the Age of Mechanical Reproduction: Drama, Gramophone, and the Beginnings of Tamil Cinema." *Journal of Asian Studies* 66 (1): 3–34.

Huq, Rupa. 1996. "Asian Kool? Bhangra and Beyond." In *Dis-Orienting Rhythms: The Politics of the New Asian Dance Music*, Sanjay Sharma, John Hutnyk, and Ashwani Sharma, eds., 61-80. London: Zed Books.

Inamdar, Hemant Vishnu, ed. 1979. *Namdevanche Abhangawani* [Namdev's *Abhangas*]. Pune, IN: Modern Book Depot Publishers.

Indian Express. 2009. "Bhimsen Joshi's Santawani to enthrall audiences again." June 30. Accessed April 15, 2012. http://www.indianexpress.com/news/bhimsen-joshis-santawani-to-enthrall-audien/483049/.

——. 2011. "Pandit Bhimsen Joshi passes away." January 24. Accessed March 25, 2011. http://www.indianexpress.com/news/pandit-bhimsen-joshi-passes-away/741459/4.

Indian Music Industry, The. 2005. "Music Market, National: Size of the Music Industry in India." Accessed September 16, 2012. http://www.indianmi.org/national.htm.

Jeffrey, Robin. 1992. *Politics, Women, and Well-being: How Kerala Became "A Model."* Houndmills, Basingstoke, Hampshire, UK: Macmillan Press.

Jensen, Klaus Bruhn. 2008. "Intermediality." In *The International Encyclopedia of Communication*, Wolfgang Donsbach, ed. Malden, MA: Blackwell Science. Accessed January 15, 2012. http://www.blackwellreference.com/public/tocnode?id=g9781405131995_yr2012_chunk_g978140513199514_ss60-1.

John, Ali Peter. 1981. "Sharon Prabhakar: will she be another actress-singer?" *Screen* 30 (44): 8.

Jones, Jacqueline. 2009. "Performing the Sacred: Song, Genre, and Aesthetics in Bhakti." Ph.D. diss., University of Chicago.

Joshi, Namrata. 2000. "Givin' It a Good Shot." *Outlook India*. April 24. Accessed August 18, 2012. http://www.outlookindia.com/article.aspx?209281.

Kabir, Nasreen Munni. 2009. *Lata Mangeshkar . . . In Her Own Voice: Conversations with Nasreen Munni Kabir*. New Delhi: Niyogi Books.

——. 2011. *A. R. Rahman: The Spirit of Music*. New Delhi: Om Books International.

Kamath, Sudhish. 2010. "Voice of the Artiste." *The Hindu*. May 28. Accessed August 18, 2012. http://www.thehindu.com/life-and-style/money-and-careers/article440410.ece.

Kapur, Akash. 2012. *India Becoming: A Portrait of Life in Modern India*. New York: Riverhead Books.

Keil, Charles. 1995. "Participatory Discrepancies and the Power of Music." In *Music Grooves: Essays and Dialogues*, Charles Keil and Steven Feld, eds., 96–108. Chicago: University of Chicago Press.

Kimmel, Michael, and Amy Aronson. 2003. *Men and Masculinities: A Social, Cultural, and Historical Encyclopedia*. Santa Barbara, CA: ABC-CLIO.

Kinnear, Michael. 1994. *The Gramophone Company's First Indian Recordings, 1899–1908*. Bombay: Popular Prakashan.

——. 2000. *The Gramophone Company's Indian Recordings, 1908–1910*. Heidelberg, DE: Bajakhana.

Kishore, Vikrant. 2011. "How Are Indian Folk Music and Dance Forms Represented in Contemporary Hindi Cinema?" Ph.D. diss., RMIT Melbourne.

Kumar, Shanti, and Michael Curtin. 2002. "Made In India: In Between Music Television and Patriarchy." *Television and New Media* 3(4): 345–366.

Kurien, Prema A. 2002. *Kaleidoscopic Ethnicity: International Migration and the Reconstruction of Community Identities in India*. Oxford, UK: Oxford University Press.

Kvetko, Peter. 2004. "Can the Indian Tune Go Global?" *TDR: The Drama Review* 48 (4): 183–191.

——. 2005. "*Indipop: Producing Global Sounds and Local Meanings in Bombay*." Ph.D. diss., University of Texas at Austin.

——. 2008. "Private Music: Individualism, Authenticity, and Genre Boundaries in the Bombay Music Industry." In *Popular Culture in a Globalised India*, K. Moti Gokulsing and Wimal Dissanayake, eds., 111–124. New York: Routledge.

Landsberg, Alison. 2004. *Prosthetic Memories: The Transformation of American Remembrance in an Age of Mass Culture*. New York: Columbia University Press.

Largey, Michael. 2006. *Vodou Nation: Haitian Art Music and Cultural Nationalism*. Chicago: University of Chicago Press.

L'Armand, Kathleen, and Adrian L'Armand. 1983. "One Hundred Years of Music in Madras: A Case Study in Secondary Urbanization." *Ethnomusicology* 27 (3): 411–438.

Leante, Laura. 2009. "Urban Myth: Bhangra and the Dhol Craze in the UK." In *Music in Motion: Diversity and Dialogue in Europe*, Bernd Clausen, Ursula Hemetek, and Eva Saether, eds., 191–207. Bielefeld, DE: Transcript Verlag.

Lelyveld, David. 1995. "Upon the Subdominant: Administering Music on All-India Radio." In *Consuming Modernity: Public Culture in a South Asian World*, Carol A. Breckenridge, ed., 49–65. Minneapolis: University of Minnesota Press.

Leyshon, Andrew. 2009. "The Software Slump?: Digital Music, the Democratisation of Technology, and the Decline of the Recording Studio Sector within the Musical Economy." *Environment and Planning A* 41 (6): 1309–1331.

Lipsitz, George. 1994. *Dangerous Crossroads: Popular Music, Postmodernism, and the Poetics of Place*. London: Verso.

Livingston, Tamara. 1999. "Music Revivals: Towards a General Theory." *Ethnomusicology* 43 (1): 66–85.

Lomax, Alan. 1968. *Folk Song Style and Culture*. Washington, DC: American Association for the Advancement of Science.

López, Ana M. 1993. "Are All Latins From Manhattan?: Hollywood, Ethnography and Cultural Colonialism." In *Mediating Two Worlds: Cinematic Encounters in the Americas*, John King, Ana M. López, and Manuel Alvarado, eds., 67–80. London: British Film Institute.

Lukose, Ritty A. 2009. *Liberalization's Children: Gender, Youth, and Consumer Citizenship in Globalizing India*. Durham, NC: Duke University Press.

Magaldi, Cristina. 2009. "Cosmopolitanism and World Music in Rio De Janeiro at the Turn of the Twentieth Century." *Musical Quarterly* 92 (3–4): 329–364.

Maira, Sunaina. 2002. *Desis in the House: Indian American Youth Culture in New York City*. Philadelphia: Temple University Press.

Majumdar, Abhik. 2004. *Bhimsen Joshi: A Passion for Music*. New Delhi: Reupa and Co.

Majumdar, Neepa. 2001. "The Embodied Voice: Song Sequences and Stardom in the Popular Hindi Cinema." In *Soundtrack Available: Essays on film and popular music*, Pamela Robertson Wojcik and Arthur Knight, eds., 161–184. Durham, NC: Duke University Press.

Manuel, Peter. 1988. "Popular Music in India: 1901–86." *Popular Music* 7 (2): 157–176.

——. 1993. *Cassette Culture: Popular Music and Technology in North India*. Chicago; London: University of Chicago Press.

——. 1995. "Music as Symbol, Music as Simulacrum: Postmodern, Pre-modern, and Modern Aesthetics in Subcultural Popular Musics." *Popular Music* 14(2): 227–239.

——. 1997. "Music, Identity, and Images of India in the Indo-Caribbean Diaspora." *Asian Music* 29 (1): 17–35.

——. 2008. "North Indian Sufi Popular Music in the Age of Hindu and Muslim Fundamentalism." *Ethnomusicology* 52(3): 378–400.

Marcus, Scott. 1992. "Recycling Indian Film-Songs: Popular Music as a Source of Melodies for North Indian Folk Musicians." *Asian Music* 24 (1): 101–110.

Marshall, Wayne, and Jayson Beaster-Jones. 2012. "It Takes a Little Lawsuit: The Flowering Garden of Bollywood Exoticism in the Age of Its Technological Reproducibility." *South Asian Popular Culture* 10 (3): 1–12.

Mathai, Kamini. 2009. *A. R. Rahman: The Musical Storm*. New Delhi: Penguin.

Mazumdar, Ranjani. 2011. "Aviation, Tourism and Dreaming in 1960s Bombay Cinema." *BioScope: South Asian Screen Studies* 2 (2): 129–155.

Mazzarella, William. 2003. *Shoveling Smoke: Advertising and Globalization in Contemporary India*. Durham, NC; London: Duke University Press.

——. 2005. "Middle Class." In *Keywords in South Asian Studies*, Rachel Dwyer, ed. School of Oriental and African Studies, University of London. Accessed April 21, 2011. http://www.soas.ac.uk/southasianstudies/keywords/.

McCann, Anthony. 2005. "Traditional Music and Copyright: The Issues." *Information and Communications Technology Law* 13 (3): 1–15.

McDowell, Stephen D. 1997. *Globalization, Liberalization and Policy Change: A Political Economy of India's Communications Sector*. London: Macmillan.

Meintjes, Louise. 2003. *Sound of Africa! Making Music Zulu in a South African Studio*. Durham, NC: Duke University Press.

Meiyappan, A. V. 1974. *Enathu Vazhkkai Anupavankal* [My Life Experiences]. Chennai, IN:

Menon, A. Sreedharan. 1978. *Cultural Heritage of Kerala*. Madras, IN: S. Viswanathan.

Menon, Ravi. 2009. *Mozhikalil Sangeethamayi* [Music in Words]. Thiruvananthapuram, IN: Mathrubhumi Books.

Mignolo, Walter. 2000. "The Many Faces of Cosmo-polis: Border Thinking and Critical Cosmopolitanism." *Public Culture* 12(3): 721–748.

Miniwatts Marketing Group. 2012. "Top 20 Internet Countries: 2012 Q1, With the Highest Number of Users." Internet World Stats: Usage and Population Statistics. Accessed September 21, 2012. http://www.internetworldstats.com/top20.htm.

Mishra, Vijay. 2002. *Bollywood Cinema: Temples of Desire*. New York: Routledge.

Mohan, Jag. 1977. *Ananda K. Coomaraswamy*. Delhi: Publications Division, Ministry of Information and Broadcasting, Government of India.

Monson, Ingrid. 1999. "Riffs, Repetition, and Theories of Globalization." *Ethnomusicology* 43 (1): 31–65.

Morcom, Anna. 2007. *Hindi Film Songs and the Cinema*. Aldershot, Hampshire, UK: Ashgate.

Mukhopadhyay, Swapna, ed. 2007. *The Enigma of the Kerala Woman: A Failed Promise of Literacy*. New Delhi: Institute of Social Studies Trust.

n. a. 1988. "Rock Bands Explode in Beat Group Contest." *Playback & Fast Forward* 3(1) (July 6): 42.

Nadkarni, Mohan. 1994. *Bhimsen Joshi: A Biography*. New Delhi: Indus Nai Dilli.

Nair, Sulekha. 2001. "Nightingale of the South." *Express India*. January 23. http://www.expressindia.com/fe/daily/20010123/fsm21016.html.

Nandy, Ashis. 1983. *The Intimate Enemy: Loss and Recovery of Self under Colonialism*. New York: Oxford University Press.

Nayar, Sheila J. 2004. "Invisible Representation: The Oral Contours of a National Popular Cinema." *Film Quarterly* 57(3): 13–23.

Negus, Keith. 1992. *Producing Pop: Culture and Conflict in the Popular Music Industry*. New York: Routledge.

Neuman, Daniel M. 1990 [1980]. *The Life of Music in North India*.Chicago; London: University of Chicago Press.

Noland, Carrie. 2009. *Agency and Embodiment: Performing Gestures/Producing Culture*. Cambridge, MA: Harvard University Press.

Ortner, Sherry B. 2006. *Anthropology and Social Theory: Culture, Power, and the Acting Subject*. Durham, NC: Duke University Press.

Osella, Filippo, and Caroline Osella. 2000. *Social Mobility in Kerala: Modernity and Identity in Conflict*. London: Pluto Press.

Pandian, M. S. S. 2007. *Brahmin and Non-Brahmin: Genealogies of the Tamil Political Present*. New Delhi: Permanent Black.

Parthasarathi, Vibodh. 2005. "Construing a 'New Media' Market: Merchandising the Talking Machine, c. 1900–1911." In *Communication Processes Volume 1: Media and Mediation*, Bernard Bel, Jan Brouwer, Biswajit Das, Vibodh Parthasarathi, and Guy Poitevin, eds., 1–21. New Delhi: Sage.

Peirce, Charles Sanders. 1960. *The Collected Papers of Charles Sanders Peirce*. Cambridge, MA: Harvard University Press.

Petshali, Jugal Kishor. 2002. *Uttaranchal Ke Lok Vadya* [Folk Instruments of Uttaranchal]. Delhi: Takshashila Prakashan.

Pinney, Christopher. 2004. *"Photos of the Gods": The Printed Image and Political Struggle in India*. London: Reaktion Press.

Pollock, Sheldon. 2000. "Cosmopolitan and Vernacular in History." *Public Culture* 12(3): 591–625.

Pollock, Sheldon, Homi K. Bhabha, Carol Breckenridge, and Dipesh Chakrabarty. 2000. "Cosmopolitanisms." *Public Culture* 12(3): 577–589.

Porcello, Thomas. 1996. "Sonic Artistry: Music, Discourse and Technology in the Sound Recording Studio." Ph.D. diss., University of Texas at Austin.

Pradeep, K. 2011. "Dance and Vyjayantimala." *The Hindu*. November 2. Accessed August 18, 2012. http://www.thehindu.com/life-and-style/metroplus/article2591559. ece.

Prasad, M. Madhava. 1998. *Ideology of the Hindi Film: A Historical Construction*. Delhi; New York: Oxford University Press.

Prasad, Vijay. 2008. "My Hip-Hop Life." In *Desi Rap: Hip-Hop and South Asian America*, Ajay Nair and Murali Balaji, eds., 3–16. Lanham, MD: Lexington Books.

Qureshi, Regula. 2006. "Female Agency and Patrilineal Constraints: Situating Courtesans in Twentieth-Century India." In *The Courtesan's Arts: Cross-Cultural Perspectives*, Martha Feldman and Bonnie Gordon, eds., 312–331. Oxford, UK: Oxford University Press.

Raghavan, V. 1959. "Methods of Popular Religious Instruction in South India." In *Traditional India: Structure and Change*, Milton Singer, ed., 130–138. Philadelphia: American Folklore Society.

Raj, Radhika, and Shubhda Khanna. 2010. "Pop No More." *Hindustan Times*, North India edition, October 2. Accessed August 18, 2012. http://www.hindustantimes.com/India-news/NewDelhi/Pop-no-more/Article1-607461. aspx.

Rajadhyaksha, Ashish. 1993. "The Phalke Era: Conflict of Traditional Form and Modern Technology." In *Interrogating Modernity: Culture and Colonialism in India*, Tejaswini Niranjana, P. Sudhir, and Vivek Dhareshwar, eds., 47–82. Calcutta: Seagull Books.

——. 2003. "The 'Bollywoodization' of the Indian Cinema: Cultural Nationalism in a Global Era." *Inter-Asia Cultural Studies* 4 (4): 25–39.

——. 2009. *Indian Cinema in the Time of Celluloid: From Bollywood to the Emergency*. Bloomington, IN: Indiana University Press.

Rajadhyaksha, Ashish, and Paul Willemen, eds. 1995. *Encyclopaedia of Indian Cinema*. New Delhi: Oxford University Press.

Rajagopal, Arvind. 2001. *Politics after Television: Hindu Nationalism and the Reshaping of the Public in India*. Cambridge, UK: Cambridge University Press.

Ram, Kalpana. 2008. "'A New Consciousness Must Come': Affectivity and Movement in Tamil Dalit Women's Activist Engagement with Cosmopolitan Modernity." In *Anthropology and the New Cosmopolitanism*, Pnina Werbner, ed., 135–157. Oxford, UK: Berg.

Ramaswamy, Sumathi. 2010. *The Goddess and the Nation: Mapping Mother India*. Durham, NC: Duke University Press.

Ranade, Ashok. 2006. *Hindi Film Song: Music beyond Boundaries*. New Delhi: Promilla & Co.

Rasmussen, Anne. 1996. "Theory and Practice at the 'Arabic Org': Digital Technology in Contemporary Arab Music Performance." *Popular Music* 15 (3): 345–365.

Ravichander, Anirudh (@anirudhravichan). 2011. "Its official! 'Kolaveri' is the most searched and played Youtube Video in India today! Thank u all!" Twitter post. November 18, 7:56 a.m. https://twitter.com/anirudhravichan/status/137242848058802176.

Rediff India Abroad. 2012. Transcripts. February 12. Accessed May 1, 2012. http://m.rediff.com/chat/trans/0212luck.htm.

Ries, Raymond. 1967. "The Cultural Setting of South Indian Music." *Bulletin of the Institute of Traditional Cultures*, Madras, 7–21.

Riley, Mary. 2004. *Indigenous Intellectual Property Rights: Legal Obstacles and Innovative Solutions*. Walnut Creek: AltaMira Press.

Sahlins, Marshall. 2004. *Apologies to Thucydides: Understanding History as Culture and Vice Versa*. Chicago; London: University of Chicago Press.

Sanden, Paul. 2009. "Hearing Glenn Gould's Body: Corporeal Liveness in Recorded Music." *Current Musicology* 88: 7–34.

Sanyal, Sanjeev. 2008. *The Indian Renaissance: India's Rise after a Thousand Years of Decline*. Hackensack, NJ; London: World Scientific Publishing Co.

Sarazzin, Natalie. 2008. "Songs from the Heart: Musical Coding, Emotional Sentiment, and Transnational Sonic Identity in India's Popular Film Music." In *Global Bollywood*, Anandam P. Kavoori and Aswin Punathambekar, eds., 203–219. New York: New York University Press.

Sarkar, Kobita. 1975. *Indian Cinema Today: An Analysis*. Delhi: Sterling Publishers.

Sawf News. 2012. "Shah Rukh Khan's Dream Project Mahabharata Takes Shape." Accessed January 18, 2012. http://www.sawfnews.com/Bollywood/68195.aspx.

Scales, Christopher. 2004. "Powwow Music and the Aboriginal Recording Industry on the Northern Plains: Media, Technology, and Native American Music in the Late Twentieth Century." Ph.D. diss., University of Illinois.

Schafer, R. Murray. 1969. *The New Soundscape*. Toronto: Berandol.

Schofield, Katherine Butler. 2010. "Reviving the Golden Age Again: 'Classicization,' Hindustani Music, and the Mughals." *Ethnomusicology* 54(3): 484–517.

Schreffler, Gibb Stuart. 2006. "Vernacular Music and Dance of Punjab." *Journal of Punjab Studies* 11 (2): 197–213.

——. 2010. "Signs of Separation: *Dhol* in Punjabi Culture." Ph.D. diss., University of California at Santa Barbara:.

——. 2011. "The Bazigar (Goaar) People and their Performing Arts." *Journal of Punjab Studies* 18 (1–2): 217–250.

Schultz, Anna. 2004. "*Rastriya Kirtan* of Maharashtra: Musical Fragments of Nationalist Politics." Ph.D. diss., University of Illinois.

Schur, Richard. 2009. *Parodies of Ownership: Hip-Hop Aesthetics and Intellectual Property Law*. Ann Arbor: University of Michigan Press.

Scott, Derek. 2008. *Sounds of the Metropolis: The 19th-Century Popular Music Revolution in London, New York, Paris, and Vienna*. New York: Oxford University Press.

Seigel, Micol. 2005. "The Disappearing Dance: Maxixe's Imperial Erasure." *Black Music Research Journal* 25 (1/2): 93–117.

Sen, Biswarup. 2008. "The Sounds of Modernity: The Evolution of Bollywood Film Song." In *Global Bollywood: Travels of Hindi Song and Dance*, Sangita Gopal and Sujata Moorti, eds., 84–104. Minneapolis: University of Minnesota Press.

Sen, Meheli. 2011. "'It's All about Loving Your Parents': Liberalization, Hindutva and Bollywood's New Fathers." In *Bollywood and Globalization: Indian Popular Cinema*,

Nation, and Diaspora, Rini B. Mehta and Rajeshwari Pandharipande, eds., 145–168. London: Anthem Press.

Shah, S. 2003. Interview with DJ Suketu, with input from Kanak Hirani-Nautiyal and Ruchita Bhardwaj. http://www.bangladeshobserveronline.com/new/2003/01/entertainment.htm. Accessed November 15, 2007.

Sharma, Chanchal Kumar. 2011. "A Discursive Dominance Theory of Economic Reform Sustainability: The Case of India." *India Review* 10 (2): 126–184.

Sharma, Devendra. 2007. "Nautanki vs. Mass Media: Exploring the Role of Community Folk Performances in the Age of New Media Forms and Technology." National Communication Association: 93rd Annual Convention, Chicago, November 14.

Sharma, Nitasha T. 2010. *Hip Hop Desis: South Asian Americans, Blackness, and a Global Race Consciousness*. Durham, NC: Duke University Press.

Shaw, Lisa, and Stephanie Dennison. 2007. *Brazilian National Cinema*. London: Routledge.

Shope, Bradley. 2007. "'They Treat Us White Folks Fine': African American Musicians and the Popular Music Terrain in Late Colonial India." *Journal of South Asian Popular Culture* 5 (2): 97–116.

——. 2008. "The Public Consumption of Western Music in Colonial North India: From Imperialist Exclusivity to Global Receptivity." *South Asia: Journal of South Asian Studies* 31 (2): 271–289.

Shresthova, Sangita. 2003. "Strictly Bollywood?: Story, Camera and Movement in Hindi Film Dance." M.S. thesis, Massachusetts Institute of Technology.

Shuker, Roy. 2005. *Popular Music: The Key Concepts*, second edition. New York: Routledge.

Sidhu Brard, Gurnam Singh. 2007. *East of Indus: My Memories of Old Punjab*. Delhi: Hemkunt Publishers.

Singer, Milton. 1972. *When a Great Tradition Modernizes: An Anthropological Approach to Indian Civilization*. Chicago: University of Chicago Press.

Singh, Harmandir. 1984. *Hindi Film Geet Kosh, Vol. 2: 1941–1950*. Kanpur, IN: Sumer Singh Sachdev.

——. 1980. *Hindi Film Geet Kosh, Vol. 3: 1951–1960*. Kanpur, IN: Sumer Singh Sachdev.

——. 1986. *Hindi Film Geet Kosh, Vol. 4: 1961–1970*. Kanpur, IN: Sumer Singh Sachdev.

——. 1991. *Hindi Film Geet Kosh, Vol. 5: 1971–1980*. Kanpur, IN: Satinder Kaur.

Smith, H. Daniel. 1995. "Impact of 'God Posters' on Hindus and Their Devotional Traditions." In *Media and the Transformation of Religion in South Asia*, Lawrence A. Babb and Susan S. Wadley, eds., 24–50. Philadelphia: University of Pennsylvania Press.

Soneji, Davesh. 2012. *Unfinished Gestures: Devadāsīs, Memory, and Modernity in South India*. Chicago: University of Chicago Press.

SPARK in Education. 2009. "Dhol di Awaz [The Sound of the Dhol] (Bhangra) Educator Guide." Accessed 21 February 2012. http://www.kqed.org/arts/programs/spark/edguide.jsp?planID=435.

Srinivasan, Gopal. 2002. "The Complete Biography of A. R. Rahman." On Gopal's Homepage (personal website). Accessed November 15, 2009. http://gopalhome.tripod.com/arrbio.html.

Srivastava, Sanjay. 2004. "Voice, Gender and Space in the Time of Five-Year Plans: The Idea of Lata Mangeshkar." *Economic and Political Weekly* (May 15–21), 39 (20): 2019–2028.

——. 2006. "The Voice of the Nation and the Five-Tear Plan Hero: Speculations on Gender, Space, and Popular Culture." In *Fingerprinting Popular Culture: The Mythic and the Iconic in Indian Cinema*, Vinay Lal and Ashis Nandy, eds., 122–155. New Delhi: Oxford University Press India.

Stivens, Maila. 2008. "Gender, Rights and Cosmopolitanisms." In *Anthropology and the New Cosmopolitanism*, Pnina Werbner, ed., 87–111. Oxford, UK: Berg.

Stokes, Martin. 2007. "On Musical Cosmopolitanism." *Macalester International Roundtable*. Accessed August 26, 2012. http://digitalcommons.macalester.edu/intlrdtable/3.

——. 2010. *The Republic of Love: Cultural Intimacy in Turkish Popular Music.* Chicago: University of Chicago Press.

Studio 440. n.d. "A. R. Rahman." Accessed Sept 8, 2011. http://www.studio440.com/projects_rahman.htm.

Subramanian, Lakshmi. 2006. *From the Tanjore Court to the Madras Music Academy: A Social History of Music in South India.* New Delhi: Oxford University Press.

——. 2008. *New Mansions for Music: Performance, Pedagogy and Criticism.* New Delhi: Social Science Press.

Subramaniam, L., and Viji Subramaniam. 1995. *Euphony: Indian Classical Music.* Chennai, Bangalore, Hyderabad, IN: East-West Books.

Supriya, Jug. 1971. Editorial. *Junior Statesman: Vol 3.* October 2: 4.

Swaminathan, Chitra. 2007. "Chilling out with ragas." *The Hindu*, February 14. Accessed August 26, 2012. http://www.hindu.com/mp/2007/02/14/stories/2007021400540500.htm.

Swanson, Philip. 2010. "Going Down on Good Neighbors: Imagining *América* in Hollywood Movies of the 1930 s and 1940s (*Flying Down to Rio* and *Down Argentine Way*)." *Bulletin of Latin American Research* 29 (1): 71–84.

Tamizhselvan, D. 1998. "An Interview with Vairamuthu." *INDOlink*. Accessed August 5, 2012. http://www.indolink.com/tamil/cinema/Specials/98/June/vaira/vairamuthu2.htm.

Tankel, Jonathan David. 1990. "The Practice of Recording Music: Remixing as Recoding." *Journal of Communication* 40 (3): 34–46.

Taussig, Michael. 1993. *Mimesis and Alterity: A Particular History of the Senses.* New York: Routledge.

Taylor, Timothy D. 2007. *Beyond Exoticism: Western Music and the World.* Durham, NC: Duke University Press.

Telecom Regulatory Authority of India. 2011. "Overview." *Annual Report: 2010–11*, 2. Accessed July 1, 2012. http://www.trai.gov.in/WriteReadData/UserFiles/Documents/AnuualReports/ar_10_11.pdf.

Théberge, Paul. 1997. *Any Sound You Can Imagine: Making Music/Consuming Technology.* Middletown, CT: Wesleyan University Press/University Press of New England.

Thomas, Rosie. 1995. "Melodrama and the Negotiation of Morality in Hindi Film." In *Consuming Modernity: Public Culture in a South Asian World*, Carol Breckenridge, ed., 157–182. Minneapolis: University of Minnesota Press.

Thoraval, Yves. 2000. *The Cinemas of India.* New Delhi: Macmillan.

Times of India. 2009. "Son Revives Bhimsen's 'Santwani.'" Pune edition, June 30. Accessed April 15, 2012. http://articles.timesofindia.indiatimes.com/2009-06-30/pune/28187911_1_programme-pt-bhimsen-joshi-shriniwas-joshi

Toynbee, Jason. 2000. *Making Popular Music: Musicians, Creativity and Institutions.* New York: Oxford University Press.

Turino, Thomas. 2000. *Nationalists, Cosmopolitans, and Popular Music in Zimbabwe.* Chicago; London: University of Chicago Press.

——. 2008. *Music as Social Life: The Politics of Participation*. Chicago: University of Chicago Press.

Vaidhyanathan, Siva. 2001. *Copyrights and Copywrongs: The Rise of Intellectual Property and How It Threatens Creativity*. New York: New York University Press.

Vasudevan, Ravi S., ed. 2000. *Making Meaning in Indian Cinema*. New Delhi: Oxford University Press.

Verma, Sukanya. 2005. "Bunti aur Babli's music Rocks!" *Rediff Movies*, April 18. Accessed October 14, 2009. http://in.rediff.com/movies/2005/apr/18bunty. htm.

Vernallis, Carol. 2004. *Experiencing Music Video: Aesthetics and Cultural Context*. New York: Columbia University Press.

von Stietencron, Heinrich, 2005. *Hindu Myth, Hindu History: Religion, Art, and Politics*. Delhi: Permanent Black.

Wallis, Roger, and Krister Malm. 1984. *Big Sounds from Small Peoples: The Music Industry in Small Countries*. New York: Pendragon Press.

Walser, Robert. 1993. *Running with the Devil: Power, Gender, and Madness in Heavy Metal Music*. Middletown, CT: Wesleyan University Press.

Weidman, Amanda J. 2006. *Singing the Classical, Voicing the Modern: The Postcolonial Politics of Music in South India*. Durham, NC; London: Duke University Press.

——. 2010. "Sound and the City: Mimicry and Media in South India." *Linguistic Anthropology* 20 (2): 294–313.

Werbner, Pnina. 2008. "Introduction: Towards a New Cosmopolitan Anthropology." In *Anthropology and the New Cosmopolitanism*, Pnina Werbner, ed., 1–29. Oxford, UK: Berg.

Widdess, Richard. n.d. "Khayāl." In *Grove Music Online*. Accessed June 29, 2012. http://www.oxfordmusiconline.com/subscriber/article/grove/music/48142.

Wolf, Richard, ed. 2009. *Theorizing the Local: Music, Practice, and Experience in South Asia and Beyond*. New York: Oxford University Press.

Wong, Avis. 2007. "Yes, we've sought permission, I don't want to be sued: Catchy track in Kelly Poon's new album based on hit Indian composer's tune." *The New Paper*, Singapore. October 3. Reproduced online at Mayyam.com. Accessed June 10, 2012. http://www.mayyam.com/talk/showthread.php?1108-ARR-News-and-other-Tidbits/page91.

Young, James. 2010. *Cultural Appropriation and the Arts*. Malden: Wiley-Blackwell.

Zager, Michael. 2003. *Writing Music for Television and Radio Commercials*. Lanham, MD: Scarecrow Press.

Zakaria, Fareed. 2006. "India Rising." *Newsweek*, March 6, 34–37.

Zarrilli, Phillip B. 2000. *Kathakali Dance-Drama: Where Gods and Demons Come to Play*. New York: Routledge.

Zeenews.com. 2010. "All My Dancing Was Extempore: Shammi Kapoor." Showbiz section, May 20. Accessed on August 20, 2012. http://zeenews.india.com/entertainment/celebrity/all-my-dancing-was-extempore-shammi-kapoor_61662. htm.

Zuberi, Nabeel. 2002. "India Song: Popular Music Genres Since Economic Liberalization." In *Popular Music Studies*, David Hesmondhalgh and Keith Negus, eds., 238–250. London: Arnold Publications.

FILMS, VIDEOS, AND MUSIC CITED

FILMS

Aah [A Sigh]. 1953. (Hindi) Directed by Raja Nawathe. R. K. Studios.

Alaipayuthey [Jumping Waves]. 2000. (Tamil) Directed by Mani Ratnam. Madras Talkies.

Albela [A Jolly Fellow]. 1951. (Hindi) Directed by Bhagwan Dada. Bhagwan Arts Productions.

Andaz [Style]. 1949. (Hindi) Directed by Mehboob Khan. Mehboob Productions.

Anmol Ghadi [Precious Time]. 1946. (Hindi) Directed by Mehboob Khan. Mehboob Productions.

Avatar. 2009. Directed by James Cameron. Twentieth Century Fox Films.

Awara [Vagabond]. 1951. (Hindi) Directed by Raj Kapoor. R. K. Studio.

Ayya [Master]. 2005. (Tamil) Directed by Hari. Kavithalayaa Productions.

Baiju Bawra. 1952. (Hindi) Directed by Vijay Bhatt. Prakash Pictures.

Band Baaja Baaraat [The Band Plays in the Wedding Procession]. 2010. Directed by Maneesh Sharma. Yash Raj Films.

Barsaat [Rain]. 1949. (Hindi) Directed by Raj Kapoor. R. K. Studio.

Basant Bahar [Beautiful Spring]. 1956. (Hindi) Directed by Raja Nawathe. R. Chandra Productions.

Bbuddah Hoga Terra Baap [Your Dad Might Be Old]. 2011. (Hindi) Directed by Puri Jagannath. AB Corp. Ltd.

Blue. 2009. Directed by Anthony D'Souza. Shree Ashtavinayak Cine Vision.

Bombay. 1995. Directed by Mani Ratnam. Amitabh Bachchan Corporation Limited.

Border. 1997. Directed by J. P. Dutta. J. P. Films.

Bunty aur Babli [Bunty and Babli]. 2005. (Hindi) Directed by Shaad Ali. Yash Raj Films.

China Town. 1962. (Hindi) Directed by Shakti Samanta. Shakti Films.

Close Encounters of the Third Kind. 1977. Directed by Steven Spielberg. Columbia Pictures.

Copacabana. 1947. Directed by Alfred Green. Beacon Productions.

Dark Knight, The. 2008. Directed by Christopher Nolan. Warner Bros. Pictures.

Delhi-6. 2009. (Hindi) Directed by Rakeysh Omprakash Mehra. UTV Motion Pictures.

Devdas. 2002. (Hindi) Directed by Sanjay Leela Bhansali. Mega Bollywood.

Dhoop Chhaon [Sun's Shadow]. 1935. (Hindi) Directed by Nitin Bose. New Theatres.

Dil Chahta Hai [The Heart Wants]. 2001. (Hindi) Directed by Farhan Akhtar. Excel Entertainment.

Dil Deke Dekho [Once You've Given Your Heart, Look Out]. 1959. (Hindi) Directed by Nasir Hussain. Filmalaya Productions.

Dil Se [From the Heart]. 1998. (Hindi) Directed by Mani Ratnam. Madras Talkies.

Dilwale Dulhaniya Le Jayenge [The One with the Good Heart Wins the Bride]. 1995. (Hindi) Directed by Aditya Chopra. Yash Raj Films.

Disco Dancer. 1982. (Hindi) Directed by Babbar Subash. Hindi.

Doll Face. 1945. Directed by Lewis Seiler. Twentieth Century Fox Productions.

Dostana [Friendship]. 2008. (Hindi) Directed by Tarun Mansukhani. Dharma Productions.

Down Argentine Way. 1940. Directed by Irving Cummings. Twentieth Century-Fox Film Corporation.

E.T. the Extra-Terrestrial. 1982. (Hindi) Directed by Steven Spielberg. Universal Pictures.

Flying Down to Rio. 1933. Directed by Thornton Freeland. Radio Pictures.

Gangaa Jamunaa Saraswathi [Ganga, Jamuna, and Saraswathi]. 1988. (Hindi) Directed by Manmohan Desai. Raam Raaj Kalamandir.

Gaucho, The. 1927. Directed by F. Richard Jones. Prod. Elton Corporation.

Greenwich Village. 1944. Directed by Walter Lang. Twentieth Century-Fox Film Corporation.

Hum Dil De Chuke Sanam [I've Already Given My Heart, Beloved]. 1999. (Hindi) Directed by Sanjay Leela Bhansali. Jhamu Sughand Productions.

Hum Tum [You and Me]. 2004. (Hindi) Directed by Kunal Kohli. Yash Raj Films.

I Hate Luv Storys. 2010. (Hindi) Directed by Punit Malhotra. UTV Motion Pictures.

If I'm Lucky. 1946. Directed by Lewis Seiler. Twentieth Century-Fox Film Corporation.

Jab We Met [When We Met]. 2007. (Hindi) Directed by Imtiaz Ali. Shree Ashtavinayak Cine Vision Ltd.

Jagte Raho [Stay Awake]. 1956. (Hindi) Directed by Shambhu Mitra. R. K. Films.

Janakan [Father]. 2010. (Tamil) Directed by Sanjeev N. R. Maxlab Cinemas and Entertainments. *Jodhaa Akbar* [The Union of Akbar]. 2008. (Hindi) Directed by Ashutosh Gowariker. Ashutosh Gowariker Productions.

Johnny Gaddar [Johnny Traitor]. 2007. (Hindi) Directed by Sriram Raghavan. Adlad Films, Ltd.

Kaadhalikka Neramillai [There's No Time for Love]. 1964. (Tamil) Directed by C. V. Sridhar. Sridhar Productions.

Kabhi Khushi Kabhie Gham [Sometimes Happiness, Sometimes Sorrow]. 2001. (Hindi) Directed by Karan Johar. Yash Raj Films.

Kaho Naa . . . Pyaar Hai [Say It Is Love]. 2000. Directed by Rakesh Roshan. Film Kraft.

Kalicharan. 1976. (Hindi) Directed by Subhash Ghai. Prithvi Pictures.

Kanoon [The Law].1943. (Hindi) Directed by Abdul Rashid Kardar. Kardar Productions.

Karan Arjun [Karan and Arjun]. 1995. (Hindi) Directed by Rakesh Roshan. Film Kraft.

Kashmir ki Kali [Blossom of Kashmir]. 1964. (Hindi) Directed by Shakti Samanta. Shakti Films.

Khazanchi [Cashier]. 1941. (Hindi) Directed by Moti B. Gidwani. Pancholi Productions.

Koi . . . Mil Gaya [Someone . . . Has Been Found]. 2003. (Hindi) Directed by Rakesh Roshan. Film Craft.

Krrish [Krrish (Kirshna)]. 2006. (Hindi) Directed by Rakesh Roshan. Film Kraft.

Kuch Kuch Hota Hai [Sometimes Something Happens]. 1998. (Hindi) Directed by Karan Johar. Yash Raj Films.

Lagaan [Land Tax]: *Once Upon a Time in India*. 2001. (Hindi) Directed by Ashutosh Gowariker. Amir Khan Productions.

Love Story. 1970. Directed by Arthur Hiller. Paramount Pictures.

Love Story 2050. 2008. (Hindi) Directed by Harry Baweja. Adlabs Films.

Mahabharat. 1988–1990. (Hindi) Directed by B. R. Chopra and Ravi Chopra. B. R. Films.

Maine Pyar Kiya [I Fell in Love]. 1989. Directed by Sooraj Barjatya. Rajshri Productions.

Major Saab [Major Sir]. 1998. (Hindi) Directed by Tinnu Anand. ABCL Films.

Mohra [Pawn]. 1994. (Hindi) Directed by Rajiv Rai. Trimurti Films.

Monsoon Wedding. 2001. (Hindi) Directed by Mira Nair. Paradis Films.

Mr. India. 1987. (Hindi) Directed by Shekhar Kapur. Narsimha Enterprises.

Mrityudaata [Executioner/Avenger]. 1997. (Hindi) Directed by Mehul Kumar. ABCL Films.

Mudhalvan [Chief Minister]. 1999. (Tamil) Directed by S. Shankar. Sri Surya Movies.

Mujhse Fraaandship Karoge [Do You Want To Be Friends]. 2011. (Hindi) Directed by Nupur Asthana. Y-Films.

Mughal-e-Azam [The Great Mughal]. 1960. (Hindi) Directed by K. Asif. Shapooji-Pallonji.

My Name Is Khan. 2010. (Hindi) Directed by Karan Jobar. Dharma Productions.

Nammal [You and I], 2002. (Tamil) Directed by Kamal. Moser Baer Entertainment.

Namoona [Model Youth]. 1949. (Hindi) Directed by Hira Singh. M.&T. Films.

Nandanam [The Flower Garden]. 2002. (Tamil) Directed by Ranjith. Bhavana Cinema.

Naya Daur [New Era]. 1956. (Hindi) Directed by B. R. Chopra. B. R. Films.

Nayak: The Real Hero. 2001. (Hindi) Directed by S. Shankar. Sri Surya Films.

New Delhi. 1956. (Hindi) Directed by Mohan Segal. Mohan Segal.

Nirala [Rare]. 1950. (Hindi) Directed by Devendra Mukherji. M.&T. Films.

Oke Okkadu [Only One]. 1999. (Tamil) Directed by S. Shankar. Hyderabad: Sri Surya Movies.

Om Shanti Om [Hindu religious invocation]. 2007. (Hindi) Directed by Farah Khan. Red Chillies Entertainment.

Paap [Sin]. 2003. Directed by Pooja Bhatt. Fish Eye Network.

Paheli [Before]. 2005. (Hindi) Directed by Amol Palekar. Red Chillies Entertainment.

Patiala House. 2011. (Hindi) Directed by Nikhil Advani. T Series.

Pennin Manathai Thottu [Touch the Heart of a Woman]. 2000. (Tamil). Directed by S. Ezhil. M. Kajamaideen.

Raaja Paarvai [Royal Vision]. 1981. (Tamil) Directed by Singeetham Srinivasa Rao. Haasan Brothers.

Rattan [Jewel]. 1944. (Hindi) Directed by M. Sadiq. Kardar Studios.

Ra.One [Ra(vanna) the First]. 2011. (Hindi) Directed by Anubhav Sinha. Red Chillies Entertainment.

Roja [Rose]. 1992. (Tamil/Hindi) Directed by Mani Ratnam. Madras Talkies.

Sainted Devil, A. 1924. Directed by Joseph Henabery. Famous Players-Lasky Corporation.

Salaam Namaste [Hello]. 2005. (Hindi) Directed by Siddharth Anand. Yash Raj Films.

Samadhi [A monument]. 1950. Directed by Ramesh Saigal. Filmistan.

Sant Tukaram. 1936. (Hindi) Directed by Vishnupant Govind Damle and Sheikh Fattelal. Prabhat Films.

Sant Dnyaneshwar. 1940. (Hindi) Directed by Vishnupant Govind Damle and Sheikh Fattelal. Prabhat Films.

Sargam. 1950. Directed by P. L. Santoshi. Filmistan.

Shabaab [Youth]. 1954. (Hindi) Directed by M. Sadiq. Sadiq Productions.

Shehnai [musical instrument of celebration]. 1947. (Hindi) Directed by P. L. Santoshi. Sasadhar Mukherjee Productions.

Sholay [Flame]. 1975. (Hindi) Directed by Ramesh Sippy. Sippy Films.

Singh is Kinng. 2008. (Hindi/Panjabi) Directed by Anees Baazmi. Hari Om Productions.
Slumdog Millionaire. 2008. Directed by Danny Boyle. Fox Searchlight Pictures.
Soldier. 1998. (Hindi) Directed by Abbas-Mustan. Tips Music.
Spider-Man. 2002. Directed by Sam Raimi. Columbia Pictures.
Swapnakoodu [Dream Nest]. 2003. (Tamil) Directed by Kamal. Lal Release.
Taal [Rhythm]. 1999. Directed by Subhash Ghai. Mukta Arts.
Tanu Weds Manu 2011. (Hindi) Directed by Anand Rai. Viacom 18 Motion Pictures.
Tees Maar Khan. 2010. (Hindi) Directed by Farah Khan. UTV Motion Pictures.
That Night in Rio. 1941. Directed by Irving Cummings. Twentieth Century-Fox Film Corporation.
Tumsa Nahin Dekha [Never Seen Anyone Like You]. 1957. (Hindi) Directed by Nasir Hussain. Filmistan.
Veer-Zaara [Veer and Zara]. 2004. (Hindi) Directed by Yash Chopra. Yash Raj Films.
Waisa Bhi Hota Hai, Part II [That Also Happens, Part II]. 2002. Directed by Shashanka Ghosh. Impact Films.
Week-end in Havana. 1941. Directed by Walter Land. Twentieth Century-Fox Film Corporation.
Yuvvraaj. 2008. (Hindi) Directed by Subhash Ghai. Eros International.

VIDEOS

"Buffalax." 2007. "Benny Lava...(WITH LYRICS) Hilarious." YouTube video, 4:39. Uploaded by "kbhurosah," February 7, 2008. Copy of "Crazy Indian Video...Buffalaxed!," originally uploaded by "buffalax" in 2007. Accessed July 10, 2012. http://www.youtube.com/watch?v=sdyC1BrQd6g.

"Buffalax." 2007. "Crazy Indian Video...Buffalaxed!" YouTube video, 4:39. Uploaded by "buffalax," August 18, 2007 (no longer available; account closed due to multiple copyright infringements). Accessed November 18, 2009. http://www.youtube.com/watch?v=ZA1NoOOoaNw.

CPDRC. 2009. "CPDRC Philippines–Jai Ho–Nov 2009." YouTube video, 4:32. Uploaded by "ThaigerBeyond," April 1, 2010. Accessed June 21, 2012. http://www.youtube.com/watch?v=FmJWJc6vsjM.

Daniels, Celia. 2008. "Shakalaka Baby." YouTube video, 4:48. Uploaded by "cdffgg2," October 29, 2007. Accessed November 9, 2009. http://www.youtube.com/watch?v=SE21tpFfRTk.

Fit Haven. 2007. "Shakalaka Baby—Fitness-Bollywood." YouTube video, 3:08. Uploaded by "FitHaven," June 8, 2007. Accessed October 4, 2009. http://www.youtube.com/watch?v=rK4Bjk3bL74

Hogan, Monica. 2008. "Shakalaka Baby BT Dance Show 2008." YouTube video, 4:17. Uploaded April 24, 2008 by "WOAHitsmo." Accessed October 25, 2009. http://www.youtube.com/watch?v=BVJ4YfteNNk.

Hsett. 2007. "Shakalaka Baby." YouTube video, 4:20. Uploaded by "hsett," May 3, 2007. Accessed October 14, 2009. http://www.youtube.com/watch?v=3wbzad3QkxI.

Ilaiyaraja. 1981. "anthi mazhai." YouTube video, 4:08. Uploaded by "raaagam," May 12, 2008. Accessed August 1, 2012. http://www.youtube.com/watch?v=J7ThzbP32QI.

Islam, Yusuf. 2005. "Indian Ocean -Yusuf Islam@Cat Stevens." YouTube video, 6:01. Uploaded by "sayembarahidup," April 18, 2007. Accessed September 15, 2009. http://www.youtube.com/watch?v=ydlnbsUIftk.

Milquiiq. 2008. "Shakalaka baby power mover 2007." YouTube video, 2:31. Uploaded by "milquiiq," April 17, 2008. Accessed October 2, 2009. http://www.youtube.com/watch?v=2SmtANvgdwc.

"Pandit Bhimsen Joshi in conversation with Dr Ashok Ranade," n.d. YouTube video file. Accessed April 10, 2012. http://www.youtube.com/watch?v=nWUXfEWWtl4.

Poon Kar Lai, Kelly. 2007. "[MV] Kelly Pan Jia Li 潘嘉丽—Shakalaka Baby [Full Version]" YouTube video, 3:42. Uploaded by "gp3," September 22, 2007. Accessed September 23, 2008. http://www.youtube.com/watch?v=mG11-U7pStw.

Rahman, A. R. 2002. "Priya Kalidas, Raza Jaffrey; Preeya Kalidas—Shakalaka Baby." YouTube video, 3:51. Uploaded by "PriyaKalidasVEVO," October 25, 2009. Accessed October 10, 2010. http://www.youtube.com/watch?v=0XsGU0jhj1w.

Rahman, A. R. 1992. "Chinna Chinna Aasai—Roja—Arvind Swamy and Madhu—HD." YouTube video, 4:56. Uploaded by "ShemarooTamil," July 8, 2011. Accessed August 2, 2012. http://www.youtube.com/watch?v=YpMK2UYmgw8.

Rahman, A. R. 1999. "Shakalaka Baby song—Mudhalvan." YouTube video, 5:19. Uploaded by "erostamil," September 23, 2010. Accessed July 1, 2011. http://www.youtube.com/watch?v=IARuN-Z3s_o.

Rahman, A. R. 2000. "Pachai Nirame." YouTube video, 5:39. Uploaded by "apinternational," November 10, 2011. Accessed August 3, 2012. http://www.youtube.com/watch?v=0xA-oWnJAWA.

Ravichander, Anirudh. 2012. "Why This Kolaveri Di Full Song Promo Video in HD." YouTube video, 4:09. Uploaded by "sonymusicindiaSME," November 16, 2011. Accessed November 23, 2011. http://www.youtube.com/watch?v=YR12Z8f1Dh8.

SMKDU. 2008. "SMKDU 5 Jati Shakalaka Baby Teacher's Day 08." YouTube video, 1:52. Uploaded by "xstellacoolx," May 16, 2008. Accessed November 1, 2009. http://www.youtube.com/watch?v=H1IonFLpuWg.

Viswanathan, M. S. 1964. "Anubavam Puthumai." YouTube video, 5:17. Uploaded by "bensigjk," March 1, 2011. Accessed August 29, 2012. http://www.youtube.com/watch?v=D50kh6B5IRw.

MUSIC VIDEOS

Maan, Gurdas. 1995. "Apna Punjab Hove." *Yaar Mera Pyar*. DVD. T-Series.

Mehndi, Daler. 1995. "Bolo Te Ra Ra." *Bolo Ta Ra Ra*. DVD. Magnasound Media Pvt. Ltd.

Sagoo, Bally. 1997. "Gur Nalon Ishq Mitha." *Bally Sagoo on the Mix: The Story So Far*. DVD. Polygram.

———. 1999. "Aaja Nachle." *Star Crazy 2*. DVD. Ishq Records.

MUSIC CITED

Abel, Roysten. 2010. *The Manganiyar Seduction*. Amarrass Records.

Akon, featuring Eminem. 2006. "Smack That." *Konvicted*. SRC, Universal, Konvict Muzik, UpFront, and Shady.

Apache Indian. 1993. "Chok There." *No Reservations*. Mango/Island Records.

Badave, Shreeyash. 2012. "Rupa Pahata Lochani." From a *kirtan* recorded by Anna Schultz on July 23, 2009, in Kothrud, Pune (Anna Schultz, *Singing a Hindu Nation: Marathi Devotional Performance and Nationalism*, New York: Oxford University Press).

Chic & His Music Makers, 1943–1945. Columbia (FB 40324, 40337, 40338, 40390, 40393, 40394, 40406, 40407, 40409, and 40446).

Chinai, Alisha. 1995. *Made in India*. Magnasound.

Cole, Nat King. 1962. "Fly Me to the Moon." *Nat King Cole Sings/George Shearing Plays*. Capitol Records 1675.

Colonial Cousins. 1996. "Sa Ni Dha Pa." *Colonial Cousins*. Magnasound.

Diabaté, Madou Sidiki. 2012. *Live in India, Amarrass Desert Music Festival*. Amarrass Records. Europe. 1986. "The Final Countdown." *The Final Countdown*. Epic Records A 7127.

Fernandes, Remo. 1998. *O, Meri Munni*. Magnasound.

Ganesh and Kumaresh. 2007. *Carnatic Chills: Ganesh-Kumaresh newage violin exotica*. Saregama India Ltd. CDNF 197274.

Gershwin, George. *George Gershwin: Porgy and Bess*. EMI Classics CDC 7543252.

Joshi, Bhimsen. 1996. "Arambhi Vandina." *Abhangvani Vol. 1*. Gramophone Company of India.

———. 2002. "Vithala Geetin Gava." *Abhangvani Vol. 2: Vitthala Geetin Gava*. Saregama [Gramophone Company of India (HMV), 1980].

———. 2004. "Teertha Vitthala, Kshetra Vitthala." *Swaranand: Bhaktirang (20 Suprasiddh Gaani)*. Saregama.

———. 2005. "Roopa Pahata Lochani." *Abhang*. Music Today.

———. 2005. "Zani Dhav Aata." *Abhanga*. Music Today.

———. 2006. *Maze Maher Pandhari*. Saregama [Gramophone Company of India, 1996].

———. 2006. "Maza Bhava Tuze Charani." *Maze Maher Pandhari*. Saregama [Gramophone Company of India, 1996].

———. 2006. "Maze Maher Pandhari." *Maze Maher Pandhari*. Saregama. [Gramophone Company of India, 1996].

———. 2006. Dnyaniyancha Raja Guru Maharao. *Maze Maher Pandhari*. Saregama [Gramophone Company of India, 1996].

———. 2006. "Jai Jai Ram Krishna Hari." *Mantra*. Times Music.

Khan, Lakha, Vieux Farka Touré, Madou Sidiki Diabaté, Nihal Khan, and Barmer Boys. 2012. *Live at Amarrass Desert Music Festival 2011*. Amarrass Records.

King, Ben E. 1961. "Stand By Me." Atco Records 45-6194.

Kronos Quartet and Asha Bhosle. 2005. *You've Stolen My Heart: Songs from R. D. Burman's Bollywood*. Nonesuch Records.

Lonely Island, The, featuring Akon. 2011. "I Just Had Sex." *Turtleneck and Chain*. Universal Republic.

MAARS. 1987. "Pump Up the Volume." 4AD/PolyGram Records.

Manmadkar, Dadamaharaj. 2000. "Rupa Pahata Lochani." From a *kirtan* performed in Pandharpur at the Manmadkar Ashram. Recorded by the family of the *kirtankar*.

Mehndi, Daler. 1995. *Bolo Ta Ra Ra*. Magnasound.

Queen and David Bowie. 1981. "Under Pressure." EMI.

Rahman, A. R. 2008. *Slumdog Millionaire* (soundtrack). N.E.E.T./Interscope.

———. 1992. *Roja* (Hindi soundtrack). Magnasound.

Sehgal, Baba. 1990. *Dilruba*. Magnasound.

———. 1991. *Ali Baba*. Magnasound.

———. 1992. *Thanda Thanda Pani*. Magnasound.

———. 1993. *Main Bhi Madonna*. Magnasound.

———. 2012. "Mumbai City."

———. 2012. "Snoop Baba."

Sehgal, Baba, and Anaida. 1997. "Hakuna Matata." *The Lion King* (Hindi). Walt Disney.

Shubhaa. 1991. *Set Me Free*. Magnasound.

Snap! 1990. "The Power." *World Power*. Ariola Records.

Vanilla Ice. 1990. "Ice Ice Baby." SBK Records.
Wonder, Stevie. 1984. "I Just Called to Say I Love You." *The Woman in Red*. Motown Records 3746361082.
Various artists. 2011. "Mitha Bol." Amarrass Records.
Various artists. 2012. "Banko Ghodo." Amarrass Records.

INDEX

maxixe, 204, 207, 208, 209, 210
Maze Maher Pandhari (2006), 287, 293
Mazumdar, Malcolm, 220, 221
McCann, Anthony, 73, 264
McLaughlin, John, 230, 240, 247, 248
media contexts, 106
media institutions, 104
mediascape, 13, 62,
mehndi ceremonies, 156
"Mehndi Laga Ke Rakhna" (2010),
    156, 157
Mehndi, Daler, 151, 152, 153, 154, 156,
    158, 163, 164, 169, 231
Mehta, Zubin, 246
Meintjes, Louise, 63, 179, 181, 189, 195,
    259, 260, 282
melodic accompanists, 189, 192
members-only dancehalls, 202, 203
Menuhin, Yehudi, 246
"Mere Dil Ki Ghadi Kare Tik Tik Tik"
    (1951), 214
"Mere Rang Mein Rangnewali" (1989),
    106, 107, 214
"Meri Jaan Balle Balle" (1964), 149,
    150, 214
migrant communities, 179, 180,
military swing bands, 215
Ministry of Information and
    Broadcasting, 144
Minogue, Kylie, 112
Mirage, 232
Miranda, Carmen, 15, 201, 202, 211,
    212, 213
Mirchi, 103
modal *raga* system, 65
modern media, 116, 143
modernization, 247
Mohanlal, 89
Mohindra College, 146
Mohra (1994), 151
Monsoon Wedding (2001), 52, 157
Morchang Studios, 258, 259, 260, 261,
    262, 263, 265, 266, 267, 268,
    271, 273
Morcom, Anna, 3, 93, 100
mountain villages, 180
Mr. India (1987), 54
mrdang, 280, 283, 287, 292, 293, 294, 297
mrdangam, 239
Mrityudaata (1997), 152

MTV Asia, 152, 160
MTV India, 161, 169, 171
MTV, 13, 14, 68, 93, 154, 169, 170, 176,
    230, 234, 235, 236, 237
Mudhalvan (1999), 67
Mughal-e-Azam (1960), 30
Mujhse Fraaandship Karoge (2011), 52
mukhda-antara, 277
mukhda, 106, 107, 109, 111
Mukherji, G. N., 119
multi-textured entertainment, 15
multiculturalism, 177
multitrack digital recording, 279
Mumbai Swing Club, 210
murli, 260
music as sound, 103
music companies, 9, 13, 104, 105, 151,
    152, 179, 182, 183, 219, 234, 235,
    311, 312, 314
music copyright lawsuits, 312
music dramas, 21, 33, 34, 117
music education, 269
music industry, 4, 9, 12, 13, 16, 31, 32,
    60, 88, 99, 103, 116, 124, 161,
    162, 164, 165, 171, 174, 175, 179,
    180, 183, 194, 217, 218, 220, 223,
    227, 235, 236, 300, 301, 304, 305,
    311, 313, 314, 315, 318
music ownership, 264
music producers, 13, 18, 106, 194, 236,
    304, 309, 312
music production software, 310
music production, 7, 8, 9, 11, 15, 17, 25,
    30, 31, 63, 172, 194, 201, 230,
    231, 301, 302, 309, 310, 312,
    316, 320
music store chains, 105
musical elements, 53, 65, 98, 100, 103,
    186, 194, 253, 302, 308, 309
musical freedoms, 256, 257, 262
musical genre, 13, 29, 57, 60, 69, 98, 99,
    103, 105, 106, 118, 119
musical hybrids, 244, 268, 272, 319
Musical Instrument Digital Interface,
    11, 47
musical instrumentation, 148
musical mediation, 77, 101
musical sound, 23, 50, 72, 98, 102, 103,
    104, 132, 231, 252, 253, 291,
    309, 318

musical style, 6, 10, 25, 29, 31, 87, 98, 99, 100, 101, 103, 104, 148, 171, 284, 287, 308
musical transformations, 108
musical-social space, 104
musicologists, 98, 147, 205
Musique Electronique, 271
My Name is Khan (2010), 57
MySpace, 266

"Na Na Na Re" (1997), 152, 154
"Nach Balliye" (2005), 158
nachar, 144
Nadkarni, Mohan, 277, 283, 284, 285
nagaswaram, 64, 72
Nair, Mira, 52, 157
Nair, Navya, 83
Nāmasiddhānta, 136
Nandanam (2002), 82, 83
Naradar, 130
Narayanan, Prashant 110
Nargis, 28, 36
narrative context, 106
National Film Award, 66
nationalism, 121, 177, 219, 220, 250
Naushad Ali, 10, 22, 23, 25, 28, 29, 202
Naya Daur (1956), 147, 149, 150, 151
Nayyar, O. P., 202
Nazareth, 232
Neelam, 35, 36
Nehru, Jawaharlal, 16, 250
Nehruvian, 220, 250
New Delhi (1956), 147
New Delhi, 146, 231, 271
New Zealand, 1, 5, 108
newspaper reviews, 125, 205
NH7, 162
Nichani, Ajay, 187
Nigam, Sonu, 151, 172
nightclubs, 15, 32, 205, 218, 220, *221*, 226, 300, 302, 314
nightlife, 16, 218, 220, 231
"Nimbura" (1999), 51
Noida, 179, 301
non-Western music, 266
North American bands, 232
North India, 13, 114, 115, 140, 172, 174, 176, 180, 181, 203, 205, 211, 230, 245, 249, 294, 301, 305
North Indian art music, 283

North Indian classical dance, 150
North Indian classical music, 276, 290, 298
North Indian film songs, 300, 319
North Indian popular culture, 167, 175
North Indian popular music, 160, 172, 196, 317
North Indian vocal music, 277
North-Central Punjab, 146

oboe, 191, 195
octapad, 184, 193
Off the Wall (1979), 231
"Oh Kedi" (2000), 158
"Oh Meri Munni" (1998), 174
Oke Okkadu (1998), 68
old Bollywood, 110
"Olichirunne" (2010), 79–80
Om Shanti Om (2007), 56
online communities, 12
oral tradition, 261
outsourcing, 301
ownership and authorship, 264, 315

Paap (2003), 112
"Pachchai Nirame" (2000), 67
Padmanabhan, N. S., 309, 312, 313, 314, 315
pahari dhun, 43
pahari, 190, 193
Paheli (2005), 51
Pakistan, 32, 112, 142, 149
Pallavi, 83, 84, 85
Panchathan Record Inn, 66, 70
Pandya, Kusumakar, 272
"Panjāb de Lok Nāchāṅ vich Mauliktā" (1992), 144
Panjabi *geet*, 180
Panjabi music, 147, 148, 157, 167, 319
Panjabi performance, 145, 146, 147, 148, 149, 151
Panjabi-ness, 148, 156
Parsi, 266
partition of India (1947), 142
Pathé, 117
Patiala and East Panjab States Union, 144
Patiala House (2011), 157
patronage, 17, 77, 120, 126, 127, 242, 245, 257, 262, 271, 273

Printed in the USA/Agawam, MA
February 10, 2014

585092.069